D0237574

Mastering Derivatives
Markets

LEEDS BECKETT UNIVERSITY
LIBRARY
DISCARDED

Leeds Metropolitan University

17 0482943 1

FT Prentice Hall
FINANCIAL TIMES

In an increasingly competitive world, we believe it's quality of thinking that gives you the edge – an idea that opens new doors, a technique that solves a problem, or an insight that simply makes sense of it all. The more you know, the smarter and faster you can go.

That's why we work with the best minds in business and finance to bring cutting-edge thinking and best learning practice to a global market.

Under a range of leading imprints, including *Financial Times Prentice Hall*, we create world-class print publications and electronic products bringing our readers knowledge, skills and understanding, which can be applied whether studying or at work.

To find out more about Pearson Education publications, or tell us about the books you'd like to find, you can visit us at **www.pearsoned.co.uk**

PEARSON
Education

Mastering Derivatives Markets

A step-by-step guide to the products, applications and risks

Third Edition

FRANCESCA TAYLOR

Prentice Hall
FINANCIAL TIMES

An imprint of Pearson Education

Harlow, England • London • New York • Boston • San Francisco • Toronto • Sydney • Singapore • Hong Kong
Tokyo • Seoul • Taipei • New Delhi • Cape Town • Madrid • Mexico City • Amsterdam • Munich • Paris • Milan

PEARSON EDUCATION LIMITED

Edinburgh Gate
Harlow CM20 2JE
Tel: +44 (0)1279 623623
Fax: +44 (0)1279 431059
Website: www.pearsoned.co.uk

First published 1996
Second edition 2000
Third edition published in Great Britain 2007

© Francesca Taylor 1996, 2000
© Pearson Education 2007

The right of Francesca Taylor to be identified as author of this work has been asserted by her
in accordance with the Copyright, Designs and Patents Act 1988.

ISBN-13: 978-0-273-70978-7
ISBN-10: 0-273-70978-X

British Library Cataloguing in Publication Data
A catalogue record for this book is available from the British Library

Library of Congress Cataloging-in-Publication Data
Taylor, Francesca.
   Mastering derivatives markets : a step-by-step guide to the products, applications and
   risks / Francesca Taylor. -- 3rd ed.
   p. cm.
   Includes index.
   ISBN-13: 978-0-273-70978-7 (alk. paper)
   ISBN-10: 0-273-70978-X (alk. paper)
   1. Derivative securities. 2. Derivative securities--Great Britain. I. Title.

HG6024.A3T39 2007
332.64'57--dc22

                                                    2006050101

All rights reserved. No part of this publication may be reproduced, stored in a retrieval
system, or transmitted in any form or by any means, electronic, mechanical,
photocopying, recording, or otherwise without either the prior written permission of the
publisher or a licence permitting restricted copying in the United Kingdom issued by the
Copyright Licensing Agency Ltd, Saffron House, 6–10 Kirby Street, London EC1N 8TS. This
book may not be lent, resold, hired out or otherwise disposed of by way of trade in any form of
binding or cover other than that in which it is published, without the prior consent of the Publishers.

10 9 8 7 6 5 4 3 2 1
10 09 08 07 06

Typeset in 11.5pt Garamond by 30
Printed and bound in Great Britain by Bell & Bain Ltd, Glasgow

The publisher's policy is to use paper manufactured from sustainable forests.

The author

Francesca Taylor

Francesca has followed each of the four basic careers within finance. She has been a corporate, a banker, a broker and a consultant. This leads her to be ideally placed to write entry level technical books and to offer independent training and product education to a range of clients.

Her career started in the Treasury department of BICC plc, one of the UK's largest companies. A typical day's work included FX and money market dealing, liaising with banks and foreign clients, constructing debt maturity profiles, managing currency and interest rate risk with derivatives.

Francesca then joined Midland Bank (now HSBC) concentrating on marketing, selling and trouble shooting the whole range of derivatives products to a client list including central banks, major and minor commercial banks, corporates and governments. One of her roles was to educate and train the bank's client base in the uses and applications of a growing number of derivative products. Francesca then became a mainstream treasury consultant, advising her clients on all aspects of currency and interest rate risk management. Notable clients included major utilities and engineering companies. Following this, she spent some time as an inter-bank swap broker with Sterling Brokers.

Francesca has trained thousands of people on Taylor Associates training courses including employees of hedge funds, clearing houses, banks, supra nationals, technology companies, corporates, risk consultancies, and UK and overseas government ministers. She has spoken at major conferences in London, New York, Hong Kong, Singapore, Malaysia and Australia.

Francesca has written a number of finance best-sellers for Financial Times Prentice Hall; she has red hair and freckles easily and lives in Surrey with her family, a Belgian Shepherd dog and one cat (the other went missing).

Qualifications include:

B.Sc. (Hons) Geology, London University

M.Sc. Management Science, Imperial College

A.M.C.T. Associate Member of the Association of Corporate Treasurers.

Contents

Author's acknowledgements   xiii

Publisher's acknowledgements   xiv

Foreword   xv

Contributors   xvii

1 Background and Development of the Derivatives Markets   1

Introduction   2

Definition and key features   3

Uses of derivatives   3

Range of derivatives   4

Increasing use of the Central Counterparty Model (CCP)   5

Risk and benchmarking   6

Market volumes   6

Users and uses of derivatives markets   7

Straight Through Processing (STP)   9

2 Market Fundamentals   11

Introduction   12

How banks generate income   12

Three key assumptions   14

Role and use of LIBOR   15

Day counts   17

Financial maths   18

Calculating forward rates   21

Marking to market   24

Yield curves   25

Quiz   26

3 Derivatives Fundamentals   29

Range of derivatives   30

What is a vanilla trade?   30

Settlement   31

Triggers		32
Liquidity and credit risk		33
Understanding the underlying		33
Benchmarks		34
Fair value		34
Dealing with derivatives		34

4 Basic Option Concepts — **39**

Introduction	40
Option pricing	52
Option mechanics	52

5 Interest Rate Derivatives – Single Settlement Instruments — **59**

Background and development	60
Single settlement interest rate derivatives	62
Financial futures contracts	63
Forward rate agreements (FRAs)	75
Interest rate options	87
Premium determinants	88
Quiz	97

6 Multiple Settlement Interest Rate Derivatives — **99**

Introduction	100
Interest rate caps and floors	102
Interest rate collars	110
Interest rate swaps	116
Quiz	133

7 Benchmarking in the OTC Derivatives Markets — **135**
Penny Davenport

Financial benchmarking for derivatives	136
Operational risk measurements for derivatives	139
Markit Annual Scorecard	140
Conclusion	141

8 Credit Derivatives — **143**

Introduction	144
What is credit risk?	145
Style of trading	146
Default data	148
The first deals	148

Range of credit derivatives 148
Credit default swaps 149
Total return swaps 158

9 Beyond a Vanilla CDS 161
Robert Reoch

Introduction 162
Credit indices 162
CDOs 167
Where next? 173

10 Currency Derivatives 175

Introduction 176
Over the counter currency options 178
Currency options: reduced premium strategies 202
Simple exotic structures 210
Currency swaps 212
Exchange-traded instruments 223
Conclusion 226
Quiz 226

11 Equity Derivatives 229

Introduction 230
Background 230
Single stocks or equity indices? 231
Stock index futures 235
Stock index options 249
Single stock options 259
Equity index swaps 263

12 Using Equity Derivatives to Create Attractive Investment Products for Personal Investors 273
Christopher C. Taylor

Equity investment 274
The development of the UK and European markets for equity-based retail products 275
Constructing a capital protected growth product with equity derivatives 277
Income paying capital-at-risk products 280
Calculation of income level 280
The risk to capital 281
The most common structural variations used in the equity derivative market 281

13 Commodity Derivatives   289

Introduction   290
Exchange-traded energy derivatives   295
Exchange-traded futures contracts   295
Exchange-traded energy option contracts   302
OTC or 'off-exchange' energy derivatives   307
OTC option products   308
OTC oil swaps   313
Overview of electricity market   317

14 Using Derivatives in Hedge Funds   321
Stuart C. Fiertz

Introduction   322
Mitigating risk   322
Increasing exposures   324
Capturing tax efficiencies   324
Manoeuvring anonymously   325
Accessing restricted markets   326
Trading non-deliverable assets   326
Shifting operational burdens   326
Executing with greater precision   327
Conclusion   328

15 Derivatives and Technology   331
Chris Horsburgh

Introduction and background   332
Hardware and software developments   333
Business drivers for change   334
Responses   336
Conclusion   337

16 Derivatives and Documentation   339

Introduction   340
Background to the International Swaps and Derivatives
Association, Inc. (ISDA)   341
Products covered by the ISDA Agreement   342
ISDA Heaven vs ISDA Hell   344

17 A brief history of straight through processing (STP) for OTC Derivatives   347
Bill Hodgson

What is STP?   348
Automation drivers and priorities   349

Message formats 349
Central clearing for OTC products 352
Innovation in trade capture and confirmation 352
Fundamental issues in processing OTC products 353
The future of STP for OTC contracts 354
The 'backlog' 355
A central infrastructure for the OTC markets: Trade
Information Warehouse 356
Conclusion 359

18 Risk and Compliance for Derivatives 361
Tony Blunden

Introduction 362
Governance 362
Risk management practice 367
Compliance practice 373
Conclusion 379

19 First Principles of Accounting for Derivatives 381
Deborah Morton-Dare

Introduction 382
Fundamental accounting concepts 382
Reporting requirements 383
Fair value and mark-to-market accounting 384
Accruals accounting and amortized cost 384
Fair value vs hedge accounting 385
Accounting treatment 385
International standards 394
Conclusion – an approach to accounting for a
new derivatives transaction 398

Glossary 401
Index 417

Author's acknowledgements

I would like to thank my publishers Financial Times Prentice Hall and everyone involved in the production of this book. To be asked to write a third edition is a great honour and we have all worked really hard to include the new areas of interest – which of course continue to change year on year.

Heartfelt thanks must go to my contributors, all of whom have full-time careers and yet still managed to find time to put pen to paper. These are:

Tony Blunden, Chase Cooper Ltd

Penny Davenport, Markit Group Ltd

Stuart C. Fiertz, Cheyne Capital Management

Bill Hodgson, DTCC Deriv/Serv

Chris Horsburgh, City Practitioners Ltd

Deborah Morton-Dare

Robert Reoch, Reoch Credit Ltd

Christopher C. Taylor, HSBC

Finally, my thanks go to everyone at home and at Taylor Associates who kept everything running smoothly whilst I wrote this.

FST

Publisher's acknowledgements

We are grateful to the following for permission to reproduce copyright material:

Figures 2.1, 5.7, 5.9, 6.5, 6.6, 6.8, 6.13 and 10.1 courtesy of Reuters; Table 6.1 with permission from BIS (www.bis.org); Figure 8.1 with permission from the International Swaps and Derivatives Association, Inc.; Tables 11.5 and 11.8 from Chicago Mercantile Exchange; Figure 12.1 ©Bloomberg L.P. All rights reserved. Reprinted with permission; Figures 12.2 and 12.5 from Arete Consulting Limited; Figure 13.1 from WTRG Economics; Figure 13.2 from *Argus Global Markets*, Argus Media Ltd, www.argusmediagroup.com; Figure 13.3 with permission from InflationData.com; Figures 13.5 and 13.7 with permission from BP Oil International Ltd; data from Euronext.liffe with permission.

In some instances we have been unable to trace the owners of copyright material, and we would appreciate any information that would enable us to do so.

Foreword

This new third edition takes into account how the derivatives market is changing. We are offering a full 360 degree look at the instruments, the products, applications and risks. This means we are including chapters on Risk and Compliance in this highly technical area as well as the first principles of Accounting for derivatives and the impact of MiFID.

What happens after the deal is done? In the last few years the global regulators became uneasy over some of the post trade practices in this market and the fresh emphasis on clarity, accuracy, consistency and speed is everywhere. New IT systems are being built or upgraded to assist banks, hedge funds and asset managers to comply with these market initiatives, and this has then led to a new breed of organizations that are providing further inputs for the downstream processing of derivatives.

We now have independent benchmarking to assist in calculating profits and losses and quantifying risks; true straight through processing (STP) is possible with the current technology but it must be carefully implemented. This has led to the increasing use of electronic templates for confirming trades and as a side effect we now have increasing usage of the central counter-party models within the OTC market place.

In a short space of time turnover in credit derivatives has more than doubled that for equity derivatives. We have therefore included a comprehensive chapter on credit derivatives together with a guest chapter on how derivatives are used in hedge funds – now estimated to be in the region of 30 per cent of the market. Equity markets continue to be risky and hedgers and traders alike are using derivatives products for protection and profit. The retail market (you and I) now wants access to these markets and we have a guest article from one of the major banks in this field. Exchange-traded instruments are undergoing a re-birth and it is no longer sufficient just to understand how the instruments work – although we provide full up-to-the-minute explanations of options, swaps and futures across the key asset classes, Rates, Currency, Equity, Commodity and Credit.

I am also incredibly lucky to have guest contributors who offer their thoughts and views on the practical side of derivatives:

Tony Blunden, Chase Cooper Limited, 'Risk and Compliance for Derivatives'

Penny Davenport, Markit Group Limited, 'Benchmarking in the Derivatives Markets'

Stuart C. Fiertz, Cheyne Capital Management, 'Using Derivatives in Hedge Funds'

Bill Hodgson, DTCC Deriv/Serv, 'A Brief History of Straight Through Processing (STP) for OTC Derivatives'

Chris Horsburgh, City Practitioners Ltd, 'Derivatives and Technology'

Deborah Morton-Dare, 'First Principles of Accounting for Derivatives'

Robert Reoch, Reoch Consulting, 'Beyond a Vanilla CDS'

Christopher C. Taylor, HSBC, 'Using Equity Derivatives to Create Attractive Investment Products for Personal Investors'.

FST

Contributors

BILL HODGSON

The Depository Trust & Clearing Corporation

Bill joined DTCC in 2004 as part of the Deriv/SERV Business Development team, the first hire into Deriv/SERV from the OTC derivatives banking community. The Deriv/SERV business provides the world's most popular post-trade processing services for OTC derivatives, serving close to 500 customers. Bill is part of the team leading DTCC's development of a trade information warehouse for credit derivatives, and spearheaded DTCC's efforts to launch an automated matching and confirmation service for interest rate derivatives in 2005, with leading dealers and buy-side firms.

Bill joined DTCC from LCH.Clearnet where he was Head of Product Development for the SwapClear Interest Rates Clearing service. Bill has extensive experience working with industry groups, amassing a wealth of experience in processing OTC derivatives trades.

Bill's prior experience includes Barclays Capital where he built and ran their OTC derivatives collateral management team and also project managed the firm through the European Monetary Union transition, as well as Merrill Lynch where he led a team selecting a global confirmations document management system, plus developed, implemented and supported a global trade capture and management platform for the OTC derivatives business.

Bill's education at Greenwich University focused on information technology and led to his early career in the development of systems for children's educational games, point-of-sale cash registers, a multi-million pound military RADAR system, oil drilling software tools, and eventually capital markets systems for repos, equities, and OTC derivatives. He spends his spare time adding yet more content to his iPod and being assistant gardener to his partner.

CHRIS HORSBURGH

City Practitioners Limited

Chris joined City Practitioners (CPL) (formerly TCA Consulting) in 2000. CPL is a leading implementer of complex asset trading systems within global financial institutions and employs over 180 experienced practitioners located in London and New York. At CPL Chris has worked with tier 1 and 2 banks helping them implement derivatives trading systems and rationalize their systems landscape so that it conforms to a logical application architecture and makes best use of developments in technology. Currently Chris specializes in the area of back office derivatives automation and workflow helping clients automate their processes reduce costs and increase their levels of STP.

Prior to CPL Chris spent 10 years with Lombard Risk Systems Limited designing, building and supporting derivatives trading systems. Chris was part of the management team that took the company from eight staff to over 150 winning two Queen's awards for exports and doing business with over 60 of the world's top 100 banks.

Chris holds a BSc in Chemistry from University College London and a MSc and PhD in Crystallography from Birkbeck College, University of London, is a member of the Institute of Project Management and is a Liveryman of The Worshipful Company of Feltmakers.

CHRISTOPHER C. TAYLOR

Director, Wealth Management Sales, HSBC Corporate, Investment Banking and Markets (CIBM)

Christopher Taylor has a BSc (Hons) in Banking and International Finance from City University in London and has been actively involved in the derivative markets since their inception. A founder member of Citibank's Financial Engineering team in the mid 1980s Christopher was highly involved in the early development of the interest rate swap and options markets in the UK. He spent a number of years as Head of Specialist Derivative Sales at Midland Montagu where he ran a cross-asset class derivative team specializing in interest rate and currency exposure management and a team dedicated to dynamic portfolio management. From there he moved to BZW, the Investment Banking arm of Barclays Bank where he was Managing Director, Head of Cross Product sales. He joined HSBC in 2003 as Head of Wealth Management Sales in London where he now runs a team whose primary responsibility is to structure and distribute capital protected equity and fund-based product to retail and institutional investors.

DEBORAH MORTON-DARE

Deborah Morton-Dare is a qualified chartered accountant who has worked in corporate finance where she gained a wide range of experience in flotations, acquisitions and mergers, venture capital, feasibility studies and rescue packages. She has set up and run her own successful manufacturing company, during this time she also acted as a financial consultant for a number of small and medium-sized companies. She assisted them in structuring and raising finance and put financial controls in place.

She now specializes in financial awareness courses at all level from beginner to advanced in a wide range of organizations.

PENNY DAVENPORT

Director, Markit Group

Penny Davenport is a director at Markit where she is responsible for global credit products, including pricing and benchmarking, and Markit RED, the reference entity data standard for the credit derivatives market.

Markit is the leading industry source of independent pricing and valuations for the global financial and commodities markets. Markit has data contributed by over 60 dealing firms, and its services are used by 400 institutions globally. Areas of product expertise include OTC derivatives (credit, equity, FX, rates, inflation, energy, power, metals and structured products), corporate bonds, syndicated loans, dividend forecasting, and index and ETF management.

Before joining Markit, Ms Davenport was a noted practitioner in the arena of OTC derivatives collateral management, with many years' experience at JPMorgan in London and New York. Ms Davenport also held the position of Head of Collateral Management at Halifax Treasury.

Ms Davenport is a frequent contributor to industry publications and conferences. She graduated in Economics from Cambridge University.

STUART FIERTZ

President, Cheyne Capital Management Limited

Stuart C. Fiertz CFA is the Co-Founder, President and Director of Research of Cheyne Capital Management Limited, a London-based alternative asset manager with gross assets under management of over $30 billion. Cheyne Capital, manages assets across a broad spectrum and is an active and pioneering user of derivatives. In recognition thereof, Cheyne Capital was named

Derivatives Week End User of The Year 2005. From 1991 to 2000 and prior to establishing Cheyne Capital in 2000, Stuart Fiertz worked in London for Morgan Stanley where he was responsible for the development and implementation of customized portfolio strategies and for credit research in their convertible bond management practice. Prior to joining Morgan Stanley, Stuart Fiertz was an equity research analyst for the Value Line Investment Survey from 1984 to 1986, and a high yield credit analyst in Boston at Merrill Lynch from 1986 to 1988 and in New York at Lehman Brothers from 1988 to 1990. Stuart Fiertz, who is a Chartered Financial Analyst and a Chartered Alternative Investment Analyst, was awarded a BA degree in Political Science and Economics in 1984 from Dartmouth College. Stuart Fiertz is a trustee of the Trialogue Educational Trust and a Director of London Stock Exchange listed Queen's Walk Investment Limited.

TONY BLUNDEN

Director of Consulting and Board member of Chase Cooper Limited

Tony's areas of focus are the identification and development of clients' needs, the development of Chase Cooper's profile and product set, and the provision of training both internally and to clients. Tony's previous client engagements have included advising and guiding clients on risk and compliance frameworks and governance, risk and control assessments, indicators of key risks, loss databases and their use, modelling of operational risk and risk reporting.

Tony has worked in the City of London for over 30 years, primarily within risk management, compliance and related areas in financial services organizations. Prior to joining Chase Cooper, Tony spent four years as a Director in Ernst & Young's Financial Services Risk Management practice.

Tony has spoken at around 50 international risk and compliance conferences and has appeared on television and radio. He is also a well known author of articles and chapters on risk management and compliance having published around 25 documents.

ROBERT REOCH

Reach Credit Partners Ltd

Robert Reoch has 20 years of experience in finance, and has been involved in the credit derivatives market since 1994. He took a pioneering role as part of the team that set up J.P. Morgan's European credit derivative business, and has since been influential in the growth and development of the global credit derivatives market. In addition to originating and structuring transactions, Robert has been an active spokesperson and contributed to the early development of the legal and regulatory framework of the market.

After 3 years building J.P. Morgan's credit derivatives business, Robert moved on to Nomura International where he was made head of credit derivatives with a mandate for rolling out the global business. Robert subsequently joined Bank of America, where he was appointed global head of credit derivatives in 1997. At Bank of America he was also mandated to build up a global credit derivatives franchise.

In response to the growing demand for independent advice on the credit derivatives industry, Robert set up a consulting practice in 2001. Drawing on their extensive experience in the sector, he and three others at Reoch Credit Partners are able to provide a range of advisory, quantitative and training services to market participants, regulators, lawyers, accountants and market intermediaries. Robert has been called as an expert witness in a number of credit derivative-related disputes.

Robert has addressed conferences and seminars on credit derivatives for over 12 years. He holds a degree in Chinese Studies and in Law from Cambridge University.

'Derivatives have been likened to aspirin: taken as prescribed for a headache, they will make the pain go away. If you take the whole bottle at once you may kill yourself.'

■ ■ ■

Background and Development of the Derivatives Market

Introduction

Definition and key features

Uses of derivatives

Range of derivatives

Increasing use of the central counterparty model (CCP)

Risk and benchmarking

Market volumes

Users and uses of derivatives markets

Straight through processing (STP)

INTRODUCTION

I am often asked, 'What exactly is a derivative?' and the temptation is to respond using expressions such as 'financial instrument' and 'risk management product'. It was only when one of our friends remarked that he thought that only musicians played instruments that I realized the need for an even simpler definition. I have now developed two definitions, first, a very simple definition (some would say overly simple).

Definition 1	Derivatives are financial tools that are used to manage risk or to take risk.

We are then faced with the follow-on question, 'What is risk?' In a financial market place risk can be related to movements in interest rates, share (or stock) prices, currency rates, oil and gas prices, even going so far as what is the risk (or possibility) that it will snow on Christmas Day? It follows then that there must be a derivative which, if it does snow on Christmas Day, or whichever date is chosen, will make a payout to the user. There is!

I may not have a party planned where I am worrying about the weather, I may just be daydreaming about snow. If it snows I will get a payout; whether I was worried about snow affecting the number of guests that could make it to the party, or whether I just think I am a better forecaster than the TV experts. Using the terminology, in the first instance I am a 'hedger' trying to protect myself from the effects of snow; in the second instance I am a 'trader' or 'speculator' who is hoping it will snow so I can reap a financial reward.

My second definition will be more familiar to those readers with a banking or finance background. American readers can liken this to 'Derivatives 101'.

Definition 2	A derivative instrument is one whose performance is based on or derived from the behaviour of the price of an underlying asset (often simply known as the underlying). The underlying asset does not need to be bought or sold and the majority of transactions are cash-settled. A premium may be due.

We use the term 'assets' – this is how we describe what the derivative is based on. Assets will include interest rates, share (or stock) prices, currency rates, oil, gas and metal prices and even credit and credit risk. We have a financial risk that the respective asset prices may be rising or falling.

Seasoned practitioners in this market may remember the terms 'off-balance sheet instruments', 'financial products', 'risk management instruments' and 'financial engineering', all meaning much the same thing. These are now collectively all covered by the expression 'derivative'. To summarize, the term 'derivative' is simply a new name for a tried and trusted set of risk management instruments. Unfortunately some market participants, not only the end-users, but also some of the firms who provide a service in these instruments, have used these derivative products to speculate wildly.

'Derivatives have been likened to aspirin: taken as prescribed for a headache, they will make the pain go away. If you take the whole bottle at once, you may kill yourself.'

DEFINITION AND KEY FEATURES

A true derivative instrument requires no movement of principal funds at maturity. It is this characteristic that makes them such useful tools to both hedge and to take risk and why, some years ago, these same instruments were known as off-balance sheet instruments. 'Off-balance sheet' signified that, as there was no movement of principal (e.g. no commitment to lend money or take deposits), they did not have to appear on the firm's balance sheet. However, with the new accounting regulations, notably FASB 133 in the USA and IAS 39 in Europe, it is arguable whether anything is actually off-balance sheet anymore. There are many types of derivative product; examples are listed in Table 1.1, together with their respective 'underlying asset'.

Derivative products and their underlying assets Table 1.1

Derivative	Underlying
Currency options	Foreign exchange
Interest rate swaps	Bond yields
Interest rate futures	Implied forward Interest rates
FT-SE 100 Futures	FT-SE 100 Index
Credit Default Swaps	Credit Risk

USES OF DERIVATIVES

Derivatives have many uses. A treasurer in a risk-averse organization may simply buy a currency option to hedge his exchange risk, while another treasurer in a profit-centred organization may well sell options to speculate and earn premium income. Stories are legion of various companies and individuals losing their shirts in the currency market due to 'unforeseen' circumstances. If they are honest, they simply sold options hoping to keep the premium and 'beat' the market – but they lost!

RANGE OF DERIVATIVES

Exchange-traded versus OTC instruments

A derivative product can be either 'exchange traded', where a contract is bought or sold on a recognized exchange, or it can be over the counter (OTC). An OTC instrument is written or created by a bank (or sometimes corporate and other financial institutions), and tailored to suit the exact requirements of the client.

1. An exchange-traded instrument

This is an instrument that is bought or sold directly on an exchange such as Euronext-LIFFE (the London International Financial Futures Exchange was bought by Euronext) or the CME (the Chicago Mercantile Exchange). There are over 20 recognized, regulated exchanges worldwide.

Each exchange-traded product has a 'contract specification', which details precisely the characteristics of the 'underlying', and the obligations of the buyer and seller at maturity. Typical exchange-traded instruments include financial futures and listed options. Trading used to be predominantly transacted via 'open outcry', which originated in the last century on the Chicago exchanges and entailed face-to-face contact, hand signals and loud verbal agreements. This style of trading conveys 'price transparency' and allows every market participant, both big and small players, to have equal access to the trade at the same price. In the last five years or so with the availability of increasingly sophisticated technology, there has been a shift away from open outcry trading towards electronic screen-based trading of these exchange-traded derivatives.

Within the exchange-traded market place there is the entity known as the Clearing House. This body is responsible for many things including the 'clearing' of trades, which will be discussed later. The Clearing House also becomes the buyer to everyone who sells and the seller to everyone who buys and they are known as a central counterparty. This is incredibly important as it means that no matter with whom you deal your ultimate counterparty will be the Clearing House. Whether you deal with a small bank, large bank, French corporate or American fund, if you deal on Euronext.liffe your eventual counterparty will be LCH.Clearnet Ltd. This is a body formed from the merger of the London Clearing House and Clearnet. In effect this removes the requirement to check individual credit lines before dealing, as the exposure will be to LCH.Clearnet, not to the firm with which you transacted, whether via open outcry or screen-based trading.

2. An over the counter (OTC) instrument

This is a financial instrument that is sold by a bank (usually), to a client and tailored to fit a specific set of requirements. Occasionally, banks will purchase these products from companies or other non-banks, but each buyer and seller must take the credit risk of their counterparty. In the event that there is a failure of any kind, each party to the trade is exposed to the risk that the other party will be unwilling or unable to proceed.

An OTC product allows much greater flexibility in terms of expiry date, reference price, amount, underlying commodity, and vast amounts of transactions are executed every day. An OTC instrument can be very simple, in which case it is known as a 'vanilla' product, or it can be exceedingly complex. The price of the trade will be agreed upon between the parties, is confidential and will involve many factors.

INCREASING USE OF THE CENTRAL COUNTERPARTY MODEL (CCP)

One of the most important distinctions between exchange-traded derivatives and OTC products is how credit risk is managed. Put simply, with an exchange-traded transaction the ultimate counterparty is the Clearing House which is a very substantial, very safe entity. In comparison, an OTC trade has credit risk linked to the counterparty itself, which may be a large company or a small company, or maybe even a bank. As the vast majority of the OTC derivatives which are dealt are the simple 'commoditized' or vanilla trades, banks are seeking ways to reduce their credit risk and exposure to each other. Given that approximately three-quarters of all derivatives are OTC, there is much development work in minimizing credit risk. One way is to use credit derivatives; another way is to make use of the CCP model where possible.

Over the last few years there have been various initiatives where a central counterparty model (which is inherently exchange driven) is adopted for OTC trades. One example is LCH SwapClear. This was formed by LCH.Clearnet and provides services to banks dealing in OTC swaps. The most important factor is that LCH SwapClear becomes the counterparty to both. Instead of Bank A and Bank B dealing with each other and taking each other's credit risk, the transaction is still executed in the same way but is then passed through LCH SwapClear which becomes the counterparty to both A and B. They are in effect no longer dealing with each other. This frees up existing credit lines and allows the banks to increase their dealing volumes, earning themselves more bid–offer spreads.

RISK AND BENCHMARKING

Banks, corporates and financial institutions need to manage their derivatives positions closely. As technology has evolved so has risk management and the science of 'risk' is becoming more and more important. We need ways to manage and measure risk, both for our own purposes and for the various regulators and accounting bodies. To monitor the value of derivatives positions it is common practice for derivatives positions to be marked-to-market at least daily, if not more frequently. To do this we compare the value of the derivative when originally transacted to what it is worth today. We also look at how this has changed compared with what it was worth earlier today and yesterday. The data used for the comparison must be independent to remove the threat of bias; this process is known as benchmarking. See Chapter 7 for more information.

MARKET VOLUMES

Each contract, whether exchange traded or OTC, will have a 'notional value', often known as the nominal principal amount (NPA). This is the amount of the underlying commodity whether financial, commodity or equity based, covered by the derivative. For example, an interest rate option with an NPA of £5 million will cover a hedging or trading transaction of £5 million, but will not be the vehicle to lend the money or take the deposit. This is assumed to be transacted separately.

The most recent survey by the BIS on the global OTC derivatives market shows that:

as at December 2005:   the total estimated notional amount of outstanding OTC contracts stood at US$298.52 trillion (inc. CDS data)

as at December 2004:   the total estimated notional amount of outstanding OTC contracts stood at US$251 trillion

as at December 2003:   the total estimated notional amount of outstanding OTC contracts stood at US$197 trillion.

Compare these figures with December 1998:

as at December 1998:   the total estimated notional amount of outstanding OTC contracts stood at US$80 trillion.

This shows a 380 per cent increase in 6 years – phenomenal growth, which shows no real sign of stopping.

USERS AND USES OF DERIVATIVES MARKETS

There are many different 'users' in this market

1. Hedgers

These may be anyone from a small to medium-sized corporation with a currency exposure that they wish to protect, to a large multinational with a $500m borrowing that needs rate protection, to a French fund manager who is worried about the domestic stock market falling. Hedgers generally will 'buy' insurance or try and establish 'fixed rates'. This is a global market and derivatives easily cross borders.

2. Traders

The banking community predominates here, although not all banks will transact or make prices (market-make) in all derivative products. The role of the trader is to create the derivative at a price, sell it to the client, run their positions at a profit, and hedge themselves. Traders will also speculate in the inter-bank market. Increasingly hedge funds are becoming active in the markets.

3. Private clients

Individuals who have funds 'under management' with one of the large financial institutions may use derivatives to enhance their yield, or perhaps to take out speculative positions. The banker or the individual in concert or in isolation may take decisions.

4. The 'retail market'

These are often ex-traders, mathematicians or individuals with money to invest who want to do-it-themselves. There is a term we now have in use – 'arcade'. An arcade is created when a firm, such as Refco, provides desks, space, technology and services, and even sometimes an element of capital for this market. They charge a monthly fee as rent and may expect a proportion of any profits that are made. Some of these arcades have hundreds of individuals trading continuously throughout the day in the exchange-traded instruments.

5. Arbitrageurs

These are individuals or banks that try to identify price discrepancies and profit from them. This is not confined solely to the derivatives market. For example, you would assume that the physical gold price will move at the same speed as derivatives linked to the gold price. This may not always be the case and there may therefore be profit opportunities from buying one and selling the other.

> 'Anyone can sell a derivative (subject to their credit), and anyone can buy a derivative (subject to their 'paying' for it).'

- Companies can sell derivatives to banks for income, and take on risk, or they can purchase derivatives and pay someone else to take their risk.

- Banks can write derivatives and sell them to clients for profit, or they can purchase them from clients for their own strategic or speculative purposes, or they can trade them inter-bank.

Typical derivatives users include:

- supranationals (World Bank, European Development Bank, African Development Bank, etc.),

- governments and government agencies,

- banks (for their own or client positions),

- companies,

- asset managers,

- hedge funds,

- high net worth individuals,

- private clients,

- arcades (where groups of individuals can hire space/rent services for a monthly fee).

Uses of derivatives

Applications for derivatives include:

- taking on credit risk without the loan,

- protecting against a possible dollar devaluation (or any other currency),

- profiting from a potential increase in the value of the euro (or any other currency),

- protecting a stock market portfolio from a downturn in the stock market,

- taking a view on the upswing of the Nikkei (or any other) stock index,

- protecting an interest rate exposure for 5 years at a fixed rate,

- choosing a FX rate to use when submitting a foreign currency tender,

- enhancing the yield on a non-performing investment,

- offering a fixed rate mortgage product,

- insuring against an upward movement in interest rates,

- fixing an investment rate now, when the investment does not start until a future date,

- speculating as a private client on the foreign exchanges with minimal risk.

STRAIGHT THROUGH PROCESSING (STP)

Volumes of derivatives have increased enormously in the last few years and the operations departments in banks sometimes struggle to keep up with deals taking place. For many market participants the quest for straight through processing – ways to streamline what happens after the dealer says 'done' – has been a dominant part of their working lives.

There are a number of stages in the life cycle of a trade; Figure 1.1 shows this in a simplified way. Historically, each stage or process had its own database and own computer system – they did not always talk to each other and each required repeated manual intervention.

Life cycle of a trade

Figure 1.1

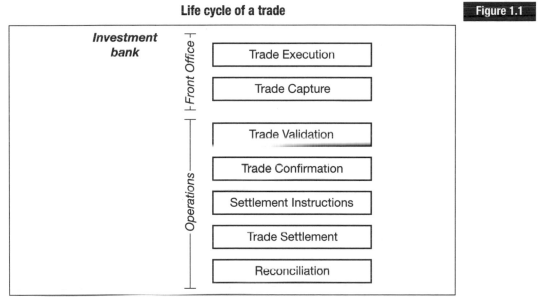

Source: Mike Simmons

STP is how we manage these processes without the need to input data more than once, e.g. full name of the client, address, legal entity, bank account details. Technology also now allows us to remove much of the paper and use electronic templates for confirmations of transactions; pricing and revaluations are more efficient. Deal capture, entry and validation can be largely automated, as are settlement instructions. For many market participants this is an ongoing project which is likely to be expensive, but in the long run it will be worth it. It is clear that technology is driving these markets. For more information see Chapters 15 and 17.

'Everyone thinks you know and understand this…. .'

■ ■ ■

Market Fundamentals

Introduction

How banks generate income

Three key assumptions

Role and use of LIBOR

Day counts

Financial maths

Calculating forward rates

Marking to market

Yield curves

Quiz

LEEDS METRCPOLITAN
UNIVERSITY
LIBRARY

INTRODUCTION

This chapter is designed for all those of you who feel that maybe, just maybe, you missed something somewhere along the line. It may help fill in some of the knowledge gaps or it may give you the urge to learn more. In my experience, a vast range of individuals want to learn about derivatives; they may have personal backgrounds ranging from a graduate with a degree in medieval history, to a trader with 10 years experience in the commodities market, to an IT specialist with 5 years with a communications company now moved into banking, to a retail bank manager on the high street. I personally prefer not to assume too much with respect to what the reader already knows. Feel free to skip this chapter – nothing is mandatory.

HOW BANKS GENERATE INCOME

If you ask anyone how banks make money, the response will probably be '... from lending money.' This is not the whole story. There are two key ways in which a bank may generate income, trading and fees.

Trading

Banks generate trading income by borrowing 'cheap' and lending 'expensive'. This allows them to use their credit standing in the market to arrange very beneficial borrowing rates (for them) and lend at higher rates, making the difference between the two prices. This holds true for any asset, from FX to loans and deposits, to equity, bonds and derivatives. The price that the bank pays for the asset is known as the BID (the lower price), the price at which it sells the asset is known as the OFFER (the higher price). In the professional markets banks will quote a 'two-way price' (the bid and the offer) to each other; this is known as 'market-making'.

Example What is the current sterling/US dollar spot rate?
Let us assume we are looking at the professional inter-bank market place.

Price quoted:
£/$ 1.8580–90, if this looks unfamiliar expand the price so it reads,
£/$ 1.8580–1.8590. Amongst market practitioners the quote would simply be, '80–90' – you are supposed to know the front figures are 1.85!

£/$1.8580 is the bid and £/$1.8590 is the offer (for the base currency which in this case is sterling.)

At 1.8580 the bank quoting the price will buy sterling and sell US dollars; at 1.8590 the bank quoting the price will sell sterling and buy US dollars. If you were a client wishing to sell dollars and buy sterling, you would deal at £/$1.8590, you are selling US dollars where the bank is buying them. The bid–offer spread works in the bank's favour but against the client. Clients can only buy where the bank sells and vice versa.

If the bank could buy and sell simultaneously it could make the difference – shown here as £/$0.0010, this is 10 'pips', and is known as the bid–offer spread; it represents the income to the bank. To the individual trader this is profit, to the bank this is income as there are a range of expenses that the bank will need to deduct, such as salaries, cost of Reuters, Bloomberg, power, premises, etc.

If the bank deals in £5 million and the bid–offer spread is 0.0010 the income is $5,000. The wider the bid–offer spread the greater the income to the bank. If the spread is too wide, the rate will not be competitive and the client will deal elsewhere. As bid–offer spreads narrow, income from this type of banking is reduced. In the traditional foreign exchange markets (dollars, euro, sterling, etc.) bid–offer spreads are small, whereas in volatile or emerging markets, e.g. China, Vietnam, there will be wider bid–offer spreads to reflect the risk; more volatility means more risk. Thus the bank needs to make additional income in these markets. If you look at the financial reports of banks they discuss trading income – this is it. Everything the bank offers to clients ultimately has two prices. The bank will always try to buy the asset as cheaply as possible and sell it for as much as possible.

Fees

If you ask a further question, 'What can banks charge for?' The short answer is everything, ranging from credit cards, to arrangement fees on loans, to fees for bond and equity issues. Fees for capital market issues such as bonds, equity and securitization are generally higher than those for loans. We must not forget advisory fees for mergers and acquisitions, privatizations, etc. Most banks will develop a business that generates income from trading and fees. Some years trading income may be good, other years not so good, therefore income from fees provides a welcome balance. Next year fee income may be down but trading income may be up, and so on.

THREE KEY ASSUMPTIONS

There are three key assumptions that are understood within the financial and derivatives markets.

1. Everything is in the price

This means that every asset that a bank trades in (loans, deposits, derivatives, FX, etc.) will need to take into account all current available data, for example:

- Prices/worries about oil price
- Terrorism
- Weather
- Politics
- Economics and statistics
- Commodity prices

This is why banks need information providers such as Reuters and Bloomberg which continuously relay information every day from the markets to the market. As information is continuously changing, prices will continuously change.

2. Euro, domestic and offshore markets

We assume that all currency is held in its country of origin, e.g. US$ in the USA, £ in the UK, in Europe. When this is so, the currencies are known as domestic and are subject to domestic, local interest rates. If a client or bank holds US$ that are in Europe or Asia, they are subject to international interest rates (not always the same as domestic US rates) and are conventionally known as Euro or offshore rates.

Example   £ in Europe is known as Euro-sterling.
Yen in Australia is known as Euro-yen.
US$ in Tokyo are Euro-dollars.
Euro outside the euro zone are known as Euro-euro.

---

3. Short selling

Large financial institutions and occasionally some trading corporates are allowed to enter into a range of transactions. This could be to:

- Buy – in anticipation of a price rising – known as 'going long';
- Sell (what they had previously bought) – to take a profit;
- Sell (what they have never had) – known as 'going short'. Why would they do this? In anticipation of a price falling.

Not all organizations have approval to 'short-sell' as it can be quite dangerous. If you purchase an asset and the price goes up, well done. If it does not go up you can perhaps just hold it for longer until the price rises – fingers crossed! However, if you agree to sell someone an asset for delivery next Friday, you must deliver it. You were hoping for the price to fall so you could buy it back more cheaply and make a profit, but if instead the price rose, it will cost you more to buy it back than you thought. Unlucky. You must deliver; if this means buying it when it is expensive, so be it.

ROLE AND USE OF LIBOR

Banks and many large organizations have funding linked to LIBOR. This is an international, commercial rate at which banks lend money to each other. It forms a reference rate for a range of different borrowings and also for derivatives. It is set in London and there are LIBOR rates available for monthly periods up to one year. Sterling LIBOR is the UK domestic rate, but there are also LIBOR rates in currencies such as the US dollar, Canadian dollar, euro and yen – these then are Euro-currency rates. As with everything in banking there is a bid and an offer.

In the UK the rates are displayed as shown:

London Inter-bank Offer Rate – London Inter-bank Bid Rate

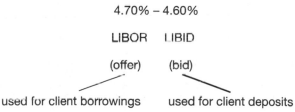

4.70% – 4.60%

LIBOR   LIBID

(offer)   (bid)

used for client borrowings   used for client deposits

LIBOR is the rate at which the market-making bank will offer to sell (lend) money.

LIBID is the rate at which the market-making bank will bid for a deposit.

There is an element of confusion about LIBOR. In the UK, the key lending rate between two banks is called LIBOR and the rate will fluctuate with supply and demand throughout the day.

Question: Does that mean that every bank will quote the same LIBOR rate at the same time?

Answer: No, it all depends upon the bank's position; is it long or short and how does this influence the rate the bank quotes?

In practice, a bank with a lot of money to lend will quote a relatively lower LIBOR rate than a bank that is itself borrowing and would rather be contacted by investors.

LIBOR fix

If LIBOR fluctuates how can it possibly be a reference rate if it is a different rate at every bank? We need a reference point for instruments such as derivatives and loans that is only going to change once a day. This is known as the LIBOR fix. Every day at 11.00 a.m. the 16 most active banks in their respective currencies send their current market rates to the British Bankers Association (BBA). This is an independent body which take the 16 rates for, say, one month LIBOR and remove the highest and lowest four rates and average the eight rates which are left. This is undertaken for overnight, 1 week, 2 weeks and every monthly period up to 12 months and then displayed on a screen (Figure 2.1).

Figure 2.1

04/24	12.07 GMT	[REUTERS]	[BBA LIBOR RATES]	Telerate Successor Page		37
[24/04/06]		RATES AT 11.00 LONDON TIME 24/04/2006				24/04 10:31 GMT
CCY	USD	GBP	CAD	EUR	JPY	EUR 365
O/N	4.79625	4.65845	3.86167	2.62625	SN0.05875	2.66273
1WK	4.84688	4.63500	4.03833	2.64788	0.06313	2.68466
2WK	4.89250	4.60875	4.04167	2.64938	0.06625	2.68618
1MO	4.97000	4.60000	4.05000	2.65413	0.07500	2.69099
2MO	5.04000	4.62125	4.07000	2.70738	0.09250	2.74498
3MO	5.10750	4.64188	4.09333	2.78163	0.11250	2.82026
4MO	5.15000	4.65375	4.11000	2.83650	0.13125	2.87590
5MO	5.19000	4.66938	4.12833	2.87775	0.15500	2.91772
6MO	5.23000	4.68125	4.15000	2.93500	0.18250	2.97576
7MO	5.25875	4.69813	4.17417	2.98213	0.21125	3.02355
8MO	5.28438	4.71750	4.19083	3.03000	0.24250	3.07208
9MO	5.30688	4.73500	4.21167	3.08088	0.27375	3.12367
10MO	5.32625	4.75625	4.23417	3.11850	0.30688	3.16181
11MO	5.33938	4.77750	4.25583	3.15088	0.34438	3.19464
12MO	5.35000	4.79750	4.27500	3.19125	0.37688	3.23557

Source: British Bankers Association, courtesy Reuters

You cannot deal at the LIBOR fix rate, although many banks benchmark their staff based on a particular LIBOR rate – it is, after all, a type of average rate. NB: The 6-month LIBOR fix is a popular index for interest rate swaps, caps and for setting the interest rate on a multi-period bank loan.

Is it just for banks?

A client who wishes to have a borrowing linked to LIBOR but is not a bank will have to pay an additional margin, e.g. 3-month LIBOR + 0.25% (25 basis points). The 25 bps is known as the credit spread.

What happens if we need to borrow for a longer term, say 5 years; how can a short-term rate like LIBOR be the key reference rate? This is because if a client borrows at a 'fixed' rate and the underlying LIBOR falls, they will feel cheated. If they borrow at a 'floating' rate and LIBOR rises they will feel the same. LIBOR is a good thermometer; it is one of several that clients will use.

DAY COUNTS

Calculating interest

Interest rates are quoted as rates per annum. A transaction with a maturity of up to 12 months will have the interest paid in arrears – at maturity. For a longer-term transaction, say 18 months, interest is likely to be paid in instalments every 6 months. Interest rates are quoted as annual rates so if a client borrows for only 3 months the amount of interest is calculated per day then multiplied by the number of days in the period.

£5 million borrowed at 4.94938% per annum for 3 months – the interest **Example** amount must be apportioned for the required number of days in that particular 3-month period. Let us assume it is 91 days. The calculation is:

$$\frac{£5,000,000}{365 \times 100} \times 91 \times 4.94938 = £61,697.75$$

This day count convention is written 'Actual/365' or A/365. It assumes 365 days in the year and 91 days in this 3-month period.

If the loan is in US$5 million, at the same rate for the same period, the interest amount will be different. This is due to the fact that US dollar calculations assume a 360 day year:

$$\frac{\$5,000,000}{360 \times 100} \times 91 \times 4.94938 = \$62,554.66$$

This day count convention is written 'Actual/360' or A/360. It assumes 360 days in the year and 91 days in this 3-month period.

Different countries have different 'day count conventions' which determine the number of days per month/year.

GB A/365

USD and EUR A/360

Question: Do I include Saturdays, Sundays and bank holidays in the calculations?

Answer: Yes, although payments must be made/received on 'good days', i.e. when the financial markets are open for business.

FINANCIAL MATHS

A. Time Value of Money (TVM)

You are familiar with the concept of interest: investors earn interest and borrowers pay interest. The financial markets provide a number of vehicles for investors and borrowers to optimize their risk and return. The rate of interest reflects the fact that cash has a current value and a decision to invest i.e. not spend the cash today, must mean that there will be a reward in the future. When an investor invests in equity or a bond or a money market instrument, he or she is forgoing the benefits of consuming a known value of money today, in return for an unknown value in the future. The investor therefore requires compensation for:

■ the period the money is invested (unable to be used elsewhere), and

■ the risk that the money may not be repaid (known as credit risk).

Generally, borrowers need to compensate the investors for both of the above factors; in the form of interest income if the investment is a loan or a bond, dividends from equity, rent from property and so on, together with an increase in the value of the original capital over time. The first is known as interest income and the second is known as capital gain. The sum of these two elements is known as the overall rate of return on the investment.

Reminder

1. Interest rates are expressed as per annum interest rates. This enables us to compare and contrast the returns on different instruments for different periods. Where there is only a single payment of interest (usually at maturity) this is known as *simple interest*.

But, what is a year? How many days in a year? Is it the same in every country? Is every month the same? What about leap years? Do I count week-ends and bank holidays?

2. What about earning or paying interest on interest? This is especially important where interim payments are not made/received, and is known as *compound interest*.

Of critical importance is the notion of Time Value of Money (TVM). All instruments have a face value (principal), a purchase price and a redemption value (which may be the same) and an interest rate. The way this all links together is Time Value of Money.

Inter-relationships between Present Value, PV, (money today) and Future Value, FV, (money in the future) are given below.

B. Future Value (FV)

$$FV = PV \times 1 + \left[i \left[\times \frac{d}{y} \right] \right]$$

where: PV = Present Value (the principal amount)

FV = Future Value

d = Actual number of (calendar) days elapsed

i = Quoted interest rate

y = Standardized year denominator (360 or 365 depending on the currency, see the previous section on day counts)

What is the FV of $10,000,000 in 91 days' time at an interest rate of 4.5%, **Example** assuming a day count 'A/360' basis?

$$FV = \$10m \times \left[1 + \left[0.045 \times \frac{91}{360} \right] \right] = \$10,113,750.00$$

What is the FV of £5,000,000 in 30 days' time at an interest rate of 5.5%, assuming a day count 'A/365' basis? **Example**

$$FV = £5m \times \left[1 + \left[0.055 \times \frac{30}{365} \right] \right] = £5,022,602.74$$

C. Present Value (PV)

$$PV = FV \times \frac{1}{\left[1 + \left[i \times \frac{d}{y}\right]\right]}$$

where: PV = Present Value (the principal amount)
FV = Future Value
d = Actual number of (calendar) days elapsed
i = Quoted interest rate
y = Standardized year denominator (360 or 365 depending on the currency, see section on day counts)

With so many debt market instruments having interest and principal payment/repayment dates in the future, we need a way of calculating the true worth of the value of those flows as at today. This is known as a Present Value calculation or 'discounting' back the cash flow. It can be likened to working backwards from the Principal + accrued interest to find out what the original Principal amount should be.

NB: This is the underlying assumption behind the concept of marking-to-market.

Example What is the PV of \$10,113,750.00 at an interest rate of 4.5%, over 91 days, assuming a day count 'A/360' basis?

$$PV = \$10,113,750.00 \times \frac{1}{\left[1 + \left[0.045 \times \frac{91}{360}\right]\right]}$$

= \$10,000,000.00

Example You are expecting to receive £100,000 in 182 days time.
What is the PV of this sum, given that current market interest rates are 5% per annum?

$$PV = £100,00 \times \frac{1}{\left[1 + \left[0.05 \times \frac{182}{365}\right]\right]} = £97,567.49$$

This means that you would need to invest £97,567.49 for 182 days at a rate of 5% to grow to £100,000.

Present Value and Future Value are related by a Discount Factor

D. Discount Factor (Df)

The expression for a Discount Factor is:

Df = [1 + I% (p.a.)]

Where the period in question is shorter than a year this becomes

Df = {1 + [I% × days/year] }

Where the period in question is more than a year (say 2 years), this becomes

Df = [1 + I%]^2

We are marking-to-market a security with a Future Value of US$100,000.   **Example**
The maturity date is in exactly 8 years' time from now and assumes that
the annual yield is 4.24 per cent for each year. What is the Present Value of
this security?

$$PV = \frac{\$100,000}{(1 + 0.0424)^8}$$

$$= \frac{\$100,000}{(1.0424)^8}$$

$$= \frac{\$100,000}{1.39403996}$$

$$= US\$71,733.96$$

CALCULATING FORWARD RATES

Fair Value calculations

Of supreme importance in the derivatives market is the ability to ascertain
whether an instrument is trading cheap or trading expensive. We ascertain this
by comparing the price on the derivative to the price where we expect it to
trade by incorporating all known current market data (known as Fair Value).

All derivatives instruments are priced by comparing the requested structure with the current market price. Ascertaining the underlying
'benchmark' for comparison prices means deciding on:

(a) the benchmark;

(b) whether to use the forward or the spot price;

(c) how to arrive at 'fair value'.

Calculating forward interest rates

For clarity we will consider how to calculate the forward price of an interest rate. This is known as a forward/forward calculation or an implied forward calculation, or even a 'fair value' calculation. It allows us to take information known today and use it to infer where a particular asset will trade on a forward date. There is a very serious drawback with this: this assumes that nothing will change, yet we know it will, so this is not a forecast. Simply, given everything we know today, *where it should be trading!*

Example | A client wants to know the rate on a 6-month borrowing of GBP 5 million, which will be drawn-down (borrowed) in 3 months' time. As financial markets change continuously, the bank is unable to guarantee the rate 3 months' in advance – unless they themselves take on this risk to moving market rates. However, the bank can calculate where the interest rate should be. They can then advise the client but unless the client wants to enter into some sort of a hedging derivative, such as an FRA in this case, there will be no guarantee.

Strategy: In simple terms, the bank can borrow the money (on behalf of the client) for 9 months at today's LIBOR rate, but the client does not want the money until month 3. This gives the bank the opportunity to invest this money for the first 3 months at LIBID. At maturity in 3 months' time, the deposit is returned with interest and is then ready and available for the client for the 6-month borrowing. This is shown diagrammatically in Figure 2.2.

Assume these interest rates are quoted in the market:

- 6 month GBP (181 days)
- 3 month (90 days)
- 9 month (271 days)

- 6 month 4.84–4.82%
- 3 month 4.81–4.79%
- 9 month 4.87–4.84%

Figure 2.2

Calculating implied forward rates

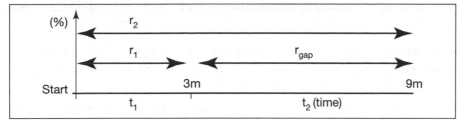

Forward/forward rates

These are generally calculated using off-setting LIBOR/LIBID rates. This is the standard forward rate break-even formula:

$$(1 + r_2t_2) = (1 + r_1t_1)(1 + r_ft_f)$$

formula 2.1

Where:

r_2 = interest rate for the long period (LIBOR)
r_1 = interest rate for the short period (LIBID)
r_{gap} = interest rate for the gap period that we are trying to ascertain
t_2 = time period from today until end of long period
t_1 = time period from today until end of short period
t_{gap} = contract period – forward gap ($t_2 - t_1$) (see Figure 2.2)

NB: As we shall quote using the number of days in the period, we shall use 'n' (days), instead of 't' (time period), and re-arrange the formula:

$$r_{gap} = \frac{r_2n_2 - r_1n_1}{n_{gap}[1+(r_1 \times n_1/365)]}$$

formula 2.1.1

using our data:

$$r_{gap} = \frac{(4.87\% \times 271) - (4.79\% \times 90)}{181 [1+(4.79\% \times 90/365)]}$$

$$= 4.85247\%$$

This is the 3 v 9 forward forward rate.

Calculating forward rates for a commodity

Let us look at one of the metals, say, copper; assume a client has asked a bank for a 6-month forward price. The current spot rate at the time of writing is US$8000 per tonne. We need to estimate, not where copper will be trading in 6 months' time, but a rate the bank can live with if it is asked to guarantee a price.

The only way the bank can do this with safety is to purchase the copper now at today's known spot rate and factor in all the additional costs (known as cost of carry), such as:

- **Financing** – how does the bank pay for the copper now if the client is not going to pay for 6 months? The money will need to be borrowed for 6 months at $ LIBOR, assume 5.0% p.a.

- **Storage** – what does the bank do with the copper for 6 months – assume it cannot be loaned to anyone else in the meantime.

- **Transport/insurance** – if appropriate.

Let us assume the additional costs (per $8,000) are:

- Finance – $201
- Storage – $50
- Transport/Insurance – $30

Total = $281 = Cost of carry

The true cost of this transaction to the bank is therefore:

$8,000 + $281 = $8,281

This is the Fair Value of the Forward. It is a break even price and a profit margin will be added. We can summarize this pricing relationship as follows:

Spot + cost of carry = Forward price (theoretical)

This indicates where the forward should be trading. If it turns out that the 6-month forward is trading higher than this we would say it is trading 'expensive'; if it was lower we say it is trading 'cheap'.

MARKING TO MARKET (MTM OR M2M)

This is a subject which is increasingly in people's minds, especially with the new Accountancy Regulations which have been introduced.

It is the way that firms, not just banks need to establish the current value for financial assets which they hold. These assets may be loans, investments in bonds or equity, or holdings in derivatives products such as swaps or options.

Simplified example

Yesterday you purchased green apples at 90 pence per pound, so you are 'long' apples. Today, at close of business, the price for the same green apples is quoted at 92 pence. Even though you have not sold them – you could have, and at a better price, thus making a 2 pence profit. This is known as a notional profit or an unrealized profit. You still have the apples. Tomorrow, the closing price may be 93 pence per pound, and then your notional profit will be 3 pence and so on. The notional profit (or loss) will fluctuate with market movements. On some days you may lose as the price falls. On a mark to market basis on the second day you had made a notional profit of 2 pence per pound.

However, the closing price must be an independent price, such as one displayed on a Reuters or Bloomberg network or via an independent market provider such as Markit; what if it was quoted at 89–91, at the close of day one. Would you have made or lost money? You would have lost 1 pence as you can only sell the apples where another purchaser will buy them, in this case at 89 pence. It is important where possible, to take into account the bid–offer spread when marking to market.

With derivatives another question arises; using the same analogy with apples, what if the only closing price we can find is for red apples? Can you use it if there is nothing else? I am afraid not.

As derivatives become more complex it is harder and harder to mark to market as there may be no published prices. In addition, many of the derivatives have cash flows stretching over a number of years into the future. These will all need to be NPV'd and compared with current prices to establish whether there is a mark to market gain or loss on the transaction.

Banks have been marking to market for years so that they know which desks are making (or losing) money – they have many established procedures for this. It is less familiar for utilities and corporations who have mostly never needed to do this before, but now under IAS 39 and FAS 133 it is needed. For further information see Chapter 7.

YIELD CURVES

I could write a whole book or at the very least an entire chapter on yield curves. But I will be brief. A yield curve is a graphical expression of interest yields against time. In the USA this is known as the 'term structure of interest rates'. There is a range of different types of yield curves, e.g. zero coupon curves, swap curves, forward curves, etc. The simplest curve is known as the par curve. It is usually drawn using the gross redemption yield on risk-free instruments such as government bonds, e.g. UK gilts and UK treasury bills, or US treasury bills and US treasury bonds. The shape of the yield curve (see Figure 2.3) is an important consideration when choosing whether or not to use derivatives. An upward sloping yield curve (positive) is one where, as the maturity lengthens, interest rates increase as investors seek higher yields for locking up their money for longer periods at fixed rates. A downward sloping yield curve (negative) is one where as the maturity lengthens, the less reward the investor gets and the cheaper borrowing becomes. This type of curve is usually an indicator of reducing inflationary tendencies. A flat yield curve indicates a stable inflationary environment – not necessarily a zero inflation rate.

Banks use the shape of the curve and how it moves with time to help them with pricing and structuring of deals.

| Figure 2.3 | **Different types of yield curve** |

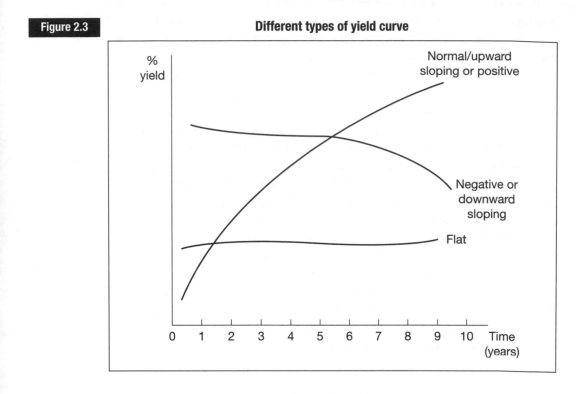

QUIZ

Questions

1. Calculate the amount of interest due on a US$5,000,000 loan for 10 days at 5.15% per annum.

2. What is the Present Value of EUR 16.2 million due in one year's time if interest rates are 2.95% per annum.

3. What is the Future Value of a £5 million asset in exactly two years' time if interest rates are constant at 4.5% per annum.

4. If GBP/USD Spot is quoted at 1.8750–60, at what rate will the bank sell USD?

Answers

1. Use A/360; US$7152.78.
2. EUR15,735,794.08, use eight figures after the decimal point on the discount factor.
3. £ 5,460,125.00.
4. £/$. 1.8750.

'Derivatives can be used for risk management or speculation, for risk mitigation, or risk taking.'

3

Derivatives Fundamentals

Range of derivatives

What is a vanilla trade?

Settlement

Triggers

Liquidity and credit risk

Understanding the underlying

Benchmarks

Fair value

Dealing with derivatives

RANGE OF DERIVATIVES

A derivative product can be used for risk management or speculation, for risk mitigation, or risk taking. The instrument itself can be bought or sold on an exchange or over the counter (OTC). There may be a premium payable for the product or it may be zero cost, and it may have one settlement or many. There are many variations to the basic 'vanilla' derivative. Let us take a few moments to clarify this.

WHAT IS A VANILLA TRADE?

A vanilla trade is the simplest form of that derivative and illustrates all the given product characteristics. The term derives from ice cream, vanilla being the simplest and easiest to obtain. For example, an option to buy gold at a pre-set price on a pre-set day will be vanilla. But if the option is to buy gold based on the average price over, say, a 3-month period, or to buy the gold over a range of dates, although this is still quite a simple structure, it may be called a simple 'exotic'. One rule of thumb is that even if just one of the rules of the traditional vanilla structure is broken, then the derivative automatically becomes an exotic. Therefore, you can have simple exotics (with only one rule broken) and complex exotics (with many rules broken).

It follows then that there are vanilla structures for all derivatives, but essentially they break down into three key financial techniques, shown in Table 3.1.

Table 3.1 **Derivatives: Key financial techniques**

	OTC	Exchange traded	Premium due
Futures	FRA	✓	No
Options	✓	✓	Yes
Swaps	✓	X	No

You will notice that an instrument known as an FRA is mentioned in the table. This is, in effect, an 'OTC financial future', where the financial future which comprises the 'raw material' is packaged to make it more user-friendly. Premiums are only required for option-based derivatives and these are priced through sophisticated computer models with multiple inputs. If a client chooses to transact an option for risk management purposes, then by paying a premium for his option, he is giving himself the chance to profit, as well as purchasing insurance for the transaction should things go wrong. Where there is no requirement to pay a premium such as on a swap or future, then a risk manager will be unable to profit, but will still have ensured a fixed rate. The old business adage 'You get what you pay for' is very relevant. An option gives a specific level of insurance as well as giving the client the chance of some profit. He or she is assured of a guaranteed worst case, if the insurance is invoked, but the best case will be dependent on how far the market has moved in their favour. If the market improves, the client will 'abandon' the option at the 'insured' rate and transact directly in the underlying cash market at a better rate.

Non-premium-based instruments 'lock' the client into a specific rate, which is fixed for the duration of the transaction, and where the client is obligated to transact. He is unable to walk away from his commitments, whatever the personal circumstances.

SETTLEMENT

At maturity all derivatives die; options are said to 'expire', futures 'go to delivery' and swaps 'mature'. At maturity there is generally a settlement, which may involve a sum of cash or the delivery of a predetermined asset. Some instruments may also contain 'triggers' which allow the user to acti vate the derivative early.

A. Single versus multiple settlement

Derivatives divide neatly into products where there is a single settlement at or during maturity, and those where there are multiple settlements throughout the transaction (see Table 3.2).

| Single and multiple settlement derivatives | Table 3.2 |

Single Settlement	Multiple Settlement
Financial futures/FRAs	Interest rate swaps
Interest rate options	Interest rate caps, collars, floors
Currency options	Currency swaps
Energy CFDs*	Energy swaps

* CFD = contract for differences

1. Single settlement

A single settlement product can only cover a specific 'tranche' or time period of the underlying. For example, one interest rate derivative is called a Forward Rate Agreement (FRA). Clients wishing to protect themselves from adverse interest rate movements use this. Consider a company that needs to cover a US$5 million borrowing for three months that commences in six months' time. It wants to protect an interest rate that will not be set until six months into the future. There will be only one settlement on this FRA, at month 6, when the reference borrowing rate (3-month LIBOR) is compared and settled against the FRA rate.

2. Multiple settlements

Alternatively, some clients may have borrowings that run for longer periods such as 5 years, where the interest rate on the loan is reset to LIBOR every three or six months in line with current interest rates. In such cases, the derivative chosen must allow for multiple fixings and multiple settlements on specific pre-determined dates. A swap or a cap may be considered.

B. Cash versus physical settlement

At maturity, derivatives may settle with a physical payment, e.g. shares or bonds – based on the underlying transaction, or on a cash basis. The vast majority will settle on a cash basis. This means that if I had the right to buy gold at $550 per ounce and the gold price at expiry was $600 per ounce, on a cash settlement basis I would receive $50 per ounce. This is also known as a settlement of differences and, in fact, some derivatives are known as Contracts for Differences or CFDs. If I had chosen physical settlement, then I would need to come up with $550 for every ounce, purchase the gold, take delivery of the gold, maybe arrange transportation, storage and insurance, and then sell the gold at $600. Arguably, there is no difference, except on a cash-flow basis and there are associated costs with physical delivery of any-thing and possible commissions for the buying and selling. Speculators tend to prefer cash settlement and hedgers tend to prefer physical delivery.

TRIGGERS

The original derivatives were designed to react to market movements; these are known as market triggers. For example, if I am the owner of an option which gives me the right to buy a particular share at £3.20, what makes me decide to use it? If the share price is now £4.00 then I can see a profit, so the increase in share price or market move has provided the trigger. Most derivatives are like this. However, credit derivatives, which are amongst the newer derivative instruments, especially credit default swaps, rely on legal triggers. This means that once a credit event notice has been published then the lawyers and the deal documentation provide the trigger. This has resulted in some interesting times and court cases!

LIQUIDITY AND CREDIT RISK

Liquidity is an important concept in any tradable instrument, especially derivatives. It is an indicator of how likely one is to be able to sell or to buy the instrument at a particular point in time. Liquidity is undoubtedly far greater with exchange-traded products, and hundreds of thousands of contracts are bought and sold each day on the major exchanges. The chance, therefore, of finding willing buyers and sellers at a particular time and price is very good. Liquidity in the 'vanilla' OTC instruments is also good, but will be spread among many types of similar but non-identical transactions. As a result of this, as deals become more complex, liquidity will start to dry up, resulting in some deals being so complex and so 'structured' that there is really nil liquidity.

> 'A frequently used expression in the market is that there is a price for buying, a price for selling, and a price for selling quickly.'

Credit risk is another important factor. It is the risk that the counterparty to the deal may go into liquidation or default in some way before the contract matures, thus making it impossible for them to fulfil their obligations. Credit risk is lower with exchange-traded products as the clearing house (which is separate from the regulated exchange) becomes counterparty to every trade, reducing exposure to individual clients. We will consider credit risk on each derivative as we describe them in the following sections.

UNDERSTANDING THE 'UNDERLYING'

'Underlying asset classes'

Each of the derivative instruments can be applied to an 'underlying asset class'. Table 3.3 shows figures based on OTC derivatives in the five primary asset classes, data has been collated by the Bank for International Settlements, Basle, Switzerland.

Total volume of OTC derivatives outstanding at June 1999 – $81.50 trillion of which   Table 3.3

- interest rates (67%)
- foreign exchange (18%)
- equity (2%)
- commodity (0.6%)
- credit (not known)

Source: BIS

The fastest growth is shown in the credit derivatives markets, although the only available data is shown for credit default swaps. Current data for CDS shows over 220 per cent growth from June 2004 to June 2005 (Table 3.4).

Table 3.4	Total volume of OTC derivatives outstanding at December 2005, − $284.819 trillion + $13.698 trillion (CDS data) = $298.517 trillion, of which:

- interest rates (72%)
- foreign exchange (11%)
- equity (2%)
- commodity (0.8%)
- credit default swaps (4.7%)
- other (9.5%) – data from non-reporting institutions

Source: BIS

BENCHMARKS

Not only can derivatives be linked to particular assets, we also need to link them to benchmarks within each asset class. This will help enable us to establish whether the derivative is cheap or expensive. Most of the time the price of the derivative is linked to the forward price of that particular asset – not the current or spot price. A currency option that matures in 3 months' time will be linked to the 3-month forward rate – not to today's current spot rate.

FAIR VALUE

Once we know what the asset is, we can calculate the forward rate or take screen data from an information provider. This allows us to establish what the benchmark rate is. A derivative that is priced at the benchmark rate will have a known value, the 'fair value' (for more information on the calculations see Chapter 2, Market Fundamentals). For example, a gold future trading at $590 an ounce when the fair value or benchmark rate is $600 an ounce is trading 'cheap' to fair value.

DEALING WITH DERIVATIVES

1a. Bank and customer credit risk – OTC transactions

OTC transactions can result in a possible two-way cash flow on the maturity date, from either the bank to the client or vice versa, dependent on who has sold (or written) the instrument and in which direction the market has moved. For example, with options, the purchaser must pay a premium for the product. If there is a default then not only is the premium lost, but also a potential profit opportunity will be lost in the transaction if the counterparty goes bankrupt. The seller (or writer) of the option must take on the risk of managing and hedging the resulting position but has received a premium.

In contrast, where a client sells a derivative to a bank or other counterparty, the client will receive the premium but then they will have the responsibility for risk managing the derivative position. This is where many companies have made losses; an instrument is sold for premium income which is regarded as a profit. This is not the case; the premium income must go towards the costs of risk managing the hedge position on the derivative. It is also easy to forget that by selling a derivative, the seller is taking on an obligation to transact in the future at a specific price.

'Derivatives can enhance the service offered by a bank to a client.'

It is not just financially naive, but absurd to run derivatives positions without some hedging. But many speculators do just that.

Consider a company which has taken a view that interest rates will not go up. This is not a risk management position but a speculative trade, and an option derivative is 'sold' accordingly. This means that if interest rates stay the same or go down, the company will make money. But if they go up, the company will lose money. As the company did not perceive that rates could go up, this was not seen as a possible outcome, so no hedging was undertaken. Eventually if rates go up, they will suffer a loss which could be substantial.

A professional trader in the market may have the same view on interest rates, but is unlikely to run the position 'naked' or un-hedged. If rates do turn against him and go up, he will either have an offsetting position to cover himself or another trade. He may not have been able to keep the entire premium but may have used some of it to buy himself cover on his derivative position. His potential loss or downside is therefore limited.

Credit risk is different from product to product and from buyer to seller, this will be explored in more detail later.

1b. Choosing your counterparty

When a client is looking for a suitable bank with which to transact business in OTC derivatives, one question he must ask himself is: 'Am I comfortable with the credit risk of the counterparty bank? In simple terms, if I transact a five-year derivative product, am I confident that if the bank is due to pay me some money on a future date in 5 years' time that they will still be around to pay it, and pay it on time?' The client is essentially taking a five-year view on the creditworthiness of the bank. Likewise, if a client wants to sell a ten-year derivative to a bank, the bank must be comfortable that if they purchase the product from the client, then the bank will receive any payment(s) due to them under the derivative in the future. They will be taking a ten-year view on the client. It is exceptionally difficult to forecast for one year, let alone ten years ahead, so a whole department has grown up in the banks devoted to this subject – the credit department.

2. Bank and customer credit risk – exchange-traded transactions

The concept of credit risk does not vanish when you look at exchange-traded transactions. The risk is still there, but all the counterparties are the same. They all turn out to be the clearing house. In London, this is LCH.Clearnet, owned 45.1 per cent by exchanges, 45.1 per cent by its members, and the balance owned by Euroclear. It is regarded as a very good risk. Whether you are buying or selling an exchange-traded instrument, it does not matter who is the client/bank on the other side of the transaction; your ultimate credit risk is always the clearing house.

3. Client relationships

Derivatives can enhance the service offered by a bank to a client. They can offer not only an extra dimension of risk management, but also permit a bank to continue dealing with a client where existing credit lines are 'full'. These are the lines that the bank credit department will allow for a particular client and will reflect the bank's appetite for his business. If the line is full, it means that the bank can transact no more business with that client. For example, if a customer wishes to transact some forward foreign exchange, but there is no more room available on the credit line, then it may be possible to sell him a currency option, without breaking the 'line' (assuming the client is willing to pay the premium). He will have the same level of hedging or risk management, but now he has some profit potential (although he must now pay a premium). The bank has no extra risk, once they have received the required premium. Offering a service in derivatives can also entice clients away from other banks, and other mainstream banking business may follow.

4. Gearing

Derivatives are often said to offer 'highly geared' positions. Just what does this mean? If a trader has a view that a particular currency is going to strengthen, then if he wishes to profit from his view, he could physically buy the particular currency, wait for it to increase in value, and then sell it at a profit. Derivatives offer an alternative. The trader could buy an option to purchase the currency at, say, a premium of 2 per cent of face value. If the currency increased in value, he could sell the option back to the writing bank (or exercise the option), and make the same profit as the original cash position (less the 2 per cent premium). But he has only laid out 2 per cent of principal for the same view on the market. So if his view turned out to be wrong, the most that he could lose is the original premium payment of 2 per cent.

A cash trade would not only need 100 per cent of the amount committed at the beginning, but there is the possibility of substantial losses should the view be wrong. So by using the derivative he could take a position up to 50 times the size (50 × 2% = 100%) for the same original cash outlay, and if he was wrong he could lose the lot. But if he was right he would make 50 times the profits. In market jargon we say this position is geared by 50 times. It could offer the market movement multiplied by a factor of 50 times. A serious profit, if you are right. If you are wrong, all that is at risk is the premium (but that in turn may be substantial).

'Anyone can sell a derivative (subject to their credit) and anyone can buy a derivative (subject to their paying for it).'

'… the test for this is that if all options were free of charge with no premium payable, most users would use them most of the time.'

■ ■ ■

Basic Option Concepts

Introduction

Option pricing

Option mechanics

INTRODUCTION

An option contract is the only derivative instrument that allows the buyer (holder) to 'walk away' from his obligations. This is unique amongst derivatives. With most derivatives and forward contracts the client is provided with a guaranteed rate; this is an obligation to deal at that rate. These products provide certainty, whatever the resulting market conditions. In contrast, option contracts allow the holder the best of both worlds: insurance when things go wrong, and when things go right, the ability to walk away from the instrument (or guarantee), and the ability to deal at a better rate in the market.

Options are available in many markets including interest rates/fixed income, currency, equity and commodity. Unfortunately, options do not come free of charge: a premium is due, usually paid upfront. The option allows a degree of flexibility; it does not completely remove all the risk (all losses and all profit). Instead it allows a degree of risk management, which is not total, controlling the risk rather than removing it completely.

In my personal opinion, options are a far superior instrument to some of the other derivatives; the test for this is that if all options were free of charge with no premium payable, most users would use them most of the time. However, the deciding factor becomes the premium. How much am I prepared to pay to have this very flexible instrument? Options can appear expensive.

Options illustrate the concept of 'asymmetry of risk'. The most that an option buyer (holder) can lose is the original premium that he or she paid, whereas profits are unlimited. To clarify this statement, if the option expires worthless then the premium is not returned to the purchaser. If the option expires with some value (we say, in the money), then should the purchaser find his counterparty has defaulted, then, yes, he or she would have lost the premium but also any gains which are due under the option – this is known as an opportunity loss. The extent of any profit on the option will be governed by how far the market has moved in his or her favour. A seller (writer) of options, in contrast, can only hope to keep the premium, but the extent of the losses are potentially unlimited.

The buyer or holder of the option is the one who has paid the premium, and he/she is the party with all the rights, i.e. the right either to buy or sell the underlying asset. Once the premium is paid, they have no further obligations under the contract. The option can be used, or not, depending on the rate on the option compared with the underlying rate in the market. The buyer will always choose the alternative that gives him the best outcome.

The seller or writer of the option has much heavier obligations. Once he has received the premium he must start to risk manage the position. In fact, hedging the option position will start immediately the deal is concluded, whereas the premium will not be received for two business days. The seller's obligations are to have 'the underlying' ready. If the option is a call, the seller must be ready to deliver the underlying. If the option is a put, the seller must take delivery of the underlying. The buyer can ask to make or take 'delivery' of the underlying, either at maturity or on any business day during the life of the transaction. This will depend upon how the option contract was originally designed.

Options can be bought or sold on an exchange in which case they are known as exchange traded or 'listed' options. Alternatively, they can be tailored to fit the exact circumstances of the client, when they are known as over the counter or OTC. If the option has a simple structure it is known as 'vanilla', a more complex option may be known as an 'exotic'. Options can be transacted in any one of the underlying primary markets, interest rates, currency, equity and commodity. Whatever the underlying commodity, all options are distinguished by the key phrase, 'the right, but not the obligation'. This separates an option from every other instrument.

> **Definition**
>
> An option gives the buyer the right, but not the obligation, to buy or sell a specific quantity of a specific financial instrument at a specific rate on or before a specific future date. A premium is due.

There are a great variety of options, not only those based on a financial commodity. There are options on such diverse assets as orange juice, pork bellies, grain, live hogs, etc. The first commonly used option-pricing model was written in the early 1970s by Fisher Black and Myron Scholes and published in the *Journal of Political Economy*. Their treatise contained many new descriptive words that are now in everyday usage – at least among options users and providers. Before we go any further, let us look at some of this terminology.

> **Terminology**
>
> **Basic option terminology**
>
> | | |
> |---|---|
> | **Call option** | The right (not the obligation) to buy the underlying. |
> | **Put option** | The right (not the obligation) to sell the underlying. |
> | **Exercise** | Conversion of the option into the underlying transaction or commodity. |
> | **Strike price** | Guaranteed price chosen by the client, which can be described as: |
> | | – at the money (ATM) |
> | | – in the money (ITM) |
> | | out of the money (OTM). |

Terminology continued		
Expiry date	Last day on which the option may be exercised.	
Value date	The date when the underlying is settled or delivered.	
American option	An option which can be exercised on any business day up to and including the expiry date.	
European option	An option which can be exercised on the expiry date only.	
Bermudan option	An option which can be exercised on selected dates.	
Asian option	An option which is linked to the average rate over a period.	
Premium	The price of the option.	
Intrinsic	Difference between the strike price and the current market value rate (depending upon whether the option is American or European style).	
Time value	Difference between the option premium and the intrinsic value, including time until expiry, volatility and cost of carry.	
Fair value	Combination of intrinsic value and time value, as calculated by the option pricing model.	
Volatility	Normalized, annualized standard deviation of the underlying reference rate.	

Terminology discussed

Calls and puts

It is possible for the bank or the customer to have bought or sold the option contract itself. It is also possible to have options to buy the underlying and options to sell the underlying. This results in a possible four-way price and likely confusion. It is because of this that we use the terms call and put.

Jargon: The client has bought a call option on the US dollar against sterling.

Reality: The client has bought the right to buy US dollars with sterling.

Jargon: The bank has sold a put option on the FT-SE 100 Index.

Reality: The bank has given someone else the right to sell the FT-SE 100 Index to them.

Jargon: The client has bought a put option on the sterling three-month future.

Reality: The client has bought the right to sell the sterling three-month future.

Jargon: The bank has sold a euro call option against US dollar.

Reality: The bank has sold someone else the right to buy euro from them with US dollars.

Exercise

This is how to convert the option that at inception is simply a piece of paper into the 'underlying commodity'. The term also tends to denote the physical movement of the underlying, unless the option is to be cash settled.

Strike price (or exercise price)

This is the rate chosen by the client. Options are not like forwards or futures where the current rate in the market is pre-determined. Instead the client can choose a rate that may be better or worse than the current market rate. This is called the strike price of the option. The strike rate must be compared with the current market rate to establish whether the client's chosen rate is better, or worse, or the same. Each option product has its own 'benchmark' rate against which the strike is measured. Some of the benchmark rates are:

■ currency options – outright forward FX rate (European style)

■ interest rate options – FRA rate (implied forward rate)

■ interest rate caps, floors (a series of options) – swap rate

■ traded energy options on futures – energy futures price.

Consider gold bullion for a moment. Assume the current price is $600 per oz. If the client chooses an option to buy gold at the same price of $600, we would say the call option was 'At the Money' (ATM): it is at the same rate as the current market. If he had chosen an option with a rate that was better for him immediately, say to buy the gold at $590 per oz, we would say the option was 'In the Money' (ITM): it is better than the current rate. If he had chosen a rate that was worse for him, say $610, the option would be described as 'Out of the Money' (OTM): worse than the current market rate.

Any strike price on any option can be described using this method. Naturally, an ITM option, which gives an advantage to the client, will be more expensive than an option that is OTM or ATM. Likewise an OTM option that gives the client a lesser degree of protection will cost less than an option which is either ITM or ATM.

At the money (ATM)	Same rate as the benchmark.	**Terminology**
In the money (ITM)	Better rate than the benchmark.	
Out of the money (OTM)	Worse rate than the benchmark.	

Expiry date

This is the last day when the buyer of the option can exercise the option into the 'underlying asset'. After this date the option will lapse. The expiry date will be agreed at the outset. It is not uncommon for options to have guide cut-off times. These are currency specific, and will often relate to a particular centre, for example, 10 a.m. New York or 10 a.m. Tokyo time. This is necessary, because most banks providing a service in options run their positions as portfolios, and manage their option risks across many option books and many currencies. If a client exercises his option with the bank, the bank will settle with him, and may then have to exercise an option they purchased from someone else, and so on.

There is no linear relationship between time to expiry and premium due (see Figure 4.1). A four-month option will not necessarily cost twice the premium of a two-month option although it will certainly cost more.

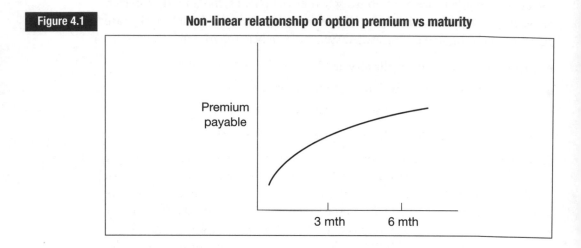

| Figure 4.1 |

Non-linear relationship of option premium vs maturity

Value date

This is the date when the underlying commodity is cash settled or delivered. For example, a sterling interest rate option written by a UK bank will have the expiry date and the value date the same. This is the same for dollar-based options written by an American bank, etc. With currency options, the settlement or delivery of the currency will result in a two-business-day value period (except US$/Canadian dollars with one business day).

American options

These can be exercised into the underlying commodity (or cash settled if previously arranged) on any business day within the transaction period up to the expiry date. If currency, it must be a business day in both currencies.

European options

These can be exercised only on the expiry date, but they can be sold back to the writing bank for fair value at any time. The names originally came from the side of the Atlantic these options were traded on. Both American and European options can be sold back to the writing bank for 'fair' value at any time.

Bermudan options

Halfway between an American and a European option, with selected exercise dates.

Asian options

An option linked to the average price over a specified period.

Premium

This is the price of the option as determined by the option pricing model. It comprises two components, intrinsic value and time value.

Intrinsic value

When the client chooses the strike price on the option, the pricing model will compare that rate with the option benchmark rate. If the option strike price is advantageous we say it is in the money (ITM). Intrinsic value is a measure of how much it is ITM.

Consider a client who wishes to buy some shares in BRIX plc. Assume the market price today is £5.00 a share. If she or he buys a call option on BRIX with a strike of £4.80 the option will be 20 pence in the money. This option has 20 pence intrinsic value. If she or he buys the call option with a strike of £5.00 it will be ATM and there would be zero intrinsic value. Equally, she or he may decide to purchase the call option with a strike at £5.10, this is 10 pence OTM. But it is impossible to have negative intrinsic value, so here the intrinsic value would again be zero.

This comparison between the strike and the benchmark rate works similarly whether the option is American or European style. The only difference is that the benchmark is slightly different. With an American option the benchmark is the current spot rate, as the client can exercise on any business day. But with a European option the benchmark is the current forward rate (to the expiry date), as the client can only exercise on the expiry date.

For the technically minded, an option's intrinsic value is measured by the present value of the amount by which it is in the money, that is, the present value (PV) of the difference between the strike of the option and the forward price of the asset. The present value is used, because we have an expiry date in the future.

Time value

The seller of the option will demand a premium in excess of the intrinsic value, as he must manage the risks he has taken on, some of which are very complex. The risks include volatility, time to expiry, cost of carry, etc.

Consider a trader wishing to purchase an option on Grape plc. Grape is trading in the market at £7.30 per share. If the option required is a call option at a strike of £7.20 with an expiry date in three months' time, there would be 10 pence intrinsic value in the option. However, the total premium for the option is 45 pence per share; then 10 pence is accounted for by the intrinsic value. The remaining 35 pence is the time value, or some traders regard this as risk premium. The reason a trader is prepared to pay an extra 35 pence for the option is because he believes that the share price will move by more than 35 pence within the next three months. Time value will decay through time, as the chance that the option will be exercised lessens.

Fair value

Fair value is the result of the premium calculation performed by the option-pricing model. The figure is a breakeven figure for the writer of the option. The premium that the client pays for the option may be adjusted upwards to allow for a profit margin.

Volatility

This is a measure of the degree of 'scatter' of the range of possible future outcomes for the underlying commodity. A volatility input is only required for options. If you wish to speculate on the level of volatility you will need to trade options. The reason that we need an input for volatility is because it is one of the key underlying assumptions in the pricing models. The original models assume that underlying financial data such as exchange rates and interest rates behave statistically with a log-normal distribution. These types of distributions are typically found in nature, for example the height of trees, the weight of children, the length of snakes, etc., and are all distributed normally. Where financial markets resemble nature can be looked at like this; where does the dollar go tomorrow – up or down? Don't know, therefore we consider it to be a 50 per cent chance of movement up or down. The volatility input into the model helps generate a prediction of how the particular target rate will move in the future: not necessarily what the rate will be as a number on a specific date in the future, but how the exchange rate or interest rate will get there. Will there be a large degree of scatter around a theoretical average or will there be very little movement? The best way to explain this is by using an example from nature.

Imagine data is being collected on the height of king penguins in Antarctica. One hundred penguins will be measured and then the data will be analysed. Once we have the data, we can calculate the average height of the penguins: this is known as the mean, and from this we assume that 50 per cent of the penguins will be shorter than this and 50 per cent of the penguins will be taller than this, but that most penguins will have a height at or around the mean height.

Many years ago a German scientist by the name of Gauss undertook some mathematical research. He showed that if you had data taken from a population with a normal distribution, once you had calculated the mean you could calculate certain 'confidence limits' or 'confidence intervals'. He worked out that if you took the mean +/– one standard deviation (the square root of the variance), you could ensure that 66 per cent of all the data readings would fall between these limits. He then further predicted that if you took the mean +/– two standard deviations, you could guarantee that 95 per cent of all the data would fall within these wider limits. This leaves you with 2.5 per cent 'tails' either side of where the data falls outside the confidence intervals.

Let us assume the penguins have been measured, the mean has been calculated at 1 m, and the standard deviation computed at a figure of 10 per cent. This would give us a normal distribution as shown in Figure 4.2.

Once you have the data, it is not too difficult to do the calculations: those of you who have studied statistics will recognize the shape of the distribution. How does all this fit in with options and option pricing? Standard deviation and volatility are the same thing.

The statistical definition of volatility is 'the normalized, annualized standard deviation of the returns of the underlying commodity'. The biggest problem in using volatility is trying to predict what the volatility level will be in the future, before there is any data to back it up.

For example, a trader trying to price a currency option in three-month US dollar/yen has to guess the shape of the normal bell-shaped curve. Will it be steep with low volatility, and most readings about the mean, or will it be very flat, with high volatility and many readings widely scattered? In fact, he is trying to guess how volatile the exchange rate will be in advance. Not an easy thing to do (see Figure 4.3).

| Figure 4.2 | **Analysis of the height of king penguins** |

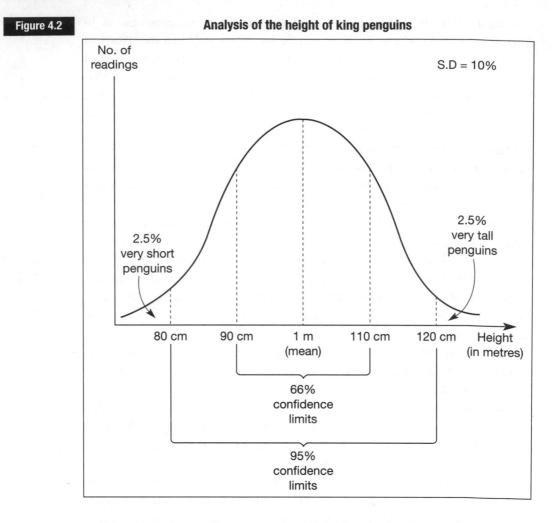

Historical data will give an idea of the level of volatility, but will not necessarily be much help in predicting a future value of volatility. The market operates using the concept of 'implied volatility'. This is where it is possible to take data from a premium already quoted, and get the model to work backwards to deduce the volatility. The relationship between volatility and premium is linear; as volatility increases so does the premium (see Figure 4.4).

The effect of different volatility levels on the shape of the normal curve

Figure 4.3

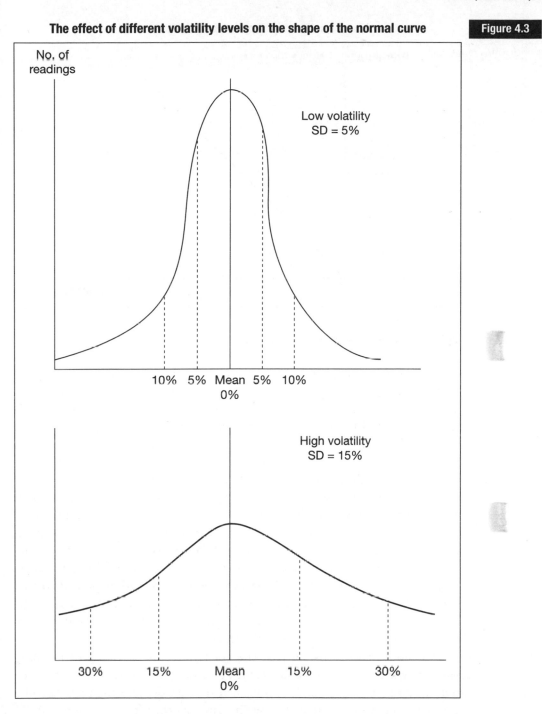

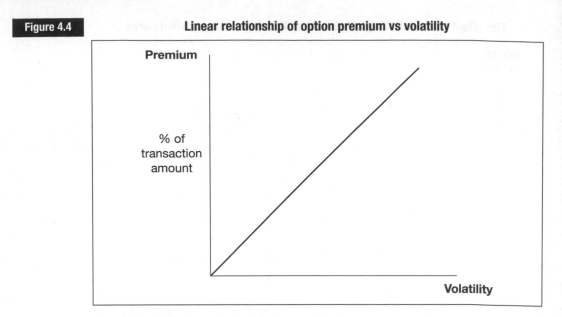

Figure 4.4   **Linear relationship of option premium vs volatility**

Volatility smiles, skew and surfaces

Since the first pricing models were developed a lot of analysis has been carried out on volatility and we now refer to terms such as 'volatility smiles' and 'surfaces'. Under the original Black and Scholes pricing models, volatility was assumed to be a constant, but instinctively we recognize that the volatility input will be different at different strike prices. The newer models focus on stochastics and mean reversion. Consider USD/JPY, if the exchange rate has been trading at around 116.00 for about 2 months, it may continue to do so, but if it breaches 119.00 it may then carry on rapidly until 123.00; volatility would therefore increase if the 119.00 level is breached. The same may be said if the US dollar weakened. If you were to plot a graph of volatility against strike price (ITM or ATM or OTM) you would generate a shape that looks a little like a smiley face (see Figure 4.5). The 'skew' (sometimes known as a 'smirk') refers to how much the shape is distorted compared with a hypothetically perfect symmetrical smile, and also to the difference in implied volatility when you compare OTM Puts and Calls. This may be due to reluctance by the trader to write Puts (or Calls).

You should then consider that the volatility of an option will not only vary by how much it is ITM or OTM, but also by the maturity. Short-dated options and very long dated options can be volatile, and the maturity of a 6-month ATM option may not be the same as that for a 12-month ATM option. This difference becomes magnified as you go further in or out of the money. If you stay with USD/JPY if you had figures for volatility up to 10 years at a range of strike prices, you could have in excess of 150 data points. This is how we then describe a volatility surface. Super derivatives have kindly let me use one of their surfaces (see Figure 4.6. NB: This is similar to the volatility smile but with a third axis which is time).

Volatility smile

Figure 4.5

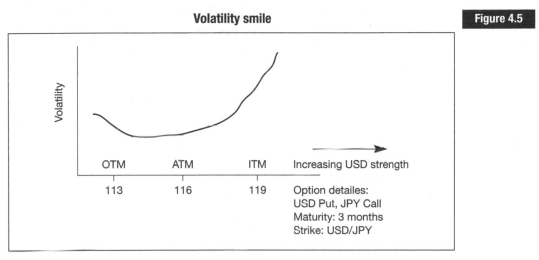

Source: SuperDerivatives

Volatility surface

Figure 4.6

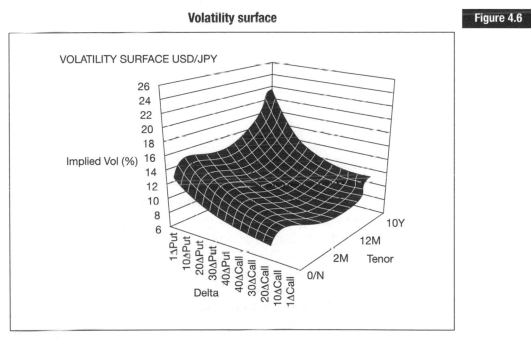

Source: SuperDerivatives

OPTION PRICING

Option pricing has evolved from the original model written by Black and Scholes in the early 1970s. There has been much tinkering with the basic formula to make it work with interest rates, bullion and currency, but the essential element of B&S confirms that financial data moves in the same way as nature, and that the normal distribution is a fair way of looking at it. The original option pricing model was based on log-normal distributions which are very different from a straight normal distribution to a statistician, but for our illustrative purposes it is close enough to be viewed similarly. However, we now recognize that the 'tails' of this distribution are statistically more likely to be significant than first thought. (NB: the 'tails' are the data which falls outside the 95 per cent confidence limits, i.e. the 2.5 per cent very short and very tall penguins.)

As a result of this in the last few years since 2000 there have been a number of new option pricing models launched onto the market that look at option pricing in a different way. The formulae they use are proprietary and their approach is different, but they are more precise.

The original option pricing model can be viewed as a 'black box' concept (see Figure 4.7), whereby a number of inputs are requested, and then the model calculates the premium. Whichever input you do not give the model, it will take the data from the other inputs and work backwards. This is how we mostly determine the 'implied volatility'. It means the volatility implied in the price. This price can come from a premium that another bank has quoted, or it can come from a price which refers to an exchange-traded option contract. Here, price transparency ensures that everyone can see the premium being quoted and traded, because the Reuters and Bloomberg and other information networks are transmitting the data around the world.

OPTION MECHANICS

The most straightforward way to understand the way options work is to draw the profit and loss profile (P/L) of the transaction at expiry. Consider the price of gold; if a trader bought physical gold bullion today in the expectation of the gold price rising, the P/L profile would look like that shown in Figure 4.8. Assume gold is currently $500 per oz.

Variable inputs for option pricing calculations

Figure 4.7

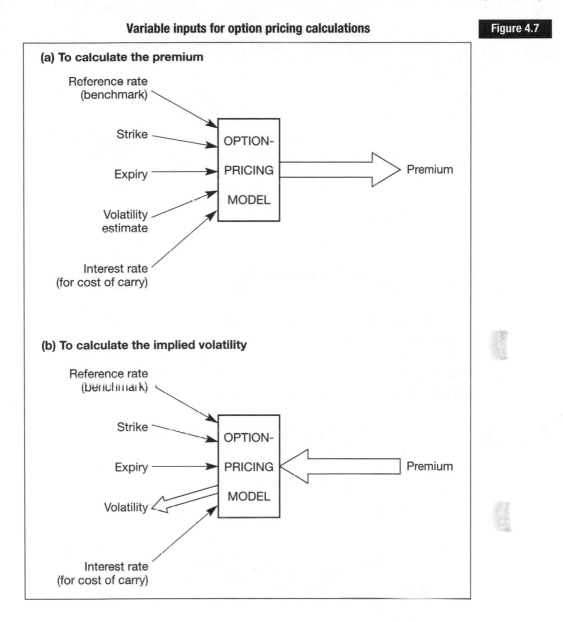

(a) To calculate the premium

Reference rate (benchmark)
Strike
Expiry
Volatility estimate
Interest rate (for cost of carry)

OPTION-PRICING MODEL

Premium

(b) To calculate the implied volatility

Reference rate (benchmark)
Strike
Expiry
Volatility
Interest rate (for cost of carry)

OPTION-PRICING MODEL

Premium

The trader has bought the gold at US$500 per ounce. If gold appreciates in value, the position will start moving into profit. But if the gold price weakens, the same position would move into loss. This is an un-hedged position, with an equal probability of profit or loss.

Figure 4.8

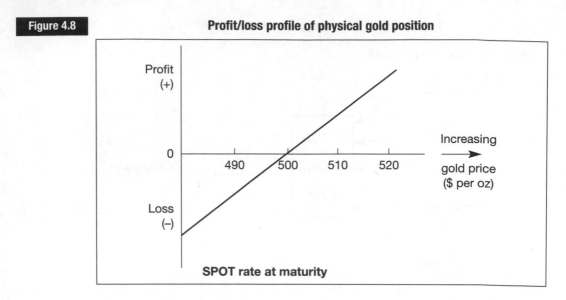

Profit/loss profile of physical gold position

Alternatively, instead of running this risk, an option could be purchased at the same level of US$500 per ounce, this would allow the same 1 : 1 profit opportunity, but where the only potential downside would be the loss of the premium paid. This would be a call option on gold: the trader has bought the option, so he is 'long' the call (see Figure 4.9).

Figure 4.9

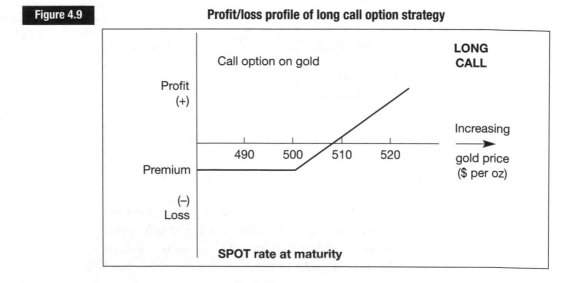

Profit/loss profile of long call option strategy

The attraction of the options lies in the limited downside risk represented by the premium, compared with the unlimited downside on the physical bullion position. Both have upside potential, although the premium cost of the option must not be forgotten.

The profile of the option resembles that of the un-hedged position, except that it starts from a negative position reflecting the premium paid. It is important to take into account the premium on the option and any associated holding or funding costs. An option purchaser may need to fund (borrow) the option premium, and an option writer must deposit the premium, so the deposit interest rate that the trader obtains must be factored into the final option premium.

The bank writing the gold call option would have a mirror-image position, where it had received the premium (see Figure 4.10).

Profit/loss profile of short call option strategy

Figure 4.10

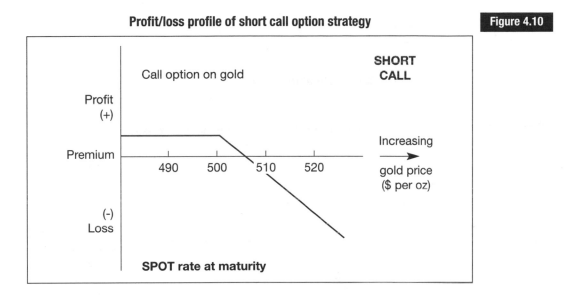

With this position, the bank that has written the option is 'short' the call option; all it has taken in is the premium, yet its potential for loss is high.

The trader has just changed his mind about the direction of the gold price. He now feels that it is going to weaken, so with his new trade he needs to buy a put option on gold (see Figure 4.11).

This P/L profile shows again that the holder of this option can lose only his premium, but can profit as long as the market moves in his favour. In comparison the writer of the option whose P/L profile is shown in Figure 4.12 is 'short' the gold put option and could lose a considerable amount.

In all, there are four basic building blocks in options: calls and puts; bought and sold.

The four strategies, long call, short call, long put, short put, are shown in Figures 4.9 to 4.12. These four strategies will allow the user to build some very complex strategies by using the options either singly or in combination. Even the most elaborate strategies can be broken down into their component parts which by definition must include these components of calls and puts, bought and sold.

Figure 4.11   **Profit/loss profile of long put strategy**

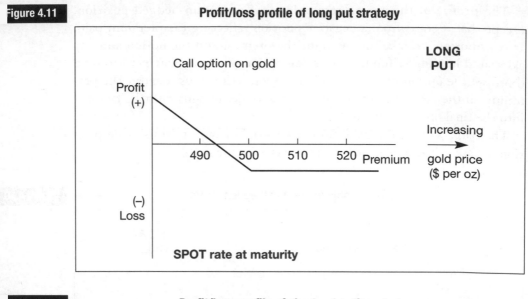

Figure 4.12   **Profit/loss profile of short put option strategy**

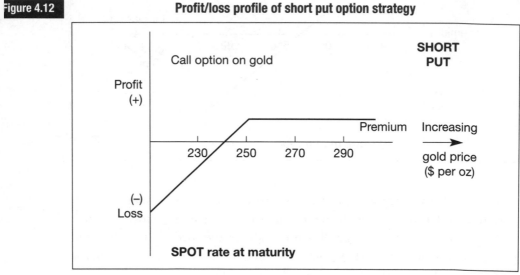

For readers who may be interested we discuss the Option Greeks (delta, gamma, theta, vega) in Chapter 10.

'There is a whole range of interest rate derivatives which can be used to cover any exposure from one week to one lasting 75 years.'

■ ■ ■

Interest Rate Derivatives – Single Settlement Instruments

Background and development

Single settlement interest rate derivatives

Financial futures contracts

Forward rate agreements (FRAs)

Interest rate options (IROs)

Premium determinants

Quiz

BACKGROUND AND DEVELOPMENT

There are whole ranges of interest rate derivatives, which can be used to cover any time period from one week to 75 years. Some of these products have only one reference fixing or settlement within that timescale, whilst others have multiple fixings. Generally, the longer the maturity of the underlying transaction, the more likely it is that the product needs to have multiple fixings. The range of instruments is shown in Table 5.1.

Table 5.1

Range of interest derivatives

Interest rate derivative	Settlement	
	Single	Multiple
Financial futures	✓	
Forward rate agreements (FRAs)	✓	
Interest rate options	✓	
Interest rate caps, collars floors		✓
Interest rate swaps		✓
Interest rate swap options (swaptions)	✓	

Interest rate derivatives can be used to hedge (risk manage), or to take risk (speculate).

What is interest rate risk?

The risk is either of increased funding costs for borrowers, or of reduced yields for investors. Short-term volatility and the unpredictability of interest rates led the banks and the financial exchanges to create 'an explosion' of financial instruments. Each of these instruments has a different set of characteristics for hedging interest rate risk on both loans and deposits, in different global currencies in both the short and the long term.

The main choices facing a borrower or depositor are the following:

■ Do nothing – and wait.

■ Fix the rate of interest by means of an option-type product, where a premium is due.

■ Fix the rate of interest by means of a zero-premium product, such as an FRA or a future.

Before a definitive choice can be made, it is necessary to look at the maturity of the underlying transaction and the range of instruments available to cover the risk. In an interest rate market, the maturity profile in any currency is generally subdivided as shown in Figure 5.1 and Table 5.2.

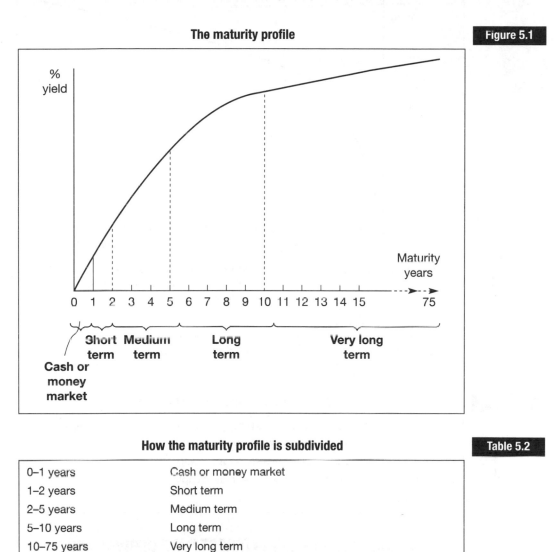

The maturity profile

Figure 5.1

How the maturity profile is subdivided

Table 5.2

0–1 years	Cash or money market
1–2 years	Short term
2–5 years	Medium term
5–10 years	Long term
10–75 years	Very long term

Risk management techniques also follow a similar pattern, as shown in Figure 5.2 and Table 5.3.

Although some of the shorter-term techniques such as FRAS and futures may have potential maturity dates over 5 years, in practice most deals are shorter than this – up to 2 years. Then when the maturity of the underlying exposure extends beyond 24 months, realistically the derivative needs to cater for multiple fixings, leading to interest rate swaps and interest rate caps.

Figure 5.2

Scope of operation of interest rate derivatives

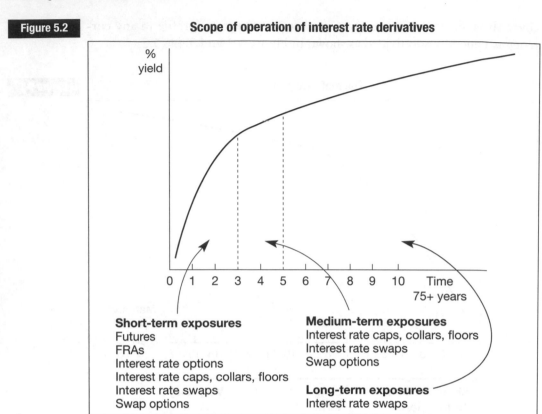

Table 5.3

Pattern of risk management techniques

0–2 to 3 years	Financial futures, FRAs, interest rate options caps, collars, floors, swaps, swap options
3–5 years	Caps, collars, floors, swaps, swap options
5–10 years	Swaps and to a lesser extent caps
10–75 years	Swaps

SINGLE SETTLEMENT INTEREST RATE DERIVATIVES

This section will concentrate upon single settlement interest rate derivatives. These are instruments that have only one settlement/fixing during the life of the transaction and are typically used to hedge or trade shorter maturities. The instruments consist of:

- exchange-traded: financial futures
- OTC: forward rate agreements (FRAs)
- OTC: interest rate options (IROs).

FINANCIAL FUTURES CONTRACTS

Introduction

Futures have been around in various guises for over 100 years. Originally based on agricultural commodities, there are now many different varieties. In the early 1970s futures trading became respectable; this coincided with the opening of 'regulated exchanges' around the world. The two oldest exchanges are both American and both based in Chicago:

- Chicago Mercantile Exchange (CME)
- Chicago Board of Trade (CBOT).

Chicago became the centre rather than New York because Chicago at the time was the main hub for the transportation of commodities from the areas where the cattle grazed and the grain was harvested to the main population centres of the East coast.

Not all futures contracts trade on all exchanges and many have contracts specifically designed for their own domestic market. Some futures contracts are international and offered globally around the world. Some even have their clearing and administration systems linked, and are known as 'fungible'. This means that you can open a position in one financial centre and close it in another; for example it is possible to sell a Eurodollar future on the CME and close out the position by buying it back on SGX (the Singapore exchange).

The London exchange LIFFE opened in 1982 and 15 years later, in June 1997, ranked the second largest in the world, turning over in excess of a million contracts per day. Now they are owned by Euronext and provide pan European coverage for listed derivatives.

Since the second edition of this book was published there has been a huge shift away from physical floor trading to electronic trading and execution; this is now cheaper per transaction and offers trading almost completely 24/7. This is now largely achieved for major users via trading platforms, which can access multiple exchanges, from Chicago Board of Trade, to EUREX to the Chicago Mercantile Exchange to Euronext-liffe.

The financial future is the building block for interest rate exposure management techniques (derivatives). Futures are primarily used by banks, other financial institutions and large multinational companies to hedge and trade interest rate positions. Some smaller companies will use futures from time to time, but there are some economies of scale that may make futures expensive for an occasional small user. Many types of futures exist globally, and this book will focus on those of a financial nature.

However, whatever the pros and contras of electronic trading when a client decides to look at using futures to hedge or take interest rate risk, he/she must choose whether they wish to protect a long-term interest rate such as that applying to a UK gilt or a US treasury bond with a 10- to 15-year maturity, or a short-term interest rate such as 3-month LIBOR.

In London the key futures on Euronext.liffe are:

- Short-term rates: EONIA – a Euro overnight rate compounded daily for 1 month, euribor, sterling, Euroswiss, Eurodollar, Euroyen (LIBOR based)
- Long-term rates: Long gilt – UK government bond, JGB – Japanese government bond
- Synthetic swaps: SwapNotes 2–10 years
- UK Equity products: FT-SE 100 and FT-SE 250
- European indices: FT-SE Eurotop 100, FT-SE Eurofirst, MSCI, AEX
- Commodities: Cocoa, coffee, corn, sugar, rapeseed, wheat
- Currency: USD/EUR and EUR/USD.

Definition	A financial futures contract is a legally binding agreement to make or take delivery of a standard quantity of a specific financial instrument, at a future date, and at a price agreed between the parties through open outcry on the floor of an organized exchange.

Definition discussed

To understand financial futures fully we need to open up this definition. With a financial future, each contract has its own specification – a type of contract description. This is so that both buyers and sellers of the future know what is expected of them and what obligations they must perform. Each future will also have a fixed 'contract amount' to make it easy to determine how many futures are required for the hedge/trade. It is not possible to trade in parts of contracts: you have to sell/buy whole numbers of futures contracts. The contract specification determines the specific financial instrument in question, and the trade will come about as willing buyers and willing sellers come together to transact business. Futures trade on every business day except public holidays, and prices will fluctuate with supply and demand. The price agreed between two traders today will be for 'delivery' on a particular date in the future. The term 'delivery' is still used although most of these contracts are no longer physically delivered (perhaps 1 to 2 per cent will go to delivery). There is usually a cash settlement of the differences between the buying and the selling price. Delivery now denotes contract expiry.

Short-term interest rate futures contracts – STIRs

Key features

Market

Futures are traded on a regulated exchange with standard contract sizes and specific delivery dates. Trades are executed by a member firm or broker physically on the floor of the relevant exchange or via a computer terminal.

Contracts

Different futures contracts are available in major currencies on each exchange. They cover both the long and short ends of the yield curve and some exchanges offer contracts on equities, equity indices and even electricity.

Pricing

It is a competitive auction-based market and prices are quoted on an index basis as a bid offer spread. For example, if the three month implied interest rate from December to March is 4 per cent, then the futures price is quoted as

$$100.00 - 4.00 = 96.00$$

Market operations

Both buyers and sellers must put up minimum levels of collateral for each open contract that they hold. This is known in the UK as 'initial margin'. The actual level is calculated by the relevant exchange in conjunction with the clearing house. The method used to calculate the level is the standard portfolio analysis of risk (SPAN) system. This was originally developed by the CME to monitor how risky particular positions had become. The level of initial margin is quoted as so much per open contract, say £750 per contract, and can change if market volatility changes. Initial margin will be returned with interest when the position is closed out.

Positions are 'marked-to-market' on a daily basis by comparing the level on the client's trade and the settlement price on the day. Profits or losses are crystallized daily. If a position loses money during the day, the client must pay his losses that day. If the position is in profit on that day, the client will receive his profit payment that day. These daily payments are known as 'variation margin'.

Credit risk

Once a trade is executed either on the floor of the regulated exchange – in an open outcry market or on a virtual exchange via a portal, both sides of the trade need to be matched. With electronic trading the matching is automatic, with open outcry a procedure needs to be followed. Once a trade has been successfully matched, the Clearing House which is a separate entity to the exchange itself, provides the clearing mechanism for the futures transactions. It is the Clearing House which will call for margin from market participants and their brokers, and ultimately each trade will eventually end up as a trade between the buyer/seller and the Clearing House. This is illustrated in Figure 5.3.

Availability

There are a number of different financial futures contracts, and it is advisable to check with the exchange in question exactly which contracts they offer.

Figure 5.3

The clearing process

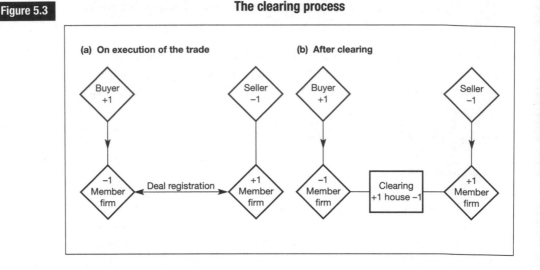

(a) On execution of the trade
(b) After clearing

Using short-term interest rate futures

To illustrate more clearly how this works, I have abbreviated the contract specification of the three-month sterling contract shown in Table 5.4. This is known colloquially as the 'short' sterling contact.

What exactly are we trading?

The short Sterling interest rate future is based on a notional 3-month deposit transaction. (NB: Notional because the future will not actually lend the client the money, just protect the interest rate).
Each single contract has a notional value of £500,000, and you can buy or sell whole numbers of contracts.

NB: All futures contracts settle to LIBOR not LIBID even though they are notional deposit transactions.

Futures contracts are available to mature in March, June, September and December, for the next five years. These are called the 'delivery' months.
The delivery date is the actual date in the month when the contracts expire. The third Wednesday in the month is usually around the 19th, 20th

Three-month sterling (short sterling) interest rate future – abbreviated contract specification

Table 5.4

Unit of trading	£500,000
Delivery months	March, June, September, December
Delivery day	First business day after the last trading day
Last trading day	11.00 hrs, third Wednesday of the delivery month
Quotation	100 minus rate of interest
Minimum price movement	0.01% known as a 'tick'
Tick value	£12.50
Hours:	07.30–18.00
Trading platform	LIFFE CONNECT

Source: Euronext.liffe

or 21st of the month, and it is on this date that the financial futures price is finally settled at the exchange delivery settlement price (EDSP). It is only on this date that the actual 3-month LIBOR fixing (at 11.00 hours) minus 100, will match the futures price.

In the market, futures traders are acting on behalf of speculators, hedgers and arbitrageurs. Some may believe that rates will increase others that rates will decrease. The bid–offer price quoted will reflect the market view of what 3-month LIBOR will be on the delivery date. Not what it is today, but what it will be in the future. This is known as the implied forward rate or the implied interest rate. Obviously some traders may think that interest rates in the future will be higher; some may think they will be lower. The actual interest rate will not be known until the delivery date when the 3-month LIBOR fixing will match the underlying futures price.

All short-term futures contracts are quoted on an 'index basis'. If the market believes that the 3-month LIBOR on 20 June 2007 will be 4.27 per cent, then the future will be trading at that point in time at 100.00 – 4.27 = 95.73. This may seem confusing, but futures contracts are designed so that you can 'buy low, sell high' and make a profit. This method of price quotation reverses the behaviour of futures prices. If a trader anticipates that interest rates are going to fall, he expects the futures price to rise. Therefore he would want to buy the future now and sell it when it was higher, making a profit on the difference between the rates. How much profit he will make depends on how many 'ticks' he has made, each tick representing a market movement of 0.01 per cent.

A futures trading transaction

At the beginning of October a trader feels that sterling interest rates will fall as year end approaches. The current 3-month LIBOR rate today is, say, 4.25 per cent, the implied forward interest rate is 4.15 per cent, this means that the futures markets look like they are already discounting (or assuming) a fall in rates. She wishes to make a profit from predicting a short-term downward movement in rates; her trading amount is £5 million.

Action

Buy 10 December 3-month sterling interest rate futures at the current trading level of 100 − 4.15 = 95.85.

Outcome

On the third Wednesday in December, the price for the DEC futures contract is 96.35 in line with the current 3-month LIBOR rate of 3.65 per cent. The trader decides to close out her position, so she will need to sell ten futures contracts, at the closing level of 96.35.

Profit or loss?

The view on the market was correct and interest rates did fall. Our trader has made a profit.

Opening futures level	95.85 (bought)
Closing futures level	96.35 (sold)
Profit	0.50, or 50 ticks

What is this profit worth in real money?

The trader has made a profit of
10 contracts × 50 ticks × £12.50 each tick = a total of £6,250.

If our trader had put on the same trade, but the view on the market was wrong, and interest rates had increased rather than decreased, she would have lost a number of ticks on the position, as she would have originally bought the futures at the same level of 95.85, but she would have then sold them lower down, resulting in a loss.

Tick values

Each tick on each futures contract has a monetary value: in the case of short Sterling futures, it is £12.50. Where does the £12.50 come from? It is the notional contract size multiplied by the length of time of the 3-month notional time deposit underlying the contract in years (i.e. 3/12) multiplied by the minimum tick size movement of 0.01 per cent.

£500,000 × 0.01% × 3/12 = £12.50

The trading units (contract sizes) and tick values for short-term contracts currently traded are shown in Table 5.5.

Table 5.5

Trading units and tick values for short-term futures contracts

Contract	Trading unit	Tick value	Tick size
Three-month Euribor	€1,000,000	€12.50	0.005
Three-month Euroyen	YEN 100,000,000	YEN 1,250	0.005
Three-month EuroSwiss franc	Sfr 1,000,000	Sfr 25	0.01
Three-month sterling	£500,000	£12.50	0.01
Three-month Eurodollar	$1,000,000	$25.00	0.01

Market structure

Each futures exchange is set up in a similar way. Members of the exchanges are those firms who have joined the 'club' and in effect paid a membership fee. The specific nature of their membership will allow them to trade futures or options or both, and will be a determining factor on how many people can be employed trading for that member company. Membership is not restricted to domestic companies and most exchanges around the world have a complex mix of nationalities and cultures, banks, institutions and others.

Matching

With electronic trading, the two sites of the deal are automatically matched. With open outcry trading there must be a buyer and a seller for the trade to take place, then the trade details are input into a trade registration system (TRS). This is an integral part of the clearing mechanism. TRS ensures that each trade has the 'other half'. Occasionally there may be an unmatched trade and it is the responsibility of each member firm to resolve these discrepancies.

Clearing

Once all the details are noted and matched, the clearing house positions itself between buyer and seller. All Euronext.liffe's contracts are cleared by LCH.Clearnet which is independent of the exchange (see Figure 5.4).

LCH.Clearnet as central counterparty

Figure 5.4

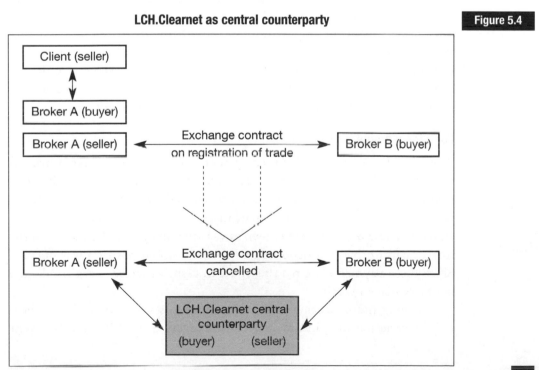

LCH.Clearnet becomes seller to every buyer and buyer to every seller. Although it is not a principal itself and never initiates a trade, after every trade it takes on the counterparty risk. It is this characteristic that makes futures so popular with market participants. LCH.Clearnet's own credit exposure is, in turn, covered by margin. Any bank can deal with any other bank or individual, whatever their credit standing in the market. They know that once the trade is electronically matched then 'cleared', their only counterparty risk is to the clearing house. Removing this counterparty risk ensures swift trading without the need to check credit lines and it offers both parties the ability to net off trades against each other. If I have bought 10 contracts from Bank A and sold 10 contracts to Bank B, my net position is zero. This feature also enhances liquidity.

Initial margins

The only way that the clearing house is able to take the credit risk of both counterparties is for each of them to put up margin or collateral at the time of trading. This is known as initial margin.

Assume the initial margin is £750 per contract on the short sterling future. If a client had opened a position of 30 contracts, he would need to deposit with the exchange 30 × £750 or £22,500. Both buyer and seller of the contracts would put up the same amount of security. This insulates the clearing house; whatever direction the market moves in, the clearing house has funds in advance to pay daily losses, should they be incurred. The extent of the daily losses should not exceed the initial margin. For example, £750 per contract represents a possible loss on a day of 60 ticks (at £12.50 per tick) or a 0.6 per cent movement in the implied interest rate. If the clearing house felt that there was potential for a greater loss due to excessive volatility in the market, it would call for increased initial margin payments from everyone with outstanding open positions. The SPAN computer program used to calculate margin amounts uses the term 'scanning risk' for initial margin.

Variation margins

At close of business every day, each open position on the exchange is marked to market and compared with the day's official settlement price. If the position is in profit, the margin account will be credited with the profit. If the position has made a loss, the margin account will be debited by that amount. These payments are known as variation margin as distinct from the initial margin that was deposited when the original position was opened. Since these payments are paid/received in cash, variation margin calls are normally made in cash.

If a client has a position which is making losses on a daily basis, there will be variation margin calls against him every day. This should prevent very large losses being run up as they are paid off daily and cannot accumulate. But Barings Bank collapsed, notwithstanding this type of safeguard is in place on all exchanges. When a trading position continually loses money, the losses are paid daily, so that funding of the position is required. When a trader calls for more and more funding due to variation margin movements, it should raise questions. If the funding of the variation margin is not forthcoming, the clearing house will start to close out the position. Barings continued to fund substantial loss-making positions on a daily basis in a falling market.

Consider a client who has taken a view that interest rates will fall. In fact he is wrong and they rise. On each day of his open position he will make a loss that he must fund on a daily basis. If the original trade was for ten contracts and the initial margin was £750 a contract, on Day 1 he would put up £7,500. At close of business that day, let us say that his position has moved against him by 20 ticks per contract:

(20 × 10 × £12.50 = £2,500)

LCH.Clearnet will debit his margin account by that amount, leaving a balance of only £5,000. If initial margin is £750 per contract, the balance of £5,000 will now support only six futures contracts. If he does not respond to the variation margin call by adding a further £2,500 to replenish his margin account, he will not have enough initial margin to maintain his position, and the exchange will close out any un-margined outstanding contracts.

Some traders regard the initial margin as a 'stop loss'. If a trader never tops up the initial margin account, then that is all the money he can lose on the position. However, with the Barings position, the variation margin from the losses was continually funded, resulting in greater and greater losses as the market continued to fall.

Hedging with short-term sterling interest rate futures   `Example`

14 February
The treasurer of a large UK company is committed to borrow £15 million on 22 June. He has no requirement for the cash today, but he has invested in a strategic venture that requires £15 million for a period of three months from 22 June. He believes that sterling interest rates will rise and is worried about the eventual borrowing rate he will incur. The 3-month LIBOR in the market today is 5.5 per cent and he feels rates will rise higher than this. The current June future is trading at 94.20 implying a future 3-month LIBOR of 5.8 per cent for the June date, so the market is already anticipating an interest rate rise. The treasurer decides to hedge using futures.

14 February – Action

Treasurer sells 30 June short sterling futures at the current level of 94.20, and puts up the appropriate level of initial margin.

Over the next few months until 22 June, the treasurer receives/pays daily variation margin as the market moves.

22 June – Action

The treasurer borrows his money from the inter-bank market at a 3-month LIBOR rate of 6.7 per cent. The same morning he lifts his hedge, and closes out his futures position. To do this, he will buy back the futures contracts at the prevailing market rate of 93.30, and receive back his initial margin plus interest.

Profit or loss?

Total profit on the futures trade is 90 ticks (94.20 – 93.30) on each of 30 contracts:

(30 contracts × 90 ticks × £12.50 tick value = £33,750)

This is not a profit overall, simply a profit on the futures 'leg' of the transaction. In the cash markets the treasurer has borrowed his £15 million at 6.7 per cent, a higher rate of interest. We need to establish whether the profit on the futures trade is enough to offset the extra interest paid on the loan.

Cash market loan

Equation 1. The amount of interest the treasurer would have paid at the original LIBOR rate of 5.5 per cent – but unachievable:

£15,000,000 × 91/365 × 5.5% = £205,684.93

Equation 2. The amount of interest the treasurer would have paid at the rate of 5.8 per cent, the implied interest rate already in the market – implied by the futures price:

£15,000,000 × 91/365 × 5.8%= £216,904.11

Equation 3. The amount of interest the treasurer actually paid at the final LIBOR of 6.7 per cent:

£15,000,000 × 91/365 × 6.7% = £250,561.64

The extra amount of interest the treasurer had to pay was £33,657.53 [Equation 3 – Equation 2]. We use Equation 2 as it reflects market sentiment for future interest rates. If we had used Equation 1, we would have been simplistically assuming that the treasurer could borrow the money in the future, but still at today's rates. This is not a realistic assumption.

To offset against this extra outgoing, the futures trade made a profit of £33,750, neatly locking the treasurer into an insurance rate of 6.7 per cent. This hedge was nearly 100 per cent effective.

As all short-term interest rate futures trade in much the same way, the same hedging techniques can be used in other currencies.

Hedging with short-term Euribor interest rate futures

2 May

The treasurer of a European multinational needs to protect the value of a forthcoming €50,000,000 deposit. The funds are the proceeds of a divestment and are expected in mid-September when the paper work is finalized. On receipt, the treasurer will invest them in a three-month time deposit. The company is worried that Euro interest rates will fall between May and September, and that they will be disadvantaged. The current 3-month rate for Euro deposits is 3.3 per cent, and the treasurer believes that rates will fall below this. The current September future is trading at 96.88, an implied forward rate of 3.12 per cent. The market is already anticipating an interest rate reduction, so the treasurer decides to hedge using futures (see Table 5.6).

Three-month Euribor interest rate future – abbreviated contract specification

Table 5.6

Unit of trading	€1,000,000
Delivery months	March, June, September, December
Delivery date	First business day after the last trading day
Last trading day	10.00 hrs, two business days prior to the third Wednesday of the delivery month
Quotation	100 minus rate of interest
Minimum price movement	0.005% – a 'half-tick' (0.01% – a full tick)
Tick value	€12.50 (or €25.00)
Trading hours	07.00 – 21.00
Trading platform	LIFFE CONNECT

Source: Euronext.liffe

2 May – Action

The treasurer buys 50 September Euribor futures at the current level of 96.88, and puts up the appropriate level of initial margin.

Throughout the next few months until mid-September the interest rates fluctuate and the treasurer receives/pays daily variation margin as the market moves.

20 September – Action

The treasurer receives €50 million and places it on deposit immediately for a period of three calendar months at a 3-month Euribor rate of 3.0 per cent. The same day he closes out his futures position. To do this he will sell back the futures contracts at the EDSP (exchange delivery settlement price) of 97.00, which exactly matches the LIBOR fixing rate. He will also receive back his initial margin plus interest.

Profit or loss?

The total profit on the futures trade is 12 ticks or 24 half-ticks (97.00 – 96.88) on each of 50 contracts:

(50 contracts × 24 ticks × €12.50 tick value = €15,000.00)

This is not a profit overall, simply a profit on the futures 'leg' of the transaction. In the cash markets the treasurer has invested his €50 million at 3.00 per cent – a worse rate of interest. We need to establish whether the profit on the futures trade is enough to offset the loss of interest income on the investment.

Cash market investment

Equation 1. The amount of interest the treasurer would have received at the rate of 3.12 per cent, the implied interest rate already in the market:

€50,000,000 × 90/360 × 3.12% = €390,000

Equation 2. The amount of interest the treasurer actually received at the final LIBOR of 3.00 per cent:

€50,000,000 × 90/360 × 3.00% = €375,000

The shortfall of interest was €15,000 [Equation 1 – Equation 2] (it is important to note that the market was already discounting lower interest rates in the futures prices). To offset against this lack of interest receivable, the futures trade made a profit of €15,000, neatly locking the treasurer into an investment rate of 3.12 per cent. This hedge was 100 per cent effective.

Practical considerations

If a client wants to trade or hedge with futures, how does he go about it? First, he will need to set up documentation, and that associated with futures may take some time. If a client is not a member of the relevant exchange, a broker will be required to transact the trades on behalf of the client. He will be acting entirely on instructions received, and will charge a fee for his services. Once the documentation is agreed with the broker, the level of brokerage must be agreed. This will depend upon many things, but especially the volume of business that is anticipated, and the level of service required of the broker. Some clients want a service which is 'execution only'; others prefer a full service offering advice, execution, clearing and maybe even risk management.

Wherever the client is around the world, he can contact his futures broker and place his bid or offer. The broker will normally transact it via a trading platform. The order may be filled immediately or it may take some time. Once the order is executed, the 'fill' details are communicated back to the client. Initial margins must be posted at close of business on that day, and maintained until the position is closed out. Variation margin must also be paid/received, until the position is closed out.

To trade and hedge with futures successfully, it is important to have an information link. The companies who offer these services are known as ISV, independent software vendors. The costs of the various services will again be dependent on the client's individual requirements, but one should not underestimate the importance of fast and accurate data.

One should never forget futures are the fastest way to make or lose lots of money!

Conclusion

Futures offer banks and other financial institutions excellent hedging and trading opportunities. Unfortunately, most companies do not have the time or the resources necessary to manage a portfolio of futures contracts efficiently. In addition to the documentation mentioned (most of which runs to a minimum of ten pages long), the user must also install systems to monitor his margins and accounting. He will also need to manage basis risk, and must agree to accept the settlement dates and the specific sizes of contracts that are fixed by the exchange. These will rarely match his own company exposure.

Financial futures are recognized as being 'unfriendly' to the occasional user. Consequently, it was only a matter of time before the banks 'packaged' financial futures into a friendlier product, known as FRAs or forward rate agreements.

FORWARD RATE AGREEMENTS (FRAs)

Introduction

Consider a businessman who is about to go away on an extended business trip, miles away from banks and information systems. He has a medium-term loan that will be re-fixed to the 6-month LIBOR rate in one month's time. He thinks he will be unable to call the bank on the loan re-fixing day to confirm the rate as he may well be in a meeting. What he needs to know today is the rate that will be applicable for his transaction. In effect, he wants to know the rate in advance. The 6-month LIBOR rate today may be an indicator of what rate he will achieve, but it is by no means a certainty. Interest rates in one month's time could be higher or lower than today, and this element of uncertainty is what the businessman would like to avoid. The bank can determine the customer's loan rate without resorting to derivatives, although they do make life a lot easier.

| Figure 5.5 | **Implied forward rates** |

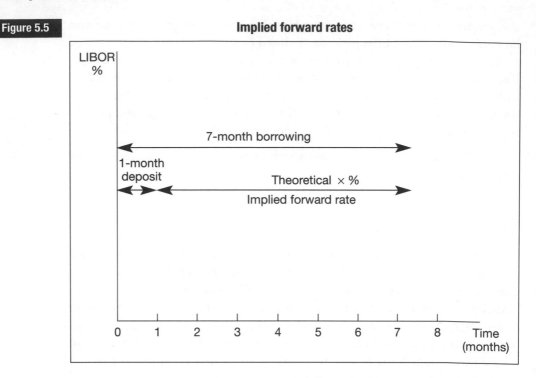

In Figure 5.5 × per cent is the rate we are trying to calculate.

The bank can do this by borrowing the money for the full seven months and investing it back for one month as the client does not need it straight away. By borrowing long and lending short, the bank has created a synthetic forward borrowing enabling it to quote a forward/forward rate of interest. However, it has transacted both the loan and the deposit physically in the cash markets. This ties up the bank's credit lines and also requires the bank to hold extra capital for the capital adequacy requirements as specified by the BIS for cash transactions. This money is in effect on permanent deposit.

In simple terms, because both transactions are in cash there is little or no profit margin for the bank, as the added cost of the capital adequacy requirement, as laid down by the regulators, makes this use of bank assets uncompetitive.

The concept of fixing interest rates into the future was well received, and other financial techniques were thus developed to allow the forward/forward interest rate to be calculated, but without the commitment from the bank to lend or take the money. With no movement of the cash principal the instrument no longer attracts the onerous capital adequacy requirements that made it so uncompetitive in the first place. The Central Bank/FSA still requires an element of 'cover' on this new transaction, but it is a much smaller amount than that previously needed. This new product is called the FRA or forward rate agreement, and it offers more profit opportunities for bankers than the original forward/forward loans. Some market practitioners also know it as an OTC future. The FRA (pronunciation to rhyme with 'bra') is quite simply a forward/forward loan or deposit given without the commitment to lend or take the money. To many users these are 'packaged' financial futures.

> A forward rate agreement is a legally binding agreement between two parties to determine the rate of interest that will be applied to a notional loan or deposit, of an agreed amount to be drawn or placed, on an agreed future date (the settlement date) for a specified term.

Definition

Definition discussed

One of the parties is a 'buyer' of the FRA, the other a 'seller'. The buyer agrees notionally to borrow the money at the FRA rate, and the seller agrees notionally to lend the money at the FRA rate. On the settlement date the difference between the FRA rate and the prevailing LIBOR rate will be settled by one party to the other in cash. The terms 'seller' and 'buyer' are used only to determine who is the borrower and who is the lender of the money, not necessarily who is providing the service. Banks can be sellers and buyers and so can customers.

We need to clarify the components. The FRA contract is legally binding and neither party can walk away. The two parties are the 'buyer' and the 'seller' of the FRA, both of whom are able to hedge against future interest rate movements. Usually one of the parties is a bank, and the other can be a corporate, financial institution or another bank. The FRA rate of interest will be that calculated on the forward/forward basis plus a profit margin, for the particular maturity required and can be derived from the financial futures markets. This FRA rate is applied to a notional loan or deposit amount. This is an important concept, because it shows that the FRA can hedge or trade an amount equivalent to, say, £5 million, but will not actually lend or take deposit of the £5 million. Currency, amount and length of transaction must be specified. The underlying loan or deposit transaction being hedged must commence in the future at a forward date, which needs to be specified. It cannot commence today. There is no uncertainty today about, say, the 3-month LIBOR; we know the rate, it was fixed in the market at 11 a.m. this morning. Products like FRAs and futures are used to hedge or trade an implied interest rate during this 'uncertainty period', before the rate is fixed in the market at 11 a.m. on the specific date. If there is no uncertainty period, no hedge is required.

As this product is based on a notional amount, the assumption is that if there is a loan or investment underlying the deal, then it is with another part of the bank or another bank entirely. The FRA will not lend the money or take the deposit. This is an important point: anyone can buy or sell an FRA subject to their credit lines – the bank providing the service in FRAs does not have the time or the inclination to check whether this is a hedge or a trade, they are not policemen. The bank 'selling' the FRA will not differentiate on price between a FRA used to hedge or a FRA used to trade. On the settlement date, a cash sum equivalent to the difference in the FRA rate and the actual LIBOR fixing rate will be exchanged. It is impossible to tell at the outset of the FRA who will pay whom the cash settlement – that will only be clear at maturity. It could be the bank paying the client or vice versa.

Key features

Insurance

The bank will guarantee (or insure) a rate of interest for a transaction which starts on a future date. The client is legally obligated to transact at that rate, so is 'locked' into the FRA interest rate; if rates move adversely, he will be protected and receive a cash settlement equivalent to the difference between the FRA rate and the LIBOR fixing, but if rates move in his favour he will be unable to profit, as he is committed to pay back a cash settlement to the other party.

Cash settlement

Principal amounts are not exchanged. The differences between the FRA rate and the ruling market rate (LIBOR) will be settled by the parties.

Profit potential

For a hedger – nil. If interest rates move in the client's favour, any difference must be repaid to the other party. For a trader, any cash received under the FRA is a profit.

Flexibility

If the FRA is no longer required, a reversing transaction may be transacted to close out the position.

Zero cost

To a hedger, but zero profit potential. The FRA will guarantee an absolute rate of interest, not better or worse.

Market structure and operations

FRAs are over the counter (OTC) instruments, and are quoted by many banks around the world. There is no requirement for them to be traded on an exchange as with futures. Each market participant will take the counterparty credit risk of the other. This is a significant point, as at the outset of the FRA trade, it is not clear who will cash settle with whom. The bank could pay the client or the client could pay the bank. So at Day 1 there is a potential two-way cash flow.

For a bank to quote a FRA rate, basic information relating to the trade is required. Consider our businessman who was going on a business trip. His underlying loan was to be re-fixed in one month's time for a period of six months (see Figure 5.6). In market jargon, this would be described as a 1s–7s exposure, possibly requiring a 1s–7s FRA to cover it. The exposure exists now, but the underlying transaction starts in one month and finishes in seven months therefore the duration must be six months. To price this we also need to know the amount and currency of the underlying loan, say £5 million. In this case, our man will ask for a 1s–7s borrower's FRA, or he could say he wishes to 'buy' the FRA.

Important dates on a FRA transaction

Figure 5.6

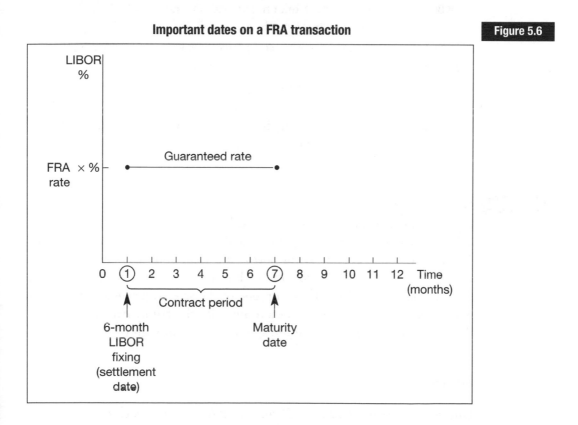

Terminology	FRA	A forward rate agreement sometimes called interest rate insurance.
	Buyer/ borrower	The party wishing to protect itself from a rise in interest rates, or profit from a rise in rates.
	Seller/lender	The party wishing to protect itself from a fall in rates, or profit from a fall in rates.
	Future rate, agreed rate, guaranteed rate	The FRA rate agreed between the parties at the outset of the of the transaction.
	Settlement date	The start date of the underlying loan or deposit, when cash settlement is made.
	Maturity date	The date on which the FRA contract period ends.
	LIBOR	London inter-bank offered rate. The rate at which banks lend funds to each other.
	LIBOR fix	The mean interest rate quoted by specified reference banks.
	LIBOR fixing date	The date when the LIBOR is checked at 11 a.m. This is the same day as the settlement date for sterling, and two business days before for currency deals.
	Contract period	The period running from the start to maturity of the under-lying loan or deposit.

Example

Hedging with sterling FRAs

Our businessman who is about to go on his business trip wishes to hedge a £5 million sterling borrowing which will take place in one month's time. The maturity of the underlying borrowing is six months. This, then, is a 1s–7s transaction. In order to comfort himself that the price quoted by his bank is competitive he will put up one of the screens provided by brokers who offer a service in FRAs, before he calls the bank. An example of a Reuters page with data from Intercapital is shown in Figure 5.7.

Strategy

Our businessman asks his bank for an FRA price to protect a six-month borrowing out of the specific rollover date, i.e. a 1s–7s. The market price for that period is 4.575 per cent. The client agrees to the rate, no money changes hands, and he is now fully protected against an adverse interest rate movement. Both the client and the bank will send confirmations. These should be checked for errors as soon as they are received, preferably by a 'third' party.

FRA quotes

Figure 5.7

02/16	16:17 GMT			[ICAP]				4914	
				GBP SHORT SWAPS			15/02	15:15	GMT
	3M FRAS		6M FRAS		12M FRAS			SHORT SWAPS	
1X4	4.565–4.545	1X7	4.575–4.555	1X13	4.610–4.590	6MA3	4.580–4.560		
2X5	4.545–4.525	2X8	4.560–4.540	2X14	4.610–4.590	9MA3	4.590–4.570		
3X6	4.530–4.510	3X9	4.550–4.530	3X15	4.610–4.590	1YA3	4.610–4.590		
4X7	4.510–4.490	4X10	4.535–4.515	4X16	4.600–4.580	15MA3	4.595–4.575		
5X8	4.500–4.480	5X11	4.540–4.520	5X17	4.610–4.590	18MA3	4.595–4.575		
6X9	4.500–4.480	6X12	4.540–4.520	6X18	4.620–4.600	1YS/S	4.555–4.535		
9x12	4.515–4.495	9x15	4.560x4.540	9x21	4.655–4.635				
12X15	4.545–4.525	12X18	4.595–4.575	12X24	4.695–4.675				
	GBP 3M TMM		GBP 6M IMM		GBP 12M IMM		GBP IMM		
1X4	4.565–4.545	1X7	4.575–4.555	1X13	4.620–4.600	MAR/MAR	4.600–4.580		
4X7	4.505–4.485	4X10	4.535–4.515	4X16	4.610–4.590	JUN/JUN	4.600–4.580		
7X10	4.495–4.475	7X13	4.535–4.515	7X19	4.635–4.615	SEP/SEP	4.635–4.615		
10X13	4.525–4.505	10X16	4.575–4.555	10X22	4.660–4.640	DEC/DEC	4.660–4.640		

Source: ICAP, courtesy Reuters

NB: The client will need to look for the 1 × 7 data. Both sides of the price are shown on this screen. Our client is a borrower in the underlying market, so he will be on the high side of the FRA quote, i.e. 4.575 per cent. An investor would be on the lower side of the price.

Outcome

Assume the 11 a.m. LIBOR fixing in one month's time is 5 per cent: this is the reference rate against which the FRA will be cash settled. This is the day when the customer will confirm the borrowing rate on his loan. It is known as the settlement date as this is the day when settlement is received. The hedge the businessman has with the bank will now come into operation. As the LIBOR rate of 5 per cent (Figure 5.8 (A)) is above the FRA rate of 4.575 per cent, the bank will refund the difference to the company, discounted back for early settlement.

NB: The amount of the settlement is paid at the beginning of the loan, not at the end when the client will pay his interest. The client is receiving his refund earlier than he needs it, so the amount is discounted at the LIBOR fixing rate on the FRA. The reasoning here is that the customer should be indifferent as to whether he receives the full amount at maturity, or a smaller amount at the beginning which he can place on deposit. The interest and principal together will add up to the original amount as if it had been paid at maturity. A fairly complicated settlement formula is used to calculate the amounts.

If the LIBOR market rate had been say 4.00 per cent (Figure 5.8 (B)), then the company would have refunded the difference to the bank, also on a discounted basis. So for nil cost, the company has obtained full interest rate protection, at a rate of 4.575 per cent, although agreeing to give up any profit.

| Figure 5.8 | **Example of sterling FRA settlement amounts** |

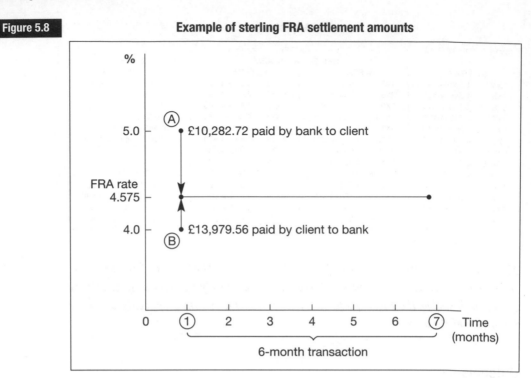

FRA settlement formula:

$$\frac{(\text{LIBOR} - \text{FRA rate}) \times \text{amount} \times \text{period (in days)}}{\text{Year} \times 100} \times \frac{1}{1 + \dfrac{(\text{LIBOR} \times \text{period})}{(\text{Year} \times 100)}}$$

LIBOR 11 a.m. fixing rate
FRA rate Rate agreed between the parties
Amount Full amount of the transaction
Period Number of days of the underlying transaction
Year 365 days for sterling, 360 for most other currencies

The first part of the formula works out the cash settlement, the second part of the formula discounts it, as the funds will be received early. Using the formula, we can calculate the amount of the settlement and who will receive it.

1. If rates had been 5 per cent on settlement:

$$\frac{(5.00 - 4.575) \times £5{,}000{,}000 \times 181 \text{ days}}{36{,}500} \times \frac{1}{1 + \dfrac{(5.00 \times 181)}{36{,}500}}$$

£10,537.67 × 0.97580537 = £10,282.72

The borrowing rate of 5 per cent was above the FRA rate when the deal was finalized so the bank will compensate the client with the amount of

£10,282.72, discounted back for early settlement. This will go towards the higher interest costs he must pay.

2. If rates had been 4.00 per cent on settlement:

$$\frac{(4.00 - 4.575) \times £5,000,000 \times 181 \text{ days}}{36,500} \times \frac{1}{1 + \frac{(4.00 \times 181)}{36,500}}$$

£14,256.85 × 0.98055018 = £13,979.56

The borrowing rate was below the FRA rate when the deal was finalized, so the client will compensate the bank with the amount of £13,979.56 (see Figure 5.8). A negative number signifies that the payment goes in the opposite direction.

Hedging with Eurodollar FRAs

Example

A European treasurer wishes to hedge the income on an investment. He will be receiving US$10 million in two months' time, and he is concerned that interest rates may fall before he receives his funds, and before he has a chance to place them on deposit. He anticipates placing them on deposit for three months.

He decides to hedge using FRAs, as they are zero cost and will guarantee for him a fixed rate for the period. This, then, is a 2s–5s transaction. The treasurer puts up the Reuters screen shown in Figure 5.9. The underlying transaction is an investment so the company will need to deal on the lower side of the price at 4.96 per cent. The company would need to 'sell' the FRA.

USD FRA rates

Figure 5.9

02/15	15:40 GMT	[REUTERS–USD FRA COMPOSITE]							02/15 10:40 61885	
	RATE	SOURCE	CTR	GMT			RATE	SOURCE	CTR	GMT
1X4	4.8800–4.9100	BROKER	A/P	15:35		1X7	5.0000–5.0200	BROKER	GBL	15:35
2X5	4.9600–4.9900	BROKER	A/P	15:35		2X8	5.0500–5.0700	BROKER	GBL	15:35
3X6	5.0300–5.0500	BROKER	GBL	16:40		3X9	5.0800–5.1000	BROKER	GBL	15:37
4X7	5.0500–5.0700	BROKER	GBL	15:40		4X10	5.1200–5.1500	BROKER	A/P	15:35
5X8	5.0700–5.0900	BROKER	GBL	15:40		5X11	5.1000–5.1200	BROKER	GBL	15:38
6X9	5.0800–5.1000	BROKER	GBL	15:40		6X12	5.1000–5.1200	BROKER	GBL	15:37
7X10	5.0800–5.1000	BROKER	GBL	15:37		12X18	4.9900–5.0100	BROKER	GBL	15:40
8X11	5.0800–5.1000	BROKER	GBL	15:40		18X24	4.9700–5.0000	BROKER	A/P	22:56
9X12	5.0600–5.0800	BROKER	GBL	15:40		1X10	5.0700–5.0900	BROKER	GBL	15:35
						2X11	5.1000–2.1200	BROKER	GBL	15:38
						3X12	5.1200–5.1400	BROKER	GBL	15:35
						6X18	5.1100–5.1300	BROKER	GBL	16:37
						12X24	5.0300–5.0500	BROKER	GBL	15:37

Source: Reuters

The treasurer will ask one of his bankers for an FRA price to protect a three-month investment starting in two months' time, i.e. a 2s–5s. The market price for that period is 4.96 per cent. The client agrees to the rate, no money changes hands, and the company is now fully protected against an adverse interest rate movement. Both the client and the bank will send confirmations.

Outcome

Assume the 11 a.m. LIBOR fixing in two months' time is 5.96 per cent: this is the reference rate against which the FRA will be cash settled. This is the day when the customer will confirm the investment rate on his deposit. As this is a Euro-currency FRA (non-sterling), settlement will be made two business days later. The hedge the company has with the bank will now come into operation.

(b) If the LIBOR rate was 4.00 per cent ((A) in Figure 5.10) below the FRA rate of 4.96 per cent, the bank will refund the difference to the company, discounted back for early settlement.

(a) As the LIBOR market rate is say 5.96 per cent ((B) in Figure 5.10), then the company would have refunded the difference to the bank, also on a discounted basis.

| Figure 5.10 | Example of a Eurodollar FRA hedge |

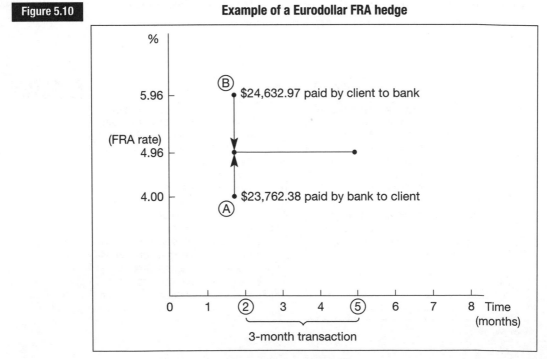

So for nil cost, the company has obtained full interest rate protection, at a rate of 4.96 per cent, although agreeing to give up any profit.

1. If rates had been 5.96 per cent on settlement:

$$\frac{(5.96 - 4.96) \times \$10,000,000 \times 90 \text{ days}}{36,000} \times \frac{1}{1 + \frac{(5.96 \times 90)}{36,000}}$$

US\$25,000 × 0.98531875 = US\$24,632.97

The actual LIBOR rate was below the FRA rate when the deal was finalized, so the bank will compensate the client with the amount of US\$23,762.38. This will go towards the shortfall of interest.

2. If rates had been 4.00 per cent on settlement:

$$\frac{(4.00 - 4.96) \times \$10,000,000 \times 90 \text{ days}}{36,000} \times \frac{1}{1 + \frac{(4.0 \times 90)}{36,000}}$$

–US\$24,000 × 0.99009901 = US\$23,762.38

The actual LIBOR rate was above the FRA rate when the deal was finalized, so the client will compensate the bank with the amount of US\$ 24,632.97 (see Figure 5.10).

This will go against the increased interest income earned on the deposit.

Practical considerations

A forward rate agreement does not require the payment of a premium, and as such will guarantee for the buyer an 'absolute' rate of cover. However, should a client wish to transact one of these for the first time, it will be necessary to contact the bank to arrange for an appropriate credit line. This will be required because the FRA allows for a 50/50 chance of a cash flow in either direction on settlement, either from the bank to the client or vice versa. It is obviously the potential risk that the client will not repay the bank when he is supposed to. The credit department of the bank will normally require the last three years' annual reports to aid them in deciding whether to grant the facility. It is usual to set up the credit line in advance of dealing.

It is advisable to consider different banks from those which may offer mainstream banking facilities, if only to spread the risk. Some clearing banks offer an excellent service in derivatives, as do some UK, Japanese, European and US houses.

It is always worth having credit lines with more than one FRA provider, as banks will quote different rates on different days. If the bank has an off day, have at least one other bank you can call for a price.

It may be worth seeking competitive quotes for individual transactions in excess of £5 million or US$5 million. Smaller deals are available, but may be at a slightly worse rate. Clients can transact for any period over one month including broken dates (non-calendar), as long as the start date of the FRA is at least two weeks forward, and the end date is not more than 60 months. FRAs are most readily available for multiples of three-monthly periods, e.g. 3s–6s or 6s–12s, but it is worth checking with your bankers for other periods. Unusual periods such as 1s–2s and 0s–1s are possible, but at a price.

Availability

FRAs are normally available in marketable amounts, from £5 million or US$5 million, in most major and some minor currencies. Some banks will make prices in smaller transactions for their own clients, sometimes as low as £1,000,000. It should be recognized that rates for smaller value transactions are likely to be worse than the rates for a 'marketable amount'.

Table 5.7 compares financial futures and FRAs.

Table 5.7		Comparison between finanical futures and FRAs
	Financial futures	**FRAs**
Documentation	Detailed, relates to exchange, broker and clearing house	Standard agreement ISDA
Margins	Initial and variation	None
Amounts	Fixed contract sizes	Any amount from £1 million
Maturity	Fixed contract dates	Any date up to five years
Liquidity	Can be problems in the back months	Good
Flexibility	Can be closed out at any time	Reversing FRA to settlement date
Restrictions	On dates, amounts, and 3-month runs	None
Bid/offer spreads	1–2 ticks	0.03-0.10 per cent
Basis risk	Between futures price and LIBOR	None
Credit risk	Margin monies placed with broker, who then places them with the exchange	With the counterparty, for cash settlement of differential
Credit lines	Not required	Required for interest rate differential

INTEREST RATE OPTIONS

Introduction

An interest rate option (IRO) is a derivative that is used to hedge either single periods of interest rate exposure, e.g. a three-month period from 1 February, or a series of sequential periods, such as three months from 1 February, and from 1 May, and from 1 August. In the latter case, a series of IROs will be needed, known as a 'strip'. It is also possible to hedge this type of longer exposure with a 'strip' of FRAs or a 'strip' of financial futures. There are two different types of interest rate options: those traded on a regulated exchange and OTC options that are custom tailored for the client. This section will focus on OTC interest rate options.

> An interest rate option gives the buyer the right, but not the obligation, to fix the rate of interest on a notional loan or deposit for an agreed amount for an agreed period on a specific future date. A premium is due.

Definition

Definition discussed

This option gives the prospective borrower or lender the chance to fix the rate of interest that will apply to their forthcoming transaction. The option instrument will let the client choose the guaranteed rate, and the writing bank will then guarantee that rate if/when required by the customer. Because this insurance is optional, and the client is not obliged to take the cover, a premium is required. The premium must be paid upfront the same day, if it is a sterling or domestic currency interest rate option, and within two days, if it is a foreign currency interest rate option transaction. Take a US dollar interest rate option written by a UK bank in London. The buyer of the option has no obligation to lend to or borrow from the writing bank. On expiry, the bank will make a cash payment to the customer to compensate for the extent (if any) to which the option strike rate is more advantageous than LIBOR.

In these circumstances the customer is the buyer of the option and must pay the premium, the bank is the seller or writer of the option, and must have the 'underlying' ready in case the client needs it. The underlying in this case is the loan or investment at a particular interest rate. However, this instrument is cash settled and at expiry, a cash lump sum will be paid equivalent to the difference between the two interest rates.

| Key features | **Interest rate options** |

Insurance protection

The client pays a premium to insure against adverse interest rate movements. The bank in return agrees to guarantee a fixed rate of interest if/when required by the client.

Profit potential

The risk of adverse interest rate movements is eliminated, while at the same time, the buyer retains the potential to benefit from favourable interest rate movements. The option can be allowed to lapse if interest rates move in the customer's favour.

Sell back

Interest rate options can be sold back to the writing bank, for residual or fair value if they are no longer required. They are not transferable, there is no secondary market.

Cash settlement

The underlying principal funds are not involved. The client is not obliged to deposit with or borrow from the same bank. On exercise, the bank will pay the difference between the option strike rate and the current LIBOR, discounted back as the early settlement.

Cash market linked

No basis risk. This means hedging 'apples with apples', not 'apples with pears'. A 6-month LIBOR transaction can be hedged with a 6-month LIBOR derivative. With futures there is a limitation in that each future is linked to a 3-month LIBOR. If you are hedging a 6-month LIBOR, then the futures hedge would not be very efficient. It would be necessary to buy twice the amount of futures contracts for a 6-month exposure, and two 3-month LIBORs do not make a 6-month LIBOR.

PREMIUM DETERMINANTS

Once a client is comfortable with the concept of options he will need to seek an indication price from an option trader or through the bank's corporate sales desk. The amount of premium that a client must pay to buy an interest rate option is determined by five factors:

- underlying price
- strike price
- maturity
- call or put
- expected market volatility.

(a) Underlying price vs strike price

With interest rate options the underlying benchmark rate against which the strike price is measured is the appropriate FRA rate. Strikes are therefore referred to as follows:

ATM	At the Money, where the strike is equal to the current FRA rate.
ITM	In the Money, where the strike is more favourable than the FRA rate, and the option premium is higher than that for an ATM.
OTM	Out of the Money, where the strike is worse than the FRA rate and the option premium is lower than that for an ATM option.

(b) Maturity

The longer the time to expiry, the higher the probability of large interest rate movements, and the higher the chance of profitable exercise by the buyer. The buyer should be prepared to pay a higher premium for a longer-dated option than a short-dated option. The premium, however, is not directly proportional to maturity.

(c) Call or put

This is important for determining whether the option is in, at, or out of the money. With interest rate options, the terms 'call' and 'put' have been replaced by 'borrowers' and 'lenders' options respectively.

(d) Expected market volatility

The higher the volatility the greater the possibility of profitable exercise by the customer, so the option is more valuable to the company, therefore the premium is higher. With interest rate options, it is not too difficult to establish a level of implied volatility. The procedure would be to find the nearest exchange-traded interest rate future, then find the option on the future, see where the price is, and use that as an input to make the pricing model work backwards.

Various market factors may lead to an increase in the option premium: these include events such as government intervention, imposition of new taxes, exchange controls, politics, or illiquidity in the market. In general terms, anything that may destabilize an interest rate or a currency will lead to an increase in volatility, so the option premium will increase.

Terminology	Strike price	Specified interest rate where the client can exercise his right to cash settlement.
	Borrowers' option	An option used to hedge against a rise in interest rates, or to speculate that interest rates will increase.
	Lenders' option	An option to hedge against a fall in interest rates, or to speculate that interest rates will fall.
	Exercise	Take-up of the option on expiry.
	Expiry date	The date when the option may be exercised, two business days before the value date if in currency, or same day if in sterling.
	Value date	The date of (settlement) payment.
	Premium	The price of the option, as determined by the option-pricing model.
	Intrinsic value	Difference between the strike price and the current market rate.
	Time value	Option premium minus intrinsic value, reflecting the time until expiry, changes in volatility, market expectations and cost of carry.

Example Hedging with sterling interest rate options

1 May

The treasurer of a medium-sized UK company has a number of loans at variable rates linked to LIBOR. His view is that interest rates will decrease, but the finance director believes the next move will be upwards. An interest rate option can cater for both eventualities, and not leave them exposed. If rates increase, the IRO will refund the difference; if interest rates fall, the treasurer will abandon the option, and the loan will be transacted at a lower LIBOR rate. One particular £5 million loan has a rollover in six months' time (on 1 November), when the LIBOR will be re-fixed for the next six months.

Current financial data:

6-month LIBOR is currently 5.25 per cent

6s–12s FRA is 5.10 to 5.00 per cent

Action – 1 May

The treasurer asks for an indication price for a borrower's option to protect (or guarantee) the present LIBOR level of 5.25 per cent. This will insure the rate of 5.25 per cent and, should interest rates fall, he will be able to profit by dealing at the lower borrowing rate – by abandoning the option cover. This will be a 6s–12s borrower's interest rate option (IRO).

NB: *This is an OTM option: although it is the same level as the current LIBOR, it is out of the money compared with the FRA rate by 0.15 per cent (5.25–5.10 per cent).*

The bank quotes an indication rate of 16 bp pa – 16 basis points per annum. A basis point is 0.01 per cent. To establish the premium due for this option, a small calculation must be made, based on the actual number of days for the option is required for. In this example, the loan rollover is six calendar months away. Assume there are 180 days in the period; after this the loan rate will be confirmed, so there is no more uncertainty. It is necessary to hedge only the uncertainty period.

£5,000,000 × 180/365 days × 0.16%

This comes to £3,945.21 payable upfront, and the treasurer proceeds with the transaction. The treasurer believed that the underlying six-month interest rate could increase or decrease by 1 per cent in the six-month period before the LIBOR was re-fixed. In which case there is a list of possible outcomes (see Figure 5.11), the extremes of which are:

1 November
(1) If the 6-month LIBOR is 6.25 per cent, the treasurer will exercise his option, giving him a net borrowing cost of 5.41 per cent.

We arrive at this from the guaranteed interest rate on the option, but we must then take into account the option premium of 16 bp. As both the

Effective borrowing costs for a sterling interest rate option | **Figure 5.11**

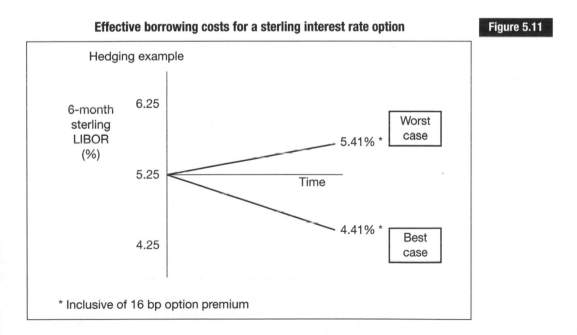

option premium and the LIBOR are quoted on an annualized basis, we can add up the two figures to arrive at a breakeven rate of 5.41 per cent.

(2) If the 6-month LIBOR falls to 4.25 per cent, the option will be allowed to lapse, and the borrowing will be funded at the new lower rate of 4.41 per cent (inclusive of premium).

The treasurer has insured against an adverse interest rate movement for a limited and known cost, and preserved his right to benefit if the cash interest rates move in his favour. This option has guaranteed for the client a worse rate. If rates go higher than the option strike of 5.25 per cent, the client will always exercise the option. So in practice the worse rate is 5.25 per cent. But if the treasurer is lucky, and interest rates fall, then he will abandon the option and borrow at the cheaper rate. There is no limit to the amount of profit he can make on the deal, the extent of the profit is limited only by how far the market moves in his favour (see Figure 5.12).

| Figure 5.12 | Sterling interest rate option example |

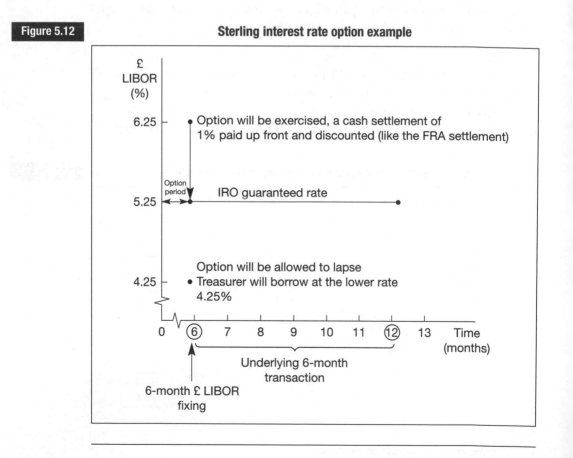

Using Eurodollar interest rate options to hedge an investment

10 April

The treasurer of a small European bank based in Paris is concerned that dollar interest rates will soon fall. He will place a six-month fixed-term deposit of US$25 million on the money market in three months' time, but is worried that by the time the funds arrive, and he can place the deposit, interest rates will have already fallen. The bank's economist disagrees with that view, and believes that rates will either stay the same, or go up.

Current financial data:

6-month LIBOR is currently 4.25 per cent

3s–9s FRA is 4.12 – 4.07 per cent

Action – 10 April

The treasurer asks for an indication price for a lender's option to protect (or guarantee) the present LIBOR level of 4.25 per cent. This will insure the rate of 4.25 per cent and, should rates rise, he will be able to profit by dealing at the higher investment rate. This will be a 3s–9s lender's IRO.

NB: This option is slightly ITM: although it is at the same level as the current LIBOR, it is in the money compared with the FRA rate by 0.18 per cent (4.25–4.07 per cent).

The bank quotes an indication rate of 55 bp p.a. – 55 basis points per annum. A basis point is 0.01 per cent. Remember this includes 0.18 per cent of intrinsic value. To establish the premium due for this option, a small calculation must be made, based on the actual number of days for which the option is required. In this example, the investment will be placed in exactly three calendar months' time. All Eurodollar calculations are based on a 30-day month and a 360-day year. In three months' time, the investment rate will be agreed in the market, so there is no more uncertainty. It is only necessary to hedge the uncertainty period from now until month three.

US$25,000,000 × 90/360 days × 0.55%

This makes US$34,375.00 payable in two business days' time. The bank treasurer assumes that the underlying six-month interest rate could increase or decrease by 1 per cent in the three-month period before the funds are available to invest. There is a list of possible outcomes (see Figure 5.13), the extremes of which are:

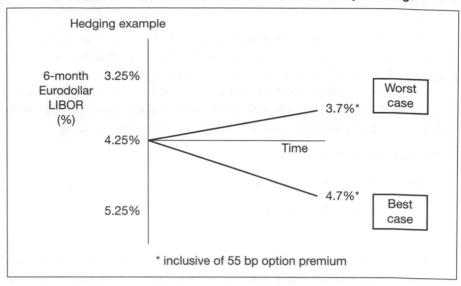

Figure 5.13

Effective investment rates for a Eurodollar interest rate option hedge

Hedging example

6-month Eurodollar LIBOR (%)

3.25%

4.25%

5.25%

3.7%* — Worst case

Time

4.7%* — Best case

* inclusive of 55 bp option premium

Action – 10 August

(1) If the 6-month LIBOR is 3.25 per cent, the treasurer will exercise his option at 4.25 per cent, giving him a net investment rate of 3.7 per cent.

We obtain this from the guaranteed interest rate on the option, but we must then take into account the option premium of 55 bp. As both the option premium and the LIBOR are both quoted on an annualized basis, we can subtract 55 bp from 4.25 per cent to arrive at a breakeven rate of 3.7 per cent.

(2) If the 6-month LIBOR has risen to 5.25 per cent, the option will be allowed to lapse, and the investment will be placed at the higher rate of 4.7 per cent (inclusive of premium).

The treasurer has insured against an adverse interest rate movement for a limited and known cost, and preserved his right to benefit, if the cash interest rates move in his favour. This option has guaranteed a worse case rate for the client who happens to be a bank. If rates go lower than the option strike of 4.25 per cent, the client will always exercise the option. So, in practice, the worst rate is 4.25 per cent. But, if the client is lucky, and interest rates rise, then he will abandon the option and invest at a better rate (see Figure 5.14). There is no limit to the amount of profit he can make on the deal, the extent of the profit is limited only by how far the market moves in his favour.

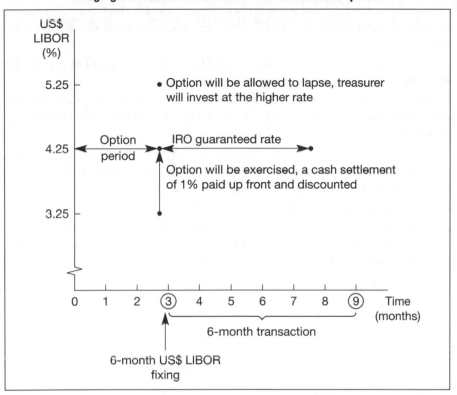

Hedging a Eurodollar investment with interest rate options

Figure 5.14

Availability

IROs are normally available in amounts from £2 million. However, some banks will make prices in smaller transactions for their own clients, sometimes as low as £500,000. Clients can transact for any period over one month, including broken dates (non-calendar dates, not whole month periods), as long as the start date of the IRO is at least about two weeks forward, and the end-date is not more than three years. IROs are usually for multiples of three-monthly periods, e.g., 3s–6s or 6s–12s, and are available in all major currencies. If the option is no longer required it may be sold back to the writing bank for residual or fair value.

Practical considerations

The real value of options is that the client can actively manage his interest rate risk, not only by choosing an instrument that can be abandoned if the market improves, but also by choosing an instrument where one can select the rate of interest; this can be ITM or OTM or ATM. The premium will be calculated according to many different parameters, but the client will always pay up if he chooses an ITM option, as the intrinsic value is a major component of the price.

There is no such thing as a free lunch. If a client needs an ITM option, he will pay for it with a more expensive premium.

Most interest rate options are European style, whereby they can be exercised only on the expiry date. This is the date when the underlying borrowing or investment transaction commences.

Occasionally, it is possible to defer the payment of the premium, and pay at maturity of the option. This would need to be arranged specifically with the credit officers at the bank, as in practice the client is asking the bank to loan him the money for the premium. The bank may wish to do this, but the interest rate for the loan of the premium is likely to be fairly high.

It is always worth seeking competitive quotes for these products. But please bear in mind that not as many banks make prices in IROs as they do in, say, 'vanilla' OTC currency options.

Table 5.8 compares FRAs and interest rate options.

Table 5.8	Comparison between FRAs and interest rate options	
	Interest rate options	FRAs
Margins	None	None
Premium	Yes	No
Amounts	Custom tailored from £500,000	Custom tailored from £1 million
Maturity	Any date up to five years	Any date up to five years
Liquidity	Fairly good	Good
Flexibility	Exercise at expiry or sell back to writing bank	Reversing FRA to settlement date
Restrictions	None, completely custom tailored	None
Bid/offer spreads	0.10–0.15 per cent	0.03–0.10 per cent
Basis risk	None	None
Credit risk	With the bank for cash settlement of the differential	With the counterparty for cash settlement of the differential
Credit lines	Not required unless option is sold	Required for interest rate differential

QUIZ

Questions

1. Using Eurodollar STIR futures, if you are speculating that interest rates are going up and you wish to speculate in a nominal amount of USD 50 million, how many futures contracts will you need and will you buy them or sell them?

2. Based on the answer to the above, if the futures settlement closing price has moved from 94.35 to 94.02 what is your daily profit or loss?

3. Using the rates in Figure 5.5 if Client A needed to hedge a £10 million investment for a 6-month period (181 days) commencing in 6 months' time, what rate would they expect to deal at?

4. Using the rate above if the LIBOR fix on the settlement date was 4.00 per cent, what is the amount of the payment, who would receive it and when?

Answers

1. 50 contracts and sell them.

2. $41,250 profit (33 ticks × 50 contracts × $25).

3. This is a 6 × 12 transaction dealing at 4.53%.

4. £25,284.76 settlement, paid on the settlement date by the bank to Client A. This is a discounted amount.

   Amount before discounting = £25,786.30.

   Discount factor = 0.98055018.

'The market for longer dated derivatives has increased enormously: "long" can now mean periods up to 40 and, in some cases, up to 75 years. The only limiting factor is credit lines.'

■ ■ ■

Multiple Settlement Interest Rate Derivatives

Introduction

Interest rate caps and floors

Interest rate collars

Interest rate swaps

Quiz

INTRODUCTION

The interest rate derivatives that we have considered so far have involved a single period of interest rate exposure: for example, a 3s–6s FRA will cover the three-month period commencing in three months' time. Once the appropriate cash settlement has been paid/received under the FRA, it has no further use. Likewise, an interest rate option, once it has been cash settled or abandoned, has no further use. However, sometimes the underlying transaction period that needs to be covered may be extended to a number of years, or it may need to have more than one re-fix or rollover during its lifetime. Where these types of exposures need to be covered, there are two alternatives (see Figure 6.1):

- Construct a 'strip' of products to cover sequential periods, for example 3s–6s, then 6s–9s, then 9s–12s, etc.

- Construct a product that allows multiple fixings, for example a two-year option product with re-fixings or rollovers every three months on pre-determined dates. Swaps could also be used (see later).

| Figure 6.1 | Different ways of hedging a longer maturity risk |

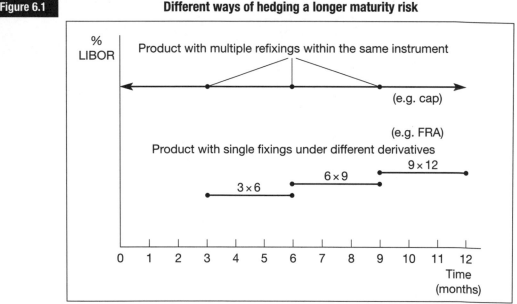

The limitation with the first solution is that each individual three-month slot of time will have a different level of interest rate cover. In Figure 6.2 we have included current market data; this could lead to problems for hedgers.

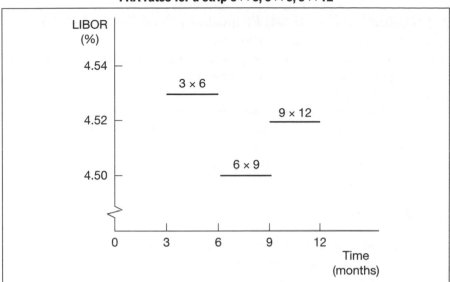

FRA rates for a strip 3 × 6, 6 × 9, 9 × 12

Figure 6.2

NB: The reason we have not included a 0 × 3 FRA is because the three-month rate today is already known to us. It was fixed at 11 a.m. this morning at the LIBOR fixing. The second solution works best for those who need the same rate across the whole period.

The market for longer dated derivatives has increased enormously: 'long' can now mean periods up to 50 and, in some cases, up to 75 years. The only limiting factor is credit lines – or used to be! We now have the ability to use the Central Counterparty model which is part of the Exchange Traded model with whch we are familiar. LCH.Clearnet, through its subsidiary company SwapClear, provides centralized clearing and settlement services and as long as both parties to the swap are members of SwapClear the transaction can be processed through SwapClear; this has the benefit of being able to net allowable swap trades against each other and it minimizes credit risk as the counterparty is now no longer Bank A, but LCH.Clearnet.

Many users of longer dated interest rate derivatives prefer to have a single 'guaranteed' level of interest, rather than many different rates for different periods. Banks now provide a service in longer dated derivatives that are 'built' from shorter dated products, and linked together to provide a guaranteed level at the same rate throughout the insured period. In essence there are two types of longer-term products that are constructed in this way: interest rate caps/floors and (options) interest rate swaps.

Interest rate caps

An interest rate cap is a series of individual interest rate options with each time period specially tailored. The strike rates/strike prices/exercise prices of each option will be identical. A premium is due and will cover the entire maturity period of the underlying transaction. The client need take up his 'insurance' only if the rate on the interest rate cap is more favourable than that currently available in the market on the rollover date. There is no obligation for him to transact, and he has profit potential in that if on a particular rollover date the rate in the market is more advantageous, he can abandon the option, and deal at the better rate.

Interest rate swaps

This is similar to a series of sequential FRAs, but all at the same interest rate. It is a zero-cost derivative, meaning that the client is obligated to transact, whatever the market conditions on each of the rollover dates. As such, it fixes the rate of interest for the whole maturity, but for the hedger allows no profit potential. More later.

INTEREST RATE CAPS AND FLOORS

Introduction

An interest rate cap is the term for an option derivative used to cover a longer-term borrowing exposure with multiple fixings. Interest rate floors are identical, except that the underlying transaction is a deposit or investment rather than a loan. A premium is required. Typically, maturities are in the two- to five-year range: much longer than this and the premiums can become prohibitive. Each cap or floor will need to have multiple settlements (fixings), with dates that are pre-agreed at the outset.

- A strip of borrower's options = an interest rate cap.
- A strip of lender's options = an interest rate floor.

Definition | **Interest rate cap**

An interest rate cap is an agreement that gives the buyer (or holder) the right, but not the obligation, to fix the rate of interest on a notional short- or medium-term loan at a specific rate (the strike) for a specified period. The bank will guarantee a maximum funding cost for the client if/when he requires it. The bank will reimburse the holder of the option for any excess funding costs over the agreed strike rate. A premium is due, payable upfront.

Interest rate floor

An interest rate floor is an agreement that gives the buyer (or holder) the right, but not the obligation, to fix the rate of interest on a notional short- or medium-term investment at a specific rate (the strike) for a specified period. The bank will guarantee a maximum investment rate for the client if/when he requires it. The bank will reimburse the holder of the option for any interest shortfall over the agreed strike rate. A premium is due, payable upfront.

Definitions discussed

To clarify the picture we need to open up these definitions. As with all option contracts we have a buyer and a seller of the option itself. Mostly, but not always, the option writers or sellers will be the major banks. Usually, the buyer of the option is a corporate or financial institution looking to risk manage its position. These derivative products are simply a series of individual options. The terms 'caps' and 'floors' are merely to identify whether the option product is on an underlying loan or investment (from the point of view of the buyer of the product). Caps and floors replace the terms 'call' and 'put'. An option-pricing model calculates the amount of premium due for these option-based products and the premium quotation itself is most often quoted on a 'flat basis'. This means that if the premium is quoted at 0.9 per cent flat, the premium payment will be 0.9% multiplied by the principal amount. If the client wants to cover a £5 million loan, the cost would be £5 million × 0.9% = £45,000, due the same day if in sterling, but two business days later if the cap were in a foreign currency. Care needs to be taken if a number of banks are quoting for the transaction: some may quote on a 'flat' basis, but, occasionally, others may quote in 'basis points per annum'. In both cases, premiums are paid upfront.

Once the buyer has paid the premium to the seller, the buyer (or holder) of the option has no further obligations. On each rollover date, he will simply compare the strike on his cap or floor with the relevant LIBOR fixing for the day and exercise his cover if it is advantageous for him to do so. In contrast, the writing bank will receive the premium, and is then obligated to hedge the banks' position, and must have the 'underlying asset' ready if and or when the client needs it. With caps and floors there will be a cash settlement on each of the fixing dates (in arrears). If the client has bought the interest rate cap or floor, he will never need to settle with the bank (except for the premium). Instead, where the underlying market has improved he will abandon the option in favour of a better rate in the money markets.

In order to ascertain whether a cap or floor is ATM, ITM or OTM, a benchmark rate is used to compare the strike on the product with current market rates. In this case, the equivalent underlying interest rate swap rate is used.

As caps and floors are multiple settlement products, the FRA reference rate that we used for single interest rate options is no longer relevant.

| Key features | **Caps and floors** |

Multiple exercise
A time series of either borrowers or lenders interest rate options with the same strike rates.

Insurance protection
The client pays a premium to insure against interest rate risk.

Profit potential
A cap or floor reduces the cost of adverse interest rate movements while retaining profit potential. The cap or floor can be allowed to lapse (abandoned), if the market has moved in the client's favour.

Cash settlement
Principal funds are not involved. The client is not obliged to deposit with or borrow from the same bank. On exercise, the bank will pay the difference between the strike rate and the relevant LIBOR. Settlement is in arrears, and is paid at the end of that particular three- or six-month period.

Cash-market-linked
There is no basis risk, because both the underlying cash transaction and the hedge are priced from the same market, i.e. LIBOR.

Premium determinants

The amount of premium payable for a cap or a floor is dependent on the same inputs that affect the pricing on any interest rate options, notably:

- strike price
- underlying price
- maturity
- volatility

(a) Strike price vs underlying price

With interest rate caps and floors, the underlying price or benchmark rate is the appropriate interest rate swap rate, taking into account the correct side of the swap, i.e. payer's or receiver's side as appropriate (see the section on interest rate swaps at the end of this chapter). It is against this reference rate that the client's strike rate is measured. Strike rates are therefore referred to as follows:

Terminology

At the money (ATM)	Where the strike rate is equal to the current swap rate.
In the money (ITM))	Where the strike rate is more favourable than the swap rate, and the option premium is higher than that for an ATM option.
Out of the money (OTM)	Where the strike rate is worse than the swap rate and the option premium is lower than that for an ATM option.

(b) Maturity

The longer the time to expiry or maturity, the higher the probability of large interest rate movements, and the higher the chance of profitable exercise by the client (buyer). The buyer should be prepared to pay a higher premium for a longer-dated option than a short-dated option, although the premium is not proportional to maturity.

(c) Expected market volatility

The higher the volatility, the greater the possibility of profitable exercise by the holder, making the cap or floor more valuable, with a higher premium as a result. In general terms, if there is high volatility in the market, then there is a strong likelihood of erratic interest rate movements; therefore there is a good chance that one of these movements may happen close to a LIBOR fixing date, and the client may therefore require compensation (dependent on the direction of the move). Various market factors may lead to an increase in the option premium, and these include events such as, government intervention, imposition of new taxes, rumours and expectations, or illiquidity in the market. In general terms, anything that may destabilize an interest rate or a currency will lead to an increase in volatility, so the option premium will increase.

Interest rate cap and floor

Terminology

Strike price	Specified interest rate where the client can exercise his right to cash settlement.
Interest rate cap	A series of options to hedge against a rise in interest rates, or to speculate that interest rates will increase.
Interest rate floor	A series of options to hedge against a fall in interest rates, or to speculate that interest rates will fall.
Multiple exercise	Take-up of the option on various fixing dates.

Terminology continued		
Rollover date	The date when the option may be exercised, two business days before the value date if in currency, or same day if in sterling.	
Value date	The date of the cash payment (settlement).	
Premium	The price of the option, as determined by the option-pricing model.	
Intrinsic value	Strike rate minus the current market rate.	
Time value	Option premium minus intrinsic value, reflecting the time until expiry, changes in volatility and market expectations.	

Example	Hedging with a sterling interest rate cap

15 September

A UK company managing director has approved the acquisition of a troublesome competitor. The treasurer needs to borrow £10 million for two years; he believes that rates will fall during the period, but is concerned at the weakness of the exchange rate, which might actually cause interest rates to move against him in the short term. The funding will come from the money markets and is linked to 6-month LIBOR. This, however, could leave the company exposed to rising rates.

Action – 15 September

The treasurer asks his bank for an indication cap price as follows:

Term	Two years
Rollovers	6-monthly LIBOR
Face value	£10 million
Strike	1 per cent away from the current swap rate (1 per cent out of the money*)
Premium	0.65 per cent of face value = £65,000 payable upfront

*This will give full protection starting at a rate of 5.65 per cent (worse (higher) than the two-year semi-annual swap rate by 1 per cent).

After checking that this premium is in line with that quoted by other market operators, the treasurer proceeds with the transaction (see Figure 6.3).

On each of the 6-monthly rollover dates commencing 15 March, the bank will settle with the company the amount by which the 6-month LIBOR exceeds the cap strike price. If the LIBOR has not risen above the cap strike price, then the treasurer will re-fix his loan at a more advantageous rate, and will keep all the benefit.

Hedging with a sterling interest rate cap

Figure 6.3

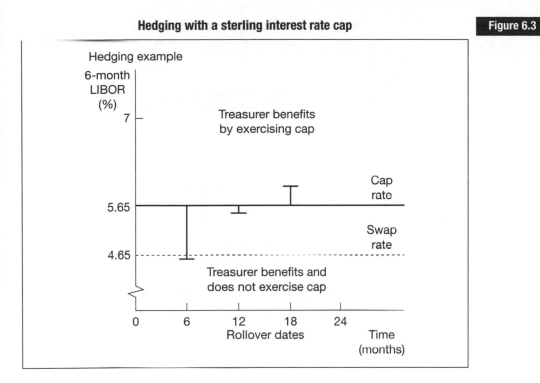

An interest rate floor is identical in operation to an interest rate cap, and protects the buyer by fixing the minimum deposit rate on an investment as shown in the following example.

Hedging with a US dollar interest rate floor

Example

1 November

A French company has just divested one of its US subsidiaries. It received US$25 million, and is about to place this on a 12-month deposit linked to floating rate 3-month money (London inter-bank bid rate). The treasurer needs to be sure that the investment rates are competitive, but he cannot wait until rates improve as his company does not allow him to speculate on the deposit rates. The company believes that rates will improve during the period, but is concerned that short-term volatility may affect the interest rate. The actual cash investment will be linked to 3-month USD LIBID. This could leave the company exposed to falling interest rates. The treasurer is aware that any derivative he uses to hedge his position will be linked to LIBOR not LIBID.

Action – 1 November

The treasurer asks his bank for an indication floor price. This will give full protection starting at a rate of 5 per cent, the same as the equivalent 12-month US dollar quarterly swap. The company decides to hedge its transaction at this rate (see Figure 6.4).

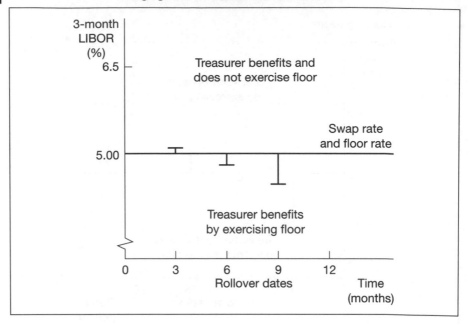

Figure 6.4 Hedging with a US dollar interest rate floor

Term	12 months
Rollovers	3-month LIBOR
Face value	US$25 million
Strike	At the money
Premium	0.35 per cent of face value = US$87,500 payable within two business days

Outcome

On each of the three-monthly rollover dates, the bank will settle with the company the amount by which the floor rate exceeds the 3-month LIBOR. If interest rates do not fall but rise, the treasurer will be able to re-fix his investment at a better rate.

Practical considerations

When a client purchases a cap or floor, his only responsibility is to pay the premium required. Once this has been paid, he has no further obligations. However, he could choose to pay the premium by selling another option product to the bank, in effect by trying to create a reduced cost strategy. He would then be opening himself up to possible risk (see the next section on interest rate collars). It is because of this risk that the banks take a very different view of client credit risk, depending upon whether the client wishes to buy the derivative, sell it outright or both.

The examples we have examined so far in this chapter involve a client buying the interest rate protection. Technically, the bank which sells the product to the client has no credit risk. Under the terms of the cap and floor agreement, the client can walk away from the product anyway, so if the client has got into difficulties, and needs to walk away, in terms of the credit risk it is the same. The client is not committed to pay anything to the bank anyway, so the bank is still in the same position.

However, if the client is a little more adventurous, he may have sold the product to the bank in return for premium. This will cause the credit department more concern, as by taking the premium the client is undertaking to 'deliver the underlying', should the purchasing bank require it. If for some reason, the client does not hedge his position, and the bank calls up to exercise its cap or floor, the client will not be in a position to deliver, and may have got himself into a serious loss position. As a consequence a bank may be prepared to sell caps and floors to their clients, but generally will not purchase these products from their clients, unless the credit risk is either collateralized or a credit line is in existence.

On a practical note, it is vital to match the cap and floor LIBOR settlement dates to the underlying rollover dates for the loan or investment, otherwise the LIBOR on the derivative may settle a day adrift from that on the underlying deal, and this may well involve losses.

When seeking prices for these products it is always worth 'going competitive', except when the principal amounts are too low (less than £1 million, or US$1 million or equivalent). In addition, different banks may credit assess customers in different ways, and so seek different cover.

Availability

Interest rate caps and floors are generally available in amounts from £5 million, and for periods up to seven years, although the majority of business is written in the two- to five-year range. They are also available in most major currencies, with both the strike rate and the rollover frequency selected by the client. Smaller transactions may be available at some banks.

> 'An interest rate cap is the term for an option derivative used to cover a longer-term borrowing exposure. Interest rate floors are identical, except that the underlying transaction is a deposit or investment rather than a loan.'

INTEREST RATE COLLARS

Introduction

In the previous section, we looked at how to cover or 'insure' the interest rate on a medium- or longer-term exposure by using option-based products. In that case, the client would need to purchase a cap or a floor, depending upon whether he wished to hedge a loan or an investment. But whatever he decided to do, he would have to pay a premium. Option cover where the client has the right to walk away from the 'insured' level will always carry a charge. In some cases, especially where the underlying transaction may be for a number of years, the premium due for this cover can be considerable.

Reducing the premium

There are a number of ways in which the client can reduce the premium payable on the cap or floor. The first alternative is usually to go 'out of the money'. Instead of having insurance at today's interest rates, where you would get an immediate payout, consider insurance about 0.5 per cent away (worse). The market then has to move further against you before you start to receive reimbursement. This is similar to a motor insurance policy with, say, a £100 excess. In that case you are still insured, but for every claim you will cover yourself, or self-insure the first £100, and if the total claim is under £100 you receive nothing from the insurance company.

It is possible to design caps and floors that are out of the money, but it should be borne in mind that you can never go so far out of the money that the option cover costs you nothing! For a borrower or an investor, even if the option is only 0.25 per cent out of the money, the premium will still be lower. But, in some cases, the client may be looking for a greater premium reduction, or is not prepared to go sufficiently out of the money. Then we need to investigate other ways of paying the premium; in other words still pay the premium, but not with money. That begs the question, how else can the client pay the premium? The only available alternative is for the client to agree to give up some of his potential profit, should the interest rates move in his favour. It must be stressed that interest rates may not move in the client's favour, and that it is only a potential profit that the client is giving up. If rates do not move in the client's favour then he has given up nothing, and he still has his insurance cover, although he will have achieved the cover at a reduced cost.

> 'An interest rate collar reduces the risk of adverse interest rate movements while retaining the client's ability to benefit from part of any favourable movement.'

The mechanics for the client giving up some profit potential involve him buying the option cover he requires and guaranteeing his insured rate (and protecting his downside), and simultaneously selling a similar second option back to the bank. This second option will have a strike rate exactly at the point where the client has agreed to give up any further profit. On the first option the premium is paid, but this will be offset by the second option where the client receives the premium. The resulting net premiums can be positive, negative or zero, depending on exactly how much profit potential the client is willing to give up. E.g. buy the cap, sell the floor.

> An **interest rate collar** is a contract between a bank and a client, whereby if the client's funding cost is greater than an agreed level, he will be reimbursed down to that level. If the client's funding costs fall below a second agreed level, the client agrees to repay any extra benefit to the bank. An upfront premium is payable, but will be lower than that for a cap or floor and can be zero.

Definition

Definition discussed

If we take the case of a borrower who wishes to cover the variable interest rate on his loan for a period of, say, three years, at a strike of 5 per cent but at reduced cost, the deal mechanics would be as follows.

The borrower would first confirm what level of insurance he wanted on the transaction. Assume he has already been quoted for a cap that is 0.5 per cent out of the money, but for him the premium quoted by the bank is too expensive given his interest rate outlook. The bank has quoted a premium of 1.3 per cent flat for the whole period, paid upfront. If he does not wish to go further out of the money, but still wants a cheaper alternative, then we have to look at these other ways of how he can pay the premium.

Let us assume that over the life of the borrowing transaction the client believes that interest rates may fall but only by, say, 1.5 per cent. He can then put that in writing, in effect guaranteeing to the bank that should rates fall below this rate of 3.5 per cent (5 per cent − 1.5 per cent), then he will take no further profit. The way he does this is to sell an interest rate floor to the bank at a strike of 3.5 per cent. Again, let us assume that the bank will pay him a premium of 0.8 per cent flat. This can go to offset the original premium that he paid on his interest rate cap at 5 per cent. The resulting net premium has now fallen, from a level of 1.3 per cent, to 1.3% − 0.8% = 0.5%.

If we go back to the definition, the original agreed strike level is 5 per cent, and if there are any LIBOR fixings throughout the life of the loan that are above that rate then the bank will compensate the client for any difference, on a cash settlement basis (in arrears, not upfront like in the FRA and interest rate options). If there is a LIBOR fix between the level of cap and floor (between 5 per cent and 3.5 per cent) then the client will be able to re-fix his loan at a lower rate than that he had insured through the cap. This is how the client makes a profit, by borrowing at a cheaper rate. But if there is a LIBOR fix of say, 3 per cent, which is below our second agreed level of 3.5 per cent, then the client can only profit down to his agreed level of 3.5 per cent, he will be unable to profit by the extra 0.5 per cent – this is the 'opportunity cost' of doing this deal.

An interest rate collar can also be used to hedge the yield on investments, in which case the client will buy the floor option and offset the premium by selling a cap.

Key features | **Interest rate collars**

Multiple exercise
A cap and a floor transacted simultaneously, with pre-agreed LIBOR fixings. The cap and floor can be exercised on each LIBOR fix.

Insurance
The client pays a premium to insure against interest rate risk. The premium will be lower as the client accepts part of the risk. He also agrees to share part of the profit with the bank. The net premium may be zero.

Profit potential
A collar reduces the risk of adverse interest rate movements while retaining the client's ability to benefit from part of any favourable movement.

Cash settlement
The principal funds are not involved. The client is not obliged to deposit with or borrow from the same bank. On each rollover date, the bank will pay the positive difference between the collar strike rates and the relevant LIBOR fix.

Cash market linked
No basis risk, because both the underlying cash transaction and the hedge are priced from the same LIBOR market.

Example | **Hedging with a sterling interest rate collar**

A large US corporation has a European subsidiary that will shortly be placing a £10 million deposit. The parent company has insisted on a three-year maturity with three-month fixings. The treasurer of the subsidiary company is concerned that interest rates may become more volatile, and does not wish to be 'locked in' to a fixed rate. Rather, he wants a product like an interest rate floor, where he can walk away from the cover, should the underlying interest rates in the market prove to be more beneficial. However, he does not wish to pay full price for the risk management strategy: instead he is investigating zero- or reduced-cost solutions. To gain an idea of current rates, he puts up a Reuters page from one of his brokers (see Figure 6.5 and 6.6).

Sterling cap prices

Figure 6.5

	STK	ATM	1.50	2.00	2.50	3.00	3.50	4.00	4.50	5.00	6.00	7.00	8.00	9.00
1 YEAR	4.60	8								1				
2 YEAR	4.67	33								15	1			
3 YEAR	4.69	69								41	7	2	1	
4 YEAR	4.67	111								69	17	6	3	2
5 YEAR	4.65	159								102	31	12	6	4
6 YEAR	4.62	208								136	48	21	12	9
7 YEAR	4.60	260								171	66	33	19	15
8 YEAR	4.57	313								206	86	45	28	22
9 YEAR	4.55	366								240	106	58	38	30
10 YEAR	4.52	420								274	127	73	49	38
12 YEAR	4.47	524							510	338	168	102	71	57
15 YEAR	4.39	675							617	422	225	145	105	85
20 YEAR	4.27	907							766	538	302	203	160	144

02/27 15:39 GMT [ICAP] 4749
[GBP CAPS – PREMIUM MIDS] 27/02 15:03 GMT

[G-ICAP GLOBAL INDEX 4900   +44 (0)20 7532 3050   OPTIONS INDEX 4740]
ICAP Global Index [4900]   Forthcoming changes [4999]

Source: ICAP (courtesy of Reuters)

Sterling floor prices

Figure 6.6

	STK	ATM	1.50	2.00	2.50	3.00	3.50	4.00	4.50	5.00	6.00	7.00	8.00	9.00
1 YEAR	4.60	8							5					
2 YEAR	4.67	33					1	5	20					
3 YEAR	4.69	69			1	2	6	17	47					
4 YEAR	4.67	111		1	3	7	17	37	84					
5 YEAR	4.65	159	1	3	7	15	32	64	129					
6 YEAR	4.62	208	3	7	14	27	52	97	179					
7 YEAR	4.60	260	5	2	23	41	76	132	232					
8 YEAR	4.57	313	8	18	34	59	102	172	290					
9 YEAR	4.55	366	12	26	47	78	131	314	350					
10 YEAR	4.52	420	17	35	61	99	162	359	413					
12 YEAR	4.47	524	28	56	92	143	224	349						
15 YEAR	4.39	675	51	93	145	217	328	495						
20 YEAR	4.27	907	101	168	247	352	513	748						

02/27 15:40 GMT [ICAP] 4750
[GBP FLOORS – PREMIUM MIDS] 27/02 15:03 GMT

[G-ICAP GLOBAL INDEX 4900   +44 (0)20 7532 3050   OPTIONS INDEX 4740]
ICAP Global Index [4900]   Forthcoming changes [4999]

Source: ICAP (courtesy of Reuters)

Our treasurer will need to buy the floor and sell the cap. The current at the money rate is just about 4.69 per cent; the treasurer wants to purchase the floor at 4.5 per cent (slightly OTM), giving a premium payable of 0.47 per cent, against this, he is prepared to give up any further profit above 5.0 per cent; so he will also sell the cap at 5.0 per cent. For that he will receive a premium of 0.41 per cent, making a net cost of 0.47% − 0.41% = 0.06%. Not quite zero cost but almost.

The total cost of this collar transaction is 0.06% × £10 million = £6,000, due the same day. This is not quite a zero-cost transaction but has reduced the premium significantly. If the client had wanted a zero-cost transaction he would have requested the bank to work out the strike of the second option – it can sometimes be too difficult and time consuming to try to establish the zero-cost line by trial and error. The bank would price the floor, work out the premium required, then make the pricing model work backwards, put in the premium and the expected volatility and the model will calculate the correct strike on the cap for that premium.

Strategy

The treasurer could purchase either of the following interest rate collars:

1.

Term	Three years
Rollovers	Three-monthly – linked to LIBOR
Face value	£10 million
Strike rate	Cap 5.0 per cent
	Floor 4.5 per cent
Premium:	0.06 per cent nett

Or, alternatively, a similar collar:

Strike rate	Cap 6.0. per cent
	Floor 4.5 per cent
Premium	0.40 per cent nett

Figure 6.7 illustrates how the collar is used.

Outcome

On each of the rollover dates, the LIBOR is fixed at 11 a.m. and compared with each of the collar rates.

(i) If LIBOR is below the floor, the bank will reimburse the difference.

(ii) If LIBOR is between the cap and floor rate, the client transacts in the cash market, neither option will be exercised.

(iii) If LIBOR is above the cap rate, the client must give back any extra benefit to the bank.

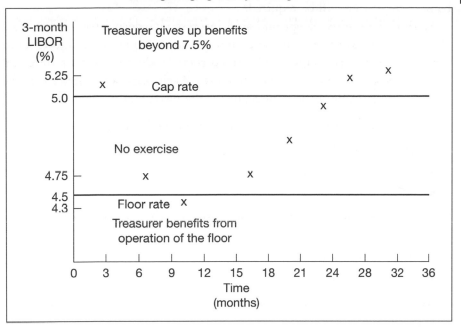

Sterling hedging example using a collar

Figure 6.7

Availability

As these interest rate collars are composite products made up of combinations of caps and floors, their availability will be identical. The only real difference is that one product is bought and one is sold; both transactions need to be carried out simultaneously.

Practical considerations

To implement a collar strategy, it is possible to execute each of the transactions with a different bank. It may happen that on one particular day, a bank may have competitive prices in caps not floors or vice versa. By contacting two different banks and asking for a selection of cap and floor prices, it is possible to 'mix and match' the hedge, so that neither bank knows the strategy is a collar; all that each bank sees is the product that they themselves have been asked to execute. When the premiums of both the cap and the floor net to zero, the product is frequently called a zero-cost collar. But is it really zero cost, or is it simply zero premium where the cost is merely being paid another way?

As one of the components on the collar is an option sold by the client to a bank, a credit line will be required.

Within the family of option-based interest rate derivatives, there is an element of confusion. When these products were originally designed some years ago, each of the larger banks called their product something different to try to make it stand out from the crowd. Each bank was hoping that its name would become the generic name for the instrument.

1. Single settlement interest rate options are also known as:

   ■ interest rate insurance

   ■ interest rate guarantees (IRGs)

   ■ options on FRAs.

2. Multiple settlement interest rate products, caps and floors are also known as:

   ■ interest rate insurance

   ■ interest rate guarantees (IRGs).

3. Reduced premium strategies using caps and floors are also known as:

   ■ zero-cost (or reduced) cost collars

   ■ zero-cost (or reduced) cost cylinders.

INTEREST RATE SWAPS

Introduction

As mentioned in the section on caps and floors, there are two different ways in which a client can protect himself against a longer-term interest rate exposure. First, there are the interest rate caps, floors and collars, and second, the interest rate swaps. The first group of products are option-based and require a premium to be paid, although not necessarily with cash. The payment of this premium gives the purchaser 'the right but not the obligation' to borrow or lend at a particular rate. But there is no compulsion. If there is a better rate elsewhere, the option product can be abandoned.

In contrast, the swap group of products are zero cost, and will tie the client into a legal obligation where he must transact at the guaranteed interest rate on the swap on his particular dates, whatever the current market rate. Obviously, this is not a problem if the current rate in the market is worse, then the swap provides a better alternative. But where the underlying market has improved, the client will be unable to benefit, as he is obliged to deal at the original rate. As we have commented before, if you do not pay a premium you cannot expect to profit.

Once the maturity of the underlying loan or deposit extends beyond five years, the liquidity in risk management instruments begins to dry up. This is due partly to the Central Bank's reserve asset requirements, and partly to the prospect of a bank tying up its credit lines, to the client and to other banks when they hedge their swap position. The chapter on credit risk will explain this more fully, but generally each derivative product carries a risk. The longer the maturity of the product, the greater the risk. As clients do more business their credit lines become full up and no further business can be transacted.

The main risk management instrument for medium to long periods is the interest rate swap, although some long-term caps are used. Premium-based products become expensive, as the maturity gets longer. An interest rate swap is similar but not identical to a series of sequential but linked FRAs, all at the same interest rate. The swap can fix the rate of interest for the whole maturity, but allows no profit potential.

Background

Swaps are probably the most flexible risk management tool around. They can cover exposures from one month (via overnight swaps) to 50 years and sometimes 75 years. They are often used by banks for their own hedging and are often combined with bond issues to achieve favourable funding costs. They can assist a borrower to find fixed rate funding if he is unable to access other lending markets. It must be borne in mind that swaps are not a method of raising finance, rather they are a way of managing an interest rate risk and possibly transform it from fixed interest rates into floating (LIBOR) interest rates or vice versa.

Table 6.1 shows how the notional volumes of major asset classes has grown from end June 2004 to end December 2005. The biggest asset class is that of interest rate contracts and swaps have the most volume. As with all tables, care must be taken when using the information. It takes many months to compile the information, and as a result it is historic before publication, but it is still the most recent available.

Table 16.1

The global OTC derivatives market[1]
Amounts outstanding in billions of US dollars

	Notional amounts				Gross market values			
	End-Jun 2004	End-Dec 2004	End-Jun 2005	End-Dec 2005	End-Jun 2004	End-Dec 2004	End-Jun 2005	End-Dec 2005
GRAND TOTAL (excluding credit default swaps – CDSs)	220,058	251,499	271,282	284,819	6,395	9,244	10,417	9,139
A. Foreign exchange contracts	26,997	29,289	31,081	31,609	867	1,546	1,141	998
Outright forwards and forex swaps	13,926	14,951	15,801	15,915	308	643	464	407
Currency swaps	7,033	8,223	8,236	8,501	442	745	549	452
Options	6,038	6,115	7,045	7,193	116	158	129	139
Memo: Exchange-traded contracts[2]	*98*	*164*	*170*	*172*				
B. Interest rate contracts[3]	164,626	190,502	204,795	215,237	3,951	5,417	6,699	5,463
FRAs	13,144	12,789	13,973	14,483	29	22	31	29
Swaps	127,570	150,631	163,749	172,869	3,562	4,903	6,077	4,864
Options	23,912	27,082	27,072	27,885	360	492	592	570
Memo: Exchange-traded contracts[2]	*49,385*	*42,769*	*53,794*	*52,300*				
C. Equity linked contracts	4,521	4,385	4,551	5,057	294	498	382	560
Forwards and swaps	691	756	1,086	1,111	63	76	88	105
Options	3,829	3,629	3,464	3,948	231	422	294	455
Memo: Exchange-traded contacts[2]	*3,347*	*3,659*	*4,553*	*5,340*				
D. Commodity contracts[4]	1,270	1,443	2,940	3,608	166	169	376	523
Gold	318	369	288	334	45	32	24	51
Other	952	1,074	2,652	3,273	121	137	351	472
Forwards and swaps	503	558	1,748	2,319	0	0	0	0
Options	449	516	904	955	0	0	0	0
E. Other[5]	22,644	25,879	27,915	29,308	1,116	1,613	1,818	1,595
GROSS CREDIT EXPOSURE[6]					1,478	2,075	1,897	2,003
Memo: Exchange-traded contracts[3, 1]					*52,830*	*46,592*	*58,517*	*57,811*
Memo: CDSa[8]		*6,396*	*10,211*	*13,698*		*182*	*264*	*346*

[1] All figures are adjusted for double-counting. Notional amounts outstanding have been adjusted by halving positions vis-à-vis other reporting dealers. Gross market values have been calculated as the sum of the total gross positive market value of contracts and the absolute value of the gross negative market value of contracts with non-reporting counterparties. The grand total excludes CDSs, which are shown separately in Tables 4 and 5. [2] Sources: FOW TRADEdata; Futures Industry Association: various futures and options exchanges. [3] Single currency contracts only. [4] Adjustments for double-couning partly estimated. [5] Includes foreign exchange, interest rate, equity and commodity derivatives of non-reporting institutions, based on the triennial central bank survey of foreign exchange and derivatives market activity. [6] Gross market values after taking into account legally enforceable bilateral netting agreements. [7] Excludes commodity contracts. [8] See Tables 4 and 5.
Source: BIS

All swaps have one common feature: one party is exchanging a benefit it has in one financial market for a corresponding benefit available to another party in another market. This is known as comparative advantage. For example, there may be two different clients, one with an advantage in the bond market, who has access to comparatively cheap long-term fixed rate money. A second client may be able to borrow on a floating rate basis

(LIBOR) from his bankers at what he considers to be a very competitive rate. Each participant in the swap market uses his most advantageous market to borrow the physical money, and then through the swap, manages to 'swap' the interest basis on which his loan is based. For example, a client may wish to borrow based on a fixed rate, but the only way he can achieve it is to borrow from the money markets on a LIBOR-based loan, a 'floating rate', and then to 'swap' into a fixed rate. A swap will allow the client to borrow wherever he likes, at the cheapest rates, and then to enter into an interest rate swap separately, to achieve the interest basis that best suits him, with the bank that has the most competitive swap prices.

There are five basic types of swap:

- Single currency interest rate swap
- Basis swap
- Currency swap
- Currency basis swap
- Cross-currency interest rate swap.

Currency swaps will be discussed in Chapter 10.

The market in swaps is made up of the world's major banks (central, commercial and investment), as well as supranationals, multinational and national corporates. Although swaps can be used for any period, the bulk of transactions are in the two- to seven-year maturity, with the longest dated swaps being placed against capital market issues for anything up to 75 years. The simplest type of swap is the single currency interest rate swap, which is also the most common. Volume increased world-wide by approximately US$15.0 trillion every half year in the period 2003 to 2005. In the period 1995–1998 the increase was only $2.5 trillion for the same period!

> An interest rate swap is an agreement to exchange interest-related payments in the same currency from fixed rate into floating rate (or vice versa), or from one type of floating rate to another. New or existing debt can be swapped.
>
> **Definition**

Definition discussed

A swap is a legally binding agreement, where an absolute rate of interest will be guaranteed. One party will agree to pay the 'fixed rate'; the other, to receive this fixed rate and pay the 'floating rate', usually LIBOR. The underlying loan or investment is untouched, and may well be with another bank. The only movement of funds is a net transfer of interest rate payments between the two parties on pre-specified dates. The interest payments are calculated on an agreed principal amount that is not exchanged. Both interest payments are 'netted off' to help minimize credit exposure.

Key features

Insurance protection

Through a swap a client can guarantee the rate of interest he will pay or receive on an underlying loan or deposit. No premium is required, and the swap can be tailored to match exact underlying requirements.

Cash settlement

It is only the interest payments that are swapped, the principal sums are not exchanged.

Funding optimization

As the underlying loan or deposit may be with another bank, the client can deal where he gets the best borrowing and investment rates. The swap will be negotiated separately.

Credit risk

The credit risk of the counterparty must be carefully evaluated, although if a bank is acting as intermediary, it will normally guarantee the credit-worthiness of each party to the other.

New or existing obligations

It is possible to swap new or existing debt.

Premium

Swaps are zero-premium instruments and a credit line will be required.

Terminology

	Interest rate swap
IRS	Interest rate swap, sometimes called interest rate insurance.
Fixed payer	The party wishing to pay the fixed rate on the swap (receiving LIBOR).
Fixed receiver	The party wishing to receive the fixed rate on the swap (paying LIBOR).
Swap rate, fixed rate, guaranteed rate	The swap rate agreed between the parties at the outset of the transaction.
Rollovers/ resets	The frequency of the LIBOR settlements, e.g. a two-year swap against 6-month LIBOR. The dates when the 11 a.m. LIBOR fix, and the fixed rate on the swap are net cash settled. Settlement is in arrears. For example, if on one reset date the fixed rate is 6.5 per cent, and LIBOR is 6.0 per cent, there will be a net payment of 0.5 per cent from the fixed rate payer.

Comparative advantage

The literature on swaps seem to imply that you cannot enter into a swap agreement unless there is 'comparative advantage' present. This is not entirely true.

The easiest way to understand the term 'comparative advantage' is to recall that the word 'swap' is not a financial term. It has come from the playground. Imagine two little boys: one has two red cars, one has two blue cars. One little boy says to the other, 'I'll swap you one of my red cars for one of your blue cars'. If the cars are identical except for colour, the swap may proceed; the key element is that both boys should be better off afterwards, each has a blue car and a red car. But if the little boy with the blue cars has very special blue cars, perhaps bigger with more chrome, then he may not wish to proceed with the swap, as he may see himself as being worse off after the swap. However, in this example, one boy has a comparative advantage in the red car market and one in the blue car market.

This seems to suggest that both of the swap participants need to have an advantage somewhere. In fact, if a client simply wishes to hedge an interest rate risk, he will deal directly with a bank which will then become his counterparty, and at the same time an intermediary between the client and perhaps another financial institution when the bank hedges his position. Swap banks make money from acting as intermediaries. A swap has no premium payable, so the client, once he has concluded the transaction, will be unable to improve the rate on his hedge, but will be obliged to transact at the swap rate, whatever the current rates are in the market.

There are two distinct types of single currency interest rate swap:

- fixed/floating single currency interest rate swap (also known as a 'vanilla' or 'coupon' swap)
- floating/floating single currency interest rate swap (also known as a basis swap).

Fixed/floating interest rate swaps: 'Vanilla'

A fixed/floating swap is so called because one party pays the fixed rate and the other pays the floating rate. To many in these markets, the term used is 'vanilla' swap. This is the simplest type of swap available, named after the simplest type of ice cream. Capital markets practitioners may call these swaps 'coupon' swaps, to highlight the fact that they are linked to an underlying bond issue, where the interest coupon is being swapped. For a swap to be known as a vanilla swap it must have the following characteristics:

- a constant notional principal amount (NPA): not amortizing (where the principal decreases) or accreting structures (where the principal increases)
- an exchange of fixed against floating interest (coupon swap)
- a constant fixed interest rate
- a flat floating interest rate (e.g. LIBOR flat)
- regular/not necessarily simultaneous payments of fixed/floating interest
- an immediate or spot start
- no special risk features such as embedded options.

Hedging with a fixed/floating US dollar interest rate swap

A UK company has agreed to purchase and equip a new hotel in the USA. Funds of $50 million are required for a period of five years, and the treasurer would ideally prefer a fixed rate of interest for the period. She considers the only fixed rate funds available to her to be too expensive. Her alternative is to borrow the $50 million on a floating rate basis from the money markets, and rollover the funds every six months. This would, however, leave the company exposed to rising rates. The company has been quoted 6-month LIBOR plus 0.5 per cent for the floating rate loan.

The company can take out an interest rate swap, which would fix the rate of interest and remove the threat of rising rates. It is important for the swap to match the underlying transaction in all respects.

In our example, the company wishes to 'pay the fixed and receive the floating' (rate). The treasurer has put up one of the brokers' screens to have an indication of current levels in the market (see Figure 6.8).

Figure 6.8	US$ swap prices

02/27 16:47 GMT	[CAP]	4903

US DOLLARS				CANADIAN DOLLARS		27/02 16:47 GMT	
	SPREAD	SWAP PRICE			SPREAD	SWAP PRICE	
1 YR	–	5.160–5.130		1 YR	–	4.235–4.205	
2 YR	41.75–38.75	5.140–5.110		2 YR	28.0–25.0	4.277–4.237	
3 YR	42.00–39.00	5.120–5.090		3 YR	29.5–26.5	4.325–4.284	
4 YR	44.50–41.50	5.120–5.090		4 YR	30.5–27.5	4.367–4.327	
5 YR	47.50–44.50	5.120–5.090		5 YR	31.5–28.5	4.409–4.369	
6 YR	48.50–45.50	5.115–5.085		6 YR	34.0–31.0	4.446–4.407	
7 YR	49.75–46.75	5.115–5.085		7 YR	35.8–32.8	4.475–4.436	
8 YR	51.00–48.00	5.115–5.085		8 YR	37.3–34.3	4.501–4.464	
9 YR	52.00–49.00	5.115–5.085		9 YR	38.8–35.8	4.528–4.491	
10 YR	53.25–50.25	5.110–5.080		10 YR	40.5–37.5	4.557–4.521	
12 YR	53.25–50.25	5.110–5.080		12 YR	46.5–43.5	4.620–4.584	
15 YR	55.50–52.50	5.120–5.090		15 YR	54.5–51.5	4.704–4.668	
20 YR	57.25–54.25	5.125–5.095		20 YR	60.0–57.0	4.766–4.730	
25 YR	58.00–55.00	5.120–5.090		25 YR	59.3–56.3	4.765–4.730	
30 YR	58.25–55.25	5.105–5.075		30 YR	58.5–55.5	4.765–4.729	

Source: ICAP (courtesy of Reuters)

Our client wishes to pay fixed, so she is on the high side of the price, i.e. at or around 5.12 per cent. This is an inter-bank screen and our client is not a bank. Her price will be higher to allow for the fact that her company credit rating is not as good as that of the bank. Let us assume that the swap trader has quoted her a rate of 5.15 per cent. This is the rate that she will pay semi-annually (this is the norm but other payment frequencies are available). In return she will receive 6-month LIBOR, which will be reset every six months in line with market rates. The dates on the swap and the underlying loan must be matched, so that the LIBOR payment received under the swap can be paid straight through to the underlying loan.

Outcome

On each of the rollover dates, which are specified in advance, the two interest payments will be calculated and offset. For example, if on the first 6-month date, the LIBOR was 5.50 per cent at the 11 a.m. fixing, we would not have one payment of the fixed rate at 5.15 per cent and another in the opposite direction of 5.50 per cent. In fact, the difference of 0.35 per cent will flow from the bank to the client. This helps in reducing the amount of credit line required, and is known as nett cash settlement (see Figure 6.9).

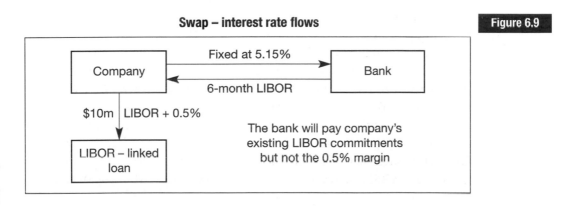

Swap – interest rate flows

Figure 6.9

Summary

(i) The client obtains fixed rate funding at 5.65 per cent (including the 0.5 per cent margin), which is better than the original 5-year fixed rate quoted.

(ii) On each rollover date, the two interest payments are 'netted off' and the balance transferred to the appropriate party.

(iii) The underlying transaction is untouched.

The example illustrates the hedging nature of swaps, without going into the complications of comparative advantage. As long as the treasurer can achieve cheaper funding via the swap, rather than direct with the bank, it will be the preferred route.

Our next example will focus more on the concept of advantages and disadvantages, and using comparative advantage.

Example

A top-rated multinational, Grady Co. can raise fixed rate sterling through a bond issue for five years at 10 per cent, but it requires floating rate funds (it wishes to borrow on a LIBOR basis). The bank has quoted a rate of LIBOR + 0.5 per cent for the funds.

Blythe Co. want to borrow for five years on a fixed basis, but their investment bankers have advised them against a bond issue at this time as their name is not presently well rated. A floating rate loan can, however, be arranged for five years at LIBOR + 0.75 per cent, but Blythe want fixed rate funds. An assumption has been made that if Blythe were offered fixed rate funds at 10.5 per cent or better, they would take them.

Summarizing the information

Grady Co. could borrow fixed at 10 per cent, but wants to pay floating at less than LIBOR + 0.5 per cent. Blythe Co. want fixed rate funding at 10.5 per cent or less, but could borrow at LIBOR + 0.75 per cent. These rates are summarized in Table 6.2. Why are these parties considering a swap at all? Grady Co. believes it has an advantage in the bond market and that the borrowing rate will reflect that. But when it asks for a quote for LIBOR-based funds, the bank wishes to charge a margin of 0.5 per cent over LIBOR, which it considers does not accurately reflect their credit standing in the market. They believe that if they can borrow in the bond market at favourable rates they can then 'swap' the advantage into the floating rate market, and achieve a lower all-in rate (i.e. lower than LIBOR + 0.5%).

Table 6.2

Summary of interest rates

	Fixed rates	Floating rates
Grady Co.	10%	LIBOR + 0.5%
Blythe Co.	10.5%	LIBOR + 0.75%
Comparative advantage	0.5%	0.25%

Question: In which market does Grady Co. have the most advantage, and Blythe Co. the least advantage?

Answer: Grady Co. has a cost advantage in both markets, as it is the better credit, but a greater advantage in the fixed rate (0.5 per cent against 0.25 per cent).

This first step will be to allow the participants to choose in which underlying market they will borrow. The swap will transform only their interest rate obligations. Grady Co. raises funds where it has the most advantage, the fixed rate bond market at 10 per cent, and Blythe Co. uses traditional funding and borrows floating rate from its bankers at LIBOR + 0.75 per cent, where it has least disadvantage.

Absolute advantage

This will show us if there is a likelihood of an interest rate swap working. There is a 0.5 per cent advantage in the fixed rate market and a 0.25 per cent advantage in the floating rate market, making an absolute advantage of 0.25 per cent (0.5% − 0.25% = 0.25%), these basis points are available to be shared among the three parties, Grady Co., Blythe Co. and the intermediary bank.

If we look at Figure 6.10(a), we can see the position before the swap, showing only the underlying cash flows.

Arrows coming out of the boxes represent interest paid, arrows coming in represent interest received.

Swapping the interest flows with the intermediary bank   **Figure 6.10**

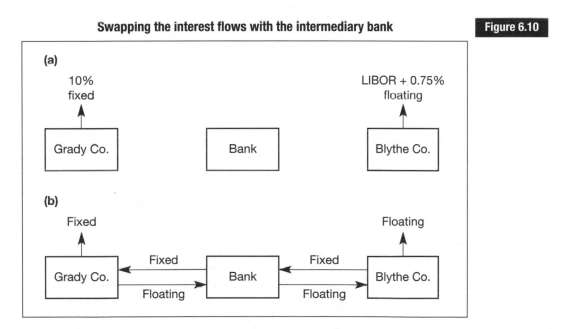

Outcome

The two participants will then swap the interest flows with an intermediary bank, as shown in Figure 6.10(b).

Grady Co. requires the bank to pay the fixed rate, which it will then pay to the bond holders, whereas Blythe Co. requires the bank to pay the 6-month LIBOR (exclusive of margin), which it will pay to the lending bank. Let us assume the swap trader has quoted a rate of 9.65 per cent to 9.60 per cent. This shows how the bank receives the fixed rate, and how the bank pays the fixed rate. If you are ever unsure on which side of the price you will be dealing, remember, the bank is going to take the profit out of the dealing spread. The bank will always want to receive on the high side of the swap, and pay on the lower side.

It is now necessary to see whether both parties are better off after the swap (see Figure 6.11).

Figure 6.11   **Actual swap – interest rate flows**

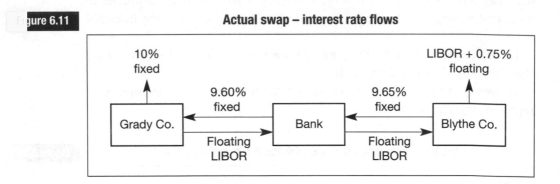

The 25 basis points are divided between the parties. The LIBOR payment is 6-monthly unless specified otherwise. The 25 points will be included in the fixed rate payment, not the LIBOR. In most cases it will be useful to draw up mini-balance sheets representing receipts and payments of interest (see Table 6.3).

Table 6.3   **Example: receipts and payments of interest**

Grady Co.		Blythe Co.	
Receipts	Payments	Payments	Receipts
9.60%	10%	LIBOR	LIBOR + 0.75%
	LIBOR		9.65%
Net cost: LIBOR + 0.40%		Net cost: 10.40%	

Grady Co. will pay 10 per cent to the bond holders but receive 9.6 per cent towards it, making a net cost of LIBOR + 0.40 per cent, a saving of 10bp.

Blythe Co. will pay and receive LIBOR so these payments will cancel out, leaving it to pay the 9.65 per cent swap rate plus its margin, a net rate of 10.40 per cent, a saving of 10 bp, but it had fixed rate funds where there were none previously available.

The bank takes a 5 bp fee for the credit risk and acting as intermediary.

Single currency basis swaps

Banks and financial institutions, which commonly engage in transactions between assets and liabilities, will from time to time experience an interest rate 'gap'. This is where there may be differing interest bases for different maturities. There are many financial institutions that borrow from the money markets and on-lend to commercial clients on a different interest basis at higher rates. There are also building societies that receive mortgage interest on a monthly basis, yet have funded themselves on a 3-month LIBOR basis in the wholesale inter-bank market. In this case both the receipt and payment are based on a floating rate but there is a mis-match. A basis swap can go some way to correcting the balance. With a basis swap both parties will be paying a floating rate of interest, of which one is often LIBOR and sometimes both. For example, one party may wish to pay LIBOR and the other a commercial paper rate; alternatively both parties may wish to pay LIBOR: one may pay 3-month LIBOR and the other 6-month LIBOR.

Hedging with a sterling basis swap

A major US bank has lent £10 million to one of its clients for 12 months. Under the terms of the facility the loan is rolled over monthly, based on 1-month LIBOR + 75 bp. The US bank's funding for this facility forms part of a much larger arrangement with one of the large inter-bank players, but the funding is based on 3-month LIBOR flat. The sterling desk manager wishes to even out the cash flow and the basis by entering into a basis swap.

Strategy

The swap bank has been asked to quote for a 1s against 3s, 12-month basis swap. The client, in this case the US bank, wishes to pay 1s (1-month LIBOR) and receive 3s (3-month LIBOR) to set off against his money market funding. Basis swaps are quite sought after, consequently they are fairly expensive, which is why the swap bank may only quote a $ rate for the US bank to pay 1-month LIBOR + 45 basis points against 3-month LIBOR flat (see Figure 6.12).

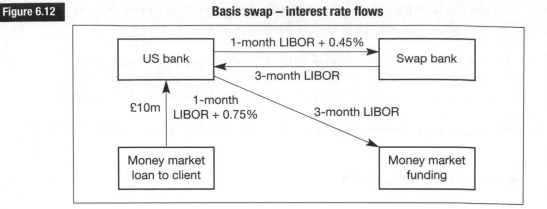

Figure 6.12   **Basis swap – interest rate flows**

The net return to the US bank, after taking into account the interest rate movements on the swap, is 0.30 per cent; this does not take into account the cost of capital or balance sheet costs.

Generally, basis swaps can involve different combinations of fixed and floating rates.

- Different maturities in the same index, 3-month LIBOR vs 1-month LIBOR.
- Same maturity and the same index, but one carries a margin: 6-month LIBOR vs 6-month LIBOR + 60 bp.
- Same or different maturities within the same index: US$CP rate (US dollar commercial paper rate) vs prime, or 3-month $ LIBOR vs 3-month bill rate.

Swap pricing

In countries where the swap market is not so well established, swap prices are quoted on an all-in basis in absolute terms (the full percentage annual yield, e.g. 5.1 per cent). Where the swap markets are well developed, such as the USA, UK and Europe, the price is quoted in two parts: a swap spread and a benchmark rate (usually a government bond such as a UK gilt, or a US treasury bond), e.g. the swap is trading at 40 basis points over the gilt. The benchmark rate will be the yield on the most liquid bond closest to the maturity date of the swap. For example, at the time of writing, the reference gilt for the five-year sterling swap is currently the 4.75 per cent of 2010 (abbreviated to '4T 10'). Quoting this way allows both parties to agree the 'spread' over the gilt, while allowing the gilt to move separately.

Sterling swap quotations

Figure 6.13

		[ICAP – GBP SWAPS & SPREADS]			
2y	4.7000–4.6600	5 08	+38.00/+34.00	SONIA	
3y	4.7250–4.6850	4 09	+39.75/+35.75	1M 4.495–4.485	
4y	4.7150–4.6650	4T 10	+42.00/+37.00	2M 4.489–4.469	
5y	4.6900–4.6400	4T 10	+39.50/+34.50	3M 4.491–4.471	
6y	4.6675–4.6175	5 12	+42.50/+37.50	4M 4.493–4.473	
7y	4.6400–4.5900	5 12	+39.75/+34.75	5M 4.500–4.480	
8y	4.6125–4.5625	8 13	+40.50/+35.50	6M 4.507–4.487	
9y	4.5825–4.5325	5 14	+38.25/+33.25	7M 4.516–4.496	
10y	4.5525–4.5025	4T 15	+37.75/+32.75	8M 4.524–4.504	
12y	4.5125–4.4425	4T 15	+33.75/+26.75	9M 4.534–4.514	
15y	4.4425–4.3525	4T 20	+33.25/+24.25	10M 4.546–4.526	
20y	4.3425–4.2125	5 25	+33.25/+20.25	11M 4.558–4.538	
25y	4.2475–4.1175	4Q 32	+36.25/+23.25	12M 4.571–4.551	
30y	4.1750–4.0450	4Q 36	+32.50/+19.50	18M 4.590–4.570	
40y	4.0950–3.9250	4T 38	+26.75/+9.75	2Y 4.644–4.624	
50y	4.0250–3.8550	4Q 55	+32.50/+15.50	SONIA	
				020 7532–3250	

Source: ICAP (courtesy of Reuters)

The benefits of this occur when there is a fast-moving market and the underlying gilt or Treasury bond may be quite volatile with the price swinging all over the place. This makes it nearly impossible for the swap trader to keep the price firm even when he is just checking the availability on the client's credit line. At least by agreeing the 'spread' over the bond yield in advance, all that is left is to determine where the gilt or bond is trading at the final moment in time, then add the dealer's spread.

The figures shown in Figure 6.13 are compiled by one of the brokers, and are indication levels of where the business can expect to be done, although the broker will not be a counterparty, simply a facilitator, putting together willing payers and willing receivers on the swaps. The first column shows the maturity, the second column the all-in prices on the swap. The third column shows the benchmark gilt, and the fourth shows the 'spread' over the gilt. The prices quoted are two-way prices. The five-year rate shows that the dealer is prepared to receive at 39.5 basis points over the gilt, and pay at 34.5 basis points over the gilt. The underlying gilt which is the 4.75% of 2010 must have been trading at a yield of 4.295 per cent, to equate to the 4.69 – 4.64 per cent rates shown in Figure 6.13.

Negotiating the deal

The most important component in a swap is the level of the swap's fixed interest rate. If the swap is quoted as a 'spread over', then the spread will be agreed first, as this is the most volatile component. A trader will then need to check that they have room on their credit lines for the counterparty, once this is cleared, then the trader will agree with the client the level of the benchmark gilt or bond, which will then be added to the spread to ascertain the all-in price. Figure 6.14 illustrates the stages in negotiating the swap transaction.

| Figure 6.14 | **Flow chart for negotiating the swap transaction** |

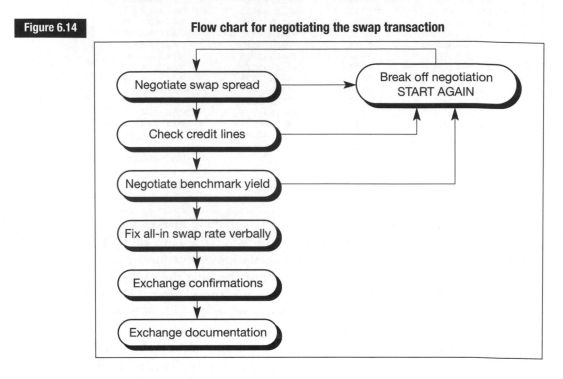

Swap variants

There a number of popular variants to the vanilla swap, these are:

- Swaptions
- Callable swaps
- Overnight swaps

A. Swaptions

These OTC products are options to enter into a swap at a later date.

| Definition | A swaption gives the buyer, the right but not the obligation, to pay or receive the fixed rate of interest on a pre-set interest rate swap. |

Example

Company A is going to issue a 10-year bond linked to a floating rate (FRN). The formalities will take 6 months to complete. As soon as the funds are received they will be swapped into fixed rate. To guard against an adverse rate movement, a 6-month European style payer's swaption is transacted.

Option period: 6 months

Underlying swap: 10 year, Company A to receive floating and pay fixed semi-annually against 6-month LIBOR.

As this is an option the holder can decide to proceed or not with the swap. If they have changed their mind they can walk away. The premium is paid up-front.

B. Callable swaps (cancellable swaps)

This is another option combined with a swap, but in this case the premium is embedded in the fixed rate of the swap and hidden.

Example

A standard 7-year swap where the client pays fixed may be trading at 4.95%. A callable swap which is callable after 3 years might mean the swap rate increases to 5.25%, but at the end of year 3 the customer can walk away from the swap with no penalties.

A simple Callable Swap (i.e. the right to cancel once only) is an Interest Rate Swap plus a bought Receivers Swaption. If, for example, there is the right to cancel a 7-year swap after 3 years, the Callable Swap is a pay fixed 7-year Interest Rate Swap plus a 3-year into 4-year Receiver Swaption where the strike rate on the swaption is equal to the rate quoted on the Callable Swap, in this case 5.25%. The higher than market swap rate for the Callable Swap is to pay for the purchased Receiver Swaption.

C. Overnight swaps

These are known as Sterling Overnight Index Swaps (linked to SONIA rates) and in Euroland as Euro Overnight Index Swaps (linked to EONIA rates). They are used to cover the very short end of the yield curve (weeks and months).

Example

A fund manager is wondering whether he should place his £5m funds on the overnight deposit market, every day for 3 months, or enter into a fixed 3-month deposit. He is worried about the variability of the overnight interest rate. Assume there are 91 days in this period. He can enter into a 3-month Overnight Swap if he wants to hedge his position (see Figure 6.15).

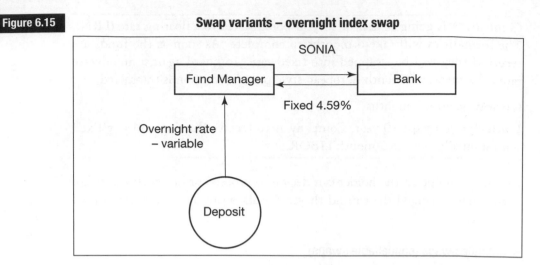

Figure 6.15

Swap variants – overnight index swap

The fixed rate quoted for this swap is 4.59% per annum and is paid once at the end of the period. The client wishes to receive the fixed rate and pay the floating rate. At maturity the British Bankers Association publishes a fixing page on the information networks. The rate is the daily overnight rate which has been compounded for the correct number of days.

If the above swap was settled today, assume the SONIA floating rate is 4.7838 settlement amount:

Pay 4.7838% × 91/365 × £5m = £59,633.67 SONIA

Receive: 4.59% × 91/365 × £5m = £57,217.81

Nett: £2,415.86

Availability

Single currency interest rate swaps are available in all major currencies for minimum amounts of US$1 million or £1 million, with no maximum amount. Periods of one to ten years are usually available, and sometimes up to 75 years.

Practical considerations

Anyone can deal in an interest rate swap, subject to credit considerations. This means that the credit department of the bank(s) with which you wish to deal need to assess their counterparty risk with you. They will need to consider the maturity and amount of any swaps you may wish to do with them, and may even specify, for example, no swaps over five years. Dealing lines and credit lines must be set up in advance. Increasingly deal execution and confirmations will be by electronic platforms.

Within the swap itself, the rollover frequency can be monthly, quarterly, semi-annual or annual. It is not necessary for the fixed payment and the LIBOR to be paid on the same day, but you must specify the frequency of all interest payments at the time of dealing. For example, a 12-month swap could be:

- Semi/semi: both payments at 6-monthly intervals.
- Annual/semi: the fixed payment annually and the LIBOR every 6 months.
- Annual/quarterly: the fixed payment annually and the LIBOR every 3 months.
- Annual/1s: the fixed payment is annual and the LIBOR is monthly.
- Quarterly/quarterly: both payments at 3-monthly intervals.

Each swap price will factor in the payment frequency, and the swap rates will be different to reflect this.

There are a number of swap providers in the market, but not all of them make a market in all currencies and all periods. It is worth shopping around. Some of the smaller banks provide a very good service in niche markets.

QUIZ

Questions

1. You have purchased a EUR 50 million interest rate cap for 5 years with 6-monthly re-sets, premium is quoted at 96 basis points flat. How much must you pay and when?
2. You have sold a £5 million 3 × 6 interest rate option with premium receivable of 0.45 basis points per annum. There are 91 days in this 3 month period and 182 days in this 6-month period. How much will you receive and when?
3. If you were a hedger worried about interest rates going up would you want to pay or receive the fixed interest on a vanilla swap?
4. To arrive at the fixed rate on an interest rate swap, you should take the yield on the appropriate benchmark bond and subtract the swap spread: true or false?

Answers

1. Premium is EUR 480,000.
   EUR 50,000,000 × 0.96%, paid up-front.
2. Premium earned is £5,609.59, due up-front.
   £5,000,000 × 0.45% × 91/365.
3. Pay fixed.
4. False. You should add the swap spread.

'Firms require an independent assessment of their financial positions to submit to desk heads, senior management and in many cases, their regulators.'

■ ■ ■

7

Benchmarking in the OTC Derivatives Markets

Penny Davenport
Director, Markit Group

Financial benchmarking for derivatives

Operational risk measurements for derivatives

Markit Annual Scorecard

Conclusion

The term 'benchmarking' is used in many different ways in the financial markets. This chapter focuses on two different types of benchmarking: frequent comparisons of a market composite price to a firm's own financial data, and reporting of operational statistics as risk measurement for regulators and management information for senior executives.

FINANCIAL BENCHMARKING FOR DERIVATIVES

Daily benchmarking

The majority of firms mark their books to market at the end of every business day. This is true of banks, broker-dealers, hedge funds and pension funds. Firms require this up-to-date assessment of their financial positions to submit to desk heads, senior management and, in many cases, their regulators or fund administrators. For example, mutual funds in the United States are stringently regulated by the US Securities and Exchange Commission (SEC) under the Investment Company Act of 1940. These '40 Act funds' have to report on their portfolios, using the most current financial data, to the SEC by 6 p.m. on a daily basis. The first part of this chapter looks at the different types of data that firms use for this daily benchmarking, and how they supplement it with additional sources for the more stringent reviews which take place at month-end.

Across the spectrum of OTC derivatives, for example, interest rate swaps, equity derivatives and credit default swaps (CDS), the most widely used type of data for end-of-day benchmarking is a dealer-contributed composite. In order to facilitate the benchmarking which benefits all participants, dealers contribute their closing prices, or where they are marking their books, to a central source. Those prices are cleaned and transformed into a single composite which is widely regarded as the price to use for marking-to-market. This data becomes easier to obtain as markets become more liquid. There are multiple sources for daily, closing prices and fixings of interest rate swaps, and other interest rate products which are widely available from the major data vendors, including Bloomberg and Reuters. One example is the BBA LIBOR fixing. The BBA LIBOR fixing is the most widely used 'benchmark' or reference rate for short-term interest rates. It is compiled by the BBA in conjunction with Reuters and released to the market shortly after 11.00 a.m. London time each day. The data is collated from contributions from reference banks which are deemed to be appropriate market representatives. The data is cleaned and published as a standard composite.

Until recently, the credit derivative markets were more opaque but Markit Group has established a data exchange for closing CDS prices which now collects pricing from more than 70 contributors and distributes a daily composite for more than 2,800 reference entities. This data is also cleaned using complex algorithms.

Snapshot of dealer contributed data points against the composite

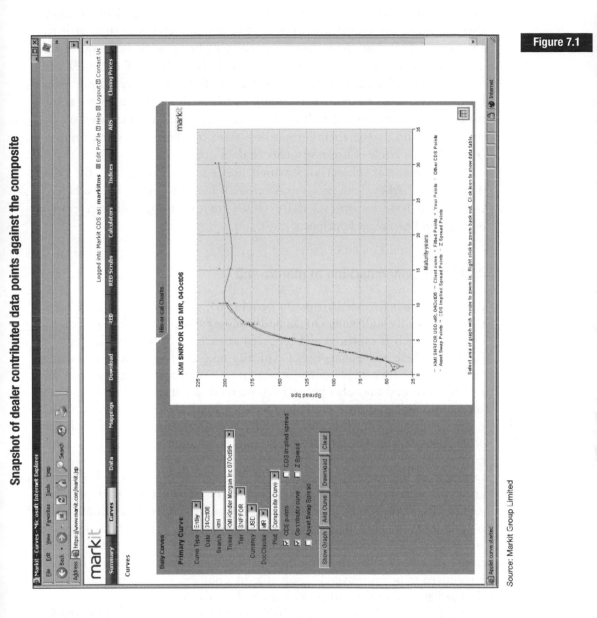

Figure 7.1

Source: Markit Group Limited

Even if a data source is considered to be the market standard for daily closing prices, firms trading OTC derivative instruments still have to apply some discretion to the data as opposed to accepting it without question. For liquid instruments or reference entities, they will typically look at where they have actually traded instruments that day, and compare that with the composite. This data may come from their in-house sources or, quite frequently, from the major inter-dealer brokers such as ICAP, GFI and Creditex. For illiquid instruments or names, firms are increasingly using forms of evaluated or modelled pricing to fill in the gaps which are sometimes left by composite data. So, firms will adjust their P&L based on the composite, and update their composites based on observable data, promoting a virtuous circle of improvements in data quality.

This element of subjectivity, which needs to be managed in the OTC derivatives markets, can be contrasted with markets which are exchange-traded and have an official daily close, for example, exchange-traded equities and future and options.

Additional benchmarking at month-end

Although most financial firms do benchmark their data on a daily basis, there are usually additional checks and analyses which are undertaken on the key data which is captured and reported at each month-end and, crucially, year-end. These additional checks typically take the form of a more manual analysis of a firm's data against a benchmark which will yield a more in-depth result and may also potentially be more accurate. One example of a service providing more detailed analysis is Markit's Totem service which compares pricing contributions from all the major banks and broker-dealers across the spectrum of OTC derivatives including interest rates, equities, foreign exchange, credit and commodities. The Totem service compares the inputs from the contributors and highlights any anomalies. The key difference between this month-end service and the daily service is the level of review that takes place. The daily services are by their nature highly automated and whilst the data cleaning is sophisticated it is standardized and rules-based. The month-end service is more manual and teams of experts pore over the data in order to highlight problems with dealer marks. This has proved to be immeasurably valuable in a number of circumstances where dealers have been mis-marked, either accidentally or otherwise.

In addition to the benefits involved in finding anomalies in dealer marks, month-end benchmarking has a further, tangible upside. IAS 39, an accounting standard of the International Accounting Standards body, requires that, for firms to be able to recognize P&L for complex derivatives at inception, their mark-to-market values need to be based on observable data. For many illiquid instruments, where there is no broker market, a dealer benchmark is the only acceptable source of observable data.

In summary, firms are benchmarking their derivatives positions on a regular basis to the rest of the market. This typically takes the form of marking to an acceptable composite on a daily basis, and may be supplemented by additional checks and balances at month-end.

OPERATIONAL RISK MEASUREMENTS FOR DERIVATIVES

This section reviews the types of operational benchmarking reviews which take place to provide regulators and management with key data, especially in the credit markets. The focus, here, is on the credit markets as they have been under the regulatory spotlight since 2005.

Monthly fed metrics

The growth in volumes in the CDS markets is well documented. The average number of CDS trades executed between the biggest dealers increased by 89 per cent between 2004 and 2005.[1] These large firms execute more than 5,000 trades a month, and the complexity of trades has increased. Following this sustained growth in volumes, backlogs developed in CDS trade processing and confirmations as the infrastructure failed to keep pace. This caused concern amongst the leading regulators, including the Financial Services Authority (FSA) and the Federal Reserve (Fed). The concerns arise because an unconfirmed trade means an incorrect reflection of risk with one or both parties to that trade, and considerable downstream implications including an inability to reconcile portfolios, valuations or collateral. This risk would be highlighted in the event of a default where the assessment of outstanding risk with the defaulted entity could potentially be a lot worse than reported and hedged against. Further, it has been shown that the cost of confirming trades increases as the time passed from trade date increases, and also that the cost of amending errors or 'confirmable amendments' also increases as time passes between trade date and the time that the error is amended.

The FSA issued a well-documented letter to all CEOs in February 2005 which requested immediate action in tackling these backlogs, and the Fed followed up by inviting 14 dealers (the Fed 14), and many leading regulators, to attend a summit meeting in September of the same year. The result of the summit was a commitment by the banks to a series of operational targets, which they would report on every month. The primary target was a

---

[1] Source: Markit Scorecard 2005

reduction in outstanding confirmations. The dealers committed to reducing the number of outstanding confirmations as a percentage of total trades by 30 per cent between October 2005 and the end of January 2006. The second milestone was to reduce the number of outstandings by 50 per cent by the end of March 2006.

In order to measure progress against targets, the dealers required the support of an independent body to collect this confidential data, collate it and report developments to the Fed on a monthly basis. Markit Group, in conjunction with Derivatives Consulting Group (DCG),[2] were selected to perform this role, which is widely known as 'The Fed Metrics'. The Fed 14 dealers submit key operational metrics to Markit within 5 days of each month-end and the metrics are submitted to the Fed within a further 3 days. An additional performance report is provided for the dealers only.

Using the metrics as a management tool, and the additional focus that the metrics provided, the dealers succeeded in hitting both targets on time. This was achieved through a series of short-term manual initiatives such as dealer lock-ins,[3] medium-term efforts such as documentation improvements including the ISDA Novations Protocol[4] and longer-term technological improvements. Following this success, the dealers then committed to achieving a 70 per cent reduction by the end of June 2006.

MARKIT ANNUAL SCORECARD

The monthly metrics are supplemented once a year by an annual benchmarking exercise known as the Markit Scorecard. The Scorecard was completed by 23 firms in 2005, as its reach is broader than the Fed 14. The Scorecard covers all aspects of credit derivatives infrastructure including business models, operations, technology, risk management and product control.

The dealers submit their data to Markit and DCG. Given the considerable amount of data which is collated, it takes some time for the collection exercise to be completed, and, of course, the analysis and summary of the data takes a considerable amount of additional time. Once the data has been compiled, each participant receives a bespoke document which benchmarks them against their peer firms.[5] The Markit Scorecard is eagerly awaited and

---

[2] Formerly Reoch Consulting, until March 2005
[3] Dealer lock-ins are lengthy meetings where portfolios of outstanding trades are reconciled and confirmed. The meeting continues until all the remaining issues have been resolved!
[4] The International Swaps and Derivatives Association (www.ISDA.org).
[5] The firms are divided into Tier 1 and Tier 2 firms.

the data is used, extensively, by the participants to inform senior management. It also plays an extremely important role in resource and financial planning for the subsequent financial year. Markit and DCG are invited, globally, to present the findings to management, at the highest levels, in order to assist them in identifying the key trends from the benchmarking, and the appropriate areas for focus in the future.

Sophisticated firms collate and circulate internal management information on a regular, typically monthly, basis anyway for their own purposes. They review trends, spot areas for improvement and use the data to make investment decisions. However, the ability to benchmark operational data against peer firms is invaluable. It provides a definite edge, particularly when working with senior management on budgetary matters. Such benchmarking requires the support of an independent, trusted party to collate, normalize and distribute the data.

CONCLUSION

Benchmarking is a fundamental part of management information in the financial markets, whether daily or monthly market information or less-frequent operational measurements. Irrespective of the type of benchmarking, the key characteristics which make it useful are:

- it is collated by an independent body which does not have an incentive to manipulate the data
- the third party is trusted to keep the data segregated and confidential
- the data is normalized and cleaned so that like is compared with like
- it is made available on a timely basis so that it is relevant.

'No longer the exotic playthings of the investment banks, credit derivatives are used to manage and exploit risks and opportunities in credit markets.'

■ ■ ■

Credit Derivatives

Introduction

What is credit risk?

Style of trading

Default data

The first deals

Range of credit derivatives

Credit default swaps

Total return swaps

INTRODUCTION

No longer the exotic playthings of the investment banks, credit derivatives are used to manage and exploit risks and opportunities in credit markets. Essentially, risk is transferred among the various participants using OTC transactions. Volumes have increased enormously; some market statisticians predicted that turnover by the end of 2006 would be in the region of US$8 trillion. It was already over US$26 trillion by June 2006 (*Source*: International Swaps & Derivatives Association, Inc. (ISDA)). The most popular credit derivative instrument is that based on a 'Single Name Credit Default Swap (CDS)' (see Figure 8.1). In everyday language this a contract which allows you to buy or sell protection on an investment linked to a single named entity, e.g. General Motors, Fiat, BMW.

| Figure 8.1 | **Credit Default Swap growth** |

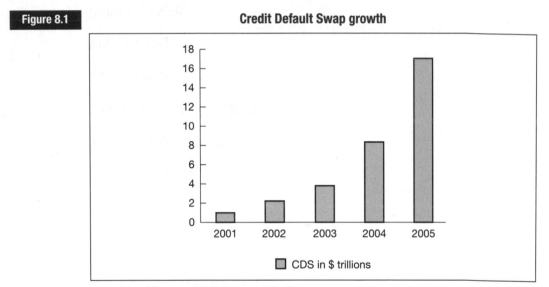

Source: International Swaps & Derivatives Association, Inc.

Not surprisingly, banks are the major users of these products, both for their own portfolio management and for trading/arbitraging credit risk across different market sectors, e.g., bonds vs term loans. Recent data from Fitch indicates that hedge funds are increasingly active in this market, possibly accounting for up to 50 per cent of the turnover. This has led the European Central Bank, amongst others, to comment about the dangers – in particular that hedge funds tended to 'deploy identical strategies' and when things go wrong there are 'disorderly exits from crowded trades'. This remains to be seen. Although the growth is credit derivatives is spectacular and now overshadows the equity derivatives markets, it is dwarfed by turnover in interest rate swap market, which is currently US$173 trillion. The main centres for credit derivative trading are London, New York and Tokyo.

WHAT IS CREDIT RISK?

Credit risk can arise in any situation where there is a contract between two counterparties giving one party a future obligation to the other. The risk being, of course, that the first party will fail to meet its obligations. This means that we need to look beyond a total default situation. Although default risk is important, credit risk also encompasses any waiver, deferral, rescheduling or any adjustment of the terms that is unfavourable to the creditor.

Credit risk actually comprises two different sorts of risk:

1. Market risk: that the price of the asset in question will rise or fall, or become more/less volatile.

2. Client specific risk: that the firm itself may run into trouble.

For example, a financier may wish to enter into an investment transaction involving corporate bonds issued by a Thai company. He is relaxed about the performance of the currency and interest rate risk but is more concerned about the possibility of a downgrade in the risk of the Thai company.

Credit derivatives also have applications beyond banks and financial institutions. Consider a manufacturer who sells custom-made machinery to one particular client. What happens if the client goes into liquidation? Not only may the manufacturer be left with the goods unsold, it will be hard to sell them elsewhere as they are designed to a specific set of client requirements.

Typically, banks and financial institutions have more experience in managing credit risk, because they lend money through corporate loans. This means that they have developed ways to manage this risk, e.g. the commercial bank can syndicate the loan or impose covenants in order to mitigate the risk. They could also seek collateral – a cash amount to cover their costs if there is a default. However, collateralization brings its own headaches, notably, has it been paid, is it sufficient, what if the market moves, marking-to-market? etc.

It is very noticeable that it is the investment banks that dominate this market rather than the commercial banks. This may possibly be due to the size of their capital market transactions and/or their tendency to hedge risks more dynamically. Hedge funds are also becoming very active and insurance companies still have their place. We tend to look at the market participants from the point of view of whether they are buying protection or selling protection.

■ Protection buyers – may own the asset (but not always) and are looking for cover.

■ Protection sellers – want exposure to the asset and will provide the cover.

At the end of 2004 (latest data available) the top 15 banks in the credit derivatives market accounted for 75 per cent of the 'sold' positions and 81 per cent of the 'bought' positions. The banks were:

2004	
1	Deutsche Bank
2	Morgan Stanley
3	Goldman Sachs
4	JPMorgan Chase
5	UBS
6	Credit Suisse First Boston
7	Lehman Brothers
8	Merrill Lynch
9	Citigroup
10	Bear Stearns
11	Barclays
12	BNP Paribas
13	Bank of America
14	Dresdner Bank
15	HSBC

Source: Fitch

STYLE OF TRADING

A credit derivative product is an over the counter (OTC) instrument which allows users to manage credit risk in the same way as they can manage currency and interest rate exposure. The 'underlying asset' is usually taken to be a publicly traded debt instrument, such as a bond issued by the debtor company, but can also be a loan or 'borrowed money'.

The market is subdivided into the following sectors:

■ investment-grade credits – top-quality government, corporate or bank bonds

■ non-investment-grade/high-yield credits/speculative – low-grade, questionable credits

■ distressed credits – bonds which are in trouble

■ emerging market credits – credits which may not be so freely traded, usually very volatile, often with liquidity/delivery problems.

Ratings

Publicly traded bonds generally have credit ratings assigned to them. The rating agencies are independent bodies that provide an assessment of the risk associated with the issuer or issue. It should be noted that rating is mandatory in the USA but not in the UK. Some large UK companies do not have ratings, but this does not indicate that they are poor credits. Rather, it shows that they have never needed one. If a bond is so popular it almost sells itself, why should the company pay for a rating? Rating agencies include Standard & Poor's, Moody's and Fitch. Large banks also have in-house systems which compute their own default data.

Table 8.1 summarizes the Standard & Poor's (S&P) credit ratings – with comments that are my own personal interpretation.

Credit ratings

Table 8.1

Investment-grade paper	
AAA	Triple A credits ... ultra safe ... often government or supranational bonds
AA+ AA AA–	High grade, good quality ... very safe ... often major bank bonds
A+ A A–	Upper–medium grade ... safe ... often medium-sized banks/corporate bonds
BBB+ BBB BBB–	Medium grade ... Reasonable quality corporate bonds
Speculative paper	
BB+ BB BB–	Low medium grade ... A little speculative
B+ B B–	Lower grade ... Very speculative
Very speculative high yield paper (used to be known as **junk bonds**)	
CCC+ CCC CCC–	Substantial risk ... Vulnerable to non-payment
CC	Possible default ... Highly vulnerable to non-payment
D	Default

NB: There is a dividing line between 'investment grade paper' and 'high yield debt' at the BBB rating level.

DEFAULT DATA

World-wide data on company defaults is imperfect, but improving. A trader may have all the public data on a company but if there is no official credit rating (from S&P, say, or Moody's), it is still far less than he would like. In comparison, the rating agencies have access to unpublished data which means that an official rating will often carry more weight. Many large companies borrow direct from banks in private transactions and publicly traded bonds may be lacking, leading to a certain amount of guesswork.

Defaults also tend to be higher in some parts of the world. In the Asia-Pacific region, when a default occurs losses can be of the order of 50 per cent of principal, whereas in the USA it is typically around 30–35 per cent. But let's be realistic. In practical terms, if a company defaults, how do you get any of your money back? The legal system in some countries can tie you up in knots for years, and even then it can be slow to gain access to the remaining assets, should there be any.

THE FIRST DEALS

Legend has it that the market started in New York in 1992/1993. Various market players claim to have transacted the first deal. Credit derivatives owe their origins to the banks' requirements to manage the large credit risk associated with their swap, bond and loan books. In order to reduce these risks swap houses began to repackage and sell on the credit risk associated with a basket of names. Early transactions were expensive and commanded a large premium, but helped free up capital which could then be used for new or more profitable business. London tends to be the dominant financial centre, and has been able to grow this product further, for four key reasons:

- the size of the international debt market
- a market-friendly regulatory environment
- liquid asset swap market
- derivative strengths.

RANGE OF CREDIT DERIVATIVES

Definition A credit derivative allows the holder to isolate and separate credit risk from market risk, thus allowing this credit risk to be either hedged, traded or transferred. A premium may be due.

Although they may be sold by different names within different banks, there are essentially three basic structures:

- credit default swaps (CDS)
- total rate of return swaps (TRS)
- credit options (CO).

The BBA has estimated that over 50 per cent of credit derivatives are default swaps in one shape or another. We will concentrate on CDS and TRS.

CREDIT DEFAULT SWAPS

> A credit default swap is a bilateral contract used to transfer the credit risk of a reference entity from one party to another. The protection buyer pays a periodic fee; the protection seller receives the fee and provides protection in the case of a credit event.

Definition

Credit default swaps enable the separation and transfer of credit risk between two parties, without transferring ownership of the underlying asset itself. They are products that allow the counterparty to hedge/gain exposure to credit risk. The nature of the default event, the reference asset, and the methods used to calculate the amount payable are specified in the swap contract, and can vary depending on the individual transaction in question. The 'underlying asset' may be a single bond or a basket of assets, and they may be categorized by their seniority or type of issue.

NB: It must be noted that most financial derivatives are triggered if there is a move in an exchange rate, an equity or bond price, however, credit default swaps have legal triggers. This makes the documentation especially important – ideally when both parties have signed and agreed the documentation!

Is this insurance?

Although this looks like insurance and resembles it closely there is a major difference! With insurance you need to own the asset and prove that you have suffered a loss. This means that you have to own the bond in question to benefit from the protection. With a CDS, you do not need to own the asset. This can be likened to insuring the car belonging to your neighbour, where you receive the payout if he has an accident! It does mean that more CDS cover may be purchased than there are sufficient, specific bonds to go round. This leads to a scramble to buy the bonds if there is a credit event and can lead to liquidity and pricing problems. Recently with the Dana credit event in 2006 and with the Delphi credit event in 2005 there was an auction process whereby the bonds were valued by auction to determine the price for cash settlement.

Hedging example

A fund manager purchased EUR 10 million of Ladbroke plc bonds last year; the entity was previously named Hilton Group but it was renamed in February 2006. This is a key component of his portfolio and he does not wish to sell the bond because if he does it could result in a tax or accounting charge. He is becoming concerned that tourism may drop and that rooms may remain empty. He wishes to buy protection and believes that although the bond has 10 years remaining, if the organization can get through the next 5 years his investment will be safe. He does not need to cover the whole of the 10-year period until maturity – just the period he wishes, be it 1, 3 or 5 years. This will be decided at the time of dealing. He decides to cover the full amount of EUR 10 million on a physical settlement basis. This means that if there is a 'credit event' in the next 5 years he must deliver the bonds and will receive in return EUR 10 million.

He puts up a screen to check where the current indicative prices are for this protection (see Table 8.2).

Table 8.2									

Derivative products and their underlying assets

Markit Ticker	Short name	Tier	Ccy	Spread 5Y	Depth	Sector	Region	Average rating
ADO	Adecco S A	SNRFOR	EUR	51.87	12	Consumer Stable	Europe	BBB
ATTINC	AT&T Inc	SNRFOR	USD	23.40	9	Comms & Technology	N.Amer	A
DCX	DaimlerChrysler AG	SNRFOR	EUR	57.59	11	Consumer Cyclical	Europe	BBB
GE-CapCorp	Gen Elec Cap Corp	SNRFOR	USD	15.80	14	Financial	N.Amer	AAA
GM	Gen Mtrs Corp	SNRFOR	USD	1052.75	9	Consumer Cyclical	N.Amer	B
HUWHY	Hutchison Whampoa Ltd	SNRFOR	USD	38.44	12	Consumer Cyclical	Asia	A
LADBRK	LADBROKES PLC	SNRFOR	EUR	141.83	13	Consumer Cyclical	Europe	BB
LLOYDS-Bank	Lloyds TSB Bk plc	SNRFOR	EUR	7.43	15	Financial	Europe	AA
PPR	PPR	SNRFOR	EUR	48.74	11	Consumer Cyclical	Europe	BBB
TKAGR	ThyssenKrupp AG	SNRFOR	EUR	62.81	10	Materials	Europe	BBB

Source: Markit Group Limited

Notes:
All spreads (quoted in bp per annum) are calculated as at close of business on 27 March 2006.
Depth refers to number of contributors for this data, and sector refers to industry sector.
Average rating is the average of the S&P and Moody's ratings adjusted for seniority, rounded to exclude (+) and (-) levels.
Hilton Group was renamed Ladbrokes plc on 23 February 2006.
Pinault Printemps Redoute was renamed PPR on 19 May 2005.

The spread can be likened to an annual insurance premium. Market convention is that this price is paid quarterly on an Actual/360 basis. For Ladbrokes plc based on the data above this would be 141.83 basis points, rounded for our example to 142 basis points. This equates to 1.42% × 91/360 × EUR 10 million = EUR 35,894.44 for a 91 day quarter. There is no bid–offer spread showing on this screen but if you assume a 5 bp spread, the price would be shown on a pricing careen as 137 bp – 142 bp. A buyer of protection must pay 1.42 per cent p.a. and a seller of the protection would receive 1.37 per cent p.a.

Where does this price come from?

There are two methods of arriving at a good approximation of where the spread will trade:

1. where Ladbrokes plc would issue a par floating rate note for the same maturity;

2. the asset swap spread of a bond with the same maturity trading near par.

This is a flawed approach in practice because we make these assumptions that we

(a) assume a common market-wide funding rate;

(b) ignore accrued coupons on default;

(c) ignore the delivery option in the CDS;

(d) ignore the counterparty risk (i.e. the bank selling the protection).

– but it does provide a starting point. The difference between where the CDS trades and where the spread over LIBOR trades is known as the default swap basis.

It is assumed that an investor carries out the four transactions in Figure 8.2 with the same financial counterparty; the investor

1. borrows the cash and pays LIBOR interest;

2. uses the cash to buy the Ladbrokes plc bond – receives the coupons;

3. swaps the coupons into LIBOR funding at a rate of LIBOR + x%; and the

4. LIBOR rate generated from the swap goes to pay off the original loan.

In this example the x per cent generated is the 142 basis points. The cash flows on the CDS are shown in Figure 8.3. Fund Manager (A) has purchased credit protection and must pay 1.42 per cent p.a. on a quarterly actual/360 basis. This payment will continue until such time as there is a credit event. This is shown as the fixed leg on the swap. If there is no credit event the contract will mature in 5 years' time. The protection buyer will not receive back the payment if there is no claim. It resembles an option premium with a digital payout – all or nothing. The floating leg of the swap is the contingent payment made by the protection seller if there is a credit event. This may be affected by physical delivery of the asset or by a cash settlement.

Figure 8.2

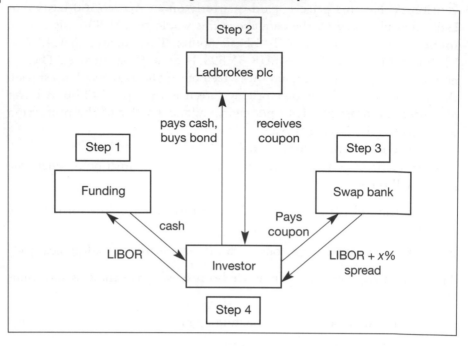

Pricing CDS via asset swaps

Figure 8.3

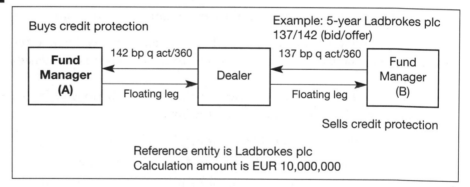

Cash flows on CDS

What happens next?

If there is a credit event the sequence of events is as follows (assume a physical delivery of bonds was agreed at the outset):

1. The protection buyer sends a Credit Event Notice (CEN) and Notice of Publicly Available Information to the protection seller; the date this happens becomes the Event Determination Date.

2. The CEN must contain facts and refer to two public sources.

3. The buyer must then deliver to the seller a Notice of Physical Settlement; this specifies the bonds/loans to be delivered.

4. The buyer must make delivery within 30 days or lose protection. Under 2003 ISDA Credit Derivative Definitions (CDD), if the bonds are not delivered, and remain undelivered 5 business days later, the seller of the protection is given 5 days to buy-in the bonds; the protection buyer cannot deliver in this period. If the bonds still remain undelivered, the protection buyer now has 5 days to deliver the bonds and the process repeats.

NB: If the protection buyer does follow these steps cover is lost. If the CEN is not received the seller does not need to pay out!

Shown below is the Physical Settlement Timeline of a Credit Derivative following a Credit Event. This is a summary of settlement procedures under the 2003 ISDA Credit Derivatives Definitions, for information purposes only.

Physical settlement timeline

Figure 8.4

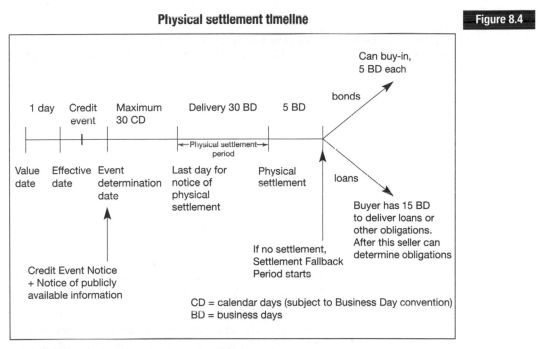

Source: 2006 International Swaps and Derivatives Association Inc.

In our hedging example, the buyer will follow the procedure we have detailed, and deliver the bonds as required under the contract. The protection seller will pay over EUR 10 million. Obviously payments of the 142 basis points per annum will cease and the last payment will be pro-rated to the date of the credit event.

Trading example

A trader is looking at the spreads on Fiat and believes that he can purchase credit protection at a competitive rate of 292 basis points per annum for

7-years cover. He does not own the bonds, but is looking for a credit event to happen. If there is a credit event he will receive a payout.

Market data

Entity	Average Rating	Spread 3Y	Spread 5Y	Spread 7Y	Spread 10Y
BMW	A	12.31	21.61	32.21	41.97
Fiat	BB	135.43	239.65	291.77	325.59
Peugeot	A	18.48	30.43	42.63	55.12
Renault	BBB	20.15	33.23	45.33	57.59
Volvo	BBB	21.46	34.66	48.85	61.43
VW	A	18.78	32.27	45.05	58.18

Source: Markit Group Limited – European Auto CDS prices
Notes:
All spreads calculated as at close of business at 27 March 2006.
Average rating is the average of the S&P and Moody's ratings adjusted for seniority, rounded to exclude (+) and (–) levels.

Market data

See Table 8.3.

Details

CDS: Euro 10 million of Fiat Group Bonds

Period: 7 years

Floating Rate: 292 bp per annum, paid on a quarterly, actual/360 basis equivalent to EUR 292,000 per annum.

After 12 months assume there is a credit event, the trader needs to buy the bonds to deliver them and receive his payout. He has a choice of two bonds which he can buy, and both have fallen in price. He will naturally buy the cheapest and deliver under the contract; assume he pays EUR 8 million for the bonds. If the cost to buy the bonds is EUR 8 million plus the premium of EUR 292,000, this makes a total of EUR 8.292 million, but he receives a payout of EUR 10 million – a profit of EUR 1.708 million. Had this been cash settlement the buyer would have received EUR 2 million from the CDS but would need to factor in the CDS spread of EUR 292,000. This is equivalent to synthetically shorting the bond; the protection buyer is long a cheapest to deliver option.

CDS contract details

As these products have legal triggers it is imperative to have detailed in the confirmation exactly what type of cover has been arranged. The confirmation must include:

- The reference entity, e.g. Ladbrokes plc
- The reference obligation, specific bond(s) or loan
- Credit Events
- Deliverable obligations
- Settlement details.

1. Reference entity

The confirmation needs to specify the exact name and legal entity; e.g. if you just refer to Ford, is it Ford Motor Company Inc. or Ltd? Is it Armstrong Holdings or Armstrong Industries Ltd?

2. Reference obligations

You have range of choices – most participants choose 'borrowed money' as this includes loans and bonds. Also noted must be the reference obligation, e.g. exactly which bond or asset is being covered, is it the bond maturing in 2012 or 2015? It used to be sufficient for the confirmation to detail the ISIN number but problems have been experienced in identifying the asset. Mark-it Group Ltd have developed a product known as 'Mark-it RED' to avoid these issues. The Reference Entity Database (RED) provides a unique nine digit alphanumeric code for each reference entity/obligation pair. It is now increasingly important to use these codes if matching the confirmations on the electronic templates used by DTCC Deriv/Serv or Swapswire.

3. Credit events

There are six credit events in the International Swaps and Derivatives Associaiton Inc. definitions; a full definition of each is found in the 2003 ISDA Credit Derivative Definitions. A credit event is required to trigger the floating payment of the swap, these are:

Bankruptcy: The 2003 ISDA definitions include a change made to the definition of bankruptcy (after Marconi).

Failure to pay: This refers to failure by the reference entity to make a payment after the expiration of an applicable grace period. This payment must be equal or greater than a specified amount normally US$1 million (specified at the start of the transaction).

Repudiation/Moratorium: This means the occurrence of a government or government official repudiating or rejecting debt and a failure to pay.

Obligation acceleration: Where one or more of the obligations has become payable prior to its normal maturity date as a result of an event of default.

Obligation default: Where one or more of the obligations has become capable of being declared due as a result of default, or similar event other than a failure to make the required payment.

Restructuring: The definition of restructuring has caused many problems. This discussion has resulted from an increase in the number of participants in the CDS market. Non-bank investors (Hedge Funds) entering the CDS market are generally credit protection sellers. They have been uncomfortable with the definitions of restructuring because it leaves too much open for discussion as to the precise meaning. Commercial banks have been using the CDS market to restructure portfolios by buying protection. Regulators have stipulated that capital relief is only applicable provided that restructuring is included in the CDS agreement; this means that restructuring is likely to remain controversial. (The Basel Committee is considering relaxing the rules provided a bank that has hedged its credit risk using CDS has a veto over any debt restructuring.) The restructuring debate focuses on the exact meaning of the legal documentation.

4. Deliverable obligations, physical settlement

If a credit event arises on the relevant type of obligation (normally borrowed money), the protection buyer delivers one of the deliverable obligations and receives from the protection seller the notional of the transaction. The delivered instrument must be a deliverable obligation (bond or loan) and must have the appropriate delivery obligation characteristics.

Ranking Pari Passu

This is the most important characteristic. The deliverable obligations must be at least as senior as the reference obligation that is defined in the confirmation. This means we cannot consider bonds which have been subordinated in any way.

5. Settlement

There are three ways that settlement works (the first two being most popular):

1. The protection seller pays the protection buyer an amount equal to the difference between the initial price and the post-default price of the reference credit. This is cash settlement but there will need to be an independent auction to determine the final price against which the CDS will be valued.

2. The protection seller pays the total notional value of the underlying reference credit, in exchange for delivery of the defaulted asset. This is physical delivery.

3. Occasionally, the protection seller pays a pre-agreed fixed percentage of the notional value of the swap.

NB: On Sept 27, 2006 ISDA announced a cash settlement protocol for vanilla credit derivatives.

Protection buyer – motivations

There are four main reasons why a financial institution may wish to transfer credit risk with a credit derivative:

1. to reduce exposure to a company or bank whose credit rating is deteriorating;
2. to free up credit lines so that higher margin business may be transacted;
3. to protect against a downgrading below a portfolio manager's internal limits;
4. to reduce credit exposures which have exceeded limits, possibly where interest rates or currency movements have exceeded expectations.

Protection seller – motivations

Again there are four principal reasons:

1. to synthesize the exposure to a client beyond market constraints, for example, if the market in a particular bond is illiquid;
2. to gain exposure to a credit that is not otherwise available, for example, where a company does not issue bonds;
3. to benefit from a higher yield which may be offered by the protection seller in a credit swap;
4. to choose a specific maturity band that is not available in the bond or loan market.

Credit default swaps

Key features

Credit rating of probable swap counterparty

It makes no sense to create a deal where you substitute a weaker credit rating for your original counterparty. Consider a bank writing (or selling) protection on a AA name, when in reality the bank is BBB – would you buy that protection? Or would you seek protection from a better credit? Guess what. You'll pay more.

The concern is that if you substitute in a lower credit as the swap counterparty, you will pay them a premium for the life of the transaction and if the AA name defaults it is quite possible the swap counterparty will as well.

Maturity

Obviously, the longer the duration of the transaction, the higher the risk and the more you will pay.

Probability of default

The higher the probability of default, the more the protection will cost, where possible independent international credit ratings will be used.

TOTAL RETURN SWAPS

 Definition | A total return swap transfers credit risk by swapping an underlying asset's specified total return (capital growth and interest) between two counterparties, in return for regular payments of LIBOR + spread. Instead of a payment in the event of a default, the total return swap guarantees the risk seller (the protection buyer) a specified economic value for the reference credit for a specified term.

In a total return swap, Bank X pays Bank Y any appreciation on the capital value of the underlying asset as well as any coupons receivable. In return, Bank Y pays Bank X any depreciation of the capital value as well as a LIBOR-linked floating margin. Bank Y is known as the 'receiver' of the total return, and Bank X is the 'payer' of the total return, similar to 'paying or receiving fixed interest' on an interest rate swap.

Bank X is guaranteed a specified capital value for the underlying, as well as a LIBOR-linked income for the duration of the swap. The credit risk for the underlying has been transferred to Bank Y, which is the recipient of the income and (any) profits generated by this asset. Bank Y is thus known as the buyer of risk, and Bank X, the seller of risk. However, Bank X retains ownership of the underlying, and must continue to fund the asset. This is shown in Figure 8.5.

Figure 8.5 | **A total rate of return swap**

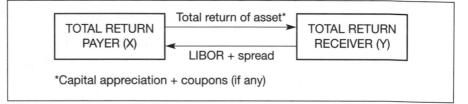

Bank X has hedged the economic risk of the asset held on the balance sheet. Bank Y is exposed to that risk, but does not have any of the other problems such as balance sheet, funding, or any of the operational complications of owning the asset.

Payers and Receivers

The payer in a TRS is also known as the protection buyer, as in the event of a market move downward where the payer receives a payment from the receiver. Likewise, the receiver of the total return is a seller of protection as they are exposed if the market moves down.

There is no credit event and no contingent payment

At the end of each three- or six-month period, payments are automatically exchanged. In the event of a default, the payment due at the end of the next period is brought forward, net present valued and the contract terminated. Occasionally physical delivery is permitted.

Maturity

The TRS can be of any maturity and is not linked to the maturity of the underlying asset.

Credit risk

A TRS is not solely linked to changes in the credit quality of the asset but also to changes to the market value. It allows the TRS receiver to be fully exposed to the bond and its cash flows without actually owning and funding the purchase, thus it is also a synthetic bond market instrument.

As well as locking in a specified economic value, total return swaps can be used to transfer the market risk of an asset off-balance sheet and lower the regulatory capital charge. Equally, it can be used for trading credits on a leveraged off-balance sheet basis. Amongst banks with the ability to take risk it is known as 'renting out the balance-sheet'. TRS transactions do not need to be linked to bonds, in fact any asset where the total return (less depreciation where appropriate) is paid across will qualify, for example, Commodities and Equity Indices as well.

For an example of a TRS readers should refer to Chapter 10, Equity Derivatives, where we have an Equity Index Swap which works in a similar fashion.

NB: For the technically minded, an interesting analogy for a total return swap is a repo transaction. One leading London house categorizes all its emerging market repo activity as credit derivative business. The primary difference is that a repo transaction is collateralized (the underlying physical credit is actually exchanged during the transaction) whereas with credit derivative products the physical underlying is never exchanged except at the termination of some transactions.

'Nobody could have predicted the stellar growth of index products, due, in part, to unprecedented demand from end-users who sought a liquid macro credit product that could be cut and diced to serve a range of services.'

■ ■ ■

Beyond a Vanilla CDS

Robert Reoch, Reoch Credit Partners Ltd

Introduction

Credit indices

CDOs

Where next?

INTRODUCTION

The basic building block of the credit derivatives market is the CDS – now a well-accepted, well understood and increasingly standardized product. One of the results of its growth and development has been improved liquidity and credit spread data for an increasing proportion of corporate borrowers. This has resulted in an associated growth of complex credit products: products which existed in theory for some time but which failed to materialize due to insufficient models to price them, insufficient data to feed the models or insufficient liquidity to enable the hedges recommended by the models.

Accompanying the growth of complex credit products has been the development of index products; here again, it was the liquidity in the CDS market that allowed these to move off the drawing board. They moved very fast: nobody could have predicted the stellar growth of index products due, in part, to unprecedented demand from end-users who sought a liquid macro credit product that could be cut and diced to serve a range of services.

In this chapter, credit indices and CDOs are introduced by focusing on their mechanics and their applications. There is a strong linkage between these two groups of products and the CDS market: the indices are derived in part from CDS activity, CDS and indices are used to hedge CDOs and CDO activity itself can drive CDS and index activity and pricing.

CREDIT INDICES

Credit indices were introduced as the next logical step in the evolution of credit derivatives products. The products improve liquidity and increase market participation by providing users with an opportunity to take exposure to or hedge liquid sectors of the global credit markets. The benefits of using credit indices can be summarized as:

- Portfolio diversification

- Ability to take a view on a market or a region

- Relative value trading or hedging purposes

- Help in reducing credit spread volatility at a portfolio level

- Increase market participation by attracting new investors.

Currently, there are two families of credit indices available in the market: CDX and iTraxx. CDX indices are primarily made up of North American and Emerging market credits. iTraxx, on the other hand, focuses on credits from Europe, Australia, Japan and the rest of Asia.

Index investors include asset managers, hedge funds, insurance companies, corporates and banks who use these indices either to diversify their portfolio or for relative value trading and hedging strategies, or both. Derivatives of the indices, such as tranches and swaptions, are also traded in the market and allow a range of trading strategies. The rest of this section will focus on the iTraxx Europe. The other iTraxx and CDX indices enjoy similar features, the main difference being index composition.

Index example: iTraxx Europe

The iTraxx Europe indices are administered by the International Index Company (IIC). The index construction process starts with a dealer poll conducted by the IIC. Each market maker submits a list of Reference Entities with the highest CDS trading volume measured over the previous six months. This is followed by a rules based construction process whereby the reference entities are mapped to an iTraxx sector and ranked by averaging the liquidity ranking of the market makers. Index rules are applied to each index family to arrive at the provisional index list (see Figure 9.1).

iTraxx index construction process

Figure 9.1

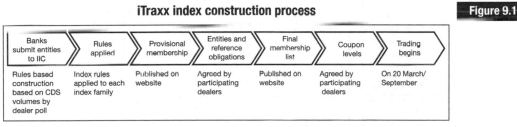

Source: IIC

Once the reference entities and reference obligations are agreed by the market makers, trading begins. New series of indices are rolled out every six months (March and September) to include the most liquid names from the previous 6-month period. The iTraxx European platform consists of a benchmark as well as sector indices with different standard maturities as shown in Figure 9.2.

Index mechanics

Consider an example where Investor A takes €25 million of exposure (protection seller) to the iTraxx Europe for 5 years on the index issue date. Assume that the premium on the iTraxx Europe is 40 basis points (bps) per annum.

Figure 9.2

iTraxx European Platform

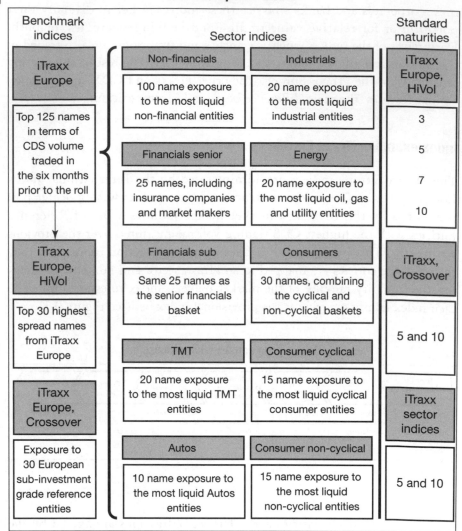

Benchmark indices	Sector indices			Standard maturities
iTraxx Europe Top 125 names in terms of CDS volume traded in the six months prior to the roll	**Non-financials** 100 name exposure to the most liquid non-financial entities	**Industrials** 20 name exposure to the most liquid industrial entities		**iTraxx Europe, HiVol**
	Financials senior 25 names, including insurance companies and market makers	**Energy** 20 name exposure to the most liquid oil, gas and utility entities		3 5 7 10
iTraxx Europe, HiVol Top 30 highest spread names from iTraxx Europe	**Financials sub** Same 25 names as the senior financials basket	**Consumers** 30 names, combining the cyclical and non-cyclical baskets		**iTraxx, Crossover**
	TMT 20 name exposure to the most liquid TMT entities	**Consumer cyclical** 15 name exposure to the most liquid cyclical consumer entities		5 and 10
iTraxx Europe, Crossover Exposure to 30 European sub-investment grade reference entities	**Autos** 10 name exposure to the most liquid Autos entities	**Consumer non-cyclical** 15 name exposure to the most liquid non-cyclical entities		**iTraxx sector indices** 5 and 10

Source: IIC

Scenario 1: No credit event

If no credit event occurs during the life of the index contract, the market maker will continue to pay a premium of 40 bps p.a. on the notional amount of 25 million to investor A as shown in Figure 9.3.

Index mechanics (no credit event)

Figure 9.3

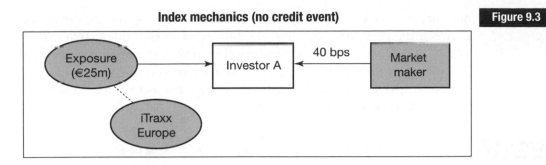

Scenario 2: Credit event

Assume that a credit event occurs on one of the reference entities in year 2. The trade is either physically settled or cash settled. In the case of cash settlement see 'Index protocol' later in this section. In case of physical settlement, Investor A pays the market maker a payment equal to the defaulted reference entity's weighting in the index (in this case 0.8% * €25 million = €200,000). The market maker in turn delivers €200,000 nominal face value of Deliverable Obligations of the Reference Entity to investor A. The notional amount of the contract is reduced by 0.8% (99.2% * €25 million = €24.8 million). Post credit event, the market maker continues to pay the premium of 40 bps p.a. to Investor A based on the reduced notional until maturity, subject to any further credit events as shown in Figure 9.4.

Index mechanics (single credit event)

Figure 9.4

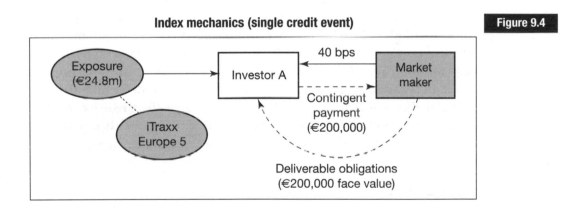

Scenario 3: Investing after the index issue date

Investor A takes €25 million exposure (Protection Seller) to the iTraxx Europe two months after the index issue date. Assume that the premium on the iTraxx Europe is 40 bps per annum and the fair value is 35 bps on the day Investor A decides to enter into the index contract. The trade is executed at the premium level: the market maker pays 40 bps p.a. on the notional amount €25 million to Investor A. To make up for the difference between the premium level and the fair value of the index, Investor A makes an upfront payment approximately equal to the present value of 5 bps accrued of the remaining life of the index settled on T+3 days. There is an agreed methodology for calculating this payment using the CDSW function on Bloomberg (see Figure 8.10).

| Figure 9.5 | Index mechanics (investing after index issue date) |

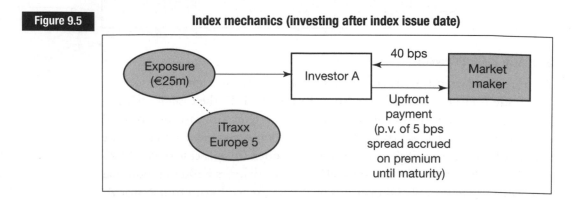

Credit fixings

Credit fixings involve a weekly fixing of the European credit indices to arrive at tradable reference and settlement rates. This methodology is currently used for the iTraxx 5yr Europe, HiVol and Crossover indices. The fixing is carried out in Europe on Fridays at 11 a.m. GMT and on quarterly roll dates (20th of March, June, September and December) at 4 p.m. GMT. The dealers electronically contribute a bid–offer price for a standard size contract to CreditEx (an inter-dealer broker), which administers the process. These two-way market contributions are then used to determine the bid, mid and offer fixings using a methodology developed by CreditEx and The Markit Group and a panel of dealer banks. These fixings are then published on a Markit and CreditEx sponsored website *www.creditfixings.com*.

Index protocol

The first index protocol was published by ISDA in May 2005 in the wake of Collins & Aikmen (C&A), a referenced name in a CDX index, filing for bankruptcy. A protocol was needed because there were not enough Deliverable Obligations of C&A outstanding to settle index trades. The protocol enabled affected index trades to be cash settled based on the value of a defaulted debt instrument (issued by C&A) as determined by an auction process.

The auction process, administered by CreditEx and Markit, involves the participating dealers submitting prices for a pre-agreed bond or bonds and determining the market price at which the affected index trades are cash settled. Since then, the protocol has undergone a number of changes to ensure a 'fair' settlement rate. A brief outline of the auction methodology is as follows:

- Dealers submit bidding agreement letters prior to the auction date. The administrators then publish the list of participating bidders, typically a week before the auction date.

- On the auction date, bidders submit their bid–offer prices with a maximum spread of 2 per cent of par for the agreed obligation(s). The bidding timeline may be extended if the number of participating bidders is less than 10.

- After the bidding process is over, the administrators determine and verify the results of the auction based on a complex set of rules that ensure a fair market mid price. The rules penalize off-market quotes by requiring high bids to be matched and traded with low offers.

- If a final price cannot be determined in the first auction, a subsequent auction is held on the same day and participants are asked to submit prices until the final price is determined. The results are published on the web.

- The Index Protocol defines the timeline for the auction methodology and settlement guidelines and all adhering parties are subject to the terms and conditions of each such protocol.

CDOs

Introduction

CDOs or collateralized debt obligations refer to the securitization of debt instruments to enable the actual or synthetic transfer of large credit-risky portfolios to investors in the form of bond issues, called tranches, which have differing risk and return characteristics. From the dealers' perspective, besides credit risk transfer, the other driving factors that lead to the widespread use of CDOs are:

- a desire to reduce the regulatory capital requirements of a bank credit portfolio;
- a desire to offload assets from the balance sheet by outright sale of debt instruments;
- the arbitrage opportunities that such structures provide.

From the investors' point of view, the key driving factors are:

■ Exposure to risks that are normally only available to banks.

■ Relative value opportunities due to attractive returns on CDOs.

The CDO market is broadly divided into those structures that do not use credit derivatives ('Cash CDOs') and those that do ('Synthetic CDOs').

Cash CDOs

The earliest CDOs in the market used a cash transfer mechanism to transfer the risk by physically selling debt instruments to a Special Purpose Vehicle ('SPV'). In a cash CDO, the debt instruments are repackaged by the SPV into various tranches of securities and sold to investors. Tranching of assets helps investors to match their specific investment needs. The SPV uses the funds received from the sale of securities to purchase debt instruments. In case of any defaults, the losses are borne by the investors in bottom-up order, i.e. from equity to senior tranche. The investors on their part receive regular interest payments generated from the cash flows from the underlying credits (see Figure 9.6).

Figure 9.6 **Basic cash CDO structure**

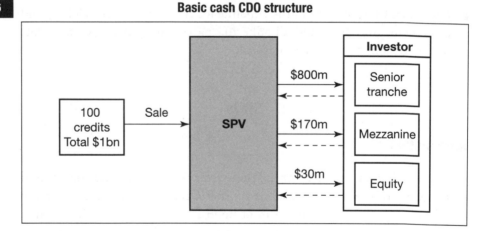

Hence, in Figure 8.11, a portfolio of US$1 billion of credits (bonds or loans) are bought by an SPV with funding raised by issuing equity, mezzanine and senior tranches of US$30 million, US$170 million and US$800 million respectively. Any losses by the SPV due to defaults by any of the credits are first absorbed by the equity tranche. Should these losses exceed US$30 million, then subsequent losses are absorbed by the mezzanine tranche and so on.

Synthetic CDOs

Synthetic CDOs use a synthetic risk transfer mechanism: only the credit risk of the reference entities is transferred to the SPV using a derivative such as a total return swap or a credit default swap. The SPV in this case holds the economic risks and rewards of the reference entities but does not legally own any debt. Synthetic CDOs also differ from cash CDOs in terms of the level of credit risk transfer. Since there is no outright sale of debt instruments to the SPV, synthetic CDOs do not generate any funds for the originating bank. The proceeds from the CDO issue are used to buy low-risk assets (the 'collateral') which are used to collateralize the swap.

The basic structure of a synthetic CDO is as follows:

- The SPV enters into a portfolio default swap with the dealer and sells protection on a pool of reference entities. For this, the dealer pays a regular premium to the SPV.

- The underlying credit portfolio is repackaged into various tranches and the SPV issues fixed maturity senior and junior mezzanine tranches. Equity and the highest tranche may be held by the dealer (i.e. never sold) or may be sold to investors.

- The SPV invests the proceeds from this issue in collateral of the same maturity as the CDO notes as shown in Figure 9.7.

- During the life of the CDO, investors receive coupons on the CDO notes derived from the cash flows from the collateral and the premium on the default swap received from the dealer.

Basic synthetic CDO structure

Figure 9.7

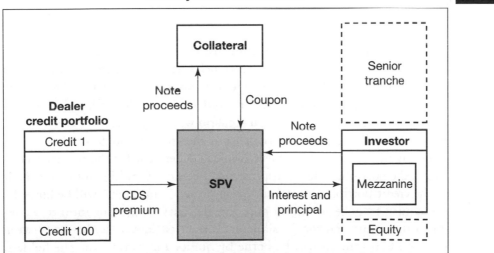

- If no credit event occurs during the life of the CDO, the investors receive the full return of principal at maturity after the collateral is sold.

- In case of a credit event, losses in excess of the equity tranche are borne by the mezzanine investors. The collateral is used to make any payments to the swap counterparty.

Tranche characteristics

Tranching is the process by which the exposure in the underlying portfolio of a CDO is redistributed and involves an assessment and prioritization of assets and liabilities in the CDO structure, replicating the corporate capital structure such that the risk and cash in-flows on the assets side are commensurate with the risk and cash outflows on the liability side as shown in Figure 9.8.

| Figure 9.8 | Loss prioritization in CDO capital structure |

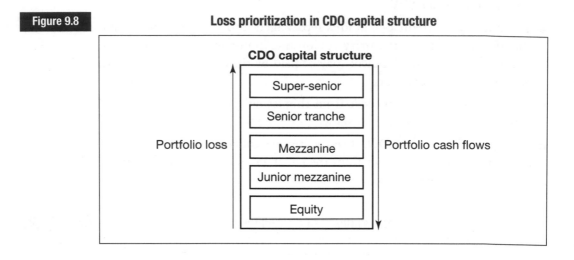

Tranching allows investors to gain customized exposure to the credit risk of the underlying assets pool. Each tranche has an attachment point and a detachment point which defines the full exposure of that tranche, i.e. the notional amount of the investment. To describe the loss allocation process in a CDO, consider a hypothetical scenario where a portfolio of credit of size €1 billion is divided into five tranches as shown in Figure 9.9.

Let us assume that the recovery rate is 40 per cent for the reference entities in the portfolio. This transpires into a loss of €6 million for each default in the credit portfolio. As default losses from 0% up to 3% will be borne by the equity tranche, it would take five defaults in the portfolio to write-down the equity tranche, also known as the first loss piece. Losses between €30 and €70 million will be borne by 'junior mezzanine' tranche holders, and so on.

Loss allocation example

Figure 9.9

Asset pool	Characteristics
No. of reference entities	100
Notional amount of protection on each credit	10m
Total portfolio size	1bn
Tranches	% of credit losses
'Equity' tranche	0%–3%
'Junior mezzanine' tranche	3%–7%
'Mezzanine' tranche	7%–10%
'Senior' tranche	10%–13%
'Super-senior' tranche	13%–100%

The tranches within the CDO structure have different characteristics from one another as described below:

- **Senior tranche**: Senior tranche notes are the least risky notes issued by the SPV and usually have a high credit rating, e.g. AAA. Thus, the coupon paid to the senior tranche is lower than the coupon paid to the other tranches. Senior tranches remain unaffected by losses in the credit portfolio until all the lower tranches are written-down due to defaults.

- **Equity or junior tranche**: The equity tranche is the riskiest piece of the CDO structure and absorb the initial losses in the credit portfolio. Thus, junior tranches pay higher coupons than other tranches. Junior tranches usually receive a low or no rating.

- **Mezzanine tranche**: Mezzanine tranche notes carry medium risk as compared with junior tranche notes and absorb losses only if the default losses exceed the detachment point of the junior tranche. Mezzanine notes holders receive coupons consistent with their credit rating.

Tranche rating

CDO transactions may be rated by more than one global rating agency such as Moody's, S&P and Fitch. Tranche ratings help investors in determining the risk and rewards associated with each tranche within the CDO structure and are one of the key features of the CDO used to attract investors. These ratings are used to determine the pricing of CDO notes. While rating a CDO transaction, rating agencies evaluate the following criteria:

- **CDO structure**: This includes analysing the issue size, interest on notes, rating level and the target cash flows.

- **Underlying assets**: This includes analysing the individual assets as well as the portfolio to arrive at the credit quality of the portfolio.

- **Portfolio management**: If a CDO is to be managed by a third-party manager, rating agencies look at the management capabilities of the manager.

Different ratings agencies use different techniques to establish the rating of CDO notes. They either use default probability of the securities or the expected loss of the securities as the key parameter to gauge the economic performance of the individual tranches. Both parameters depend on the level of subordination in the CDO structure. For example, the 'junior mezzanine' tranche will be affected by defaults if losses exceed the equity tranche. Thus, the detachment point of equity tranche acts as the threshold limit for the 'junior mezzanine' tranche. Rating agencies use this 'probability of losses exceeding the threshold limit' to establish the rating level of the tranche.

CDO classification

CDOs structures are classified in a number of ways: typically by specifying the deal motivation, whether the portfolio is static or managed, whether the transfer mechanism is cash of synthetic, the underlying assets and the extent to which all or part of the capital structure is placed:

- **'Balance sheet' or 'arbitrage'**: 'Balance' sheet CDOs are mainly driven by a bank's desire to seek regulatory capital relief and credit risk reduction via transfer of credit risk. 'Arbitrage' CDOs on the other hand allows dealers to take advantage of relative value opportunities in the market.

- **'Static' or 'managed'**: 'Static' CDOs have a fixed portfolio composition meaning the underlying credits are held until maturity irrespective of any deterioration in the quality of the underlying credit whereas the portfolio composition in a 'managed' CDO may change depending on the performance of the underlying credits and involves a third-party manager who actively manages the portfolio.

- **Underlyings**: CDO structure classified on the basis of type of underlying debt instruments. Currently, there is a wide range of underlyings available in the market that can be used in a CDO. These include leveraged loans, bonds, ABS, CDOs or credit indices.

- **Capital structure**: Classification based on the extent to which the capital structure is placed to the investors, i.e. single tranche CDO or multi-tranche CDO. Single tranche CDOs are preferred over traditional multi-tranche CDOs due to quicker execution of deals as the whole tranche is sold to just one investor. There is no need for a ramp-up period in a single tranche CDO structure as the portfolio is built synthetically.

Advantages of CDOs

Compared with similar rated corporate bonds, CDOs offer better returns that are uncorrelated with other markets such as equity markets. The structure not only helps create a market for illiquid assets but also provides exposure to a well-diversified portfolio of assets that investors would not be able to invest in directly. The structure not only allows dealers to tailor risk and reward to match investor specifications, but also helps them broadly to distribute credit risk throughout the capital markets.

WHERE NEXT?

Due to the combined liquidity and standardization of both the CDS and the Index markets, the scope for the third sector – complex credit products – continues to broaden. This sector will continue to be dominated by CDOs and it is likely that these will further evolve and grow. Beyond CDOs the complex credit sector is already seeing other products including options, constant maturity and principal protected products.

The growth and development of the CDO market is being driven by two factors. On the supply side, in the search for new opportunities and better margins the dealers are introducing a broader range of reference entities. ABS and leveraged loans are new additions to the synthetic structures and there is no reason why other instruments such as corporate receivables could not be added. In addition, due in part to Basle II, a new bank credit risk management culture is emerging resulting in increased loan portfolio management using credit derivatives.

On the demand side, investors are looking for more supply and better returns and there is broad acceptance that innovative synthetic structures are an effective way to achieve this. With the dealers providing an effective mechanism to match supply with demand there is every indication that the CDO and index markets will remain robust and continue to grow.

'. . . the products used to risk
manage a position are the very
same products that can be used to
speculate.'
■ ■ ■

Currency Derivatives

Introduction

Over the counter currency options

Currency options: reduced premium strategies

Simple exotic structures

Currency swaps

Exchange-traded instruments

Conclusion

Quiz

INTRODUCTION

There is a range of currency derivatives covering both short- and long-term exposures; in this context a short-term exposure may be only a few days. A long-term exposure may be linked to a foreign currency bond that could have a 10- or 20-year term. It almost goes without saying that the products used to risk manage a position are the same products that can be used to speculate. Most trading or speculative positions, as opposed to hedging positions, are likely to be of short duration, usually within the year and mostly within a few months or weeks. A hedger wants to remove or manage his currency risk. A trader wants to take currency risk in the hope of making a profit.

What is currency risk? The risk to a hedger is of either receiving a smaller amount of the base currency than expected, or paying out more of the base currency to purchase a required amount of foreign currency. For example, a UK company may have sold some goods to the USA; their base currency is sterling, but they have agreed to receive payment in US dollars in 3 months' time. If their sterling price (including profit margin) to the buyer was £250,000, they would need to convert this amount to US dollars for invoice purposes. Let us assume that they choose the current exchange rate on the day, which is £1 = US$1.60. This means that when they send their invoice to the US buyer it will state that US$400,000 is due in three months' time. If the company does not hedge its currency exposure on this invoice, it could make a profit or a loss on the transaction. A profit is unlikely to cause a problem (but in some companies it may), but a loss will certainly be unwanted. If the company decides not to hedge its position on the foreign exchanges it is running a risk.

It is impossible to predict the direction of an exchange rate with confidence, so we must assume one of two things can happen. The rate can increase or decrease against the base currency, which in this case is sterling. In three months it is not impossible for the currency rate to move five cents in either direction. The spot rate of exchange (the rate quoted today for value two business days later) could have moved as follows by the end of three months:

US$ increases (strengthens) to £1 = US$1.5500

US$ decreases (weakens) to £1 = US$1.6500

The company needs to receive £250,000 for the transaction. If it does not hedge its position, it will be compelled to accept the exchange rate on the day the dollars arrive.

- If the dollar has strengthened to US\$1.5500, the company will receive £258,064.

- If the dollar has weakened to US\$1.6500, the company will receive £242,424.

In the first instance the company has made a windfall profit, in the second case it has not received what it needed for this transaction. They may end up selling the goods at a loss. Yet, the client has paid what he was asked to, and the company quoted the dollar equivalent on the day. No one is to blame, but world-wide events have changed either the value of sterling or the value of the US dollar. This is why currency risk must be accepted as a way of life for companies which both export and import goods. In the case of an importer, he may need to buy euro to pay a supplier and budgets on the piece of equipment costing, say, £175,000. But, when it comes to payment date, and the company buys the euro on the foreign exchanges, they cost £195,000.

Different companies view foreign exchange risk in different ways. There are two extreme views. First, the company whose view is that 'we make widgets, we do not speculate on the foreign exchanges'. In that case they would hedge every single transaction denominated in foreign currency, either by using forward foreign exchange contracts, or by using currency options. Forward foreign exchange has been around for years: it involves the bank guaranteeing a rate of exchange for the client, at no cost. However, the client is then obliged to deal at that rate, whatever the spot rate of exchange is at maturity, and as we have seen, the spot rate could have moved into a profit position. A client who sells all his currency against forward transactions will have guaranteed rates, but be unable to profit from market moves.

The currency option provides an alternative method of hedging that allows the client not only to hedge his risk and guarantee a rate of exchange, but also to make a profit if the market moves in his favour. But a fee, or premium, is payable for the product, whereas a foreign exchange forward transaction costs nothing.

Secondly, there is the company that wishes to profit from their currency transactions, and may deliberately not hedge any of their currency exposures. They may in some cases actively seek foreign exchange risk as a means of enhancing income. The danger here is that the commercial side of the business, which may be profitable in its own right, could be over-shadowed by foreign exchange losses if some bad decisions on the currency are taken.

In a bank, a foreign exchange trader wishes to take risk by buying and selling currency for a profit. He may have a short-term view on the direction of the US dollar, or a long-term view on some other currency. He will then position himself accordingly, by either buying or selling the currency now, in order to reverse out of the deal later, hopefully making money in the process.

'A hedger wants to remove or manage his currency risk. A trader wants to take currency risk in the hope of making a profit.'

The trader can use the traditional foreign exchanges and deal in either the spot or forward markets, or he can use derivative products to support his view.

Table 10.1 shows a range of currency derivatives.

Table 10.1	Range of currency derivatives	
	Exchange traded	OTC
Currency futures	✓	
Currency options	✓	✓
Currrency swaps		✓

Most liquidity in currency derivatives is present in the over the counter market (OTC). The main reason for this is historic. For many years the major banks that were active in foreign exchange both for their own hedging and trading purposes, and for client business, had only the global FX market in which to operate. Spot and forward foreign exchange is technically OTC, and the volumes are enormous. In April 2004 the BIS calculated that the average daily volume of foreign exchange transacted through London is in the region of $753 billion – approximately one-third of the global turnover. When the derivatives market started to become popular, the idea of buying and selling currency derivatives on an organized exchange was anathema to most traders. As a result, the liquidity in currency derivatives traded on organized exchanges was never that good. However, in the last few years there has been a re-birth of foreign exchange futures and options as the banks seek liquidity from additional market players.

OVER THE COUNTER CURRENCY OPTIONS

Introduction

Risk management with regard to foreign exchange revolves around one concept: that the actual out-turn amount of a foreign currency transaction needs to be known in advance. Quite simply, how much sterling have I generated with this foreign currency, or how much sterling must I pay for this foreign currency? Until 1971, estimating sterling proceeds was not too much of a problem. Most currencies were linked officially or unofficially to the US dollar, which, in turn, was tied to the gold price. This meant that trying to forecast a foreign exchange rate was not too difficult, as there was little or no movement. After 1973, things became considerably more complex as the major currency relationships finally disintegrated with the OPEC oil crisis. Forecasting exchange rates is now something which is reserved for bank economists and end-of-year competitions.

The two main reasons why it is hard to forecast a rate are:

- Currencies tend to deviate away from anticipated trend paths.
- Continuing short-term volatility affects the currency values.

The simplest way for a client with a currency exposure to hedge against foreign exchange risk is to sell or buy the currency forward using a foreign currency forward contract. This entails the client calling the bank and requesting a forward foreign exchange rate for, say, 3 months; this will be guaranteed by the bank. The client, however, will have no flexibility. The rate is fixed so that whatever the rate of exchange when the dollars arrive or the yen is paid away, the client will transact at the pre-determined forward rate, even if the current exchange rate in the market offers a better alternative. The forward contract is an obligation, but it costs nothing except perhaps a lost opportunity should the foreign exchange rate improve. The currency option is an alternative hedging mechanism. It allows both risk management and the chance for the holder of the option to take a profit if the underlying foreign exchange rate moves favourably.

An option is one of the three derivative tools used for both risk management and speculation – the others are swaps and futures. The basic option concepts and terminology have already been covered in a previous chapter. If readers are unfamiliar with options, then they may find it advantageous to look through Chapter 4.

Options

Options have been around for hundreds if not thousand of years. Details of an early option taken out by Thales and relating to an impending olive harvest were referred to by Aristotle in Ancient Greece. More recently, in the 1700s in Holland, there was a scandal relating to options on tulip bulbs. In the early 1970s options on financial instruments were developed and both the corporate market, the banks and the exchanges claim the glory for inventing the currency option. Nevertheless, a paper published in 1972 by Fisher Black and Myron Scholes, is probably the one single thing that made options commercially available.

Definition A currency option gives the buyer, the right but not the obligation, to buy or sell a specific amount of currency at a specific exchange rate, on or before a specific future date. A premium is due.

Definition discussed

This option gives the client the ability to fix the exchange rate that will apply to a forthcoming transaction. The client need not progress with the option if he can find a more advantageous exchange rate elsewhere. The option instrument will let the client choose his guaranteed rate of exchange (the strike) and then the writing or selling bank will guarantee that rate if or when required. Because this option provides a kind of optional insurance or guarantee, the client is not obliged to take the cover so a premium or fee is required. This is normally paid within two business days, in either of the currencies of the option. Some banks may take the premium payment in a third currency, but it is at their discretion.

In these circumstances, the customer or client is the buyer of the option and must pay the premium, and the bank is the seller or writer of the option. It is the bank who must have the 'underlying' foreign exchange ready in case the client requires it. The bank will also need to hedge any risks on the option position. The underlying in this case is the receipt or payment of one currency against another currency. Options can be cash settled at expiry or they can be sold back at any time during the life of the transaction for residual or 'fair value' (see Glossary). Alternatively, the currency can be physically delivered or paid to the writing bank and the client will receive the counter-currency at the strike rate previously agreed under the option. It should be noted that there may not always be a positive benefit on the option, and some options will expire worthless. The currency option is more flexible than the traditional forward foreign exchange contract, and gives the buyer (holder) of the option four alternatives, the choice of:

- when to exercise
- whether to exercise
- how much to exercise
- the exercise price (strike).

When?

There are two styles of 'vanilla' currency option: an American option and a European option. Under an American-style currency option a greater flexibility is offered. Consider an American-style US$ put option against sterling: the holder can exercise the option on any business day until the expiry date for value two business days later. This allows him to deliver dollars to the bank at the rate agreed on the option on any day in the period. By comparison, under a European-style option, the holder can only exercise on the actual expiry date (for value two business days later). A European-style option therefore resembles a traditional forward FX deal.

With the FX forward contract, the currency must be delivered on the maturity date. If a client has sold forward some dollars for sterling against a two-month forward contract, and the dollars do not arrive in time, the forward contract must still be honoured, even at the expense of buying the required amount of currency from the market, possibly at a worst rate, and then delivering it under the forward contract. With the European-style currency option, if the dollars do not arrive, the option is simply abandoned, or if there is value remaining it can be sold back to the writing bank and the residual (fair) value realized.

Occasionally, the underlying exposure that the option is covering may be shortened, or for some reason the option is no longer required; then, the option can be sold back to the writing bank for fair value. If the underlying exposure is lengthened, it is not possible to extend the option at the same strike, or to roll it over into a new deal, as these practices are open to fraud. If the option maturity needs to be extended, the most effective way to do this is to sell the original option back to the bank for fair value, and take out a new transaction covering the fresh maturity date at the current prevailing market conditions.

Whether?

An option will be exercised by the holder only if it is profitable for him/her to do so. Where the spot exchange rate on maturity remains more favourable than the option strike price, the option will be allowed to lapse, and the underlying transaction will be effected in the spot market. This is known as 'abandoning the option'.

How much?

When the currency option is originally established, it is for a specific amount of a reference currency, and it is upon this figure that the premium is based. This is a notional maximum amount of currency. If the resulting currency receipt/payment turns out to be for a lesser figure, it may be possible (in some cases) for the excess cover to be sold back for fair value to the writing bank. Should an excess amount of currency arrive there is no provision for additional cover under the original option.

Strike

The strike of the option is chosen by the client at the outset. The premium that is due for the option will be a function of how the strike relates to the current market price and various other inputs (see Premium determinants).

Key features

Currency options

Insurance protection

A premium is paid by the buyer of the option to the writing bank, which in turn guarantees a fixed rate of exchange if/when required by the holder.

Profit potential

The option eliminates any chance of currency loss: the only outflow of funds relates to the premium payment. If the underlying market movement is in the holder's favour, then upside potential is available. An option profile exhibits 'asymmetry of risk'. The most that a holder can lose is the option premium; the most he can profit is limited only by how far the market moves.

Sell-back

The option can be sold back in whole or in part, for fair value to the writing bank. This is not a negotiable piece of paper and cannot be on-sold to a third party.

Premium

A premium is due, based on a series of variables that are input into an option pricing model, derived from the original Black and Scholes model.

Premium determinants

There are a number of major factors that affect the premium due on a currency option:

- strike price compared with the underlying price
- maturity
- put or call
- expected currency volatility
- interest rate differentials
- style – American or European.

(a) Strike price vs underlying price

For European style options, the benchmark against which the strike on the currency option is measured is the appropriate forward foreign exchange rate, known in the market as the 'outright forward'. For American-style options we use the current spot rate.

Table 10.2 illustrates the concept of 'in/at/out of the money'.

Illustration of the concept 'in/at/out of the money' Table 10.2

Client purchases option to sell dollars against sterling		Client purchases option to buy dollars against sterling
$1.40	IN THE MONEY	$1.60
$1.50	AT THE MONEY	$1.50
$1.60	OUT OF THE MONEY	$1.40

Note: Assume the current forward rate of dollars against sterling is £1 = US$1.50.

Using European options as an example, strike prices are generally referred to as follows:

Terminology

At the money (ATM) Where the strike is equal to the current outright forward rate.

In the money (ITM) Where the strike is more favourable than the outright forward rate, and the option premium is higher than that for an ATM option.

Out of the money (OTM) Where the strike is worse than the outright forward rate and the option premium is lower than that for an ATM option.

(b) Maturity

The longer the time to expiry, the higher the probability of large exchange rate movements, and the higher the chance of profitable exercise by the buyer. The buyer should be prepared to pay a higher premium for a longer-dated option than a short-dated option. The relationship between the premium due on an option and the maturity of the transaction is not a linear relationship, i.e. the premium due for a 6-month option is not double that of a 3-month option.

(c) Put or call

This will relate back to whether the currencies are at a premium or a discount to each other (see the section on Interest rate differentials).

(d) Volatility

It is the volatility element that differentiates one bank's price from another. All other premium determinants are matters of fact that are available to market participants simultaneously. If a client purchases an option with high volatility, he has purchased an asset with a high possibility of profitable exercise. See Chapter 4, Basic Option Concepts, for a fuller discussion of volatility.

Implied volatility

This is the current volatility level implicit in today's option prices. It can be derived from both exchange-traded options and OTC options. It is published by the information providers such as Reuters. An example is shown in Figure 10.1.

Figure 10.1

OTC option volatility

	GBP/USD	EUR/USD	USD/CAD	USD/JP¥	EUP/JP¥
		[TFS – ICAP]			4948
		[FX CURRENCY OPTIONS – INDICATIVE VOLS]			14/03 16:40 GMT
1W	6.25–7.00	6.90–7.65	6.40–7.15	8.70–9.45	7.35–8.10
1M	7.15–7.50	7.55–7.80	7.10–7.40	8.90–9.20	7.70–8.10
2M	7.35–7.65	7.75–8.00	7.20–7.50	8.75–9.05	7.70–8.05
3M	7.50–7.80	8.10–8.35	7.25–7.55	8.75–9.00	7.75–8.10
6M	7.80–8.10	8.55–8.75	7.45–7.70	8.70–8.95	7.90–8.20
1Y	8.05–8.30	8.80–9.00	7.55–7.75	8.65–8.85	8.00–8.30

ICAP Global Index [4900]   Forthcoming changes [4999]

Source: ICAP, Courtesy Reuters

Historical volatility

It is possible to analyse the spread of movements of the underlying commodity by recording, for example, the closing prices of US$/JP¥. If these prices were plotted on a graph a type of scatter pattern would emerge. Volatility is in effect the definition of this scatter, 'the normalized, annualized, standard deviation of the underlying price'.

While this type of analysis allows historical data to be examined, it can only ever indicate future prices, it will not be able to predict them, but rather give an idea of where they should be, taking into account how the commodity has moved in the past.

When an option trader has to price an option, he will need to input a level for volatility in percentage terms. This can be quite difficult, as in effect he is being asked to guess the way a currency pair will perform in the future. We earlier saw that the premium/maturity profile was non-linear: but the profile of premium/volatility is linear, as shown in Figure 4.4, i.e. the higher the perceived volatility, the higher the premium. Higher volatility implies a greater possible dispersion of prices at expiry.

(e) Interest rate differentials

Forward foreign exchange rates are calculated using the interest rate differentials of the two currencies concerned. Currencies are said to be at a premium or discount to each other, reflecting whether the forward points are added or subtracted from the spot rate. This differential will affect the premium due on an option.

Interest rates affect option pricing in two ways:

(a) By affecting the forward price of the asset and hence the intrinsic value.

(b) By affecting the present value calculations within the option-pricing model, and ultimately the present value of the option premium.

(f) American or European

Generally, an American-style option gives the holder greater flexibility. If the client wishes to call a currency with a higher interest rate (discount currency), the American-style option will be more expensive. If the client wants to call a premium currency the price of the American and the European option will be the same.

Currency options   **Terminology**

Call option	The right (not the obligation) to buy foreign currency.
Put option	The right (not the obligation) to sell foreign currency.
	It is always safer to specify both the currencies in order to avoid confusion.
Exercise	Conversion of the option into the underlying transaction.
Strike price	Exchange rate chosen by the holder. Prices can be described as:
	● at the money (ATM)
	● in the money (ITM)
	● out of the money (OTM).
Expiry date	Last day on which the option may be exercised
Value date	The day on which the currency is delivered.
Premium	The price of the option.
American option	An option which can be exercised on any business day, up to and including the expiry date.
European option	An option which can be exercised on the expiry date only.
Intrinsic	Difference between the strike price and the current value market exchange rate.
Time value	Difference between the option premium and intrinsic value; including the time left until expiry, volatility, forward points and including market expectations.
Fair value	Combination of intrinsic value and time value, as calculated by the option-pricing model.
Volatility	Normalized, annualized standard deviation of the daily SPOT rate for the exchange rate concerned.

Terminology discussed

It is very important to specify whether you are the buyer or seller of the option and whether you are selling or buying the underlying currencies. Potentially, there could be a four-way price, which is why we need the added terms of puts and calls. There are also a number of different ways in which people describe options. Some talk about 'calling' or 'putting' the foreign currency, others about calling or putting the dollar. There is added confusion when you consider cross-currencies, for example, if the currencies are euro/yen, which one is foreign? It is always safer to specify both sides, not just to call the euro, but to call the euro and put the yen; then there is no possibility of confusion. The option premium calculated by the pricing model can be divided into two parts, intrinsic value and time value. The intrinsic value is measured by the present value of the amount by which it is in the money.

Example	A European-style US dollar put, sterling call, is used to cover a dollar receivable against sterling in three months' time:

Forward outright rate for three months is $1.77

Option strike rate is $1.74

Intrinsic value is present value (PV) of $1.77 – $1.74 = PV of 3 cents

Intrinsic value provides the minimum price at which the option will trade and relates to the relationship between the strike price and the spot rate.

The time value component of the option expresses the risk premium in the option and is a function of several variables:

- the time to maturity;
- the interest rate differential between the two currencies (cost of carry);
- the volatility of the currency pair.

To the option writer, this risk premium is highest when the option is 'at the money', because at this point there is the greatest uncertainty over whether the option will expire worthless or have some value at maturity.

If the option moves 'into the money', the writer can be more sure the option will be exercised, if it moves 'out of the money' the opposite applies. The more deeply 'in' or 'out' of the money the option moves, the greater the confidence of the option writer in the final outcome, for example, will it or won't it be exercised?

In simple terms, the longer the time to expiry, the more an option is worth. As time passes, the option writer can define the risk more accurately, and in the last few days before expiry the time value diminishes rapidly. The time value of an option decays as expiry approaches. Time value decay follows a particular pattern and the rate of time value decay is called Theta, which is one of the option Greeks, to be discussed later.

Comparisons of currency options against forward foreign exchange

Table 10.3 summarizes the main differences between OTC currency options and traditional forward foreign exchange.

Comparison between currency options and forward contracts **Table 10.3**

Currency options	Forward contracts
Right to buy or sell	Obligation to buy or sell
No obligation to deliver	Must deliver on/before maturity
No loss possible – excluding premium	Unlimited opportunity loss possible
Eliminates downside risk and	Eliminates downside risk – but no
retains unlimited upside potential	upside potential
Perfect hedge for variable exposures	Imperfect hedge for variable exposures

A forward contract is perfectly acceptable as a hedging product if you have complete information at your disposal; you know the amount, the currencies, and when – to the day – the currency will be paid/received: 'the end of the month' is not acceptable, it is too vague. In everyday business, the luxury of complete information is not always available, dates and amounts have to be estimated, and some clients simply pay late. In those circumstances an option is the perfect alternative. It is not zero cost like a forward, but it is immensely flexible, and some options can be designed to have very low premiums.

Using a currency option to hedge a receivable

2 April

A major British company has won an export order in Thailand. Delivery and payment will be in three months' time and will be in dollars. The treasurer is not sure exactly on which day the money will be available in his account, however, he is not expecting to be paid weeks in advance! He is worried that the value of the dollar may fall (depreciate) before he receives his invoice amount of US$1,250,000. If he does nothing and the value of the dollar falls, he will not realize sufficient sterling from the resulting foreign exchange conversion, but if the value of the dollar increases he will be very happy. He is not sure in which direction the dollar will move, but under his own strict internal guidelines he is not allowed to do nothing. If he transacts a forward contract with one of his bankers, he must give up any windfall profits, but if he transacts an option, he has insurance if things go wrong and profit opportunities if things go right.

Action – 2 April

The treasurer will ask for an indication level on a dollar put, sterling call option, European-style, strike = at the money, and an expiry date in three months' time (2 July) for value two business days later. The current financial information is available:

£/US$

Spot rate: 1.7500

Outright forward rate: 1.7450.

The strike on the option will be at the money forward (ATMF), at $1.7450. The premium due for this option is, say, 1.20 per cent of the dollar amount. The total premium is 1.2 per cent of $1,250,000 which is US$15,000, and must be paid to the bank two business days (known as value Spot) after the deal is struck. The option can now be filed or put in a drawer for three months until expiry.

Action – 2 July

The dollars arrive on time. The treasurer will call his bank to check the current level of the spot exchange rate. If the dollar has strengthened (appreciated) to, say, US$1.6950, then the option will be worthless and will be abandoned, and the transaction will be effected in the spot market. If the dollar has depreciated to say US$1.7950, the client will exercise the option at the agreed rate of $1.7450. The treasurer will need to call the bank and confirm that he wishes to exercise his option, as exercise is not always automatic. Under the option, the treasurer will deliver $1,250,000 and receive sterling at US$1.7450, giving a sterling out-turn of £716,332.38. Technically the option premium should be deducted to work out the breakeven rate (to be absolutely correct, the net present value (NPV) of the premium). This would give a net sterling out-turn of £716,332.38 less the amount of the option premium in sterling (for premium conversion purposes, the spot rate is always used:

US$15,000 divided by £/$1.7500 = £8,571.43) – a total figure of £707,760.95

giving a net rate inclusive of premium of 1.7661.

As Figure 10.2 shows there is always a best and worst case, indeed the nature of FX means that no one knows how far or how fast a currency will move.

A 5-cent move in the three-month period has been used for the purposes of illustration.

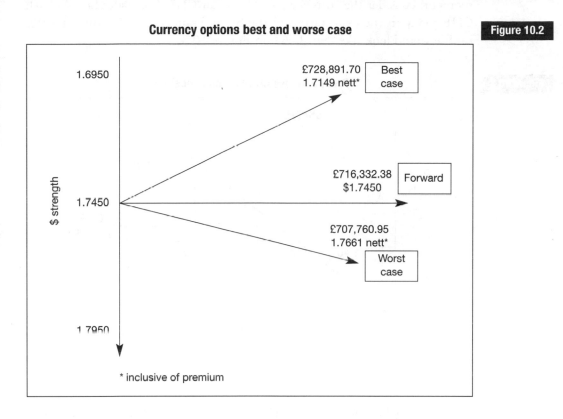

Currency options best and worse case

Figure 10.2

If the client had chosen a traditional forward contract and been lucky with the receipt of the dollars on the correct date, he would have achieved at best (or worst) a rate of $1.7450, and an out-turn of £716,332.38.

The option will always be the second best alternative in hindsight. If the client knew with 100 per cent certainty that the dollar was going to depreciate, he would sell forward, a hedging alternative that would cost nothing and allow no profit. But if you are not expecting to profit, you have given up nothing. If the client knew with 100 per cent certainty that the dollar would appreciate, he would do nothing and simply sell the dollars at the better rate when they arrived in three months' time. The option allows the client to get the best possible outcome, the 'insured' rate when required, or the profit when the market moves favourably, but a premium is required.

Option mechanics

So far we have looked at options in the very simplest terms. They are, however, quite complex and each type of option has a particular 'signature'. The most straightforward way to understand the way options work is to draw the profit and loss profile (P/L) of the transaction. Forget options for a moment: consider the currency pair US dollar/CHF. If a trader bought cash CHF today in the expectation of the Swiss Franc strengthening, the P/L profile would look like that shown in Figure 10.3.

| Figure 10.3 | Profit and loss profile – cash position |

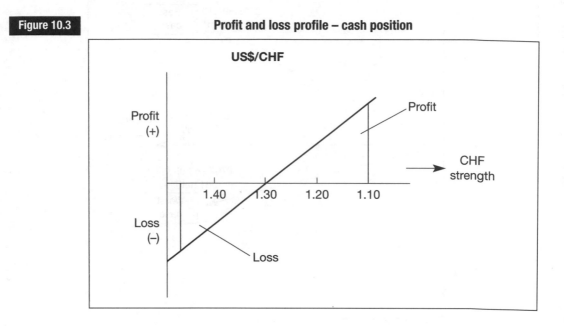

If a trader had bought the CHF at US$/CHF 1.30, then as the Swiss Franc appreciates, and the dollar weakens (towards $1.20), the position will start moving into profit. Likewise if the CHF depreciates, and the dollar strengthens, the same position would move into loss. This is an un-hedged position, with an equal probability of profit or loss.

Alternatively, instead of running a spot risk, an option could be purchased, with a strike of US$/CHF 1.3000, which would allow the same 1:1 profit opportunity, but where the only potential downside would be the loss of the premium paid. This would be a Swiss Franc call, put on US dollars. The option has been bought, so the trader is 'long' the call (see Figure 10.4).

The profile of the option mirrors that of the un-hedged position, except that it starts from a negative position reflecting the premium paid. It is important to take into account the premium on the option and any associated interest rate costs. An option purchaser may need to fund (borrow) the option premium, and an option writer must deposit the premium, so the deposit interest rate that the trader obtains must be factored into the final option premium. There are also associated opportunity costs that should not be overlooked.

Profit and loss profile – CHF call option – long call

Figure 10.4

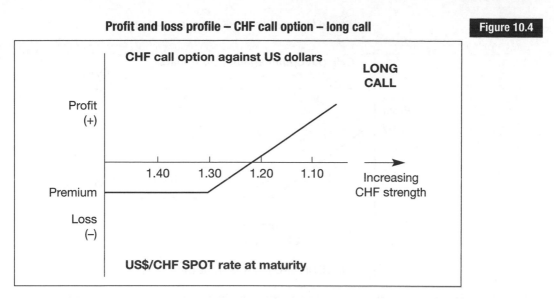

Profit and loss profile – CHF call option – short call

Figure 10.5

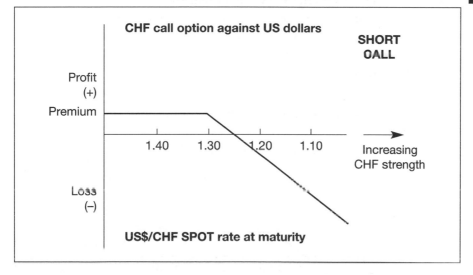

The bank writing the Swiss Franc call option shown in Figure 9.4 would have a mirror image position, where they had received the premium: this is shown in Figure 10.5.

With this position the bank that has written the option is 'short' the call option. All they have taken in is the premium, yet their potential for loss is comparatively high.

Let us now assume that the trader has changed his mind about the direction of the Swiss Franc. He now feels that it is about to weaken, so with his new trade he needs to buy a CHF put, US dollar call option (see Figure 10.6).

Figure 10.6	**Profit and loss profile – CHF put option – long put**

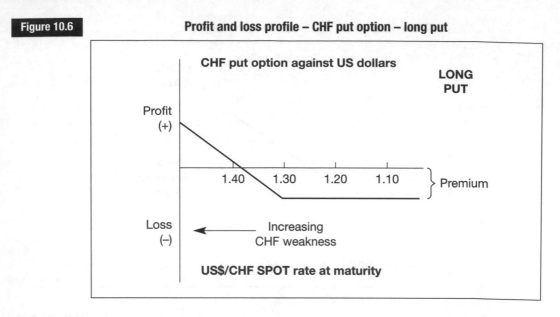

The profit and loss profile shows again that the holder of this option can lose only his premium, but can profit as long as the market moves in his favour. In comparison, the writer of option shown in Figure 10.7, who is 'short' the Swiss Franc put option, could lose a considerable amount, if no hedging is undertaken.

Figure 10.7	**Profit and loss profile – CHF put option – short put**

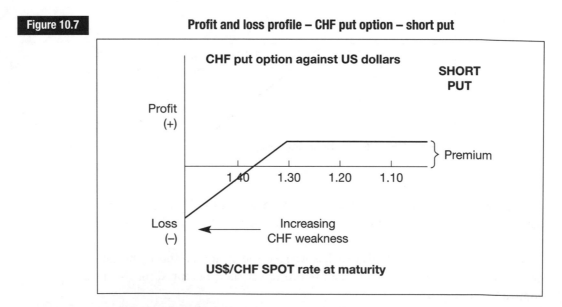

In all, there are four basic building blocks in options: calls and puts, bought and sold. The four strategies, long call, short call, long put, short put are shown in Figures 10.4, 10.5, 10.6 and 10.7.

Basic workings of currency options

The following rules apply:

1. The option is exercised only when it is advantageous for the holder.
2. If the ruling spot rate is more favourable, the option will be abandoned.
3. The downside risk is protected, with a 1:1 gain, if the market moves favourably.
4. The writer of the option is obliged to deliver the 'underlying' if the option is exercised.

Put/call parity

The profit and loss profile of a forward contract is similar to the profile of the unhedged position.

Profit and loss profile – put – call parity

Figure 10.8

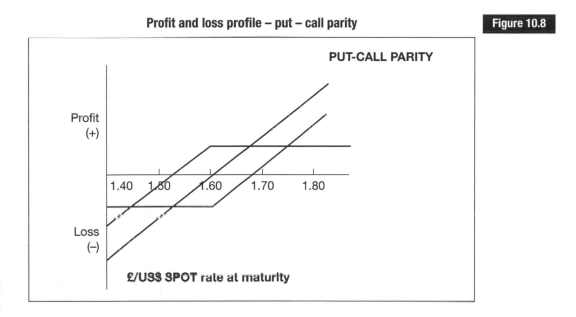

Figure 10.8 superimposes the profiles of a European-style long call and European-style short put upon the forward. You can see that once the premiums are netted off, then the combined strategy of buy a call and sell a put at the same strike price equal buying forward. Similarly, buying a put and selling a call at the same strike price equal selling forward. These are known as synthetic forward positions.

Using currency options to speculate

A private client believes that the yen will appreciate against the dollar over the next month. He is prepared to put on a position equivalent to US$10 million. He has no desire to hold either currency physically and no requirement for flexibility on the date, so he will purchase a one-month European-style option that he can sell back, but will not need to exercise. When the option is sold back to the option writer, the currency gain, if there is one, will be factored into the sell-back price. This obviates the need for physical foreign exchange transactions.

Current financial information:

US$/Yen

Spot rate	115.00
Outright forward rate	114.00

Strategy

The client will purchase a European-style yen ATM call, US dollar put in US$10 million for expiry in one month's time. Option premium is calculated at 0.8 per cent, which is US$80,000 or JP¥ 9.20 million, payable within two business days of the transaction date. This option has one calendar month to run. The client must decide when he believes he has the maximum profit on the deal. Let us assume that three weeks after inception, the option trade is showing a healthy profit. The strike on the ATM option was originally set at $/JP¥ 114.00, the spot rate is now 111.50 and the client does not think there will be much more movement, so wants to close out his position and take a profit. As this is a European option, all he has to do is to call the writing bank and ask them to 'buy back' the option. They will calculate the buy-back premium through the option-pricing model. The buy-back premium will incorporate the FX gain and will also incorporate any residual time value.

Figure 10.9 shows the different risk profiles. The long yen call option against dollars, with limited loss illustrating asymmetry of risk, and the unhedged or spot position, with a potential unlimited profit or unlimited loss.

Early exercise

If the private client had purchased a more expensive American-style option, he could still have sold it back at any time, but why pay for exercise flexibility if you never want to exercise? The private client had no need for either of the physical currencies, so exercise is not required; he simply wanted to profit from his view on exchange rates.

Using options to speculate – profit and loss profile of US$/yen position

Figure 10.9

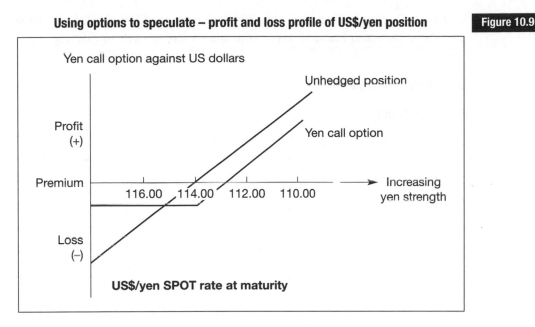

The other problem with exercising an option early is that all the client or trader would receive is the intrinsic value; that is, the amount by which the option is in the money, the amount by which the option is better than the underlying market rate. If there had been any time value left, this would be lost. Instead of early exercise, it is always better to sell back an option. This ensures that the time value component is always included in the sell-back premium.

Another consideration for using European options and selling them back, is that if the client chose to exercise the option, it would be necessary for him to take delivery of the physical yen and pay for them with physical dollars, simultaneously needing to sell the yen back into the market to crystallize the profit. In that case the transaction costs on the foreign exchange deals may be significant on their own.

Trading volatility

Options are the only product*, derivative or otherwise, where volatility is an input. We have discussed volatility at some length, and we have looked at how a hedger and a trader may use options, either to risk manage a currency position or to speculate on the direction of a currency. It is also possible to trade or speculate on volatility. This does not mean we are trying to forecast the direction on an exchange rate, rather, we are trying to forecast a 'slow-down' or a 'speed up', or an increase or decrease in uncertainty.

---

* not including vol or variance swaps/options

Mostly it is banks that trade volatility, and corporates would need very clear mandates from their board of directors to allow them to trade in this way.

Volatility strategies

The long straddle

A trader takes the view that volatility will increase; it often does at the beginning of a new financial year when everyone is back in the market, 'bright-eyed and bushy-tailed'. The direction of the market is unknown, but the trader feels definitely that it will move. If he thought the currency would strengthen, he would buy a call option; if he thought it was going to weaken, he would buy a put option. In fact, he will buy both the call option and the put option. This will entail paying two premiums. But if the market moves far enough, one of the options will be heavily in the money, and when it is sold back, will more than cover the cost of the two original option premiums, and allow for some profit.

If the market strengthens, the call option goes ITM. If the market weakens, the put option goes ITM (see Figure 10.10). Whichever option goes in to the money you sell it back, hoping that the profit on the one option will cover the cost of the two premiums. As long as the market moves, you make profit with this strategy. You will make most money if there is a big swing in one direction quickly, then when you sell the option back, you can recover some time value. You will lose most money – both your premiums – if the market does not move at all.

| Figure 10.10 | **Long straddle** |

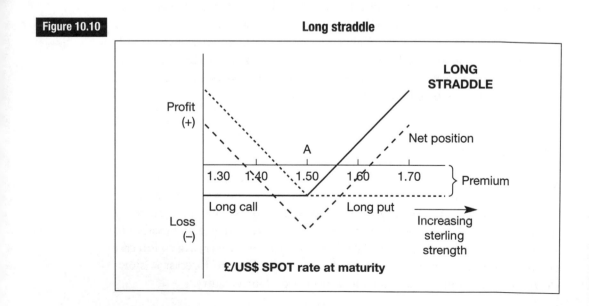

The short straddle

It is early December. In the run-up to Christmas and New Year many banks' trading operations tend to quieten down, staff go on holiday, and it is rare for big positions to be put on at this time. If a speculative position goes wrong, it may be hard to trade out of as liquidity will be lower.

A bad position may affect the dealer's bonus that he has earned that year, and which is paid annually, based on profits up to 31 December; the last thing he wants to do is something risky that may lose him money. Bearing this in mind, you would expect volatility to decrease; fewer players in the market and smaller positions. But should you buy a call or a put? The call would be the right option if you thought the currency was going to strengthen, the put option if you thought the currency would weaken. But your view on volatility will not give you a guide as to the direction of the currency.

The answer is that you sell both the call and the put, ATM, receiving two option premiums (see Figure 10.11). This is a high-risk strategy. In this example, you have taken in two expensive premiums, but if the view on the market is wrong and volatility increases, not decreases, then there is a possibility of serious loss. In effect you will have sold options at, say, volatility of 9 per cent and have to buy them back to close out the positions at 12 per cent, making a loss. You will make most profit if the volatility decreases or remains the same, and you will lose if the market exchange rate moves by even a small amount in either direction. The extent of the loss will be realized only at expiry or sell-back: potentially, it could be very big indeed; it will be limited only by how far the market moves (in either direction).

Short straddle

Figure 10.11

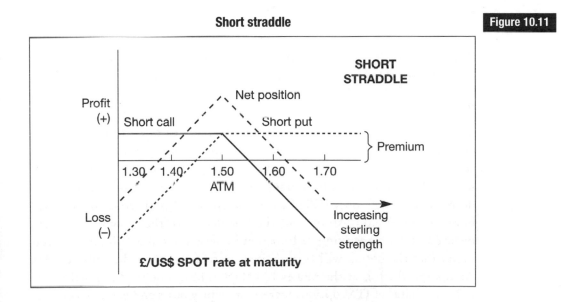

Each of the volatility trades described can be used in any of underlying markets, interest rates, equity, commodity and, of course, currency.

Availability

The OTC currency option is very liquid and most commercial banks will have an option service that they offer to clients. The large international banks will offer a service in many currencies, while some smaller banks will concentrate on niche markets. The minimum transaction size for a currency option will vary from bank to bank, but is likely to be in the region of US$250,000 or equivalent. To be assured of a competitive price the size of the transaction will ideally be in excess of US$250,000.

Option Greeks

The option-pricing model needs a number of inputs so that it can calculate option premium. Only the strike will remain fixed, all the other variables will change with the market or with the passage of time. Each variable changes in a distinct way and these lead us to sensitivity ratios which are known as the option Greeks. They define how the particular variable changes while all the others remain the same. The four most important option Greeks are:

- delta
- gamma
- theta
- vega.

Those of you with a classical education may not recognize vega as a Greek letter. It probably came from 'Star Trek'!

Delta

The definition of delta is: 'The change in the option premium for a unit change in the underlying exchange rate'. This is an important measure as it shows how the price of the option will change as the underlying market moves. The values of delta ranges from zero to one. An option which is deeply out of the money (OTM), with no chance of profitable exercise, will have a delta of 0.00. An option which is deeply in the money (ITM) will behave like the underlying cash market because there is a 100 per cent certainty that the option will be exercised, in this case the delta will be 1.00. An option which is at the money (ATM) will have a delta of approximately 0.5. The deltas of ITM options increase as expiry nears and exercise becomes more certain. Deltas of OTM options decrease as expiry nears and the option looks like being abandoned.

Delta is also considered as the 'hedge ratio'. This means that the delta on a particular option can meaningfully help hedge the position. Consider a trader who has bought an ATM Swiss Franc call, US dollar put option in CHF 10 million, with a one-month expiry. As the underlying spot rate moves, so the option will become worth more or less, it will not stay ATM. If the option goes into the money, the trader will exercise the option, and the writing bank must have the CHF10 million ready for him. If the option at expiry is OTM he will not exercise it and the writing bank needs to hold zero CHF. On the day of purchase, when the option is still ATM, the chance of profitable exercise is deemed to be 50 per cent, the delta is 0.5. The option writer therefore needs to hold 50 per cent of the underlying CHF ready for the buyer, should he require it at expiry. The option writer will buy in 50 per cent × CHF 10 million. A week later, assume the spot market has moved and the delta is now 60 per cent, or 0.6: the option writer needs to buy in another 10 per cent of cover. The next day the market moves back to 55 per cent, or 0.55: the option writer needs to sell 5 per cent of the cover, and so on. Every time the position is re-hedged the trader must pay away the bid–offer spread.

This procedure is known as delta hedging: it is time consuming and costly. If the position is delta neutral, or delta hedged, the volatility has been locked in. Option portfolios that are not exposed to small movements in the underlying exchange rate are said to be delta hedged or delta neutral (see Figure 10.12).

Delta of a call option at various points

Figure 10.12

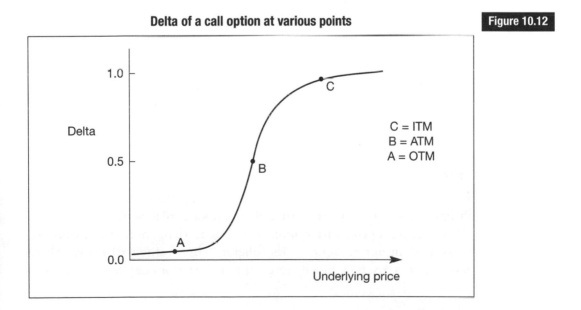

Gamma

The definition of gamma is: 'The rate of change of delta for a unit change in the underlying exchange rate'. The more frequently an option portfolio needs to be re-hedged the higher will be the gamma. It reflects how much and how fast the hedge ratio changes. Options with a small gamma are easy to hedge, because the hedge ratio will not change much as the spot rate moves. Options with a high gamma, such as short-dated ATM options, can be treacherous to manage and very costly. Imagine the last day of an option's maturity: it is still ATM, a very small move in the underlying spot rate, say +0.0005, may swing the option ITM. In which case the option writer needs to have 100 per cent of the underlying ready for the option holder not if, but *when* he exercises. Twenty minutes later the spot rate has moved back –0.0007, the option is now OTM. The option writer now needs to hold 0 per cent cover. Every time the market moves, even in very small amounts, the delta may swing from zero to one, with nothing in between: this is the classical high gamma position. Figure 10.13 illustrates the gamma of a call option.

Figure 10.13	**Gamma and delta curves**

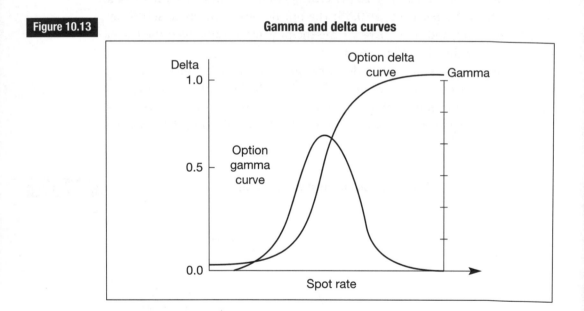

Theta

The definition of theta is: 'The change in the option premium for a given change in the period to expiry (usually the passage of a day)'.

Long-dated options have more time value than short-dated options, because as an option ages, so its inherent time value will decay. Theta describes exactly how much time value is lost from day to day, and is a precise measure of time decay. At inception an option will have 100 per cent of its time value. Consider a 90-day ATM option. How much time value has been lost after one day – assuming everything else remains constant? Answer: 1/90. The next day, the option loses 1/89, and so on. So in the early part of an option's maturity, it retains most of its time value. Time decay is almost constant for about two-thirds of the option's life. The decay increases in the last third of the option's life, and in the last week it loses progressively one-seventh, then one-sixth, then one-fifth, etc., of the time value that is left. Theta is highest in ATM options close to expiry.

The graph of time value decay is best illustrated with ATM options, as in Figure 10.14.

Time and value decay

Figure 10.14

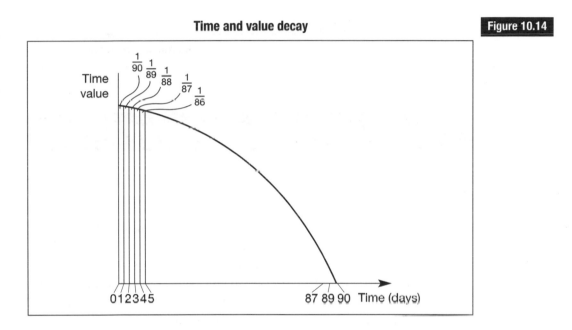

Vega

The definition of vega is: 'The change in the option premium for a 1 per cent change in volatility'. This is a straight-line relationship. As volatility increases, so does uncertainty, and so does the premium. An option with a high volatility gives the holder a greater chance of profitable exercise than an option with low volatility (see Figure 10.15).

Figure 10.15

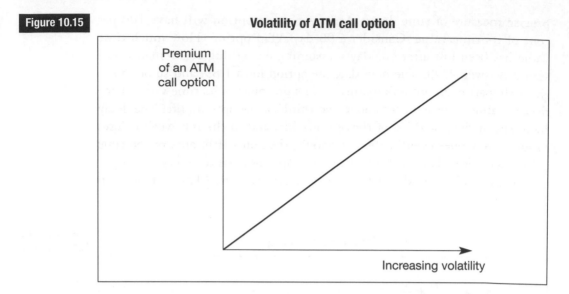

Volatility of ATM call option

Premium of an ATM call option

Increasing volatility

CURRENCY OPTIONS: REDUCED PREMIUM STRATEGIES

Introduction

In the previous section we looked at how to cover or 'insure' the exchange rate on a currency deal by using option-based products. Then the client would need to purchase a call or a put, depending upon whether he wished to sell or buy the underlying currency. In any event, a premium is due, and as volatility in the currency option market is quite high, the premium can sometimes be quite large. Some currency pairs are especially volatile and expensive to cover. Even if the premium is accurate, and all of the banks in the market are making the same price, it may still be too high for the client, based on his own perceptions of where the currency may move during the transaction period. In these cases another alternative is needed to make the strategy economically viable for the client. We need to consider some way of reducing the premium. In fact, there are a number of ways, but we shall examine only three of them:

■ out of the money options
■ currency collar options
■ participating forwards.

Premium reduction strategies – out of the money options

There are a number of ways that the client can reduce the premium payable on a currency option. The immediate choice is usually to 'go out of the money'. Instead of the client having insurance at today's spot or forward rates, he may take his option cover, at say, 2 cents away, this would make the option 2 cents out of the money. The foreign exchange market will then have to move a little further against the holder before the option becomes valuable. Calls and puts are often transacted out of the money, but it is never possible to go so far out of the money that the option cover costs nothing! For a dollar receiver, even if the option is only 0.5 cents out of the money, the premium will be lower than that for an at the money option. However, in some cases the client may be looking for a greater premium reduction than he can attain solely by going out of the money, or perhaps he is not prepared to go sufficiently out of the money to achieve the reduction he is looking for. Then we need to investigate other methods of premium reduction; in other words still pay the premium, but not with money. That begs the question, how else can the client pay the premium? The only available alternative is for the client to agree to give up some of his potential profit under the option, should the exchange rates move in his favour. But it must be stressed that exchange rates may not move in the client's favour; it is only a potential profit that the client is giving up. If rates do not move in the client's favour, he has given up nothing, and he still has his insurance cover, although he will have achieved it at a reduced cost.

Currency collar options (cylinder options)

A currency collar will involve the client buying the call or put option cover he requires to guarantee his insured rate, and simultaneously selling the opposite option back to the bank. This second option will have a strike rate exactly at the point where the client has agreed to give up any further profit. On the first option the premium is paid to the bank, but this will be offset by the second option with the premium that is received from the bank. The resulting net premiums can be positive, negative or zero, depending on exactly how much profit potential the client is willing to give up. The collar option exhibits put/call parity.

> **Definition**
>
> A collar option gives the client the right, but not the obligation, to sell or buy his currency at a particular exchange rate on or before a specific future date. Should he be able to transact at a rate which is better than a second pre-determined level, the client agrees to give up any further profit. Premiums can be positive, negative or zero. The collar option involves a combination of two options: one bought and one sold. Both transactions are simultaneous, and tailored to fit the exact currency profile.

Definition discussed

Let us take the case of a client who wishes to sell US$1 million and buy Sterling three months forward. The current forward rate is £/US$1.60. The client is familiar with the concept of options, yet feels they are too expensive, given his outlook on the currency.

First, the client needs to confirm with the bank the strike on the option that he wishes to buy (although he considers it too expensive at the moment). He will need to buy a US dollar put, sterling call option, and let us assume that option is already 3 cents out of the money, but the premium quote of 1.1 per cent of the dollar amount is still too expensive for him. He does not wish to go further out of the money, but still wants a cheaper alternative. In that case the bank will need to examine other ways in which he can pay the premium. Let us assume that over the three months the client believes that the dollar/sterling exchange rate may fall – the dollar strengthens (he can profit), but only by 3 cents. The client can then put that in writing, in effect guaranteeing to the bank that should rates fall below this second rate (3 cents lower than the current forward rate) he will take no further profit. The way he does this is to sell the opposite option – a US dollar call, sterling put option to the bank at strike of £/US$1.5700. The bank will price the option at this strike price and pay him, say, 0.9 per cent of the dollar amount. This can go to offset the original premium that he paid on his option. The resulting net premium has now fallen, from a level of 1.1 per cent, to 1.1% – 0.9% = 0.2%.

| Key features | **Multiple product** |

Multiple product
A collar option consists of two options which offset each other, transacted simultaneously. On one the premium is paid, on the other the premium is received.

Insurance
The client pays a premium to insure against currency risk. The premium is lower as he accepts part of the risk himself, he also agrees to share part of the profit with the bank.

Profit potential
A currency collar reduces the risk of adverse currency movements while retaining the client's ability to benefit from part of any favourable movement.

Cost
A cheaper hedge than a standard option. The client selects the degree of risk he is prepared to take and the level of profit he is prepared to give up and the final net premium may be, positive, negative or zero, depending upon exactly how the two premiums offset.

22 October

A UK exporter has sold some goods abroad and will receive US$1.5 million in three months' time. He wishes to use an option to protect his profit potential should the dollar rise (appreciate). The current forward rate is $1.55, and the exporter wishes to hedge his budget rate of $1.60. The exporter has telephoned his bank, and they advise that the premium for a standard option with a strike of $1.60 is 1.3 per cent (of the dollar amount), which the exporter considers too expensive.

Action – 22 October

The exporter buys an OTM option for three months to sell dollars and buy sterling at $1.60 – client buys a dollar put, sterling call option. Simultaneously, the client sells an OTM option to the bank for three months to sell them dollars and receive sterling – client sells a dollar call, Sterling put option. The strike price of the option written by the client is dependent on the size of the premium he wishes to pay. Our exporter has requested a series of different strikes for the option he will sell to the bank. He could sell any one of them but is looking for a zero-premium strategy. In which case (see Table 10.4) for the figures, the zero-cost line will involve the bought dollar put at $1.60 and the dollar call sold at $1.51. It is at this point that premiums net exactly to zero.

Example: figures

Table 10.4

Client buys option with strike at	Premium payable (%)	Client sells option with strike at	Premium earned (%)	Net cost/ benefit (%)
$1.60	1.3	$1.40	0.3	Client pays 1.0
$1.60	1.3	$1.45	0.75	Client pays 0.55
$1.60	1.3	$1.47	1.10	Client pays 0.20
$1.60	1.3	$1.51	1.30	Zero cost

Outcome

By executing a transaction (at $1.60 and $1.51), the exporter has insured against an adverse currency fluctuation for nil cost, while still allowing himself any profitable movement up to a limit of $1.51 but not beyond.

There are a number of possible outcomes as shown in Figure 10.16.

Figure 10.16

Zero-cost collar option

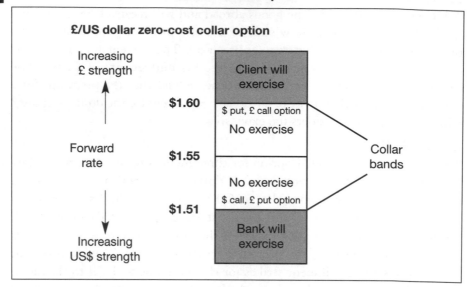

- No exercise takes place if the spot rate at maturity is within the collar bands (between $1.51 and $1.60).

- If the dollar depreciates above the cap rate, the exporter will exercise his option (anything over $1.60).

- If the dollar appreciates below the floor rate, the bank will exercise the dollar call option they have bought from the client (anything below $1.51).

Put/call parity

The notion of paying for one option by selling another illustrates the very important concept of put/call parity. As we saw earlier, a synthetic forward contract can be created by buying a call, and selling a put option – or vice versa, if they have the same strike price which is ATMF (at the money forward). The two premiums will be exactly equal and will offset. A forward contract is also zero cost. If we extend the theory a little, examine what will happen if the option bought by the client and the option sold by the client move equally out of the money: if both the put and the call are 1 cent OTM, then technically their cost will again equate to zero, so this will be another zero-cost structure. There are an almost infinite number of possibilities, for zero-cost collars, as long as each option is equally OTM, and the volatility is not different. The theory breaks down a little when you start to realize that the option trader will have a bid–offer spread between buying and selling options, this and his profit margin mitigate against a zero-cost collar being exactly equally distant either side of the current forward rate.

Participating forwards

These can also generate a zero-cost structure for a client, and also involves buying one option and selling the other. In this case, however, the option strike rates are the same, but the principal amounts on each option are different.

Consider a client who wishes to hedge the receipt of US$5 million against Sterling in six months' time. He wishes to achieve a zero- or reduced-cost strategy, but his expectation on exchange rates is that they may well come a substantial way in his favour – the dollar will strengthen. If he transacts a collar structure he would, of necessity, give up all further profit beyond a certain level, and he has already checked with the bank where that level is.

Current financial information shows:

£/US$

Spot rate	1.6000
Forward rate	1.5900
Zero-cost collar strikes	1.6200 and 1.5700

The client is certain the dollar will strengthen below 1.5700 and he still wants to profit beyond this level.

Strategy

The client will buy the option he requires in the normal way. He will purchase a US dollar put in $5 million, sterling call option, strike 1.6200 (OTM), expiry six months, the premium for this option is 1.9 per cent of the dollar amount. He still needs to pay the premium. To pay it, he will sell an option to the bank as before. But the option he sells will be a US dollar call option, sterling put option, expiry six months. The option written by the customer will have the same strike as the first option – $1.6200. It is therefore 3 cents in the money (ITM), and as such the bank will pay a high premium. Let us assume they will pay 3 per cent for this. This is more than enough to pay the original premium of 1.9 per cent.

The principal amount on the second option needs to be adjusted to reflect this, and we want to match the dollar amount of the premium as closely as possible.

Option 1
US dollar put, sterling call   Premium paid 1.9% = $95,000

Option 2
US dollar call, sterling put   Premium received 3% = $150,000

Principal amount required:
1.9% ÷ 3% = 0.6333
0.6333 × US$5,000,000 = US$3,166,666

The principal amount on the second option needs to be only US$3.167 million, for the premium receivable to be $95,000 (at a rate of 3 per cent). The amount of participation will increase the further OTM the option strike is pitched.

There will be a range of possible outcomes (see Figure 10.17).

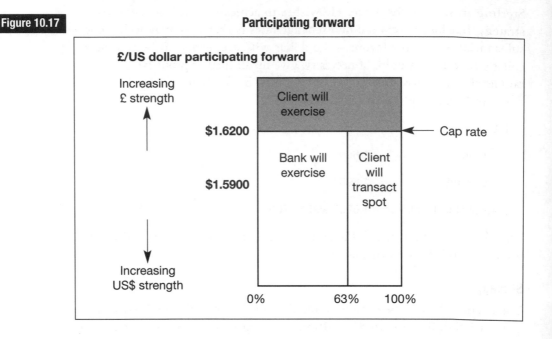

Figure 10.17 **Participating forward**

1. If the dollar weakens above the cap rate, the client exercises his option (anything over $1.62), to sell the full amount of $5 million.

2. If the dollar strengthens to anywhere below the 1.6200 cap rate, the bank will exercise the option they have bought from the customer, also at 1.6200. This option has a principal amount of $3.167 million which leaves the client a balance of $1.833 million which needs to be sold spot. In practical terms 63 per cent of the transaction amount is locked in at $1.62, while the rest can be sold spot at whatever is the best rate in the market.

A zero-cost structure of this type allows the client more flexibility, especially where he believes there is likely to be a large movement of the currency, as part of the principal amount will always need to be sold spot.

Practical considerations

The most effective collar options are written when the option purchased by the client has a strike price OTM compared with the outright forward, and where both the options are European style. This is because the customer must be absolutely sure that he has the underlying currency, should the bank exercise the option they have bought from him. At least if both options are European there is no danger of the customer exercising, and then the bank asks to exercise their option some days later when the dollars in this example have already been converted into sterling at an earlier date. This structure is not advisable for uncertain or seasonal cash flows.

As this strategy involves the client writing an option to the bank, the risk is similar to that of a forward foreign exchange deal, and a forward line or treasury derivatives credit line will be required.

Minimum amounts on these zero-cost structures will vary; with collars the minimum amount is likely to be around US$500,000 or equivalent. For participating forwards, the amounts are higher, as the second option is only a proportion of the underlying principal. The minimum is likely to be about US$750,000, but check with the banks. It is not necessary for both options to be transacted by the same bank. It is perfectly feasible to buy one option from one bank, and sell the other to another bank. Care must be taken with lines and internal dealing mandates.

It is an interesting discussion point whether companies who are not allowed to sell 'naked' options outright to a bank (as a speculator) will be allowed to transact a collar structure which is a hedge with a lower all-in cost. Both positions involve selling options – one to speculate, the other for reduced cost risk management.

As with the interest rate derivatives, where options are concerned, there are a wealth of different names for the same thing. Reduced premium structures can also be known as:

- zero- (or reduced) cost collars
- zero- (or reduced) cost cylinders
- range forwards.

Setting up a facility with a bank

What does a potential user of OTC currency options need to do before he can pick up the telephone and deal?

A client will need to set up credit lines with one of his banks. If he always wishes to purchase options, his only responsibility will be to pay the premium, in that case the credit risk to the bank is minimal. If sometimes he may want to sell options, the risk assessment is more complicated, but is generally regarded as being similar to the risk on forward foreign exchange. A good rule of thumb is that if you have a forward line with the bank, they will almost certainly let you sell options to them. If you are able to trade only in the spot market with them, they might specify they will only sell options to you, not buy them from you.

Not all banks will offer a service in every possible pair of currencies, so shop around and ensure that the banks with which you deal will be able to cater for all your requirements. If, from time to time, you need to cover an exotic pair of currencies, see if they will be able to help.

There are many banks making prices in the market, so make sure you are getting competitive quotes; either ask two banks to quote for the business, or check with brokers or information screens.

Realistically, the minimum deal size for a good price is about US$500,000 or equivalent; anything smaller than this, and the banks may charge an extra premium.

Make sure that you understand the documentation; if not, ask the bank to send someone to explain it to you.

Once the option facility is established, and there are deals on the book, be careful of exercising early. If a client buys an American-style option, he has the possibility of exercising the option early, and physically delivering or paying the currency early. If he does this he will lose any remaining time value, but will gain the intrinsic value. If the option is sold back, the sell-back premium will include intrinsic value and any remaining time value.

SIMPLE EXOTIC STRUCTURES

A. Bermudan options

These are options where the buyer has the ability to exercise on selected dates rather then, any date (American style) or only on the expiry date (European style).

B. Asian option

This is an option where the buyer will choose whether to exercise or not based on the average rate over a period, rather than the rate on the expiry date only. These are typically cheaper than European-style options as the volatility component is smoothed.

C. Barrier options – e.g. knock-ins

Knock-ins

i. Up and in

If the market goes up and reaches a pre-set trigger point, the option appears.

Up and in   Example

Consider a knock-in call option with a strike price of EUR 100 and a knock-in barrier at EUR 110. Assume the option was purchased when the underlying was at EUR 90. One of two things will happen:

(a) If the option expires with the underlying at EUR 103, but the underlying at no time reached the barrier level of EUR 110 during its' life of the option, the option would expire worthless.

(b) If, on the other hand, if the underlying first rose to the EUR 110 barrier, this would cause the original option to knock-in (with a strike at 100). It would then be worth EUR 3 when it expired with the underlying at EUR103.

---

ii. Down and in

If the market goes down and reaches a pre-set trigger point, the option will disappear (terminate)

Down and in   Example

Consider a put option with a strike of EUR 100 and a knock-in barrier at EUR 90, assume the option was purchased when the underlying was 110. One of two things will happen:

(a) If the option expires with the underlying at 96, but at no time did it reach 90, the option will expire worthless.

(b) If the underlying fell to 90, the option knocks-in (with a strike of 100). It will then be worth EUR 4 when it expires with the underlying is at 96.

Knock-in options reduce potential upside from large moves and are cheaper to purchase as there is a chance that the trigger will not be reached.

Knock-out options disappear when a pre-set trigger point is reached.

CURRENCY SWAPS

Introduction

The currency swap market developed in the early 1960s in the UK, and was originally used as a means of avoiding exchange controls. When the Exchange Control Act was abolished in 1979, it did little to affect the growth in these instruments. The currency swap that we are familiar with today has grown out of the two techniques known as parallel loans and back-to-back loans.

Parallel and back-to-back loans

A US multinational company might need sterling for its UK subsidiary, and a large UK company may have surplus sterling but need dollars for its US operations. With the parallel loan, each company would lend the other equivalent amounts in each currency for the same maturity. Figure 10.18 shows that in the UK, the UK company will lend £10 million to the US company and receive in return 5 per cent interest per annum. In contrast, in the USA, the US company will lend US$16 million to the UK company and receive 3 per cent fixed per annum. The rate of exchange used is £/US$1.60.

There were a number of problems with this arrangement, mostly concerned with securing an adequate right of set-off in the event of default by one of the parties, and the complex documentation involved.

| Figure 10.18 | Parallel loans |

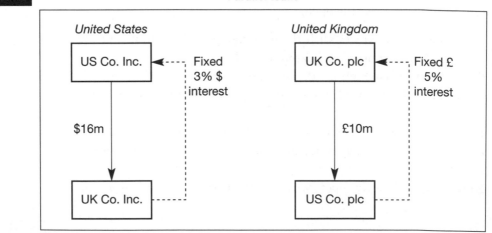

The currency swap that we are familiar with has grown out of the two techniques known as parallel loans and back-to-back loans.

The back-to-back loan (see Figure 10.19) was then introduced to try to overcome some of the obstacles and to simplify the structure. This newer structure was only partly successful, but it was some time before the currency swap was developed in the 1970s, incorporating the best features of both parallel and back-to-back loans (see Figure 10.20). In 1981 the World Bank did a highly publicized currency swap with IBM which ensured that the currency swap became respectable. Since then the market has grown, although it is still considerably smaller than that for single currency interest rate swaps. As at December 2005, the outstanding amounts were US$8.50 trillion, for currency swaps, against US$172.869 trillion, for interest rate swaps (*source: Bank for International Settlements*). The reasons why the growth of the currency swap market has been much slower centres upon the following points:

- Currency swaps involve an exchange of 100 per cent of principal, resulting in a much higher credit risk weighting. Their uses are very much confined to currency hedging, rather than speculation.

- Higher capital requirements have been imposed on currency swaps than interest rate swaps.

- There is less liquidity in the currency swap market so a bank would find it harder to hedge its positions.

Back-to-back loan

Figure 10.19

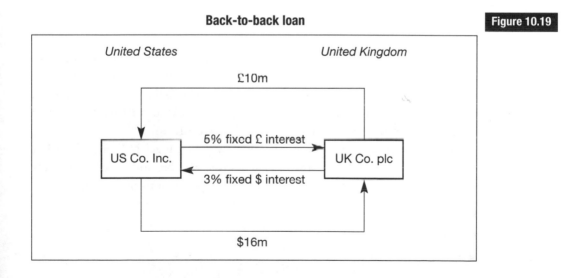

Figure 10.20 **Currency swap**

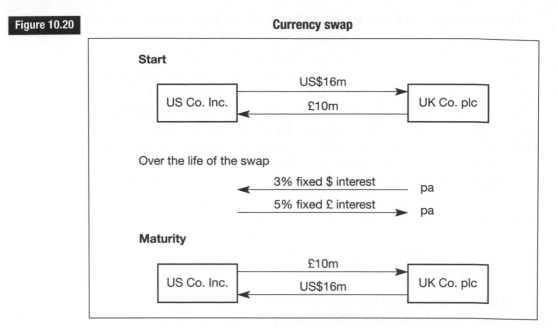

Definition

A currency swap is an agreement between two or more parties to exchange interest obligations/receipts, for an agreed period, between two different currencies, and at the end of the period to re-exchange the corresponding principal amounts, at an exchange rate agreed at the beginning of the transaction.

Definition discussed

Currency swaps differ from interest rate swaps in that they involve an exchange of interest in two currencies, and also involve an exchange of principal amounts. They therefore impinge on the balance sheets of each counterparty. As a result, currency swaps are used almost exclusively to hedge a risk, rather than to trade a speculative position.

Like an interest rate swap, a currency swap is a legal obligation, and at the outset each party has to agree what its role will be, and on what interest basis it will pay and receive. There are three types of currency swap:

- fixed/fixed
- fixed/floating
- floating/floating.

The interest rates are determined in advance, either as a fixed rate, e.g. 10 per cent per annum, or a specified floating rate such as six-month dollar LIBOR. At maturity the two counterparties will exchange the principal amounts. The exchange rate used is set at the beginning of the transaction.

Dragon Bank, a UK bank, wishes to enter into a commitment to exchange US$80 million for sterling in three years' time. This deal is rather large for a traditional forward contract, and so Dragon Bank is looking at using currency swaps. Bank Georgia is prepared to take the other side of the swap.

The sequence of activities will be:

(1) Over a period of three years Dragon Bank to pay Bank Georgia (a US Bank – the swap counterparty) a stream of US dollar interest on US$80 million. The interest payments will be at a rate agreed at the outset.

(2) Also over three years, Bank Georgia pays to Dragon Bank a stream of sterling interest on £50 million, at an interest rate agreed at the outset.

(3) Dragon Bank and Bank Georgia to exchange at the end of the period the principal amounts of US$80 million and £50 million on which interest payments are being made. Exchange rate also agreed at the outset as £/US$1.60 (see Figure 10.21).

Principal and interest obligations

Figure 10.21

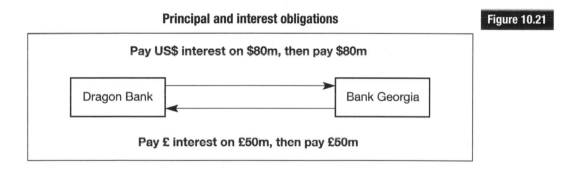

Cash flows on the swap with no initial exchange

If there had been an initial exchange, each counterparty would borrow their home currency and then enter into a spot deal with the other party to convert it into the counter currency (see Figure 10.22).

Figure 10.22   **Cash flows on a currency swap**

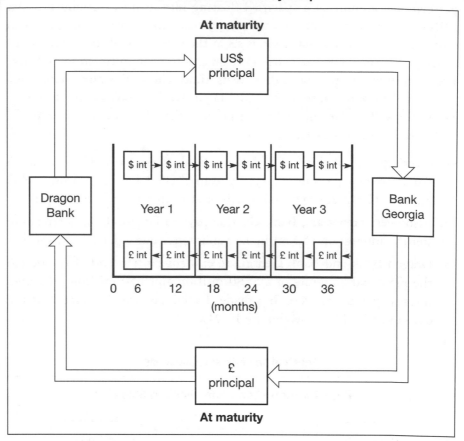

Key features   Maturity
A currency swap provides a simpler, more liquid solution to long-term
FX exposure than can be provided through conventional foreign exchange
markets.

Size
Large amounts can be accommodated within one transaction avoiding the
need for repeated recourse to the markets.

Confidentiality
Identities of swap participants need not be revealed in the market.

Bypass mechanism
Currency swaps can be used to bypass exchange controls (where they still
exist) and help clients gain access to restricted markets.

Key features
continued

New or existing obligations
It is possible to swap new or existing commitments.

Initial/final exchange of principal
Principal amounts can be exchanged at the start of a currency swap.

This is normally where the swap is associated with a new borrowing, or where one of the counterparties needs the principal amount of one of the currencies being swapped.

A swap with an initial exchange, using the previous example, would need Dragon Bank to sell the sterling spot for dollars to Bank Georgia. The exchange rate does not need to be exactly the spot rate and is often rounded to the nearest 'big figure' (e.g. $1.5997 becomes $1.60). The sterling sold spot by Dragon Bank initially would be borrowed by them specifically for swapping into the dollars, and vice versa. At maturity there would be a re-exchange of currencies at the original exchange rate.

The sterling principal repaid to Dragon Bank by Bank Georgia would be used to repay the sterling borrowing, and the sterling interest received during the swap will be used to service the debt repayments on the loan. The borrowings which are taken out to fund the initial exchange are separate from the swap itself. Where a swap has initial as well as final exchange, the credit risk is substantially reduced.

True derivatives?

A currency swap is not a true derivative as it will always involve a final exchange of principal. Market convention, however, deems that it should be treated as one.

Terminology

Currency swap	
Payer	The party wishing to pay the agreed currency.
Receiver	The party wishing to receive the agreed currency.
Swap rate, guaranteed rate	The swap interest rate agreed between the parties at the outset of the transaction.
Rollovers/ resets	The frequency of the LIBOR settlements, e.g. a 2-year Euro swap against 6-month $ LIBOR. Dates when the swap rates are net cash settled. Settlement is in arrears.

Range of swap types

- A traditional currency swap would keep the fixed interest rates constant and simply swap into a different currency (fixed US$ vs fixed yen).
- A cross-currency swap will swap fixed for floating as well as crossing the currency (fixed US$ vs floating sterling). These are also known as cross currency coupon swaps.
- A currency basis swap, will swap two different floating rates in two different currencies (floating sterling vs floating euro).

Occasionally the terms asset and liability swaps are used. These terms merely denote whether the interest flows at the start come from an asset or a liability.

Liquidity considerations

There is less liquidity in currency swaps than in interest rate swaps, and because of this, it is sometimes necessary to go through a third intervening swap, usually a fixed/floating US dollar swap, to end up at the interest and currency basis required by both parties. These multi-legged swaps are sometimes known as cocktail swaps, or tripartite swaps.

In Figure 10.23, the bank is trying to hedge a swap in yen and dollars that it has just undertaken with client A. The only way it can protect itself is to use another yen/dollar swap for the correct maturity from the inter-bank market, but this is matched only on the yen side not on the dollar side. So an intervening fixed/floating dollar swap is installed with another swap bank in the inter-bank market.

Figure 10.23	Tripartite swap

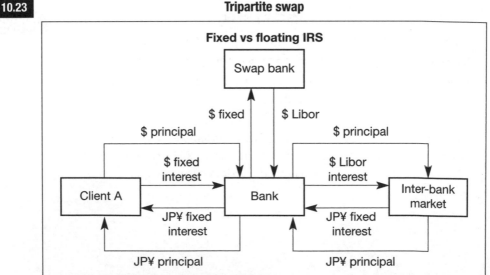

Currency swap quotations

It is banking practice for the 6-month US$ LIBOR to be the standard index for the floating rate, in both cross-currency coupon swaps, and cross-currency basis swaps. Given the complexity of currency swaps with their interest payments in various bases in one currency and their principal repayments in another, care must be taken when asking for prices. It is a good idea to specify both sides of the deal, for example: 'I wish to pay 6-month yen LIBOR against 5-year fixed dollars'. Then there can be no confusion.

Currency swaps are generally quoted as inclusive prices, e.g. 5.18 to 5.28 per cent: on one side the client is a payer, and on the other side he receives, but what exactly?

- Cross-currency coupon swaps – paying and receiving refer to the fixed rate, the floating rate is assumed to be 6-month dollar LIBOR.
- Currency basis swaps – both sides of the swap need to be identified.
- Fixed vs fixed currency swaps – both sides of the swap must be specified.

Hedging with a fixed/floating currency swap

A UK communications company with mostly sterling revenues has borrowed fixed rate dollars to finance the purchase of plant and machinery from the USA. It expects the dollar to appreciate, owing to sustained interest rate rises. But an increase in the value of the dollar would increase the amount of sterling required to repay the original loan. The sterling equivalent cost of interest payments may also increase. A currency swap is being considered. The swap would fix the rate at maturity where the UK company could exchange sterling revenues for the dollars needed to repay the borrowings. This would hedge the exchange risk. The communications company also believe that sterling interest rates may fall, but not by very much. Consequently they could, through the swap, take a view on their own domestic interest rates as well as hedge their currency risk. They could swap from the fixed rate dollars needed to repay the dollar loan into floating rate sterling. This would be described as a cross-currency coupon swap. It does, however, open the company up to an interest rate risk, an element of speculation. The simplest structure will not involve an initial exchange of principal and in any case the original borrowing was taken out years ago. The UK communications company will contact their swap bank and they will:

- Fix the currency rate at which the principal will be exchanged at maturity (probably the spot rate).
- Agree the interest rates for the swap.

The UK communications company will pay a stream of sterling floating rate interest and receive a stream of fixed dollars from the swap counter-party. The dollar interest received will be used to service the underlying dollar borrowings. The sterling interest paid on the swap will come from UK earnings, and will reduce if LIBOR rates fall.

At maturity, the UK company will pay a sterling principal amount through the swap and receive in return a dollar principal amount. The exchange rate used for the conversion will be the one both parties agreed to at the outset. The UK company will fund the payment of sterling principal from accumulated sterling earnings, and will use the dollars it receives to repay the original dollar borrowings (see Figure 10.24).

Figure 10.24	Example: currency swap cash flows

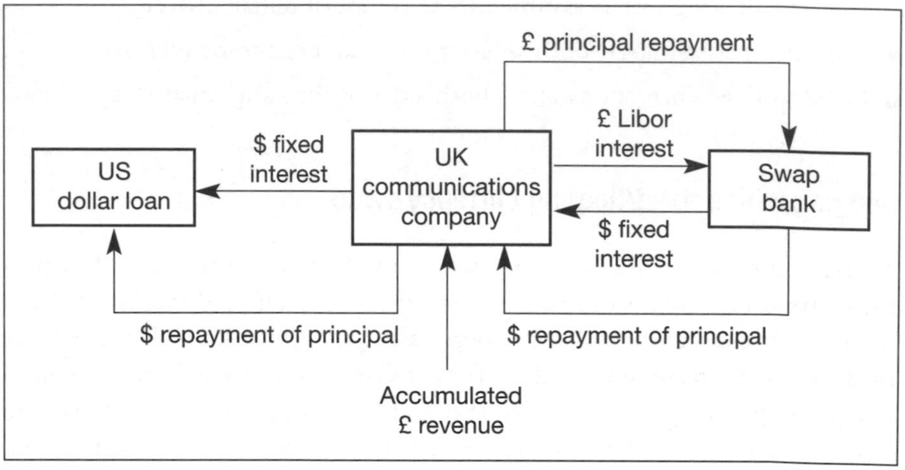

Both currency swaps and forward foreign exchange allow a hedger to pro-tect himself against future movements in exchange rates. The instruments are similar, and both take account of interest rate differentials, but do so in different ways.

Comparison of currency swaps and forward foreign exchange

Consider a company, Corporate X, which wishes to sell forward US$16 mil-lion for sterling. A currency swap will involve throughout its maturity an exchange of streams of dollar and sterling interest, and then finally at matu-rity, the exchange of principal of, say, $16 million and £10 million, corresponding to an exchange rate of $1.60. Under the currency swap treat-ment we would see the flows illustrated in Figure 10.25.

Currency swap cash flows

Figure 10.25

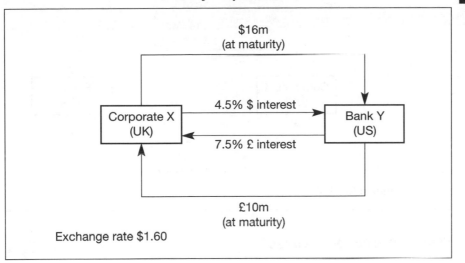

The swap

- Involves exchange of interest and principal.
- The exchange of principal takes place at a rate agreed at the start of the swap, usually (but not always) the spot rate.

Outright forwards

With an outright forward deal the interest rate differential is accounted for in a different way, by including the difference in the currency conversion rate.

- No interest amounts are exchanged, only principal.
- The exchange of principal amounts takes place at maturity, but at a rate different from the spot rate.

In our example the forward rate of $1.4749 would mean that at maturity, the principal amounts would be £10 million and $14.751 million. This would compensate for the lack of interest flows during the life of the deal (see Figure 10.26). The implied forward points for the deal are:

$1.6000 – $1.4749 = 0.1251

If the cash flows were to be compared between the swap and the outright forward, they would equate to the same thing. The two instruments have equal net present values. A normal yield to maturity rate is used to discount the cash flows on the swap, but a zero-coupon interest rate is used for the outright forward. In summary, outright forward deals reflect the interest differential in the FX rate, whereas with currency swaps there is an exchange of interest cash flows and the FX rate is untouched.

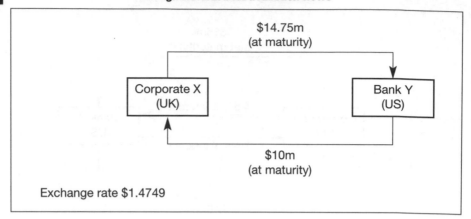

Figure 10.26

Outright forward FX deal cash flows

$14.75m
(at maturity)

Corporate X
(UK)

Bank Y
(US)

$10m
(at maturity)

Exchange rate $1.4749

When to use currency swaps

Currency swaps can be used to hedge foreign exchange risk, and on occasions allow the client to take a view on the strength or weakness of his own domestic currency. However, as we have already seen, the over-riding rule of when to use swaps is that both counterparties (and the bank) should be in a better position after the swap. It follows, then, that there are circumstances when a currency swap should not be contemplated. These are:

■ When the existing currency of a foreign currency liability is expected to depreciate. This would reduce the amount of domestic currency required to repay the liability, which is a good thing.

■ When the existing currency of a foreign currency asset is expected to appreciate. This would increase the domestic currency value of the asset, also good.

■ When the currency into which the liability is to be swapped is expected to appreciate. This would increase the amount of domestic currency required to repay the liability, which is to be avoided.

■ The currency into which an asset is to be swapped is expected to depreciate. This would reduce the domestic currency value of the asset, also to be avoided.

Availability

Currency swaps are available in most major currencies and some cross-currencies, in minimum amounts of £5 million or US$5 million (or equivalent). Smaller amounts may be available on request, but there will be a price to pay included in the swap rate. Periods of up to 15 years are possible, but due to the heavy nature of the credit risk, the majority of deals are transacted for seven years and under.

Practical considerations

Any counterparty can deal in a currency swap, subject to credit considerations. Unfortunately, the credit risk on these deals includes not only the possible interest rate movements, as in interest rate swaps, but also the potential movement between the two currency exchange rates for entire maturity. The risk to the counterparty bank is therefore very much higher. The credit department of the swap bank will need to assess its counterparty risk with the client. They will need to consider the maturity and amount of any swaps the client may wish to execute, and may even specify a terminal maturity, say, nothing longer than seven years. Dealing lines and credit lines must be set up in advance.

In addition to credit lines, the documentation is quite onerous for those dealing with swaps for the first time. The market has adopted the International Swaps and Derivatives Association (ISDA) document, which is a master agreement that must be set up in advance of the first deal. This is not a precondition as such, but the documentation is quite long, and company lawyers and solicitors may need to spend some time examining the main document. All swap deals are dealt 'subject to docs': if the documentation cannot be agreed within a fairly short period, the swap will be cancelled.

Within the swap itself, the rollover frequency can be monthly, quarterly, semi-annual or annual. It is not necessary for the fixed and floating payments to be paid on the same day, but the client must specify the frequency of all interest payments at the time of dealing. Each swap price will factor in the payment frequency, and the swap rates will be different to reflect this.

There are a number of currency swap providers in the market, but not nearly as many as in the interest rate swap market. As a consequence, swap counterparties may be harder to find, and the product is certainly less liquid.

EXCHANGE-TRADED INSTRUMENTS

Foreign exchange futures

With respect to exchange-traded products, the instrument which is having a re-birth at the moment is the FX future. The FX future was originally developed in 1972 and was one of the first ever financial futures contracts. However, the traditional FX markets are so deep and so liquid that the FX future never really took a large market share as most participants stayed in the market they knew well – the OTC Spot and Forward FX markets.

In the last few years as profit margins in FX are squeezed and additional liquidity is sought, market participants have started to look again at FX futures. As most FX business is transacted in the Spot market and futures always have a delivery date in the future (similar to a forward contract) there always appeared to be a mis-match. However, the Chicago Mercantile Exchange (CME) developed a way of trading FX futures which were linked to Spot FX – the CME made it easy to remove the forward points – thus it became equivalent to a Spot FX contract, at least if you bought and sold during the contract period and did not go to delivery. It is known as the CME E-quivalent® contract.

Table 10.5

Simplified contract specification for CME British pound future

CME® British pound futures	
Trade Unit	62,500 pounds sterling (British pounds)
Point Descriptions	1 point = $.0001 per pound sterling = $6.25 per contract
Contract Listing	Six months in the March Quarterly Cycle Mar, Jun, Sep, Dec.
Trading venue: Floor	
Hours	7:20 a.m.–2:00 p.m.
Listed	All listed series
Limits	No limits
Minimum Fluctuation	Regular 0.0001 = $6.25
	Calendar spread 0.0001 = $6.25
	All or none 0.0001 = $6.25
Trading venue: CME® Globex®	
Hours	Mon/Thur 5:00 p.m.4:00 p.m.; Sun & Hol 5:00 p.m.-4:00 p.m.
Listed	All listed series plus 3 calendar spreads
Strike	N/A
Limits	No limits
Minimum Fluctuation	Regular 0.0001 = $6.25
	Calendar spread 0.0001 = $6.25

Source: CME®

The contract specification shows the trading times for both floor trading and via Globex® which is their electronic platform. Volumes increased by 65 per cent in 2005 as this contract became popular.

The spot equivalent contract, known as the E-quivalent®, is traded on-line and can be found at www.cme.com/e-quivalents (see Figure 10.27).

CME® E-quivalents®

Figure 10.27

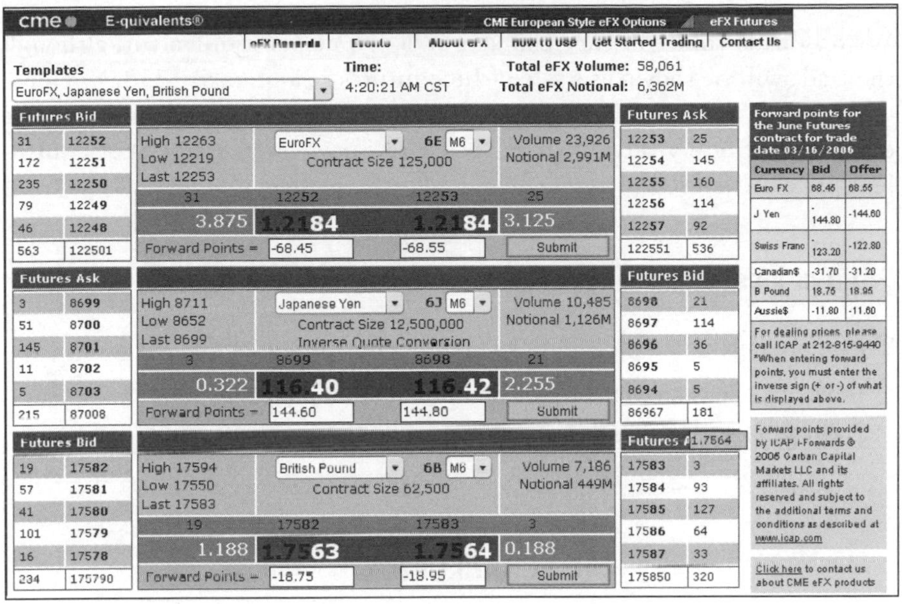

Source: CME®

At the bottom of Figure 10.27 you can see the British pound contract – the other currency is assumed to be the US dollar. With this contract, the contract size is equivalent to £62,500, and when this screen was printed GBP/USD was quoted at a spot equivalent rate of 1.7563–64. On the far right-hand side there is a table of forward points. Data is for the next deliverable month, which is the June delivery date. The forward points for June are shown 18.75–18.95, meaning 0.001875–0.001895, and as US interest rates are currently higher than sterling rates these points are added to create the forward price. But as we are looking for the spot equivalent, we need to remove them to be left with spot rate. At the bottom of Figure 9.27 you can see they are shown with a negative sign to remove them from the quotation.

Although you would be buying or selling the June future – you are effectively trading spot if you remove the forward points.

Trading with FX futures, 16th March

Example

My view: USD will strengthen, GBP will weaken.

Strategy: We need to sell GBP futures contracts – assume 100 contracts, equivalent to £6.25 million. If USD strengthens, one pound will buy less USD and the exchange rate will become numerically smaller. We are looking for the rate to fall towards GBP/USD 1.7300 or below. We will need to put up margin for collateral and be marked-to-market every day (see Chapter on Financial Futures for more information).

Outcome – 20th March

We originally sold 100 June contacts at 1.7563 (spot e-quivalent, although the trade will be shown as a sale of June futures at a price of 17582).

Although we could hold these contracts until June, we decide to close out the position by buying them back a few days later, at the spot equivalent price of 1.7480.

Profit or loss?

This represents a profit of 83 ticks (1.7563 minus 1.74880).

Profit of 83 ticks on each of 100 contracts at $6.25 per point

= $51,875.00 profit

CONCLUSION

In my opinion FX futures are a valuable tool to enhance liquidity and the ability to trade Spot FX.

QUIZ

Questions

1. You believe that the USD will strengthen against GBP in the next 3 months. Will you buy a call or a put on GBP?
2. You have been quoted 1.15% for the premium on a 6-month, $5 million call option against GBP. Spot rate is £1.7500, forward rate is 1.7510. What is the amount of premium in sterling and when must it be paid?
3. Would you sell a straddle when you thought volatility was going up or going down?
4. If you were an exporter of goods to the USA and were going to be paid in USD in 3 months' time and the dollar was expected to appreciate, is this good or bad? Would you want to hedge with an option or a forward contract?

Answers

1. Put on GBP, call on USD.

2. £32,857.14, paid value spot – 2 business days. $57,500 divide by $1.7500

3. Going down.

4. Good, as the dollars will be worth more when they arrive. You would need to hedge with an option to benefit from an up-side move. A forward contract will merely give you a fixed rate.

'Firstly, how does "the market" move? Secondly, how do the individual shares that make up the market move? Derivatives are available to cover both alternatives.'

■ ■ ■

11

Equity Derivatives

Introduction

Background

Single stocks or equity indices?

Stock index futures

Stock index options

Single stock options

Equity index swaps

INTRODUCTION

The derivatives that are used to hedge against equity risk or to speculate upon it are the same as the derivatives that we have studied in previous chapters. There are only three classifications of derivatives: futures, options and swaps. When we apply these techniques to equity the results are:

- stock index futures, universal stock futures
- options on stock index futures or options on single stocks
- equity index swaps or single stock equity swaps.

Equity derivatives can be exchange traded or OTC, with exchange traded futures and options making up the majority of transactions. OTC equity swaps are a very important part of this market, gaining in popularity all the time. However, credit risk is very different with OTC equity products such as equity swaps and options, as we shall see later. Many OTC equity derivatives deals are proprietary. The only gauge we have of the scope of general OTC equity derivative activity is from the BIS survey, which shows that notional amounts have increased from US$3.7 trillion to US$5.1 trillion in 18 months (as at 2005).

BACKGROUND

When people discuss equity, they generally mean stocks and shares. In the UK we talk about owning shares in a company, and in the USA we refer to common stock. An equity investor is participating more fully in the risks of that business than any other type of investor in the same company. This is because a rate of return is not guaranteed to the equity investor, neither is there a maturity date for the investment or a fixed redemption amount. Should the company experience difficult trading conditions and not make the expected profit, there will be no share of the profits for the investor. The income that the equity investor receives is known as the dividend, and it can be as high or as low as company fortunes permit. Some years there may be no payment at all. To counter these perceived disadvantages, the investor is allowed to vote at company meetings on matters of policy and also to have a say in electing the board of directors. Never forget that the owners of the business are the shareholders, but the controllers of the business are the board of directors. It is this conflict that can sometimes cause problems, especially when a large block of shares is owned by one person who wants a say in his investment. Really, what he wants is a say in running the company, but unfortunately the board of directors running the company may disagree with him.

When an investor wishes to liquidate his holdings in a company he must sell his shares in the secondary market, as there is no redemption date. At the time of the sale, the market share price can be anywhere, and will react to supply and demand. The efficiency of the secondary market is paramount, as investors must be confident that they can sell or buy shares at any time.

There is another important difference between equity and the other underlying primary markets that we have examined so far. With equity the cash market is a lot less liquid. Consider the global equity market; this is split into equity in different countries, denominated in different currencies. Within each country there are different sectors, with many different companies in each sector. If an investor is trying to hedge against a movement in a stock with equity options, the bank writing the option could have problems in hedging its own position, especially if the transaction size is large. They may need to buy or sell quantities of stock for the hedge position, at times when the market may be very tight and illiquid. Contrast this with, say, dollar/yen currency options; the inter-bank market world-wide will make prices in spot dollar/yen, liquidity will never be a problem. But how many market makers are there in an individual share, in a particular country? The answer must be a lot less.

SINGLE STOCKS OR EQUITY INDICES?

When you examine equity risk further, it can be subdivided into two sections. First, how does 'the market' move? Secondly, how do the individual shares that make up the market move? Derivatives are available to cover both alternatives. As we have already discussed, an individual company may be in distress and its share price may fall, but the stock market as a whole may be increasing in value. This is an important point. Are we looking to hedge or speculate on the 'market' or on an individual equity? The answer lies in the different motivations of the user.

A portfolio manager holds a number of different stocks and will generally be more concerned about the performance of them as a group, than about how a single one of them performs – although he would always hope that the individual share prices will increase too. To counteract the effect of a single share performing badly, the portfolio manager will need to have a diversified portfolio of different stocks that are unrelated. If one stock goes down another may go up. Generally about 60 per cent of the risk that affects individual shares relative to the index can be eliminated with about ten reasonably uncorrelated stocks. If the number of stocks in the portfolio is raised to 20, all but 10 per cent of this risk can be removed (see Figure 11.1).

| Figure 11.1 | Systematic and unsystematic portfolio risk |

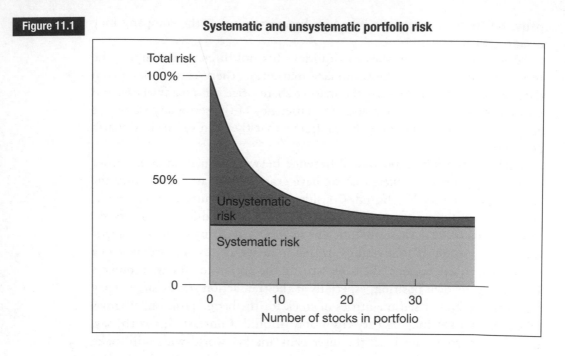

This type of derivatives user will prefer to hedge or to speculate on the performance of an index which contains many shares.

A private client may well hold substantial amounts of single stocks, and be concerned about how those stocks perform individually. He will then be looking to use derivatives on that particular stock, either using an exchange-traded option if available or by using OTC products such as swaps or options.

Futures

A hedger looking to protect himself from a fall or a trader looking to profit from a movement in the stock market can use futures on the appropriate index, e.g. FT-SE 100 or S&P 500®. A single stock hedger or trader will use Universal Stock Futures (USF), however, not every company has a specific USF.

Options

There are exchange-traded options on most of the indices (options on futures), and also options on some single stocks, although each exchange will offer a different selection. If a client needs an option on a company where there is no option quoted on the exchange, he will be compelled to go to one of the OTC providers in the market.

Swaps

Equity swaps are by definition an OTC derivative, and can be completely tailored to the specific requirements of the client. Equity swaps can be constructed with stock indices and individual shares against a LIBOR interest rate.

Equity indices

A stock index tracks the changing price of a hypothetical portfolio of stocks. It is used to measure a stock market's performance. The price of each stock is weighted by the stock's market capitalization. This 'value weighted' approach means that movements in stocks with large market capitalizations can have a disproportionately large impact on the index. This is important for two reasons. First, movements in the index will mirror changes in the market portfolio. Secondly, a portfolio can be constructed to match the index and 'index track' it.

There are four main market indices used in the UK:

1. FT Ordinary Share Index (or FT 30)

Based on 30 actively and highly capitalized companies representing British industry. It is calculated on a real-time basis while the market is open.

2. FT Actuaries All Share Index (FTA)

A weighted arithmetic index, used to create a benchmark for measuring the performance of a market portfolio.

3. FT-SE 100 (Footsie)

Used to support the FT-SE 100 future. A weighted arithmetic index based on the top 100 UK companies by market capitalization. The component shares are reviewed quarterly. This index covers about 65 per cent of the FT Actuaries All Share Index.

4. FT-SE 250 (the Mid-Cap)

Introduced to support the FT-SE 250 future, comprising the next largest 250 companies by market capitalization.

In the USA there is a range of market indices but the three main ones are as follows:

1. The Dow Jones Index

Equivalent to the FT 30 index, it is un-weighted but calculated arithmetically.

2. The S&P 500®

Equivalent to the FTA, based on the 500 major stocks listed on the New York Stock Exchange (NYSE). It includes 400 industrials, 40 utilities, 20 transportation companies and 40 financial institutions. This index accounts for nearly 80 per cent of the total market capitalization on the NYSE.

3. The NASDAQ 100 Index

Mostly technology and non-financial shares; the 100-share index was launched in 1985, with a base of 250.

Each index has its own characteristics; some assume that stock dividends are re-invested and the value of the index is adjusted accordingly; others do not. For example, the DAX index, which is the German market index, covering 30 stocks, assumes that dividends are re-invested, but in neither the FT-SE 100 nor the American indices does this occur. Table 11.1 lists the major global equity indices.

Table 11.1   **Major global equity indices**

Country	Name	Stock Exchange	Level in Mar 06
Americas			
Argentina	MerVal	Beunos Aires	1804
Brasil	Bovespa	São Paolo	37491
Canada	S&P TSX Composite	Toronto	12190
Chile	IPSA	Santiago	2190
Mexico	IPC	Mexico City	19132
USA	S&P 500	NY	1302
	DJIA	NY	11215
	NASDAQ	NY	2337
Asia/Pacific			
Australia	ASX All Ordinaries	Sydney	5071
China	Shanghai Composite	Shanghai	1294
Hong Kong	Hang Seng	Hong Kong	15880
India	BSE 30	Mumbai/Bombay	11307
Indonesia	Jakarta Composite	Jakarta	1322
Japan	Nikkei 225	Tokyo	17045
Malaysia	KLSE Composite	Kuala Lumpur	926
New Zealand	NZSE 50	Wellington	3695
Pakistan	Karachi 100	Karachi	11620
Phillipines	PSE Composite	Manilla	2180
Singapore	Straits Times	Singapore	2521
South Korea	KOSPI Composite	Seoul	1338
Sri Lanka	All Share	Columbo	2250
Thialand	SET	Bangkok	730
Taiwan	Taiwan Weighted	Taipei	6546

Europe				Table 11.1 continued
Austria	ATX	Vienna	4096	
Belgium	Bel 20	Brussels	3920	
Czech Republic	PX50	Prague	1528	
Denmark	OMXC 20	Copenhagen	391	
France	CAC 40	Paris	5212	
Germany	DAX 30	Frankfurt	5940	
Italy	MIB Tel	Milan	29298	
Netherlands	AEX General	Amsterdam	469	
Norway	OSE All Share	Oslo	456	
Russia	RTS	Moscow	1400	
Slovakia	SAX	Bratislava	412	
Spain	IBEX 35	Madrid	1283	
Sweden	OMX	Stockholm	1063	
Switzerland	SMI	Zurich	8000	
Turkey	ISE	Istanbul	42540	
United Kingdom	FTSE 100	London	5994	
Pan-European	DJ Euro STOXX 50		3518	
	FTSE Eurotop		2914	
	Euronext 100		895	
Africa/Middle East				
Egypt	CASE 30	Cairo	2191	
Israel	TA 100	Tel Aviv	844	

Other equity products – hybrids

Some instruments are unique in having multiple characteristics. The general name given to these types of products is hybrids. For example, a convertible bond starts life as a bond, but when certain pre-determined conditions are satisfied, it can convert into equity. This gives the owner of the bond the chance to move into equity if he so desires at a later date. A preference share pays a level of guaranteed dividend, resembling a bond structure. It is also easy to embed equity derivatives into, for example, Eurobonds, providing an 'equity kicker'. These products, together with warrants, rights issues and convertibles, fall outside the scope of this book.

STOCK INDEX FUTURES

Introduction

Stock index futures started to trade in the early 1980s. The underlying commodity is the basket of shares that make up the index. The index itself conveys information about stock market movements, but says nothing about the relative level of the index. This is because the initial value of the index was chosen arbitrarily.

For the index to be used correctly as a hedging mechanism, it needs to be assigned a monetary value for each point of movement. With the FTSE 100, this value is £10 per full index point or £5.00 per tick (half-point), and with the American S&P 500 index, it is US$250 per full index point. This monetary value is also known as the index multiplier. If the value of the FT-SE 100 on a particular day is 6120, then the 'cash value' of the index is £10 × 6120 which equals £61,200. In simple terms, if you hold a portfolio of shares which exactly matches the FT-SE 100 basket of shares, you will need one future to cover each £61,200 of portfolio. Tomorrow the cash value of the index may have changed, and more or less futures will be required. Consider a fund manager who is managing a portfolio worth £5 million. He will need the following number of futures if he wishes to hedge his position.

$$\frac{5,000,000}{61,200} = 81.70 \text{ futures contracts (round up to 82)}$$

As with all futures contracts it is not possible to trade in a fraction of a contract, so the figure will need to be rounded up or down. On any particular day the formula used to calculate the number of futures for hedging purposes is:

$$\frac{\text{Total value of portfolio}}{\text{FT-SE 100 Index level} \times \text{Index multiplier}}$$

It is not too difficult to choose a basket of shares that corresponds to the FT-SE 100 Index without resorting to having to purchase the exact 100 shares in the index, although there may be an element of 'tracking error'. This occurs when the make up of the index is different, and may not exactly match the movement of the FT-SE 100. For example, assume that the FT-SE 100 is standing today at 6110: if a portfolio manager exactly replicated the FT-SE 100 Index by purchasing the individual shares in the correct weightings, it would cost him approximately £61,100 (excluding transaction costs). The behaviour of this basket of shares would exactly match the performance of the index. If the index moved from 6110 to 6160, the arbitrary cash value of the index would increase from £61,100 to £61,600 and the value of the basket of shares would increase by the same amount. If, on the other hand, the portfolio manager had a basket of shares where most of them matched fairly closely those stocks of the FT-SE, but also included some highly volatile, say, pharmaceutical stocks, then this portfolio will be more volatile than the FT-SE 100. It will outperform the FT-SE 100 on the way up; it will reach a higher figure or make a greater incremental profit. It will also outperform the index on the way down – it will fall further and lose more money.

A stock index future is an agreement between two parties to compensate each other for movements in the value of a stock index over the contract period. The value of the stock index is defined as being the value of the index multiplied by a specific monetary amount (the index multiplier).

Definition

Definition discussed

As with all futures contracts traded on a regulated exchange, there is a contract specification that determines the role of each person in the transaction. Stock index futures do not have the specific contract sizes that are common in other futures contracts. The value of a stock index future will vary from day to day as the FT-SE 100 Index rises and falls.

Index level 6000 – value of one futures contract is £60,000 (6000 × £10)
Index level 6250 – value of one futures contract is £62,500 (6250 × £10)

Example

The future can either be bought or sold; if you believe that the index will fall, you sell the future, if you think the index will rise, you will buy the future. Profits or losses are determined by how many ticks profit is made or lost between the buying and selling prices, and contracts are settled not with the delivery of a basket of shares, but with cash settlement. Less than 2 per cent of futures contracts ever reach delivery or contract expiry; the rest of them are closed out well before.

Index futures contracts

Key features

Market
Futures are traded on a regulated exchange with contract sizes based on market levels and specific delivery dates. Trades are executed by a member firm or broker, physically on the floor of the relevant exchange.

Contracts
In the UK, there are a range of futures contracts, including the FT-SE 100, which covers the top 100 companies by market capitalization, and the Mid-Cap 250 which covers the next 250 companies after the top 100. In the USA, there are various indices, the S&P 500, the Dow Jones etc., and in Japan there is the Nikkei; almost every country has its own index (see Table 11.1).

Pricing
This is a competitive auction-based market, and prices are generally quoted as a bid–offer spread in index points. Once a trade has been executed, the price is then widely disseminated through various information networks, providing world reference levels.

Key features   Market operations

Both buyers and sellers must put up minimum levels of collateral for each open contract that they hold. This is known as initial margin. The actual level is calculated by the relevant exchange and can change if market volatility changes. Initial margin will be returned with interest when the position is closed out. Positions are 'marked-to-market', and profits or losses are crystallized daily. If the position loses money during the day, the losses must be paid that day. If the position is in profit, a payment will be received that day. These daily payments are known as variation margin.

Availability

There are many index futures contracts worldwide, each primarily designed for its own domestic market, for further details, contact the exchange direct.

Cash settlement

At maturity or 'delivery' there will be a cash settlement of the differences, based on the exchange delivery settlement price (EDSP) and the level of the futures contracts. The EDSP is based on the intra-day auction held at the London Stock Exchange on the last trading day of the particular contract. There is no requirement to deliver or take delivery of the underlying physical securities.

Using index futures

To illustrate more clearly how this works, the abbreviated contract specification of the FT-SE 100 future is shown in Table 11.2.

Table 11.2   **FT-SE 100 Index future – contract specification**

Unit of trading	Value at £10 per index point (e.g. value £65,000 at 6500)
Delivery months	March, June, September, December
Delivery day	First business day after the last trading day
Last trading day	As soon as practical after 10.15 (London time) on the third Friday of the delivery month
Quotation	Index points (e.g. 6500)
Minimum price movement	0.5
Tick value	£5.00 per half-tick (£10 per full tick)
Trading hours	08.00 – 17.30 (London time)

Source: Euronext.liffe

What exactly are we trading?

Traders, hedgers and arbitrageurs will buy or sell these futures contracts depending on whether they believe the level of the FT-SE 100 Index will rise or fall.

An index futures trading transaction

It is mid-March, and all the recent economic data suggests that the stock market is about to rally. Today the June FT-SE 100 Index future is quoted at 6555, and the equity trader believes that the market will advance further. She wishes to make a profit from predicting this upward movement in share prices. Her trading amount is a notional £5 million.

Action – 10 March

Buy the required amount of June futures based on the following formula:

$$\frac{\text{Total value of portfolio}}{\text{FT-SE 100 Index level x index multiplier}}$$

Substituting in the numbers:

$$\frac{£5,000,000}{6555 \times £10} = 76.27 \text{ futures contracts (round down to 76)}$$

Outcome

On the third Friday in June, the exchange delivery settlement price (EDSP) on the June FT-SE future is 6735. The position 'will go to delivery', so her position will be marked against the EDSP at 6735.

Profit or loss?

The view on the market was correct and the FT-SE rose. Our trader has made a profit.

Opening FT-SE 100 futures level	6555 (bought)
Closing FT-SE 100 futures level	6735 (sold)
Profit	180 points

What is this profit worth in real money?

The trader has made a profit of

76 contracts × 180 index points × £10.00 each full point

= £136,800

If our trader had put on the same trade, but her view on the market direction was wrong, and the stock market had fallen instead of rallied, she would have lost on the position, as she would have originally bought the futures at the same level of 6555, but she would have then sold them lower down, resulting in a loss.

Market structure and operations

The operation of the equity futures market is identical to other futures markets, the only difference being that the underlying commodity upon which the future is based is different. The transactions take place in a regulated exchange such as Euronext or CME, where the market participants are able to buy or sell the futures contracts as required. Each contract is subject to a contract specification which details the responsibilities of the buyer and the seller. The transactions must be executed through a broker or through a member firm, either on the floor of the exchange or via an electronic platform, such as Globex™. Once the contracts have been sold or bought, the trade is registered and then the contracts will be 'cleared'. At this stage, the clearing house becomes counterparty to both buyer and seller. The different underlying commodity will not prove to be a problem, as these contracts will be 'cash settled'. In effect, the parties will compensate each other for movements of the index. These contracts can also be known as contracts for differences or CFDs. Market practitioners who use equity futures tend to be asset managers, portfolio managers, unit and investment trust managers, as well as pension fund managers, hedge funds and other holders of equity. For further information on futures market structure and operations, see Financial futures contracts in Chapter 5.

Initial and variation margins

As with all futures contracts, initial and variation margins must be paid according to the specific regulations of the exchange. With the LIFFE FT-SE 100 Index future, the initial margin at the time of writing is £1,795.00 per contract for both buyers and sellers. This initial margin must be maintained throughout the open contract position, but is repaid on maturity or close out plus a small level of interest. This initial margin is placed first of all with the broker who is executing the business, and then placed by him with the clearing house on behalf of particular client trades. Most exchanges worldwide operate a 'netting' system, where a client's complete portfolio is evaluated with contracts offsetting each other. The overall margin requirement is then notified to the client. In London the system used is the standard portfolio analysis of risk (SPAN) system – currently working on London SPAN version 4. This was originally developed by the Chicago Mercantile Exchange to monitor how risky a client's position becomes.

	Margin	account (£)

Day 1

Buy 40 DEC FT-SE 100 contracts
at 6430
Initial margin paid @ £1,795 per
contract £71,800
Futures settlement price is 6410
Trading loss = 20 index points
(6430 – 6410)
× 40 contracts × £10 per
point = (£8,000)   £63,800   (Original £71,800 balance less
the £8,000 daily loss)

Margin call £8,000   £71,800   Balance back-up to £71,800 the
from the clearing house   minimum required to support 40
contracts

Day 2

Futures settlement price is 6470
Trading profit = 60 index points
(6470 – 6410)
× 40 contracts × £10 per point
= £24,000   £95,800   Profit of £24,000 added to the
balance on the margin account
This profit can be withdrawn, as
long as the balance does not fall
below that required to support
40 contracts

Day 3

Futures rally further to 6510
Trading profit = 40 index points
(6510 – 6470)
× 40 contracts × £10 per point
= £16,000   £111,800   Profit of £16,000 added to
margin account

Sell 40 contracts at 6510   £111,800   Balance returned to client on
to close out   close out

Total profit on this trade: (–£8000, +£24,000, +£16,000 = £32,000)

In the last example, the trade was profitable. It is possible to ascertain the
final profit/loss on a futures position only at close out, when all the variation
margin payments can be added together to give an overall figure. On days
where the position makes a profit, the balance on the margin account will be
credited with the profit. Technically, the extra monies on the margin account
can be debited by the trader as long as the balance on the margin account
equates to £1,795 per contract of open position. If not, the clearing house

will call for extra margin to support the open position: this is known as a 'margin call'. If the extra margin monies are not forthcoming, the exchange will close out the extra futures contracts that are unsupported by margin.

Example

Hedging with FT-SE 100 Index futures

23 June

A pension fund manager has made some respectable gains over the spring and summer months on his £20 million portfolio of shares. His portfolio matches the FT-SE 100 Index almost exactly, although he only has 40 shares in it. His target for the year is to increase the value of the portfolio by 20 per cent, and so far he has managed 12 per cent with careful stock selection and a general increase in the value of the stock market. Now, market intelligence suggests that the index may be in for a sharp reversal, and he wishes to hold on to his 12 per cent gain so far. He is considering using index futures to protect his profit, and immunize him from further moves in the market up until the end of September.

Assume his market information comes from yesterday's copy of the *Financial Times*. The current level of the FTSE is 6300 and the Sep and Dec futures closed the previous day at 6343 and 6402 respectively (see Table 11.3). He carries out a desk exercise on the deal, assuming a possible 100-point movement in either direction.

23 June – Action

Pension fund manager sells SEP FT-SE 100 futures at 6343, according to the following formula:

$$\frac{\text{Total value of portfolio}}{\text{FT-SE 100 current index level} \times \text{index multiplier}}$$

Substituting the numbers:

$$\frac{£20,000,000}{6300 \times £10} = 317.46 \text{ futures contracts (round to 317)}$$

Table 11.3

Possible extract from the *Financial Times* showing index futures levels

■ **FT-SE 100 INDEX FUTURES** (LIFFE) £10 per full index point

	Open	Sett price	Change	High	Low	Est. vol	Open int.
Sep	6235.0	6343.0	+141.0	6373.0	6231.5	25762	177471
Dec	6325.0	6402.0	+141.0	6404.0	6325.0	522	8093
Mar		6452.0	+141.0			0	1976

■ **FT-SE MID 250 INDEX FUTURES** (LIFFE) £10 per full index point

	Open	Sett price	Change	High	Low	Est. vol	Open int.
Sep		6033.0	+1.0			0	6047
Dec		6073.5	+3.5			0	0

The position will require initial margin of £665,945 as collateral. The fund manager expects to hold the position for three months, so should consider the opportunity loss on the interest of his margin money: for example, could he get a better rate of interest on his deposit elsewhere? Almost certainly.

I. Assuming a 100-point fall in the index

From the current cash level of 6300, giving an EDSP of 6200.

> **Action – 23 June**
> Sell 317 SEP futures at 6343
> **Action – 20 September**
> Buy 317 SEP futures at EDSP of 6200
> Profit = 143 index points (6343 – 6200) × 317 contracts × £10 per
>   point
>   = £453,310, plus the return of the initial margin.

Normally the profit/loss on the position is paid daily. For clarity, these figures assume that the monies are paid in one block on contract delivery.

But is this enough profit on the futures transaction to offset the fall in the value of the physical stocks?

A 100-point move down to 6200 represents a move of 1.58 per cent on the portfolio, a reduction in value from £20,000,000 to £19,684,000, a fall of £316,000. The futures profit more than offsets the loss. This is because the SEP future is already trading away from the cash level at a premium of 6343. This does not mean that the market believes that the FT-SE is going to rally, but reflects the cost of carry on the position – essentially the cost of funding the position less the dividend income from the shares.

II. Assuming a 100-point rise in the index

From the current cash level of 6300, giving an EDSP of 6400.
> **Action – 23 June**
> Sell 317 SEP futures at 6343
> **Action – 20 September**
> Buy 317 SEP futures at EDSP of 6400

Normally the profit/loss on the position is paid daily. For clarity, these figures assume that the monies are paid in one block on contract delivery.

> Loss = 57 index points (6343 – 6400) × 317 contracts × £10 per point
>   = £180,690 plus the initial margin will be returned

The underlying portfolio will increase in value by 100 points or 1.59 per cent, from £20,000,000 to £20,318,000 – a profit of £318,000 – and the futures hedge will lose £180,690. Not such a bad outcome.

Given the overriding concern to protect the 12 per cent increase so far (and his bonus), and given his view that there is a greater probability that the index will fall rather than rise, the pension fund manager decides to hedge using the futures market.

This example illustrates how it is possible to be 'long of the cash market' and 'short of the futures market'. This fund manager cannot sell the stocks in advance of a stock market fall, as then he will have no portfolio to manage. Even if he has the mandate to sell the stocks, he will have to sell them individually, and take into account the transaction costs of selling the physical stock, and selling stock in a falling market is never a good idea. Using futures is especially good where there is expected to be a sharp movement. Why sell the shares today to buy them back two weeks later? In that case, transaction costs will need to be paid twice.

Cash futures relationship

The futures in the example are trading at a premium to the cash market, but are they trading significantly higher or lower than we would expect from ruling market conditions? It is possible to calculate a theoretical or fair futures price (FFP).

Fair futures price = cash index level + net cost of carry
The net cost of carry can be ascertained by:

$$r \times n/365 - (d \times p)$$

where r = funding rate
n = number of days
d = expected annual dividend yield on the FT-SE
p = proportion of the annual dividend paid out during the maturity period of the futures hedge

Using these data, we can infer the following relationship, giving a theoretical value for the futures:

Fair futures price = spot index + cost of funding – dividend income
Assume 3-month LIBOR is 5 per cent and that the futures hedge is going to run from 23 June to 20 September – a total of 89 days. Assume also that the historic yield on the FT-SE 100 is about 3.75 per cent with dividends paid equally throughout the year.

Fair value of the SEP future
Fair futures price = spot index + cost of funding – dividend income
= 6300 + (6300/365 × 0.05 × 89) – (6300 × 0.0375/4)
= 6300 + (76.81 – 59.06)
= 6300 + (17.75)
= 6317.75

It is normally the case that dividend yields on the FT-SE 100 are below money market rates. In this case you would expect the future to trade at a premium relative to the cash market. If the premium is significant, then arbitrageurs will come in and try to profit from the discrepancy. They will buy the stock and short (sell) the futures, rather like our pension fund manager, but he was already long of the stock to start with. In this case, the current futures price of 6343 is trading at a premium of just over 25 points to the theoretical value, making it expensive to buy, but quite a good proposition if you wished to sell. Calculations are based on a 365-day year for FT-SE 100 transactions and a 360-day year for most other indices.

Stock betas

In the example, the portfolio was similar to that of the FT-SE 100 Index and had a close correlation. But consider a portfolio with many volatile recovery stocks. This will almost certainly react differently to changes in market sentiment from a traditional FT-SE portfolio. It will be more volatile, it may be twice or three times as volatile, needing twice or three times the amount of futures to cover it. In these circumstances the stock betas need to be examined to achieve a realistic hedge. These are similar but not identical to a measure of volatility, and indicate how much riskier a stock is compared with the FT-SE 100.

The FT-SE 100 Index has an overall beta of one, and individual shares have their own betas, which can be found through Bridge, Bloomberg and other information providers. Each portfolio needs to have the betas of the individual shares weighted by the amount of the holding and added up to establish the beta of the portfolio. The futures hedge should then be 'beta weighted' to reflect the different volatility inherent in the non-market portfolios.

A fund manager has a portfolio of four shares, with individual betas as shown in Table 11.4.   **Example**

Example: fund manager's portfolio   Table 11.4

Company	Beta	Amount of holding	
Company A	0.96	£2,000,000	
Company B	0.63	£1,500,000	
Company C	1.4	£750,000	
Company D	1.95	£2,250,000	
Total value of portfolio		£6,500,000	=

To calculate the beta of the portfolio:

$$\frac{(0.96 \times 2{,}000{,}000) + (0.63 \times 1{,}500{,}000) + (1.4 \times 750{,}000) + (1.95 \times 2{,}250{,}000)}{6{,}500{,}000}$$

$$= \frac{(1{,}920{,}000 + 945{,}000 + 1{,}050{,}000 + 4{,}387{,}500)}{6{,}500{,}000}$$

$$= 1.27731 \text{ (round to 1.28)}$$

A beta of 1.28 suggests the portfolio is 1.28 times more volatile than the FT-SE 100 Index. To calculate the number of futures required to hedge the position accurately, we need to amend the original formula.

Original formula:

$$\frac{\text{Total value of portfolio}}{\text{FT-SE 100 Index level} \times \text{index multiplier}}$$

Amended formula:

$$\frac{\text{Total value of portfolio} \times \text{portfolio beta}}{\text{FT-SE 100 Index level} \times \text{index multiplier}}$$

(A) Assuming the FT-SE Index still stands at 6300, and using the figures above, if we do not beta weight the hedge, then the number of futures contracts we need are:

Original formula:

$$\frac{\text{Total value of portfolio}}{\text{FT-SE 100 Index level} \times \text{index multiplier}}$$

$$= \frac{6{,}500{,}000}{6300 \times 10} = 103.17 \text{ futures contracts (round to 103)}$$

(B) If we do weight the futures hedge we shall need:

Amended formula:

$$\frac{\text{Total value of portfolio} \times \text{portfolio beta}}{\text{FT-SE 100 Index level} \times \text{index multiplier}}$$

$$= \frac{6{,}500{,}000 \times 1.28}{6300 \times 10}$$

$$= 132.06 \text{ futures contracts (round to 132)}$$

Nearly 30 more futures contracts are required to 'beta-weight the hedge'. This will incur extra initial and variation margin costs, but will offer a tighter hedge. The extra contracts are not taken out for speculative purposes but rather to reflect the increased volatility in the underlying portfolio.

Trading with S&P 500 futures

23 March

A US fund manager is holding a portfolio matching almost exactly the make-up of the S&P 500. He wishes to execute an additional trade to enhance the performance of his portfolio. The present level of the index is, say, 1290, and the index multiplier is US$250 per full index point. The Chicago Mercantile Exchange web page gives historical and live data and shows that the June future closed yesterday at 1314.60 (see Table 11.5).

CME® S&P® 500

Table 11.5

cme® s&p 500® futures
settlement prices as of 03/22/06 07:00 om (cst)

MTH/ STRIKE	OPEN	---- DAILY ---- HIGH	LOW	LAST	SETT	PT CHGE	EST VOL	---- PRIOR DAY ---- SETT	VOL	INT
JUN06	1307.40	1315.90	1304.80	1314.80	1314.60	+710	30K	1307.50	33217	648275
SEPT06	1320.00	1325.90	1317.00A	1325.00A	1325.20	+710	152	1318.10	32	6136
DEC06	- - - -	1335.10B	1326.60A	1334.60B	1335.70	+710		1328.60	4	628
MAR07	- - - -	1345.50B	1337.00A	1345.00B	1346.10	+710		1349.00		55
JUN07	- - - -	1355.90B	1347.40A	1355.40B	1356.50	+710		1349.40		42
SEP07	- - - -	1366.40B	1357.90A	1365.90B	1367.00	+710		1359.90		1
DEC07	- - - -	1376.90B	1368.40A	1376.40B	1377.50	+710		1370.40		2
MAR08	- - - -	1387.40B	1378.90A	1380.30D	1388.00	1710		1380.90		
TOTAL						EST. VOL			VOL	OPEN INT.
TOTAL							30821		33253	655139

Source: CME.com

The fund manager believes that the index could rise as far as 1450 over the next few months, and he wishes for additional profit over and above his existing holding, which will also increase in value if he is right. He wishes to put on a trade in a notional amount of US$5 million. Assume that the initial and variation margins are paid and maintained as specified by the regulations on the exchange.

Action – 20 January

The fund manager needs to calculate how many futures to trade, by using the following formula:

$$\frac{\text{Total value of portfolio}}{\text{S\&P 500 Index level} \times \text{index multiplier}}$$

$$= \frac{5,000,000}{1290 \times \text{US\$250}}$$

= 15.50 futures contracts (round to 16)

If the fund manager thinks the index will rally, he must buy the futures contracts and sell them later, when they are hopefully trading at a higher level. He will need to buy 16 June S&P 500 futures contracts: these are currently trading at 1314.80.

Action – 20 April
The fund manager has experienced a short-term rally with his position, but it looks like the index may now retrace, and the chances of further gains are limited. He decided to close out his position by selling the futures back at the current level of 1398.1.

How much profit has the fund manager made?

Opening level   1314.80 (buy)

Closing level   1398.10 (sell)

Total profit   83.3 index points

In cash terms, a profit of 83.3 index points $\times$ 16 contracts $\times$ US$250 per point value = US$333,200.

NB: This profit excludes costs due to funding the initial margin, brokerage, clearing and other transaction costs.

Availability

Index futures contracts are available world-wide, in many countries and in many currencies covering various domestic indices (different baskets of shares). Each exchange will offer a slightly different range of futures contracts. Should a client wish for an index future based, not on the FT-SE 100 or the S&P 500, but on the client's own specific combination of shares, it is possible to construct the customer's own index or basket of shares that will track his portfolio exactly. This would need to be effected in the OTC market.

Practical considerations

Any potential user of equity futures will need to set up documentation which is market specific and based on the particular exchange where he wishes to trade. For further details on general futures documentation, see Chapter 5.

Initial and variation margins must be posted as required and initial margins can be very expensive. Eventually the initial margin will be returned to the client plus interest, but the interest on the margin deposit is inferior to that obtained elsewhere in the money markets. In some cases it is possible to put up the collateral required in another form, such as shares that are already held or gilts/bonds.

Administration of a futures hedge needs competent people to manage the various daily transfers between accounts. Bank charges may also be significant on each transfer, and combined with the brokerage required for the trade to be executed in the pit, as well as clearing fees, may all erode possible profits.

When the FT-SE 100 Index does not mirror accurately the make-up of the particular portfolio, 'tracking error' will exist. This can be positive or negative, with the basket of shares either outperforming or underperforming the FT-SE 100 Index. Ideally all futures (and options) hedges should be beta weighted to reflect the variety within different types of portfolios.

Universal Stock Futures, which are futures linked to a single share operate in a similar fashion.

STOCK INDEX OPTIONS

Introduction

Both stock index futures and options started to trade in the 1980s. In May 1984 both contracts commenced at LIFFE. The index options that we discuss in this chapter are exchange traded and based on an underlying stock index. In the UK the most widely traded index is the FT-SE 100 basket of shares; in the USA the most widely used index option is based on the S&P 500.

Readers who are unfamiliar with basic option concepts may find it useful to refer to the section on *basic options* in Chapter 4 for background information. As previously discussed, an option contract is the only derivative instrument that allows the buyer (holder) to 'walk away' from his obligations. One of the key principles behind stock index futures and options is cash settlement. This is the process used at expiry (or exercise), whereby cash differences reflecting a price change passes hands, rather than a physical delivery of the underlying basket of shares. As with all option contracts, if the holder of the index option is a hedger with an underlying exposure to the market, he can be considered to have bought insurance against adverse market movements, without the obligation to deal. In contrast, a trader using options to speculate on an index move will have no underlying market exposure. For example, the holder of a call option will be hoping the market will rally so that he can exercise the option and make a profit. This is an important point; hedgers who have bought options can (but not always do) make a profit if they have not needed the option as insurance. Because then the stock index must have moved to favour their underlying position. With a trader who has no underlying position, the option itself needs to become more valuable for him to make a profit.

Unfortunately, options do not come free of charge. A premium is due, usually paid upfront. The option allows a degree of flexibility; it does not completely take away all the risk, i.e. all the losses and all the profit.

Instead it allows a degree of risk management which allows for risk control, not risk removal. Options exhibit 'asymmetry of risk'. The most that an option holder can lose is the original premium that he paid, whereas the amount by which he can profit is unlimited, being governed only by how far the market has moved in his favour. A seller of options, in contrast, can hope to keep only the premium, but the extent of his losses are potentially unlimited. Simplistically, buyers of options have rights, but no obligations, and writers of options have obligations, but no rights.

Definition

A stock index option gives the holder the right, but not the obligation, to buy or sell an agreed amount of an equity index at a specified price, on or before a specified date. A premium is due. The option will be cash settled, unless physical delivery is elected at expiry.

Definition discussed

An index option gives the client, who may be a portfolio manager or equity hedger, the chance to secure the level of the stock market in advance. The holder of the option chooses his own level for the index (the strike), from those specified by the exchange. As this transaction provides a level of insurance that is optional, a premium is required which must be paid upfront to the seller on the business day following the trade. The premium is quoted in 'index points' per contract. With exchange-traded options the premium itself is margined.

Table 11.6 gives the abbreviated contract specification for the FT-SE 100 Index option (European-style exercise).

Most open option positions will be closed out or exercised prior to expiry. Remaining open positions are automatically closed out at the exchange delivery settlement price (EDSP).

Table 11.6 **FT-SE 100 Index option European-style exercise – abbreviated contract specification**

Unit of trading	Valued at £10 per index point (e.g. £65,000 at 6500)
Expiry months	March, June, September, and December plus such additional months that the nearest four months are available for trading
Exercise day	Exercise by 18.00 hrs on the last trading day
Settlement	Settlement is the first business day after the expiry day
Last trading day	As soon as practical after 10.15, third Friday of the expiry month
Quotation	Index points
Minimum price movement	0.5 index points
Tick value	£5.00 (per half-point), £10 per point
Trading hours	08.00 – 16.30 (London time)

Source: Euronext.iiffe

Example

The holder of 25 FT-SE 100 call options at a strike of 5950 wishes to hold his position until expiry. The calls were originally bought at a premium of 35 points, making a total cost of £8,750 (£10 × 25 × 35). The EDSP is calculated at 6024, when the holder will receive a profit of 74 points (6024 – 5950), on each of the 25 contracts at £10 per full point, a total of £18,500. This must be offset against the premium paid, resulting in an overall profit on the deal of £9,750.

Premiums on exchange-traded options are 'margined', and are dealt with in a different manner from OTC option premiums.

Margined premium

Example

(*courtesy of Euronext.liffe*)

Day 1

A fund manager sells two FT-SE 100 Index call options at a premium of 144 index points, a total premium due to him of £2,880 (£10 × 144 × 2). At close of business the option premium is at 142 points.

Day 2

The fund manager will receive £2,880 from the original option sale which will be paid into his LCH account. The clearing house will calculate the profits/losses on the day with the SPAN system. Under the SPAN scenario, the maximum loss on the position is calculated at £270 per contract, a total of £540. The value of the position at close is worth £2,840 (2 × 142 × £10). This amount is known as the net liquidation value or NLV. The total margin liability is, therefore, £2,840 + £540, a sum of £3,380. The margin liability is offset against the premium received leaving a total of £500 to be paid to the clearing house. At close of business the option premium has risen to 148 index points.

Day 3

The fund manager is still short two FT-SE option contracts. The total margin liability due today (for yesterday's movements) will again be calculated by SPAN plus the NLV. SPAN calculates the maximum loss to be £285 per contract, and the NLV is £2,960 (2 × 148 × £10). Total margin liability at close of Day 2 and payable on Day 3 is £3,530 (£2,960 + (2 × £285)). But £500 was paid on Day 2 and LCH is still holding the premium payment of £2,880. The amount due is £3,530 – £500 – £2,880: a balance of £150.

The fund manager closes his position at a level of 142 index points.

Day 4

There will be no margin liability, as LCH will pay the client £690: £2,880 premium less the £2,840 which is owed for purchasing the two contracts (2 × 142 × £10), plus the £650 the fund manager has lodged with the LCH (£150 + £500). A net profit of £40 (see Table 11.7).

Table 11.7

Summary of margin flow on FT-SE 100 Index options

Action in the market		Margin flow						
Day	Action	Position at close	Day	Premium due from LCH	SPAN	NLV	Total margin liability	Cash flow
1	open position	short 2 contracts at 142	2	£2,880 2×144×£10	£540 2×£270	£2,840 2×142×£10	£3,380 £540+£2,840	–£500 £3,380–£2,880
2		short 2 contracts at 148	3		£570 2×£285	£2,960 2×148×£10	£3,530 £570+£2,960	–£150 £3,530–£3,380
3	close position	long 2 contracts at 142 Net flat	4	£2,840 premium due to LCH				+£690 £3,530–£2,840
				Net profit of 2 index points on two contracts				+£40 £690–£650

Source: Euronext.liffe

Stock index options

Insurance protection

The client pays a premium to insure against adverse movements on the index. The clearing house agrees to guarantee the agreed rate if/when required by the client.

Profit potential

The risk of adverse stock market movements is eliminated while, at the same time, the buyer retains the potential to benefit from favourable movements. The option can be abandoned or exercised, or sold back into the market, dependent upon market movements.

Sell back

Open positions can be netted off via the clearing house.

Exercise

As the counterparty to each deal is the clearing house, if a client wishes to exercise the option, he is assigned a counterparty at random.

Cash settlement

Different index options are settled against different underlying prices. For example, options on the Chicago Board Options Exchange (CBOE) are settled against the corresponding index. Options on the Chicago Mercantile Exchange (CME) are settled against the S&P 500 future. Cash settlement allows participants to take profits from favourable movements without having to deal physically in the underlying stocks. Other types of settlement would be unsatisfactory in terms of:

■ inconvenience

■ time

■ expense

■ reduced contract efficiency

■ potential market distortion.

Regulators in the USA stipulate cash settlement as an essential criterion for an exchange-traded stock index contract.

Options traded in London may be settled physically if this is elected at expiry.

Premium determinants

The amount of premium payable by the purchaser of an index option is determined by the following factors:

- underlying price
- strike price
- maturity
- put or call
- dividends
- cost of carry of the position
- expected market volatility.

(a) Strike price

Different stock index options are marked against different underlying prices (see cash settlement earlier in this chapter). Strike prices are referred to as follows:

Terminology		
At the money (ATM)	Where the strike price is equal to the underlying price.	
In the money (ITM)	Where the strike rate is more favourable than the underlying price, and the option premium will be higher than that for an ATM option.	
Out of the money (OTM)	Where the strike rate is worse than the underlying price and the option premium will be lower than for an ATM option.	

(b) Maturity

The longer the time to expiry or maturity, the higher the probability of large index movements, and the higher the chance of profitable exercise by the buyer. The buyer should be prepared to pay a higher premium for a longer dated option than a short-dated option, although premium is not proportional to maturity.

(c) Put or call

This will affect whether the strike is in or out of the money, and also the final market price due to supply and demand swings.

(d) Dividends

The effect of dividends on option pricing can be difficult to factor in. Are they assumed to be continuous or non-continuous? The 1970s Black–Scholes option-pricing model assumes that dividends are spread evenly throughout the year, so many traders use a different binomial model that allows dividends to be explicitly built in.

(e) Cost of carry of the position

As this option is based on the underlying index future, the cost of carrying the position is a relevant factor. As shown in the previous chapter, a fair value can be calculated for the futures price. This is a function of the cost of borrowing the money to pay for the stocks that make up the index, for the exposure period.

(f) Expected market volatility

The higher the volatility the greater the possibility of profitable exercise by the customer. The option is more valuable to the client and the premium is higher.

Various market factors may lead to an increase in the option premium; these include events such as corporate failures, new taxes, political stability, exchange controls, or general illiquidity in the market.

Index options

Terminology

Strike price	Specified index level rate where the client can exercise his right to cash settlement.
Call option	The right to buy the specified index.
Put option	The right to sell the specified index.
Exercise	The take up of the option at or before expiry.
Expiry date	The last date when the option may be exercised.
Value date	The date of payment (settlement) as determined by the exchange EDSP.
Premium	The price of the option, as determined by an option pricing model or the market.
Intrinsic value	Strike price minus the current market rate.
Time value	Option premium minus intrinsic value, reflecting the time until expiry, changes in volatility, and market expectations.

Hedging with a stock index option

23rd March

It is the beginning of spring, and an American fund manager is concerned about a possible fall in world stock markets. She has a number of portfolios, but the one that is causing her most concern moves fairly closely in line with the S&P 500 Index. If she were certain of the downward fall, she could use futures which would cost nothing in terms of an upfront cost, but could actually lose her money if her view of the market were wrong. However, there are certain factors in the market which lead her to believe that there may be major takeovers that could push index levels upwards. She decides to hedge her position using index options, and called up the CME page on the internet to gain an idea of where prices were trading (see Table 11.8).

Table 11.8

CME® S&P 500® options May Puts

cme® s&p 500® options
settlement prices as of 03/23/06 07:00 pm (cst)

MTH/ STRIKE	OPEN	HIGH	LOW	LAST	SETT	PT CHGE	EST VOL	SETT	VOL	INT
1220	3.50	3.50	3.50	3.50	3.30	UNCH	45	3.30	530	2421
1225	4.10	4.10	4.00	4.00	3.60	−10	60	3.70	95	2357
1230	- - - -	- - - -	- - - -	- - - -	4.00	UNCH	15	4.00	1	349
1235	- - - -	- - - -	- - - -	- - - -	4.30	−10		4.40	298	314
1240	4.80	5.00	4.80	5.00	4.80	UNCH	84	4.80	7	10517
1245	5.50	5.50	5.50	5.50	5.30	UNCH	15	5.30		4014
1250	6.10	6.50	6.10	6.50	5.80	UNCH	87	5.80	189	2882
1255	- - - -	- - - -	- - - -	- - - -	6.40	UNCH		6.40	3	5
1260	- - - -	- - - -	- - - -	- - - -	7.10	UNCH	5	7.10	4	374
1265	8.10	8.10	8.10	8.10	7.90	+10	15	7.80	29	29
1270	- - - -	- - - -	- - - -	- - - -	8.80	+20		8.60	1	235
1275	9.80	9.80	9.80	9.80	9.80	+30	17	9.50	58	1267
1280	- - - -	- - - -	- - - -	- - - -	10.90	+40		10.50	10	280
1285	- - - -	- - - -	- - - -	- - - -	12.10	+50		11.60		8
1290	- - - -	- - - -	- - - -	- - - -	13.50	+60		12.90		27
1295	- - - -	- - - -	- - - -	- - - -	15.00	+70		14.30		4
1300	- - - -	- - - -	- - - -	- - - -	16.70	+90		15.80	18	454
1305	- - - -	- - - -	- - - -	- - - -	18.50	+100		17.50	5	5
1310	21.00	21.00	21.00	21.00	20.50	+120	15	19.30		1
1315	- - - -	- - - -	- - - -	- - - -	22.70	+130		21.40		40

Source: CME.com

The cash level of the S&P 500 Index is 1275, and the value of the portfolio is US$7.5 million.

Action – 10th September

First, she would need to calculate the number of options contracts for the hedge. Using the same formula for futures, as each option is based on a single index future, and, assuming a 1:1 correlation with the index (beta =1), she calculates the need for 24 option contracts.

Amended formula

$$\frac{\text{Total value of portfolio} \times \text{portfolio beta}}{\text{S\&P 500 Index level} \times \text{index multiplier}}$$

$$= \frac{\$7,500,000 \times 1}{1275 \times \$250} = 23.53 \text{ contracts (round to 24)}$$

She needs to buy put options. If she used the May put option at a strike of 1275, this would mean a cost of 9.8 index points in premium, making a total premium cost of US$58,800 (24 contracts × 9.8 index points × $250). This option is at the money. She decides to draw an expiry profile for the option strategy, and includes on the diagram the underlying portfolio where she was long of the stocks (see Figure 11.2).

Profit and loss profile of the option strategy   Figure 11.2

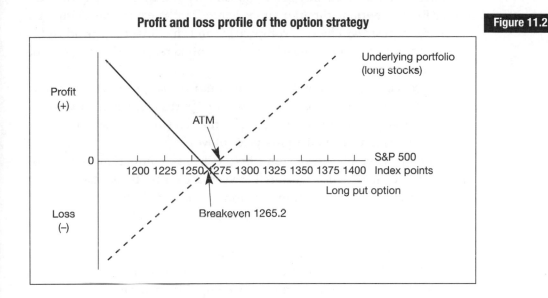

From this she could see that her total exposure would be to the premium which would be lost if the option was not exercised, giving a possible downside on the option of US$58,800, but if that were the case, then the value of the underlying portfolio would have increased. By exactly how much would be unknown until the option expiry date. Alternatively, if she were right and the stock market did fall, then the loss in value of the portfolio would be offset by the increase in value of the option. In this case the breakeven level will be 1275 − 9.8 points = 1265.2. For this strategy to be worthwhile, she would need to assume a market move of at least of 9.8 index points. Given that she thought the index might swing by +/− 30 points, this was perfectly acceptable. She called her broker and transacted the hedge.

Availability

Each of the major exchanges worldwide has an index futures contract, and most have an option on the index. For precise details on all the options contracts, it would be necessary to contact the exchange or a broker for exact specifications.

Practical considerations

Any potential user of exchange-traded equity options will need to set up documentation which is market specific and based on the particular exchange where he wishes to trade. For further details on general documentation, see Chapter 5 on financial futures contracts.

A buyer of options has only one responsibility and that is to pay the premium. Buying options through an exchange can be expensive. Although the premium costs will be very competitive and the bid–offer spread tight, the cost of execution and the corresponding brokerage on the deal cannot be ignored.

With exchange-traded options the premium is margined. This is not as straightforward as the OTC market where a writer or seller of options receives single payment upfront, and may result in further minor receipts/payments as the underlying price moves.

Administration of the options hedge needs competent people to manage the various daily transfers between accounts. Bank charges may also be significant on each transfer, and combined with any brokerage required for the trade to be executed in the pit, as well as clearing fees may all erode possible profits.

Using options on the FT-SE 100 for short-term portfolio management should always be more cost effective than transacting in the underlying physical 100 stocks, as dealing costs and stamp duty may be significant.

When calculating how many option contracts to use on an index portfolio, it is always advisable to 'beta weight' the hedge, in just the same way as when calculating how many futures to use. This will assist in making the hedge more effective, and allow for the fact that most portfolios do not track an index exactly. When the FT-SE 100 Index option does not mirror accurately the make-up of the particular portfolio, 'tracking error' will exist. This can be positive or negative, with the basket of shares either outperforming or underperforming the FT-SE 100 Index.

Should a client need to hedge a different basket of shares to that of, say, the FT-SE, there are over the counter banks which specialize in designing customer-tailored baskets of shares, and then constructing OTC futures and OTC options to cover them.

SINGLE STOCK OPTIONS

Introduction

Exchange-traded options on specific equities add an extra dimension to equity risk management. These single stock options complement existing trading and hedging using futures and options on stock indices. Each stock exchange or futures exchange will have options on their own specific equities. Generally these cover the major corporations in that country.

In London, the standard contract size is 1,000 shares, and these options must be physically settled by delivery of the specified equity.

One call option on Company XXX shares would give the holder the right to purchase 1,000 shares in that company. A seller of that option, on exercise, would be required to deliver 1,000 shares of Company XXX. Table 11.9 shows the specification of the Euronext option contract.

	Equity options – abbreviated contract specification	Table 11.9

Unit of trading	One option normally equals rights over 1,000 shares
Expiry months	**January cycle** (J): means the three nearest expiry months from Jan, Apr, Jul, Oct cycle **February cycle** (F): means the three nearest expiry months from Feb, May, Aug, Nov cycle **March cycle** (M): means the three nearest expiry months from Mar, Jun, Sep, Dec cycle
Exercise/ settlement day	Exercise by 17.20 on any business day, extending to 18.00 for all series on the last trading day. Settlement is four business days following the day of exercise/last trading day
Last trading day	16.30 (London time) third Friday of the expiry month
Quotation	pence per share
Minimum price movement (tick)	0.5 pence per share/£5 per contract
Tick value	£5.00 per half point and £10.00 per full point
Trading hours	08.00 – 16.30 (London time)

Source: Euronext.liffe

A single stock option gives the holder the right, but not the obligation, to buy or sell an agreed amount of a specific equity at a specified price, on or before a specified date. A premium is due. The option will be physically settled.

Definition

Definition discussed

A single stock option gives the client, who may be a portfolio manager or equity hedger, the chance to guarantee the exact level of a particular share price. The holder of the option chooses his own guaranteed price (the strike), from those available on the exchange, and a premium is due. This must be paid upfront, by the buyer, and credited to the option seller on the business day following the trade. The premium is quoted in pence per share, based on a 'parcel' of 1,000 shares. With exchange-traded options the premium itself is margined (see example earlier in this chapter for *stock index options*). The expiry dates are arranged quarterly. These options are American style, and can be exercised on any business day, up to and including the expiry date. On exercise of an equity option, the exchange will randomly assign sellers to buyers, each of whom will receive an assignment notification. Writers are required to settle the underlying share transaction by the settlement date of the current account, as with any other share transaction.

Key features

Single stock options

Insurance protection

The client pays a premium to limit his risk to adverse movements on the particular stock. The writer and then, ultimately, the clearing house agrees to guarantee the agreed rate if/when required by the client. The premium is the maximum cost of this transaction to the client. If the market moves adversely, the option will be exercised.

Profit potential

The risk of adverse stock market movements is eliminated while, at the same time, the buyer retains the potential to benefit from favourable movements. Call options can be bought to profit from rising share prices and put options to profit from declining prices. Both calls and puts can be sold for a more aggressive strategy.

Sell-back

Open positions can be netted off via the clearing house.

Exercise

As the counterparty to each deal is the clearing house, if a client wishes to exercise the option, he is assigned a counterparty at random.

Physical settlement

The option is physically settled, with each contract supporting 1,000 shares, or such other number as determined by the terms of the contract.

Key features continued

Flexibility

Changes in portfolios can happen very quickly. It may be more prudent to cover specific shares in particular circumstances rather than use the index derivative. It may be more judicious to buy put options on a share for a short period, than for a fund manager to sell the stock today, and then buy it back a week later.

Leverage (gearing)

Because of the low option premium needed to establish a market position in the underlying security, any given change in the share price can produce a much larger percentage change in the value of the option, than in the value of the shares.

Premium determinants

The amount of premium payable by the purchaser of an equity option is determined by the same factors as influence the stock index:

- underlying share price
- strike price
- maturity
- put or call
- dividends
- cost of carry of the position
- expected market volatility.

The only factor which needs highlighting concerns the payment of dividends. The holder of a stock option is not entitled to receive any payment of dividend declared on the underlying security unless the option is exercised before the stock was made ex-dividend.

Example

Example of a 'covered call'

Enhancing portfolio income using single stock options

It is January, the beginning of the year and a UK fund manager wishes to start the year on a profitable note. Unfortunately, the stock market seems to be going nowhere and immediate gains look a little fanciful. The portfolio has within it a number of shares on which traded options can be transacted, and which are available in market amounts. The fund manager decides to use his holding of 455,000 shares in Barclays Bank, equivalent to about £3.12 million. He believes that the share price will not fluctuate much and decides to sell 'covered calls'. The option is covered as the fund manager already holds the underlying stock.

The current Barclays Bank share price is £6.85, and the March call option with a strike of £7.00 is trading at 50 pence per share. The fund manager decides to sell 400 contracts, receiving in a premium of £200,000 (400 contracts × 50 pence per share × 1000 shares per contract). He draws himself a sketch to clarify the position, including the underlying asset holding, where he is long of the stocks (see Figure 11.3). He chooses to sell out of the money options to give himself some protection if there is a small upswing in the share price. Ideally, our fund manager does not want to part with the shares and certainly wants to keep the forthcoming dividend. He does not want these options to be exercised against him, but he does want to enhance his income, and is prepared to take the risk.

| Figure 11.3 | **Profit and loss profile of the option strategy** |

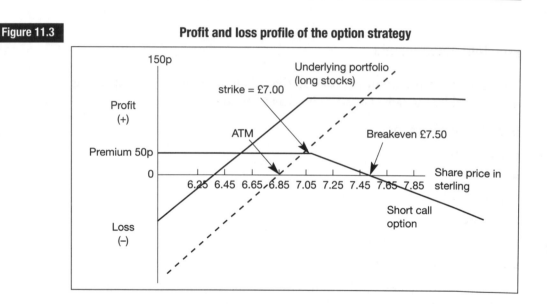

The fund manager draws up a list of potential outcomes:

(a) The market goes nowhere, he keeps the premium and the option is not exercised. Total income = £200,000 + dividends.

(b) The share price swings above £7.00 and the option is exercised. He will lose the stocks, but at a much higher price where he is fairly happy. This strategy can be regarded as a 'target sell price'. Total income £200,000 + an increase in the value of the shares from £6.85 to £7.00, a profit of 65p per share (+ 50p option premium), possibly plus dividends if these are received before exercise.

(c) The share price falls to £6.35. The option remains unexercised, and the underlying value of the shares drops by 50p, but this is offset by the premium received under the option. Dividends will also be received.

Availability

Not all exchanges offer single stock options. For precise details on availability it would be necessary to contact the exchange or a broker for exact specifications.

Practical considerations

A buyer of options has only one responsibility and that is to pay the premium. Buying options can be expensive. Although the premium costs will be very competitive and the bid–offer spread tight, the cost of execution and the corresponding brokerage on the deal cannot be ignored. If the manager of a large pension fund transacts hundreds of contracts a month, he will undoubtedly pay less brokerage per ticket than a smaller company.

Selling options on anything can be risky. The previous example of a covered call illustrates how to enhance performance of a portfolio, but in this case the fund manager is already holding the stock. As such he has no hedging to do, unlike a bank, which, if it sold the option 'naked', would need to delta hedge the resulting position.

Using options and indeed futures on the FT-SE 100 for short-term portfolio management should always be more cost effective than transacting in the underlying physical 100 stocks, as dealing costs and stamp duty may be significant.

A client may have the view that the stock market is going to fall, but at the same time believe that a particular share represents good value. On the one hand, he could buy the share and then either sell futures on the FT-SE, or, on the other, buy put options on the index while still purchasing the target share.

EQUITY INDEX SWAPS

Introduction

An equity index swap is similar to an interest rate swap and has evolved from it. Both transactions are obligations where each party swaps a cash flow. With an index swap, at least one of the cash flows is determined by reference to the performance of an equity index (with or without the inclusion of dividend payments). With an interest rate swap the cash flow is determined by reference to an interest rate. It is not necessary for both rates to be tied to the equity index, and it is quite common for one of the rates to be linked to a floating interest payment such as LIBOR. For example, a US client may wish to receive the return on the S&P 500 (the US index), and pay away 6-month US dollar LIBOR. Alternatively, he may wish to pay or receive interest in a foreign currency, against the FT-SE 100. An equity index swap may involve only a single currency or may involve a second or cross-currency arrangement.

The equity swap itself provides a mechanism whereby a client can hedge or take equity exposure at relatively low cost, for either a longer period than that available by using futures, or with lower administration costs. In some cases it is also possible to design transactions to offer tax advantages. Other types of transactions can synthesize exposure to other markets. For example, a 'vanilla' swap on the FT-SE 100 Index against LIBOR is an exact replication of an investor switching out of a Sterling deposit account and into the constituent stocks of the FT-SE 100 Index, or vice versa. The underlying equity cash market is not as large or as liquid as, say, the interest rate or currency markets, so the big players in equity swaps will generally be the global securities houses that have a trading capability in the various stock indices and their components. This is a similar structure to a Total Return Swap which also includes dividends.

Definition | An equity index swap is an obligation between two parties to exchange cash flows based on the percentage change in one or more stock indices, for a specific period with previously agreed reset dates. The swap is cash settled and based on notional principal amounts. One side of an equity swap can involve a LIBOR reference rate.

Definition discussed

The two parties to an equity swap are likely to be a bank and an investor who may be a fund manager or an insurance company. There is a substantive difference between equity swaps and interest rate swaps: equity swaps are more risky. Consider an equity swap transaction where the bank has agreed to pay the fund manager the percentage increase in the S&P 500 Index, based on a notional amount of US$10 million. What happens if the S&P 500 falls over the period? Then the fund manager must pay the bank on the equity index leg (as the market has moved in the opposite direction) and, if the other side of the swap involved a LIBOR payment, the fund manager would also have to pay that. So instead of cash flows going in opposite directions, which is what we are used to with interest rate swaps, they both flow from the fund manager to the bank.

Or another example: a swap may have involved a client receiving the percentage change in the FT-SE 100, against paying 3-month LIBOR minus 20 basis points. If the index level decreased, the client would pay the negative percentage change in the FT-SE 100, and pay LIBOR less the 20 basis points. The 20 basis points spread is attached as an 'offset' to the LIBOR level and reduces funding costs, but realistically if the index fell 5 per cent, the 20 bp is largely irrelevant and can help immunize the client from falls in the index. The swap is cash settled and payments are netted, as in interest rate swaps. Where one leg of the swap is linked to LIBOR, it is market practice to use 3-month LIBOR.

Example

A portfolio manager holds a selection of equities that trades very closely in correlation with the FT-SE 100 Index. He believes that the short-term returns from this portfolio are likely to disappoint him as he expects the stock market to decline. He is unwilling to sell the cash equity portfolio and buy the shares back later, due to the significant dealing costs he will incur. He does feel that UK interest rates will rise, and he decides to enter into an equity swap for one year where he pays the percentage change in the FT-SE 100 and receives 3-month LIBOR (see Figure 11.4).

Equity swap cash flows

Figure 11.4

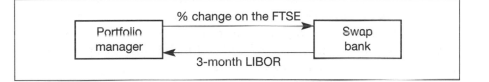

Equity index swaps

Key features

Cost effective
Through an equity swap, a client can invest directly in a stock market portfolio, and replicate cash investments without having to purchase/sell the underlying shares in the correct quantities. An equity swap avoids any requirement to pay stamp duty and other associated taxes and also negates the need for safe custody of certificates, etc.

Net cash settlement
It is only the cash flow payments that are swapped. The principal sum is not exchanged but is used as a reference point.

Index tracking
An equity swap has a 100 per cent correlation to the underlying index on which it is based. This is a great advantage for index-tracking fund managers. Through the swap they can maintain capital exposure and receive dividend income, but avoid the pitfalls of trying to achieve this through holding a basket of stocks. The more complex the underlying index, the harder it will be to track it, and therefore the greater the benefit of using the index swap.

Efficient portfolio management

An equity swap allows the portfolio manager to stabilize a portfolio without the need to change the make-up of the portfolio, to allow for changes in share prices or market capitalizations. The purchaser of an equity index swap transfers the responsibility of managing an index portfolio over to the issuer of the swap. For a passive fund that is seeking only to replicate or track the performance of a particular index, an equity swap is ideal since the objective is achieved without any of the administrative burden.

An equity swap allows the fund manager to receive LIBOR if he believes that it will offer him a better return than the index portfolio he is holding, without the need to sell the stocks and invest in the money market. Alternatively, consider a two-year swap on the German DAX index, priced at LIBOR – 75 basis points. This is quoted with no dividend flow, as with the DAX the dividends are assumed to be re-invested. A buyer of this swap would receive the performance of the DAX over a two-year period while passing through interest income on the principal amount at 75 basis points less than money market rates.

Exposure to a foreign index

Allows the fund manager to exchange the return on the FT-SE 100 Index portfolio that he is physically holding, for, say, the return on the S&P 500, or any other foreign index, without the requirement to sell the stocks, and without worrying about local taxes and politics. He may choose to hedge the associated foreign currency risk or not.

Credit risk

The credit risk on an equity index swap is similar in some ways to that of an interest rate swap, in that principal amounts are not exchanged, and in some cases one of the 'legs' of the swap can be an interest rate. The other leg, however, can sometimes behave in such a way as to cause problems. The risk is significantly greater because:

■ Swings in equity indices can be much larger than moves in interest rates.

■ Equity index movements can be negative.

Collateral

Because of the volatile nature of the credit exposure to the client, bank swap counterparties will call for collateral to be lodged as security for the swap transaction.

Principal amounts

As the swap may involve the paying away and/or receiving the change in the relevant equity index, it is possible for the notional amount to change to reflect this. The client can either capitalize the profits and losses, thereby

Key features
continued

varying the notional amount, or he can keep the notional amount fixed and dispose of profits as income and losses as expenditure on the swap.

Resets

An equity swap is reset at various intervals throughout its maturity, and this is how capital payments are exchanged between the parties. In reality the net payment is made up of three elements. There may be a capital appreciation of £500,000 on the underlying holding, plus dividend income of £100,000, less interest payments of £175,000. In those circumstances, there would be a net payment of £600,000 less £175,000, an amount of £425,000 paid to the index receiver of the swap. The frequency of resets is usually every three or six months. With wholly sterling swaps, it is usual for the closing level of the index to be taken against that day's prevailing LIBOR 11 a.m. fixing rate. If the counter currency is non-sterling, the LIBOR fix will be two business days earlier.

Terminology

Equity index swap

EIS	Equity index swap, sometimes called portfolio insurance.
Index payer	The party wishing to pay the percentage change in the index.
Index	The party wishing to receive the percentage change in the receiver index.
Swap rate, fixed index rate, guaranteed rate	The swap rate agreed between the parties at the outset of the transaction, typically expressed as offset around the LIBOR rate.
Rollovers/ resets	The frequency of the LIBOR settlements, e.g. a one-year swap against 3-month LIBOR. Dates on which the payments flow between the counterparties.

Example

A synthetic stock market investment

A UK fund manager is considering what action to take regarding the maturity of his £10 million fixed rate money market deposit. Should he roll it over for another year, or should he invest the money elsewhere, probably in equity? He could buy shares in major companies to create a portfolio which mirrors the FT-SE 100 Index, but he would need to pay all the relevant transaction costs. He believes that over the next year the FT-SE 100 Index will rally and offer a better rate of return than a simple money market deposit. He decides to investigate the use of equity index swaps, and summarizes the basic information received from his bankers:

Current FT-SE 100 level	6000
3-month LIBOR	4.5 per cent
Spread to investor	10 basis points (10bp)
Payment frequency	Quarterly
Maturity	12 months
Underlying deposit	Linked to 3-month LIBOR

By using the swap illustrated in Figure 11.5, the total return/cost to the client will be the increase/decrease on the FT-SE 100 over the reference level of 6000. For simplicity he assumes a fixed notional amount of £10 million.

The fund manager decided to carry out a 'what-if' scenario (ignoring dividends):

Figure 11.5   **Equity swap cash flows**

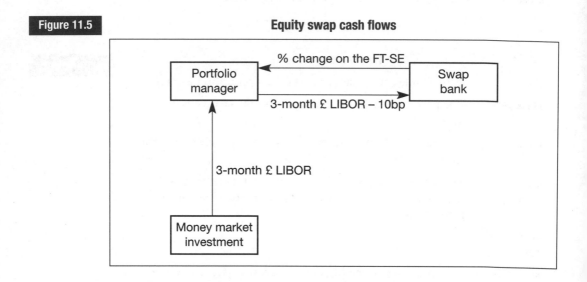

(a) The market rises 400 points in the first quarter

FT-SE 100 Index has risen from 6000 to 6400, a rise of 6.66 per cent. The bank must pay the fund manager this increase, an amount of:

(6.66% × £10,000,000) = £666,000

The fund manager has also gained by 10bp on his funding, an amount of:

(0.10% x £10,000,000 × 91/365) = £2,493

Making a total receipt of £668,493.

(b) The market falls by 300 points in the second quarter

FT-SE 100 Index falls from 6400 to 6100, a fall of 4.68 per cent. The fund manager must pay this decrease to the bank, but will still gain the 10 bp spread on the funding. A total payment of:

(4.68% × £10,000,000) – (0.10% × £10m × 92/365)

Making a total payment of £465,480.

(c) The market rises to 6575 in the third quarter

FT-SE 100 Index has risen from 6100 to 6575, a rise of 7.78 per cent. The bank must pay the fund manager this increase, an amount of:

(7.78% × £10,000,000) = £778,000

The fund manager has also gained by 10bp on his funding, an amount of:

(0.1% × £10,000,000 × 91/365 = £2,493

Making a total receipt of £780,493.

(d) The market rises to 6700 in the last quarter

FT-SE 100 Index rises from 6575 to 6700, an increase of 1.9 per cent. The bank will pay this to the fund manager, an amount of:

(1.9% × £10,000,000) = £190,000

The fund manager has also gained by 10bp on his funding, an amount of:

(0.10% × £10,000,000 × 92/365) = £2,520

Making a total receipt of £192,500.

If the fund manager had left his money on deposit, he would have achieved 3-month LIBOR over the period, assuming the LIBOR rates had moved as shown in Table 11.10.

Example: LIBOR rates and day count   Table 11.10

	LIBOR rate	Maturity
Commencement date	4.5%	91 days
Month 3	4.75%	92 days
Month 6	4.75%	91 days
Month 9	4.5%	92 days

The equivalent return using the LIBOR rate for each period is:

Quarter 1	£112,191
Quarter 2	£119,726
Quarter 3	£118,424
Quarter 4	£113,424

A total income of £463,765, equivalent to 4.637 per cent (ignores possible re-investment of interest income).

By using the equity index swap, the stock market move, in addition to the 10 bp spread on the funding represents a total return of:

+£668,493 − £465,480 + £780,493 + £192,500 = £1,176,006

This is equivalent to a straight interest rate of 11.76 per cent (ignores the possibility of re-investing the interest income).

The return through using the index swap is over twice as high.

Availability

Different banks each offer a different service in equity index swaps. This is very much a new and growing market with continual new developments.

Practical considerations

Other index derivatives such as options and futures can also reduce administrative charges, but none of these instruments can exactly replicate the returns of the equity investment. The equity swap is the only instrument which provides the actual dividend flow: all other instruments factor in the anticipated dividend flow.

By purchasing an equity index swap, the investor transfers the responsibility of managing an index portfolio over to the issuer of the swap. For a passive fund that is only seeking to replicate or track the performance of a particular index, an equity swap is ideal since the objective is achieved without any of the administrative hassle.

Credit risk is a complex problem when dealing with equity index swaps. Each bank will look at this in a different fashion, some will require credit lines, some will require collateral, some will require both. If a bank requires collateral, it may take stocks of bonds and equities as well as cash. Try and avoid giving cash, the opportunity cost is very high.

Many of these swaps are tax driven and most of them will have tax implications. It would therefore be prudent to discuss those issues with a tax specialist in advance of executing the deal.

FT-SE 100 stocks are highly liquid with the ability to trade out of a cash position very quickly. This is not the case with equity index swaps. If a client wishes to terminate an index swap early, there is likely to be a substantial penalty possibly in the region of 2 to 3 per cent of the notional principal amount.

Equities are perpetual, and an investor holding them simply has to wait for his interest. The holder of an equity swap has a term instrument which on a future date will mature, possibly requiring a further swap.

'Now investors, ranging from small retail savers to large institutions can share in the benefits of rising equity markets without placing capital at risk.'

■ ■ ■

Using Equity Derivatives to Create Attractive Investment Products for Personal Investors

Christopher C. Taylor
Director, Wealth Management, Sales, HSBC

Equity investment

The development of the UK and European markets for equity-based retail products

Constructing a capital protected growth product with equity derivatives

Income paying capital at risk products

Calculation of income level

The risk to capital

The most common structural variations used in the equity derivative market

EQUITY INVESTMENT

Equity markets have delivered healthy returns to investors for prolonged periods over the past 20 years or so (see charts of FTSE100 between 1990 and 2006). However, there have been times when share prices have fallen sharply, resulting in substantial capital erosion for those who have committed funds to the market. The steep decline in global equity markets starting in 2001, for example, shocked many investors who had grown accustomed to capital growth throughout the sustained bull markets of the 1980s and 1990s and many remain reluctant to re-enter the market (see Figure 12.1).

| Figure 12.1 | FTSE100 between 1990 and 2006 |

Source: ©2006 Bloomberg L.P. All rights reserved. Reprinted with permission.

Aversion to taking equity market risk evident amongst some groups of investors has been the main driver to the development of the multi-billion dollar market for capital protected equity products. Now, investors, ranging from small retail savers to large institutions can share in the benefits of rising equity markets without placing capital at risk.

Banks and financial institutions can now offer capital protection combined with potential to benefit from the positive performance of equities and/or equity market indices by using equity derivatives. Indeed, as a result of the flexibility of derivative instruments, any desired combination of risk and reward may be accommodated ranging from full capital at risk strategies with geared upside to more conservative products focusing on capital preservation.

THE DEVELOPMENT OF THE UK AND EUROPEAN MARKETS FOR EQUITY-BASED RETAIL PRODUCTS

Early market development

The first retail-based capital protected equity products appeared in the early 1990s in the UK wrapped as life bonds. These were simple structures offering stock market growth with 100 per cent capital security, or as one product's promotional literature put it, 'Stock market appreciation, or your money back'.

The main stimulus to these early financial products was the emergence of a market in equity derivatives as derivative technology, by now well established in other asset classes such as fixed income and foreign exchange, was applied to the complex world of equities.

Over the next decade the UK market for capital protected products grew strongly with participation from most domestic banks, building societies, life companies and other leading financial institutions with significant investment interest being derived from the increasingly important independent financial adviser (IFA) sector. As volumes increased and derivative technology became more sophisticated, so the diversity of products and payoffs broadened. In particular, and some would say to the market's detriment, a trend emerged for products generating high levels of income as opposed to an accumulation of value. These products also placed capital at risk in the event of a fall in the market, a feature that became highly controversial when the markets turned.

Elsewhere in Europe the market for these type of products grew more slowly but as we approached the new millennium the European structured retail product market experienced massive impetus from the move to a single currency, as economies throughout the region converged and interest rates in many participant countries plummeted. As a consequence of euro convergence, investors in countries such as Spain, Italy and France, who had grown used to high interest rates, suddenly found that they were receiving yields of 2 and 3 per cent. They demanded higher returns from their banks and financial advisers who turned to equity markets as a potential source of double digit returns.

The structured retail product market in the twenty-first century

Within a short space of time investment activity in a number of countries in Europe far surpassed that of the UK with Italy, and Germany being the most prolific. Figure 12.2 shows the total investment in structured retail products throughout Europe in 2005 in a market estimated to exceed EUR142 billion.

| Figure 12.2 | Leading structured retail product markets in Europe 2005 |

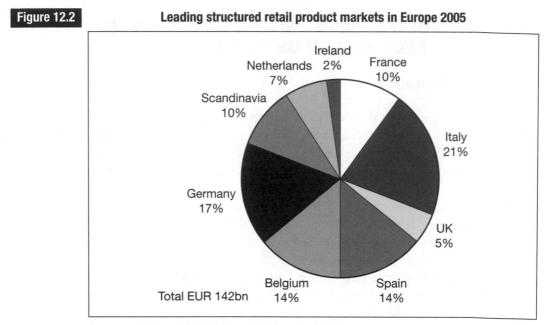

Source: www.StructuredRetailProducts.com. Arete Consulting Limited

Figure 12.2 deals with investments offered to the retail markets only in the leading retail markets in Europe. Similar structured investments are also offered on a more bespoke basis to high net worth individuals and institutional investors. If these figures were to be taken into account, countries such as Switzerland and Luxembourg would feature prominently due to prolific private banking activities within these nations.

The US market with its highly developed mutual fund sector and easy stock market access does not sell packaged equity derivatives to retail investors to the same extent as is the experience in Europe. Products are typically of a one- or two-year maturity with less than half those issued being fully principal protected.

Other parts of the globe, most notably Asia, have experienced similar market growth to that seen in Europe with 2005 sales in the US being half of those recorded in Europe (source: StructuredRetailProducts.com) and with emerging wealth and prosperity in the most populous region of the globe this market is expected to grow strongly in the future.

Today the use of equity derivatives to provide safe access to equity investment is truly a global phenomenon.

CONSTRUCTING A CAPITAL PROTECTED GROWTH PRODUCT WITH EQUITY DERIVATIVES

Capital protected equity investment products incorporate two features: capital protection and the ability to participate in equity gains. The capital protection feature is achieved by investing a proportion of the funds in a cash investment on a zero coupon basis (i.e. interest rolled up and paid out at maturity). The equity participation is then ensured via the purchase of an equity option with the remainder of the investment. The objective here is to ensure that 100 per cent of the funds invested can be repaid at maturity whatever happens to the underlying equity reference benchmark (usually a stock index, basket of indices or basket of equities) while at the same time providing investors with the opportunity to profit from a rise in the markets.

Factors that determine the extent to which an investor can benefit from a rise in the market whilst still keeping capital secure

1. Interest rates

Taking a simple example of a 5-year 100 per cent capital protected investment linked to the S&P500, the first factor that will determine the overall pricing of the structure is the level of interest rates. The optimum method of providing full capital protection is to place funds on deposit. Quite simply, a sum is invested on day one that will grow to equal at maturity the total capital amount committed by the investor. Logically therefore, the higher the rate of interest, the smaller the proportion of funds required to guarantee 100 at maturity.

So, if the total amount placed by investors in an investment product is US$10m and the 5-year zero coupon rate is 5.16 per cent the equity derivative structurer will need to invest US$7.74m on day one in order to generate US$10m in five years time. Figure 12.3 demonstrates the effect of zero coupon rates in relation to what proportion of total funds need to be invested to preserve the capital value.

Figure 12.3

Cost of $10m in 5 years' time depending on interest rates

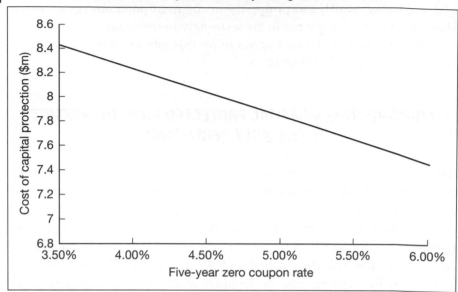

Following on from this point it is easy to comprehend why in these types of product the full capital sum is only protected at maturity, since before this date the zero coupon investment will not have grown to the required size. In the case of early redemptions therefore, the size of the capital sum available for repayment will depend heavily on how long the investment has been in place.

Returning to our example, with US$7.74m fully committed to safeguarding the capital element this leaves an amount of US$2.26m. This sum will be used to purchase the equity derivative which will give the structure its investment performance. However, before the option can be purchased a portion of this residual amount must be set aside to pay for administration costs.

2. Fees

Packaging, marketing, administering and settling retail products is a labour-intensive enterprise and the fee levels charged by providers may vary between 2 per cent and 7 per cent depending on the product, its maturity and its wrapper (i.e. legal vehicle- deposit, ISA, Life Bond, Fund, MTN, etc.).

NB: Large institutional trades or transactions for high net worth individuals in private banks will not require the same level of administration so fees will be substantially lower.

Let us assume for the sake of this example that total fees are 3 per cent. Once these have been deducted, US$1.96 million will remain for the purchase of the option.

3. Option cost

In order to provide participation in the appreciation of the index a call option will need to be purchased. The price of this option will be determined by the usual variables that affect option pricing – strike price, maturity, forward pricing, volatility etc. So it follows that in times of high volatility options cost more and consequently the funds available for purchasing the option buy less of the option than they would if volatility were to be lower and the call option cheaper.

One further factor that also affects the option price is the method used to ascertain the reference price at maturity. Typically structured equity investments are subject to an *averaging methodology* which avoids the risk of the option payout being adversely affected by a sudden, sharp fall in the market at or close to maturity. Products of three years and less usually have a three- to six-month averaging period whilst longer term deals will often be subject to 12-month weekly averaging. Not only does this smooth the risks when approaching maturity but also, conveniently, averaging has the additional benefit of cheapening the option. Some product structures in the European market place are subject to full averaging or as it is sometimes termed 'asianing'. This significantly reduces the option cost but also impairs performance as an investor can only benefit from the average rise in the market over the investment period.

Let us assume that in our example a five-year at-the-money S&P500 Call for US$10m with 12-month weekly averaging costs US$2.02m. Since we only have US$1.96m to spend on this option this will mean that the option purchased will not produce the opportunity to participate in the full appreciation of the index. Instead, this product will deliver 97 per cent participation* ($1.960/2.02 \times 100 = 97$).

Summary of pricing factors

1. Zero coupon rate
   - ■ Determines how much needs to be invested to produce 100 per cent at maturity.

2. Level of fees charged by provider
   - ■ This is deducted from the funds available to spend on the option.

3. Option cost
   - ■ This will determine the level of participation. If cost is greater than amount available to spend then investor will have less than 100 per cent participation.

---

* If the option costs less than is available to spend then participation will be higher than 100 per cent – a concept that is sometimes difficult for some investors to comprehend.

INCOME PAYING CAPITAL-AT-RISK PRODUCTS

Investors in equity-linked structured products usually expect to benefit from any rise in the market in the form of capital appreciation and do not generally receive payments that can be construed as income as dividends are not paid. Hence these structures are often termed 'growth products'. It is nevertheless possible to structure equity-based transactions that generate income. However, it should be noted that these often involve placing capital at risk.

The most commonly utilized mechanism for generating income is called a reverse convertible and operates as follows. Basically, income is generated in two ways. First, all funds collected from investors are placed on deposit at current yields thereby producing quasi money market returns (similar to the zero coupon element of a standard growth structure). Secondly, returns are enhanced through the writing of put options on the equity market and the premium earned is paid out in the form of annual interest.

Quite obviously, the writing of these put options means that the investor's capital is at risk as, if the market is lower at maturity than at commencement, the option writer will have to compensate the option buyer with the difference between the strike price and the market level at option expiry.

Example Income product

Terms

Total investment	£10 million
Benchmark	FTSE100
Term	5 Years
Fees	3%

CALCULATION OF INCOME LEVEL

- The writing of an at-the-money put option on an underlying of £10 m earns £1.07 m (to be distributed as income).

- Using a zero coupon rate of 5.16 per cent a total of £7.775 m is required to deliver £10 m at maturity

- After the deduction of 3 per cent fees there would be a surplus of £2.994 m which would be used to purchase an annuity stream that would deliver annual income of 7 per cent. This level of income would be determined by discount factors from 1 to 5 years (Table 12.1).

Derivative products and their underlying assets

Table 12.1

	Discount factors:	Income paid	Present Value
Year 1	94.84%	700,000	663,880
Year 2	89.95%	700,000	629,624
Year 3	85.31%	700,000	597,135
Year 4	80.90%	700,000	566,323
Year 5	76.73%	700,000	537,101
			2,994,063 total

The product provider would solve for the income paid per annum which has a present value equal to the remaining available investment.

THE RISK TO CAPITAL

If at maturity the FTSE100 reference level is higher than that at commencement of the product then 100 per cent of the investment will be repaid. However, if the level is lower there will be a one-to-one reduction in capital.

Some structures incorporate downside, one touch triggers whilst others introduce gearing of over 100 per cent. Both of these embedded options are designed to increase the income paid at the expense of capital security.

THE MOST COMMON STRUCTURAL VARIATIONS USED IN THE EQUITY DERIVATIVE MARKET

With the imaginative use of equity derivatives, returns may be altered to produce a variety of different payoffs. The most commonly used are as follows.

Minimum return

There is no doubting that potential returns from equity investment are high, however, the actual payoff will be determined by the performance of the stock market or markets in question. Many investors, although attracted to the prospect of high returns, find the prospect of earning nothing if the market is lower at maturity to be relatively unpalatable. This problem can be overcome by guaranteeing a minimum return at maturity.

So, instead of promising 100 per cent participation in a 5-year FTSE100 linked product a structure can be created that pays either a minimum return of 20 per cent at maturity or 50 per cent of the appreciation in the index, whichever is the greater. Although the investor may take comfort from the fact that his funds will generate a guaranteed minimum return, it should be noted that in order to establish a fixed minimum the upside potential is reduced. In this case if the market was subject to strong appreciation the investor would only benefit from half the market gain (Figure 12.4).

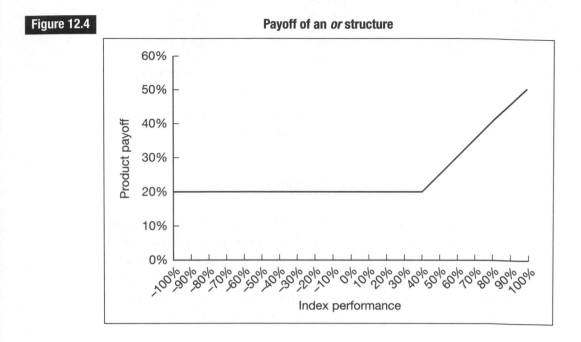

Figure 12.4

Payoff of an *or* structure

For non-retail investors, minimum return structures can be tailored to produce higher or lower minimums depending upon the investor's personal risk versus reward parameters.

A variation on this theme is a so-called 'and' payoff as opposed to the 'or' structure described above. With an 'and' structure the investor receives a guaranteed return *and*, in addition, a certain percentage of any appreciation in the market.

Definition   **Underlying equity derivative – '*or*' structure**

Investor is long an out-of-the-money call with strike dependent on minimum return and participation levels.

For above example:

Strike – 100% + (20%/50%) = 140%

Capped call

Equity derivative returns can be enhanced by capping the overall payout. On the face of it this may not initially appear to be an attractive proposition, however, if the transaction is constructed realistically participation levels can be increased without the cap being breached.

With a capped call structure the investor is actually writing an out-of-the-money call that constitutes the cap, i.e. he/she agrees to forgo gains above a defined market level in exchange for a premium. This premium is not actually paid out but instead is reinvested in the structure to boost participation rates.

For example, let us say a 5-year vanilla call on the Eurostoxx50 would give participation of, say, 60 per cent in the rise in the market at maturity. This participation level would be increased to 80 per cent if returns were to be capped at a maximum return of 140 per cent (Figure 12.5).

Payoff of a capped call structure Figure 12.5

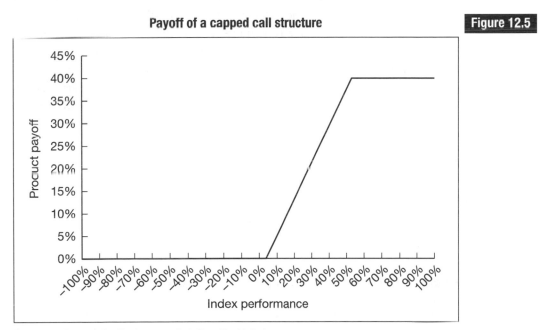

Source: www.StructuredRetailProducts.com. Arete Consulting Limited

From a product selection perspective it follows that a capped call structure is most attractive when a modest rise in the market is expected.

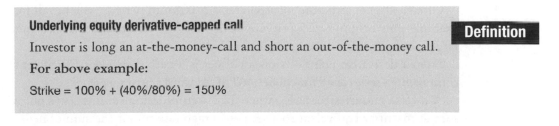

Underlying equity derivative-capped call Definition

Investor is long an at-the-money-call and short an out-of-the-money call.

For above example:

Strike = 100% + (40%/80%) = 150%

Auto-callable (or early release)

Many investors place a high value on liquidity and view the fact that most structured equity investments are for 5 years or longer as a negative factor. One way of potentially shortening the maturity of the investment is to include an auto-callable feature.

An auto-callable feature is essentially a European barrier option written by the investor such that if on a set date in the future the equity market is above a defined trigger level, then the structure will automatically terminate and funds will be paid back to the investor together with a specified return.

For example, a 5-year investment against the Dow Jones Global Titans 50 Index may incorporate an auto-callable feature after 3 years whereby if on the 3-year anniversary the market has risen by 20 per cent or more, the structure will automatically terminate. If the auto-callable feature is not triggered then 105 per cent of the appreciation of the index will be paid to the investor.

It should be noted that since the investor is writing the early termination option an implied premium will be earned. This will not be paid out but will be invested in the structure to produce enhanced product terms.

Some products have multiple triggers giving, for example, an annual opportunity for early termination at gradually increasing levels.

Definition	Underlying equity derivative – auto-callable
	Investor is short a knockout call with rebate.

Cliquets and reverse cliquets (also known as ratchet options)

With a cliquet option the investor receives a return determined by the sum of a sequence of periodic settings (sub-periods) which are combined to pay a return at maturity.

For example, the performance of the S&P 500 is measured every three months and each reading is compared with the previous quarter's setting and is added to (if positive) or subtracted from (if negative) a running total.

Often a cliquet structure incorporates a maximum periodic rise or fall for example plus or minus 2.5 per cent which has the effect of smoothing out large movements from one reference period to another.

From a derivative point of view a cliquet is a path dependent instrument comprising a series of at-the-money (ATM) forward starting options.

A reverse cliquet structure, rather than accumulating returns, pays out a sum at maturity equivalent to a set percentage rate minus the sum of negative settings.

Underlying equity derivative – cliquets   **Definition**

Investor is long a series of forward starting calls and puts most commonly including local caps and a global floor.

Digital option (also known as a binary option)

A digital option is very simple to understand since its payout is determined by a defined trigger (or set of triggers). Basically, the structure pays out a fixed amount if the market is above (or below) a specified level at maturity or on specified reference dates. If it is not, there is no payout.

Example

A 3-year product linked to a basket comprising 10 stocks of leading petrochemical companies will pay 30 per cent at maturity if the basket is higher at maturity than at inception.

Digital structures are generally used when a rise or fall in the market is expected but the magnitude of the move is uncertain. The size of the payout can be increased by introducing a higher digital strike price, for example paying a set return if the market rises by more than 5 per cent or 10 per cent (Figure 12.6).

Payoff of a capped call structure   **Figure 12.6**

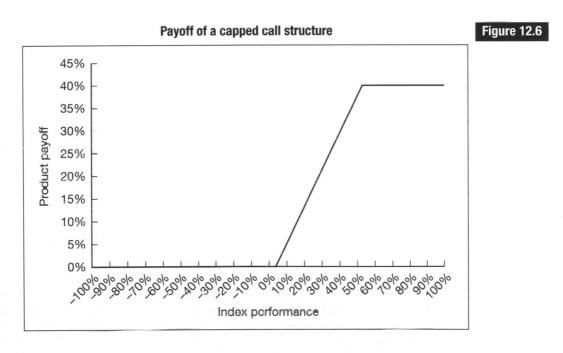

<table>
<tr><td>Definition</td><td>Underlying equity derivative – digital</td></tr>
</table>

Investor is long a digital or 'binary' option.

Other variations

The structures above are the most common equity derivative variations but there is now such a wealth of technology available to product structurers that an almost infinitesimal range of payoffs can be created. Indeed, some quite exotic structures are now available, many with equally exotic names – Altiplano, Himalaya, Podium, Rainbow, Napoleon, Airbag, Serenity, Wedding Cake to name but a few. The range of alternatives is mind boggling and the pace of innovation simply continues to accelerate driven by advancements in equity derivative expertise.

In the previous edition we wrote: 'The collapse of the oil price from US$25.60 in December 1996, to US$10.90 in December 1998, led many corporations to discontinue their oil hedging. Now, with prices much higher, the negative impact on the balance sheets will start to show.'
– How things have changed, in 2005 and 2006 prices reached over US$70 per barrel!

■ ■ ■

Commodity Derivatives

Introduction

Exchange-traded energy derivatives

Exchange-traded futures contracts

Exchanged-traded energy option contracts

OTC or 'off-exchange' energy derivatives

OTC option products

OTC oil swaps

Overview of electricity market

INTRODUCTION

The commodity markets are generally accepted to comprise energy (oil, gas and electricity) and metals (precious metals which include, gold, silver, platinum, and base metals which include copper, aluminum, zinc, lead, nickel and tin). In addition, there are the agricultural or soft commodities ('softs') which include grain, peanuts, soybean, orange juice, pork bellies, sugar, cocoa and coffee, etc. Whilst we tend to focus on energy and metals, one item of miscellaneous information is that soybean exports from the USA to China are greater than the export of airplanes to the same country.

Each of these commodity markets can potentially use derivative instruments for risk management and trading, but it is the energy and metals markets which are at present the most well developed and where there are most parallels with other financial derivatives markets. This chapter will focus on the oil-based energy derivatives with a brief overview of electricity.

The key question is, 'What determines the price of oil?' As with any other commodity, the supply and demand pulls will make the price cheaper or more expensive, but with oil there is another factor that cannot be ignored. This is simply that the oil price, or changes in the oil price, can make or break the economy of a country and, for many, oil is a cash equivalent. Consequently, politics and politicians are also integral factors.

Crude oil has no intrinsic value. It is valuable only in relation to the value of the products that can be made from it. What constitutes a 'best value' crude oil to a refiner will depend on its quality and availability, the location of the refinery and geographical and seasonal differences between the markets to be supplied. If absolute prices were stable, then these factors alone would be sufficient to determine confidently the prices of particular crude oils. However, in practice, oil prices are volatile (40 per cent volatility is not uncommon) and general market uncertainty can swamp the perceived value of a crude oil.

The value of any particular crude oil is compared with the 'benchmark' or 'marker crude' for pricing in the final area of importation. The oil will then be sold at a premium or a discount, to the value on the day of the marker being used. The level of the premium or discount will relate to the crude oil itself, while the outright level of price is decided by the price level of the marker. In general, light crudes yield more gasoline and high-value products than heavy crudes.

As in all markets where derivatives are available, there is a choice of using exchange-traded products with their strict contract specification, yet superb liquidity; or the over the counter (OTC) instruments which can be specifically tailored to the client's own requirements. OTC instruments are sometimes known as 'off-exchange' instruments. Most of the major oil companies have now consolidated their downstream activities, and markets have been created for independent brokers and traders. Price projections in the oil market are difficult, if not impossible; consequently the risk management of long and short positions is crucial to the long-term performance of the industry as a whole.

Background to the oil market – a brief timeline

Oil has been seeping out of the ground literally for geological ages, usually without the local population being too concerned. If anything, it was regarded as an inconvenience, but occasionally oil could be used as a tar-based product for waterproofing. However, in the middle of the nineteenth century its usefulness as a fuel for light and heat came to people's attention. Edwin Drake is credited with the founding of the modern oil industry, when he made the first commercial discovery of crude oil in Pennsylvania in 1859.

More recently, in the 1950s and 1960s, the oil industry experienced a period of rapid growth. Investment in oil exploration and development led to a massive expansion in production activity. As a result, oil was abundant and relatively cheap, and fuelled the post-war economic recovery among the major industrial nations. In 1957 the US government imposed import controls; this meant that it was impossible for US companies and consumers to import foreign-produced oil. It also meant that the US oil companies were forced to market and sell all their non-US produced oil, notably that extracted from Middle Eastern, North African and other regions outside the USA, to Europe. By the time the US government oil controls were eventually lifted in 1971, the oil majors had established highly lucrative European markets.

During this period the oil business was dominated by the major international oil companies, through their ownership of both production and refining capabilities. From the production wellhead, oil was shipped in company-owned or chartered tankers to company-owned and operated refineries. The refined products were then distributed through company outlets. This left very little room for traders and speculators and the oil companies were usually involved in oil trading only as a means of managing their temporary surpluses or deficits.

To put all this into context: up until the early 1960s, the major oil companies were charging only US$1.80 a barrel, making their money by continually increasing their production levels. Their only worry seemed to be how long the oil would last before all the reserves had been exhausted.

Twelve years later the prices were between ten to fifteen times greater. This had come about partly because of the US insistence that only US oil could be used in the USA, and partly because the traditional US oil reserves had started to diminish and new supplies were not yet available. The USA had, in fact, changed from being a net producer of oil and had become a large oil importer.

Growing demand for oil in the USA and Western Europe, combined with oil supplies that were increasingly concentrated in the Middle East, meant that the governments of the oil-exporting countries (OPEC) were able to seize and manipulate the oil pricing mechanism in 1973/1974. This effectively ended the growth period.

In the 1950s and 1960s the market was generally in surplus with prices being determined by what the oil producers could make from their refining and marketing of oil products. In the 1970s and 1980s with the OPEC leaders capitalizing on the relative scarcity of crude oil, prices rose between ten- and twenty-fold from their 1960 levels.

The various 'oil shocks' in the mid to late 1970s brought about the decline of OPEC. Incidentally, it also brought about the demise of the Bretton Woods agreement used to peg the value of the US dollar to the gold price. It has been argued that OPEC's downfall was self-inflicted. Higher oil prices slowed economic growth and increased fuel conservation. It also meant that oil exploration accelerated, and the search for fresh supplies became ever more important. Importers world-wide would not or could not afford the high price of oil and turned instead to oil substitutes. The various oil crises that followed in those years also allowed other non-OPEC oil producers to compete in the oil export market, where before the cost of their oil had been prohibitively expensive. These factors taken together led for a time to a downward oil price spiral for both crude oil and petroleum products. Now the 'free market' is not dominated by one group of producers or consumers, but instead volatility and uncertainty are characteristic of today's environment.

Historically, the spot market for oil has covered only the small amount of oil left over from the fixed price term contracts of the major oil companies. By the mid 1980s spot and spot-related trading accounted for about half of all the international trade.

The main known reserves at the time of writing, recoverable under current economic conditions, are in the Middle East (approximately 50 per cent) which is mostly in Saudi Arabia, and Canada which now includes the Athabasca Oil Sands (not really oil but a semi-solid called bitumen). However, many countries are unwilling to make known the exact extent of their reserves and Antarctica is protected from exploration by international treaty.

In the previous edition of this book I wrote:

'... But the collapse of the oil price (West Texas Intermediate) from US$25.60 in December 1996, to US$10.90 in December 1998, led many corporations to discontinue their oil hedging. Now, with prices much higher, the negative impact on the balance sheets will start to show.'

How things have changed, in 2005 and 2006 prices exceeded US$70 per barrel!

Over the last few months oil prices have hit historic highs, mostly as a result of increased activity in the USA and Far East, combined with exceptionally low excess capacity. Shown in Figure 13.1 is how the price of WTI traded on NYMEX has fared over the last few years. In Figure 13.2 we have a snapshot of oil prices in March 2006.

WTI price performance

Figure 13.1

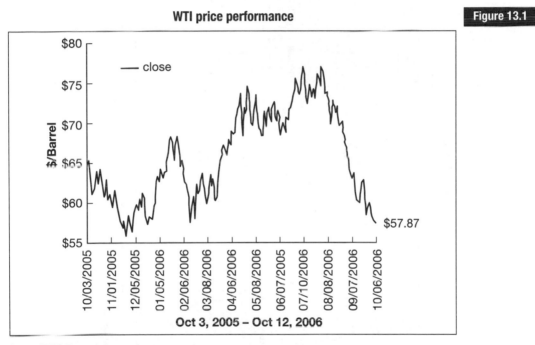

Source: WTRG Economics, www.wtrg.com

The most prominent derivative is the future linked to the West Texas Intermediate (WTI) grade of oil. This is traded on NYMEX for delivery at Cushing, Oklahoma. In 2006 a rival contract for WTI started trading at the ICE (Intercontinental Exchange) in London and is currently trading about 196,000 contracts per day (notional of $11.76 billion per day).

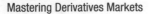

Figure 13.2

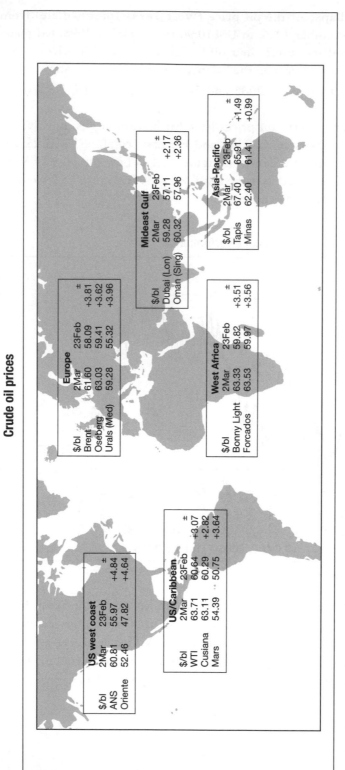

Crude oil prices

US west coast

$/bl	2Mar	23Feb	±
ANS	60.81	55.97	+4.84
Oriente	52.46	47.82	+4.64

US/Caribbean

$/bl	2Mar	23Feb	±
WTI	63.71	60.64	+3.07
Cusiana	63.11	60.29	+2.82
Mars	54.39	50.75	+3.64

Europe

$/bl	2Mar	23Feb	±
Brent	61.60	58.09	+3.81
Oseberg	63.03	59.41	+3.62
Urals (Med)	59.28	55.32	+3.96

West Africa

$/bl	2Mar	23Feb	±
Bonny Light	63.33	59.82	+3.51
Forcados	63.53	59.97	+3.56

Mideast Gulf

$/bl	2Mar	23Feb	±
Dubai (Lon)	59.28	57.11	+2.17
Oman (Sing)	60.32	57.96	+2.36

Asia-Pacific

$/bl	2Mar	23Feb	±
Tapis	67.40	65.91	+1.49
Minas	62.40	61.41	+0.99

Source: Argus Global Markets, Argus Media Ltd, www.argusmediagroup.com

EXCHANGE-TRADED ENERGY DERIVATIVES

Introduction

The major exchanges where energy derivatives are traded are the New York Mercantile Exchange (NYMEX), the IntercontinentalExchange (ICE) in London and SGX, the Singapore Exchange (merger of Stock Exchange of Singapore and SIMEX – the derivatives trading exchange). NB: The ICE, an Atlanta based organization, purchased the International Petroleum Exchange in May 2001.

NYMEX introduced the first energy-related futures contract in 1978, and now trades a variety of different futures contracts, e.g. No. 2 Heating Oil, light sweet crude oil, natural gas, unleaded regular gasoline, propane, etc.

EXCHANGE-TRADED FUTURES CONTRACTS

As with all futures contracts, positions can be taken to mitigate (hedge) risk or to take it actively as a trader (speculate). A trader may simply have a view on the direction of a particular oil price and wish to take out a futures position that will allow him to profit from his view (or not). A hedger, however, may seek to take an equal and opposite position in the futures market to offset as much of the price risk as possible on his physical contracts. For example, if we pay US$60 for a barrel of oil today and then we sell it tomorrow at US$50, we have lost US$10. If we hedge the position we will try to guarantee the price at which it will be sold, in effect to 'lock in' the price.

To illustrate how futures have been used for risk management and price control, we can look back as far as the Gulf War of 1990–91. Traders were able to manage their price risk using futures to smoothe out 'price shocks'. This, combined with the willingness of the International Energy Agency (IEA) to release oil from stocks already held to make up for possible shortfalls, meant that oil prices did not fluctuate as wildly as during the oil crises of the 1970s. Oil prices still moved, but not catastrophically. Figure 13.3 shows the average annual crude oil price from 1946 to 2006, both in nominal and inflation adjusted form.

| Figure 13.3 | Inflation adjusted monthly crude oil prices (1946 – present) in December 2005 in dollars |

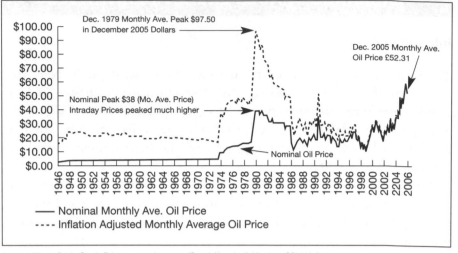

Source: Illinois Basin Crude Prices – www.ioga.com/Special/crudeoil_Hist.htm CPI-U Inflation index – www.bis.gov
© www.inflationData.com

For futures and options markets to be successful, they need price volatility and liquidity allowing participants to trade in and out of positions on a regular basis. But for the resulting hedge to be successful, the future (and the option) and the underlying oil price need to move closely together. Unfortunately, as with all futures contracts, but especially in the commodity market, a pricing feature exists called 'basis'. This describes the differential that exists between the futures price of the commodity and the equivalent cash market price. The basis is continually changing and is in practice difficult to hedge. It reflects such variables as storage and transportation costs, interest rates, market sentiment and supply and demand. The only firm certainty is that by the expiry date of the futures the cash market price and the futures price will converge.

At this point it is worth defining our terms.

Terminology		
	'Long' the physical	A company which produces oil or has bought crude and is holding it in storage for delivery or use at a later date.
	'Short' the physical	A company with an obligation to deliver crude at a future date at a fixed price when it does not already own the physical.
	'Long' the future	A client who has bought futures to open a position.
	'Short' the futures	A trader who has sold futures without previously owning them.

In order for a company to hedge oil price risk, it will need to 'short the futures' if it is 'long the physical', and vice versa. But, by using futures contracts as opposed to options they will not be allowed to participate in a profitable movement, as futures hedge 100 per cent of all risk – profits as well as losses.

Table 13.1 gives a summary of basic hedging techniques using futures.

Basic hedging techniques   **Table 13.1**

Physical position	Price risk	Futures position	Result
LONG	Falling prices	SHORT	Short hedge
SHORT	Rising prices	LONG	Long hedge

Exchange of futures for physicals (EFPs)

This is the mechanism used to exchange a position in the futures market for an equivalent position in the physical market, and vice versa. It is a complicated procedure, but in essence it allows the pricing to be separated from the supply. It is also possible to have exchange of futures for swaps (EFSs), which involve a similar procedure whereby futures contracts are exchanged for oil swaps.

> An energy futures contract is a legally binding agreement to make or take delivery of a standard quantity of a specific crude or product cargo at a future date and at a price agreed between the parties through open outcry on the floor of an organized exchange. Cash settlement can be arranged for particular futures contracts.   **Definition**

Definition discussed

As with all futures contracts there is a rigid contract specification that the participants must adhere to. It explains what is expected of the buyer and seller of the future and what obligations they must perform. Each future will also have a fixed 'contract amount' to make it easy to determine how many futures are required for the hedge or trade. The price agreed between two traders today will be for 'delivery' on a particular date in the future. The term 'delivery' is still used, although many of these contracts do not now have to be physically delivered. There is often an opportunity to cash settle the differences between the buying/selling price and the final price at maturity or close out. In fact, 'delivery' really denotes contract expiry. On most of the oil exchanges the 'open outcry' method of trading is used. This conveys an element of price transparency, allowing every trader equal access to the same trade at the same price. For further details on the open outcry method of trading, see the chapter on *financial futures contracts*.

Key features

Energy futures contracts

Market
Oil futures are traded on regulated exchanges with standard contract sizes and specific delivery dates. Trades are executed by a member firm or broker.

Contracts
Different contracts are available on each exchange; each is standardized to enhance liquidity.

Pricing
It is a competitive auction-based market, and prices are generally quoted as a bid–offer spread, either in dollars and cents per barrel or per tonne, or in cents per US gallon (pricing for propane and natural gas is a little different). Once a futures trade has been executed, the price is then widely disseminated through various information networks, such as Reuters and Bloomberg.

Market operations
Both buyers and sellers must put up minimum levels of collateral for each open contract that they hold. This is known as initial margin, and can be viewed as a good faith deposit. The actual level is calculated by the relevant exchange in conjunction with the clearing house. The method used by most exchanges is now the SPAN 4 (standard portfolio analysis of risk v4) system. This was developed by the Chicago Mercantile Exchange to monitor how risky a client's position becomes.

Once the initial margin is placed with the clearing house it will accumulate interest, and will be returned with interest when the position is closed out. The level of margin due on a futures contract can change if market volatility changes. When the Iraq/Kuwait Gulf War blew up in 1990, initial margins had to be reviewed as a matter of some urgency. You can see from Figure 13.4, that just as the US operation Desert Storm commenced the initial margins had increased to US$6,000 per contract (lot), equivalent to US$6 per barrel.

Futures positions are 'marked-to-market' daily, and profits or losses are crystallized daily. If the position loses money against the daily settlement price, losses must be paid following the close of the trade. If the position is in profit on that day, then payment will be received. These payments are known as variation margin.

Credit risk

Key features continued

The ICE and other major oil exchanges function in a similar way to Euronext.liffe. The trade is executed and matched and LCH.Clearnet which is an entity separate from the exchange itself provides the clearing mechanism. It is the clearing house which will call for margin from market participants and their brokers, and ultimately each trade will eventually end up as a trade between the buyer/seller and the clearing house.

Availability

There are a number of different oil and gas futures contracts, and it is advisable to check with each exchange exactly which contracts they offer. Table 13.2 lists an abbreviated contract specifications for the electronic Brent Crude future, still known as IPE.

A Brent futures hedging transaction

Example

2 November

A trader has bought a cargo of 500,000 barrels of Brent Blend crude oil, for which he paid US$56.20 per barrel. He has agreed to sell it in mid-January time on a Platt's-related basis. Platt's is a well-established journal in the market and provides reference rates for many different types of oil and oil products, now owned by Standard & Poor's. A Platt's-related trade is based on a continuously variable oil price. It is similar to a LIBOR fix in the interest rate market. He is concerned that oil prices may fall and he will therefore make a loss. To hedge this position he will need to sell futures to protect against this anticipated fall in prices. He will close out the futures position at the time he sells the cargo.

Figure 13.4

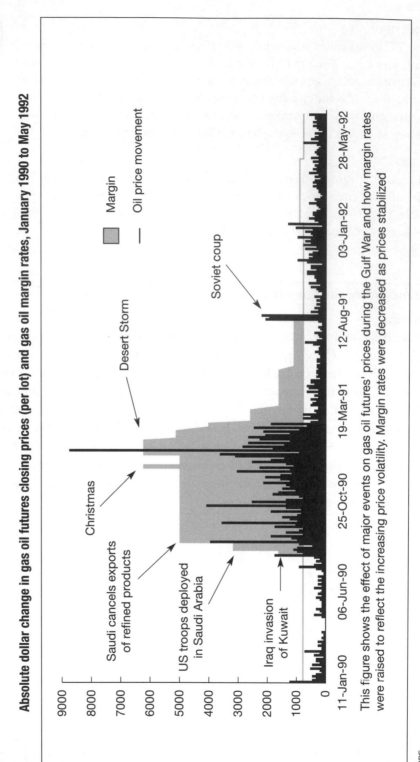

Absolute dollar change in gas oil futures closing prices (per lot) and gas oil margin rates, January 1990 to May 1992

This figure shows the effect of major events on gas oil futures' prices during the Gulf War and how margin rates were raised to reflect the increasing price volatility. Margin rates were decreased as prices stabilized

Source: IPE

IPE Brent Crude oil future – abbreviated contract specification*   Table 13.2

Unit of trading	1,000 barrels of crude (42,000 US gallons)
Delivery months	30 consecutive months then half-yearly out to 7 years
Expiration date	Trading will cease at the close of business on the business day preceding the 15th day of the month prior to the first day of the delivery month
Quotation	US$ and cents per barrel
Minimum price movement	One cent per barrel equivalent to a tick value of US $10.00 per barrel
Trading hours	01.00 – 22.00 Local London Time (LLT), Monday–Friday

* For further contract details, contact ICE.
Source: ICE

Assume the trader sells 500 Brent January futures contracts at a price of $55.90. He will put up the initial margin of US$700 per contract – a total of US$350,000 and the position will be marked-to-market on a daily basis with profits and losses crystallized on a daily basis.

Action – 17 November

The trader sells his cargo at a Platt's reference price of US$55.30, making a loss of 0.90 cents per barrel or US$450,000. However, the futures trade has made a profit which will go some way to offset the loss on the physical position. He buys the futures back at the current market level of US$55.30.

Profit from the futures hedge

2 November	Sell 500 contracts at US$55.90
17 November	Close out position by buying the futures back at the current market price US$55.30
Profit	(60 ticks × 10 cents × 500 contracts) = US $300,000

The hedge is not 100 per cent effective but has narrowed the loss on the transaction to US$150,000 (US$450,000 less US$300,000). This loss of US$50,000 can be accounted for by the narrowing of the basis.

EXCHANGE-TRADED ENERGY OPTION CONTRACTS

Introduction

Energy options were launched by all the major exchanges in the mid to late 1980s. They are options on the underlying futures contract and, by using a combination of futures and options, even the most complicated risk scenarios can be hedged.

As previously discussed, an option contract is the only derivative instrument that allows the buyer (holder) to 'walk away' from his obligations. With energy options, when the option is exercised, it results in the holder being long or short an energy futures contract, which is then usually cash settled. In effect the holder of one call option on the energy future will, on exercise, be long one energy future. An upfront premium is due. The option allows a greater degree of flexibility than a futures contract in that it does not completely take away all the risk, i.e. all the losses and all the profit. Instead it allows a degree of risk management that allows for risk control not risk removal. Options also exhibit 'asymmetry of risk', such that the most that an option holder can lose is the original premium that he paid, whereas the most by which he can profit is unlimited, the amount of profit governed only by how far the market has moved in his favour. A seller of options, in contrast, can only hope to keep the premium, but the extent of the losses is potentially unlimited. Put simplistically, buyers of options have rights, but no obligations, and writers of options have obligations, but no rights.

'It has been estimated that the total volume of crude oil trading on NYMEX and the ICE is equivalent to well over ten times world oil consumption.'

| Definition | A traded energy option gives the holder the right, but not the obligation, to buy or sell an agreed amount of energy futures at a specified price, on or before a specified date. A premium is due. The option will be cash settled against the corresponding energy future. |

Definition discussed

An energy option gives the holder, who may be an oil refiner, the chance to secure the oil price in advance. The holder of the option will choose his own guaranteed rate (the strike) from those specified by the exchange that are in multiples of 50 cents per barrel. A premium is required, which must be paid upfront, to the seller of the option on the business day following the trade. Energy options are American style, allowing the holder to exercise on any business day in the contractual period. NYMEX options and futures on light sweet crude oil are used to hedge positions where the underlying is West Texas Intermediate (see Table 13.3). Most open option positions will be closed out or exercised prior to expiry. Remaining open positions are automatically closed out by the exchange.

NYMEX light sweet crude oil option – abbreviated contract specification*	Table 13.3

Unit of trading	One NYMEX division light sweet crude oil futures contract
Trading months	Current year and the next 5 years
Strikes	20 strike prices above and below ATM, the next 10 in increments of $2.50. The ATM (at the money) strike is that nearest to the Previous day's close on the futures contract
Exercise/ settlement day	Exercise by a clearing member not later than 16.30, or 45 minutes after the underlying futures settlement price is posted, on any business day, up to and including expiry
Last trading day	Three business days before the underlying futures contract expiry
Quotation	Dollars and cents per barrel
Minimum price movement	1 cent per barrel
Tick value	US$10 per contract
Trading hours	10.00 – 14.30 (New York) 9.45 – 15.10 (trading pit)

* For further contract details, contact NYMEX direct

Most open option positions will be closed out or exercised prior to expiry. Remaining open positions are automatically closed out by the exchange.

Traded energy options	Key features

Insurance protection

The client pays a premium to insure against adverse oil price movements. The clearing house agrees to guarantee the agreed rate if/when required by the client.

Profit potential

The risk of adverse oil price market movements is eliminated, while at the same time, the buyer retains the potential to benefit from favourable prices. The option can be abandoned or exercised, dependent upon market movements.

Sell-back

Traded energy options cannot be sold back to the exchange, but an opposite position can be transacted at the current market rate with another counterparty.

Key features
continued

Exercise
As the counterparty to each deal is the clearing house, if a client wishes to exercise the option, he is assigned a counterparty at random.

Cash settlement
The option is cash settled against the corresponding energy future. This allows participants to take profits from favourable movements without having to deal physically in the underlying cargo.

Premium determinants

The amount of premium payable by the purchaser of a traded energy option is determined by the following factors:

- underlying price compared with strike price
- maturity
- put or call
- cost of carry of the position
- expected market volatility.

(a) Strike price

With energy options, the underlying benchmark against which the strike is measured is the appropriate energy futures price. Strikes are therefore referred to as follows:

Terminology

At the money (ATM)	Where the strike is equal to the current futures price.
In the money (ITM)	Where the strike is more favourable than the futures price, and the option premium higher than that for an ATM option.
Out of the money (OTM)	Where the strike is worse than the futures price and the option premium is lower than for an ATM option.

(b) Maturity

The longer the time to expiry, the higher the probability of large oil price movements, and the higher the chance of profitable exercise by the buyer. The buyer should be prepared to pay a higher premium for a longer-dated option than a short-dated option.

(c) Put or call

This will affect the whether the strike is in or out of the money, and also the final market price due to supply and demand swings.

(d) Cost of carry

As this option is based on the underlying energy future, the cost of carrying the position is a relevant factor. As shown in the previous section on futures, a fair value can be calculated for the futures price. This is a function of the cost of borrowing the money to pay for the oil for the full exposure period.

(e) Expected market volatility

The higher the volatility the greater the possibility of profitable exercise by the customer, so the option is more valuable and the premium is higher. This may well be different from the level of historic volatility, which could be higher or lower. Various market factors may lead to an increase in the option premium, such events as oil company failures, new taxes, political stability, exchange controls, or general illiquidity in the market.

	Energy option	**Terminology**
Strike price	Specified energy futures price where the client can exercise his right to physical settlement. This will be specified as ATM, ITM or OTM compared to the futures price.	
Call option	The right to buy the underlying future.	
Put option	The right to sell the underlying future.	
Exercise	The take-up of the option at or before expiry.	
Expiry date	The last date when the option may be exercised.	
Value date	The date of (settlement) as determined by the exchange.	
Premium	The price of the option, as determined by an option pricing model.	
Intrinsic value	Strike rate minus the current market rate.	
Time value	Option premium minus intrinsic value, reflecting the time until expiry, changes in volatility, and market expectations.	

Example | Hedging with an option on light sweet crude oil

4 January

An oil producer fears an oil price decline, due to warm winter weather and is worried that he may have to sell his oil too cheaply on the market. He anticipates he will sell approximately 1,000 barrels a day in January at a price of about US$45 per barrel. His expected receipts on 25 days of production are US$1,125,000. The oil producer could use futures that would cost nothing in terms of an upfront premium, but could actually lose him money if his view of the market was wrong. However, there are certain factors in the market that lead him to believe that there may be a short-term market shortage which may well push up prices temporarily. He wishes to profit if the market moves in his favour, but he also wishes to protect his downside.

Action 4 January

The current level of the February future is US$44.67 per barrel. The oil producer decides to buy 25 February put options on the NYMEX light sweet crude oil future with a strike at US$45.00 per barrel. This is slightly 'in the money' and the cost will reflect this. His Reuters screen shows that the last trade went through at 59 cents per barrel, the same as yesterday's closing price. Volatility is currently stable, and our oil producer decides to deal through his broker at 59 cents per barrel – a total premium cost of US$0.59 × 25,000 barrels = US$14,750.

February

There are two possible outcomes, oil prices can rise or they can fall. Let us assume that the oil price can move +/– US$5.00.

First, if oil prices rise to US$50.00 the producer will abandon his option and sell his oil at the higher level. This would realize him 25,000 × $50.00, which equals US$1,250,000, an improvement of US$125,000 over his original estimate. But his option premium cost him US$14,750, which must be deducted to give the final figure of US$1,235,250, equivalent to US$49.41 per barrel.

Secondly, if oil prices had fallen to, say, US$40.00 from their original level, he would exercise the option to sell his oil at US$45.00, netting an income of US$1,110,250 after premium costs. This is absolutely the worst case, if oil prices fall to US$5.00 a barrel, the producer will still be able to guarantee a rate of US$1,110,250 by utilizing the option, an effective rate of US$44.41 per barrel.

The oil producer has insured against an adverse oil price movement for a limited and known cost, and preserved his right to benefit if the oil spot market rates move in his favour. This option has guaranteed for the client a worst rate of US$44.41. If rates fall lower than the option strike of

US$45.00, the oil producer will always exercise the option. So in practice the worst rate is US$44.41. But, if the oil producer is lucky, and oil prices rise, then he will abandon the option and sell his oil at the higher price. There is no limit to the amount of profit he can make, it is constrained only by how far the market may move.

Practical considerations

Using exchange-traded oil derivatives to hedge positions will offer the client liquidity, a tight price and the comfort of dealing with an established exchange and clearing mechanism. Unfortunately, commodities of all sorts can suffer very violent swings in the underlying, and on occasions illiquidity in the spot market will cause problems.

It is very rare to achieve a hedge that is 100 per cent effective, owing to the pricing disparity known as 'basis', which in practical terms is almost unhedgeable.

Commodities are prone to 'backwardation'. In simple terms, this means that the price of oil on the spot market is more expensive than the price quoted for forward delivery. This seems to be the 'wrong way round'. With any commodity, storage, transportation and funding costs almost always mean that forward prices should be more expensive than spot prices which do not include all the above extra costs. But it can happen on some occasions that spot prices are bid up. This relationship needs to be monitored very closely during the life of any hedge.

Documentation for all exchange-traded products will be standardized, although the brokers through whom most market participants will deal will each have their individual terms and conditions for dealing. It is always advisable for the lawyers to have sight of the paperwork before signature, so allow sufficient time for this before dealing is due to commence.

OTC OR 'OFF-EXCHANGE' ENERGY DERIVATIVES

Introduction

Because of the many different types of oil and oil products, dealing 'off-exchange' is popular with users and producers who wish to hedge or trade a particular variety of oil or oil product where there is as yet either no exchange-traded contract available or it has some limitations.

For example, a client may wish to hedge his exposure for a longer period, or to purchase an option with a different strike from that offered by an exchange, or execute an energy swap where there is no exchange-traded equivalent. The providers of OTC energy derivatives will generally be the large oil companies such as Exxon Mobil, Total, Royal Dutch Shell and Elf, together with the investment banks such as Morgan Stanley, Lehman Brothers and Barclays Capital.

Available OTC products are energy options and other option related products such as oil caps and collars, and oil swaps. The credit risks attached to OTC products are always greater than the credit risks attached to exchange-traded derivatives and need careful consideration. An OTC transaction is a bilateral arrangement where each counterparty must bear the other's credit risk. Dealing on an exchange immunizes both counterparties from this risk, as once the transaction is executed, both parties are in legal contract with the clearing house, rather than each other.

OTC OPTION PRODUCTS

The option products that are most frequently used in the oil market are caps and collars. These have exactly the same structure as those in the interest rate markets, but are typically used to cover a shorter time horizon.

The cap will have multiple settlements (fixings), with dates that are pre-arranged at the outset. Options with a single settlement are known as puts (the right to sell) and calls (the right to buy), and perform in exactly the same way as options on stocks or options on currency. For further details on options see *basic option concepts* in Chapter 4.

Definition An energy cap gives the buyer (or holder) the right, but not the obligation, to fix the oil price, on a notional amount of product cargo at a specific rate (the strike) for a specified period. The writer of the cap will guarantee to the holder a maximum price level if/when required, and will reimburse the holder of the cap for any excess cost over the agreed strike rate. A premium is due, payable upfront or monthly.

Definition discussed

To clarify the picture we need to open up this definition. As with all option contracts there is a buyer and a seller of the option itself. A cap is simply an option with more than one fixing. Mostly, but not always, the cap writers or sellers will be the major oil companies and banks. Usually the buyer of the cap is a consumer or user of oil or oil products, such as an airline, or a transport company, or in some cases an institution looking to risk manage its positions.

The client needs to choose a strike price for the cap which best reflects his actual fuel costs. One noticeable difference between an interest rate cap and an oil cap relates to the fixing or rollover dates. With an oil cap, the client's floating reference rate is not a particular price on a particular date (as with interest rate caps), such as 6-month LIBOR on 21st March, but the average oil price over the period, usually a month. This strike price, index price or fixed rate will be guaranteed for the client if/when he requires it. A reference rate needs to be agreed at the outset for the floating side of the cap: this can be linked to a Platt's (now owned by McGraw-Hill) rate, or a futures price +/– some premium. The actual monthly averages in the market, as published in Platt's for example, will be compared with the strike rate on the cap, and a payment of the difference will be made by the appropriate party. Caps with average monthly fixings are sometimes known as 'Asian options'. The benchmark used to compare the strike on the oil cap with the current market rates is the equivalent underlying oil swap rate.

Energy caps

Key features

Multiple exercise
A time series of individual energy options with the same strike rates.

Insurance protection
The client pays a premium to insure against adverse oil price movements. Premium can be paid upfront or monthly.

Profit potential
A cap reduces the risk of adverse price movements while retaining profit potential. The instrument can be allowed to lapse (abandoned) if the market has moved in the client's favour.

Cash settlement
Principal funds are not involved. The client is not obliged to make or take delivery from the writing oil company. On exercise, the writer will pay the difference between the strike rate and the average oil reference rate. Settlement is usually five business days in arrears after the end of the month.

Premium determinants

The amount of premium payable for an oil cap is dependent on the inputs into the pricing model that are:

- underlying price compared with strike price
- maturity

- expected market volatility
- market conditions.

(a) Strike price

With energy caps the underlying benchmark is the appropriate oil swap rate, taking into account the correct side of the swap, i.e. payer's or receiver's side as appropriate (see the discussion on *interest rate swaps* in Chapter 6). It is against this that the client's strike rate is measured. Strike rates are therefore referred to as follows:

Terminology	At the money (ATM)	Where the strike is equal to the current swap rate.
	In the money (ITM)	Where the strike is more favourable to the swap rate, and the option premium higher than that for an ATM option.
	Out of the money (OTM)	Where the strike is worse than the swap rate and the option premium is lower than that for an ATM option.

(b) Maturity

The longer the time to expiry or maturity, the higher the probability of large price movements, and the higher the chance of profitable exercise by the client (buyer). The buyer should therefore be prepared to pay a higher premium for a longer dated cap than for a short-dated cap.

(c) Expected market volatility

The higher the volatility the greater the possibility of profitable exercise by the client, so the cap is more valuable to the company, therefore the premium is higher. In general terms if there is high volatility in the market, then there is a strong likelihood of erratic oil price movements.

(d) Market conditions

Various market factors may lead to an increase in the option premium and these include events such as government controls, strikes, imposition of new taxes, rumours, or illiquidity in the market. In general terms, anything that can destabilize the oil price will lead to an increase in volatility, so the option premium will increase.

OTC OPTION PRODUCTS

	Oil caps	Terminology
Strike price	Specified oil price where the client can exercise his right to cash settlement. This can be ITM, ATM or OTM.	
Multiple exercise	Take-up of the option on various fixing dates.	
Settlement date	Usually last business day in the month.	
Value date	Five business days after the settlement date.	
Premium	The price of the option, as determined by an option pricing model.	
Intrinsic value	Strike rate minus the current market rate.	
Time value	Option premium minus intrinsic value, reflecting the time until expiry, changes in volatility, and market expectations.	

Hedging with an energy cap

Example

A Singaporean shipping company needs to purchase bunkerfuel for one of its small subsidiaries. The company estimates that it will need to buy 1,000 metric tonnes per month for September, October and November, and wishes to 'cap' its fuel costs. The index that best suits this customer is based on Singapore IF 180 which is currently trading at US$345/t. (NB: Bunkerfuel is used in car ferries and similar vehicles.)

Strategy

The company starts to gather prices from the market makers for a cap with a strike of US$350/t. This is a little OTM, and a major oil company has offered a cap to the shipping company at a premium of US$4.5/t, making a total monthly premium cost of US$4,500. This will give full protection starting in September at a price of US$350/t.

Outcome

If the monthly average price is below the strike, the shipping company will buy its fuel at a cheaper price in the market; if the average monthly cost is higher than the strike, the oil company will compensate the company for any excess over and above this rate.

Figure 13.5

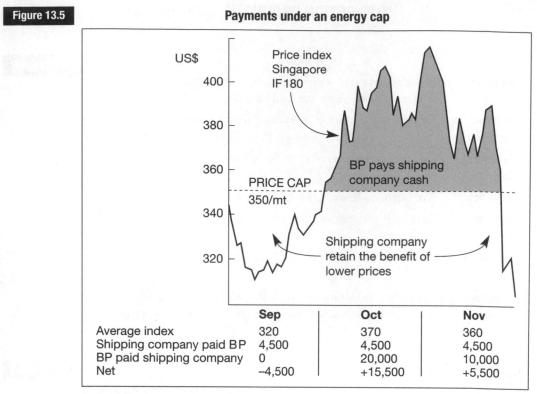

Payments under an energy cap

	Sep	Oct	Nov
Average index	320	370	360
Shipping company paid BP	4,500	4,500	4,500
BP paid shipping company	0	20,000	10,000
Net	−4,500	+15,500	+5,500

Source: BP Oil International Ltd

An oil cap will therefore fix the shipping company's bunkerfuel costs at a maximum level of US$ 350/t (see Figure 13.5). The breakeven rate will be achieved at cap price + option premium, a level of US$354.50.

An oil floor is identical in operation to an oil cap, and could protect an oil producer from falling prices by fixing the minimum sale price, for a pre-determined period. However, they are only likely to account for about 35 to 45 per cent of total cap and floor turnover.

Availability

Energy caps and floors are generally available in notional amounts from 1,000 barrels of crude, and 500 metric tonnes for oil products, although deals between market makers will obviously be larger. Increasingly, business is being written in non-dollar-based currencies such as the euro.

Practical considerations

Most energy caps and floors are for periods up to two years, and occasionally up to five years and will generally have resets every month or every quarter based on the average rate throughout the period. References for the floating rate must be agreed in advance, and there are a number of different oil indices to choose from.

When a client purchases a cap or floor, his only responsibility is to pay the premium required. Once this has been paid, he has no further obligations. However, he could choose to pay the premium by selling another option product to the bank, in effect trying to create a reduced cost strategy. He is then opening himself up to possible risk. These composite products are known as collars, and the premium due can be reduced down to zero. They involve the simultaneous trading of the cap and the floor, and are similar in operation to collars in the interest market.

Where the client buys the cap or floor, a credit line is not required as the client is under no obligation to deliver anything. However, if he wishes to sell the product, or to transact one of the collar strategies, a credit line will be required and this needs to be set up in advance.

OTC OIL SWAPS

Introduction

Oil swaps are one of the fastest growing products on the market. The mechanics of oil swaps follow those in other swap markets. The big players continue to be the major oil companies, and the large international banks, most of whom have an interest rate swap capability. Maturities are most likely to be in the one to five-year period, occasionally longer with quarterly or semi-annual resets.

In Asia, most oil hedging is carried out using swaps, but in the USA more OTC options are transacted.

> An agreement between two parties to exchange cash flows based on an agreed oil index price for a specified period at agreed reset intervals based on the average price for the period, as noted by a pre-specified independent authority.

Definition

Definition discussed

This is a legally binding agreement where an absolute oil price level will be guaranteed. One party will agree to pay the 'fixed index rate'; the other to receive this fixed rate, and pay the 'floating rate' based on the monthly average movement of the same index. The underlying sale or purchase transaction is untouched and may well be with another institution. The only movement of funds is a net transfer of payments between the two parties on the pre-specified dates. However, with oil swaps it is possible to link the swap with a particular physical cargo. The cash flows are calculated based on an agreed notional amount with a cargo which may or may not be delivered.

Key features

Oil swaps

Insurance protection
Through a swap a client can guarantee the rate at which he will purchase (or sell) a pre-specified amount of oil or oil products for a pre-determined period. No premium is required.

Cash or physical settlement
It is normally only the index-linked cash flows that are swapped, with the notional amount of cargo not exchanged. However, physical settlement can be arranged but must be agreed in advance.

Funding optimization
As the underlying commitment to buy or sell the oil may be with another institution, the client can deal where he gets the best prices. The swap will be negotiated separately.

Credit risk
The credit risk of both counterparties must be carefully evaluated, as each will bear the other's credit risk.

Premium
Swaps are zero-premium instruments and a credit line will be required. On some occasions the client will need to collateralize the swap, that is, to secure the credit risk with cash, either in the form of a deposit, or by way of a variable letter of credit. These arrangements need to be finalized before dealing commences.

Terminology

Oil Swaps

Fixed payer	The party wishing to pay 'fixed' on the swap, and protect itself from a rise in prices.
Fixed receiver	The party wishing to receive 'fixed' on the swap, and protect itself from a fall in prices.
Swap rate, fixed rate, guaranteed rate	The oil swap rate agreed between the parties at the outset of the transaction.
Resets	Dates when the monthly average floating rate is compared to the fixed rate on the swap. The differences are net cash settled. Settlement is usually five business days in arrears.

Hedging a Brent Crude exposure with an oil swap

15 May

A major European refiner is worried that the price of Brent Crude is rising again and he needs to hedge approximately 150,000 barrels per month for one year, commencing in June. The current swap price for the period is US$65.00 per barrel.

Strategy

The company can take out an oil swap which would fix the price of Brent Crude and remove the threat of rising oil prices. It is important for the swap to match the underlying transaction in all respects. In our example, the company wishes to 'pay the fixed and receive the floating' (rate). The company is happy to hedge at the current levels, and a major oil company has offered the swap at the current rate of US$65 per barrel against monthly average as quoted by Platts or Argus (see Figure 13.6).

Oil swap cash flows

Figure 13.6

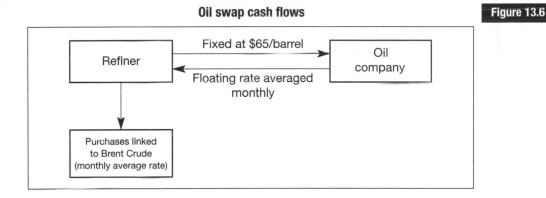

Outcome

On each of the pre-specified reset dates, the two cash flows will be calculated and offset. If at the beginning of July when we are calculating the settlements for June these were the rates:

Fixed: US$65/barrel

Average monthly rate: $67.20

There would be a net payment of US$2.20 per barrel from the oil company to the refiner, a total of US$330,000 on 150,000 barrels. This offsets the extra US$2.20 per barrel which must be paid in the underlying market. Had the monthly average rate been US$64.50, then there would be a net cash settlement of US$0.50 per barrel from the refiner to the oil company.

This illustrates that, as with all swaps, the swap rate becomes an absolute guaranteed rate for the transaction. No improvements on the price level are possible. All risk has been hedged away, even the risk of making a profit.

Example

Using a Swap to fix the price of Diesel

Last October Company X fixed the cost of diesel purchases in Germany for the following January and February, by entering into a swap with BP. The index chosen was ULSD 50ppm Rotterdam Barges swap for 5,000 metric tonnes per month. The swap rate was US$220/MT. (Summary terms – Table 13.4.)

Table 13.4

Summary terms

Fixed price payer:	End-user
Floating price paper:	BP
Product:	ULSD 50 ppm Rotterdam Barges
Duration:	01 Jan – 28 Feb
Volume:	5,000 MT/mth (total 10,000 MT)
Fixed price:	$220/MT
Floating price:	Average of mean of Platts
Settlement:	5 days after pricing month

Figure 13.7

Oil swap

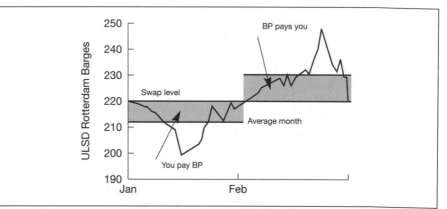

Source: BP Oil International Ltd

Settlement

1. In January the average monthly index price is equal to $213/MT, this is $7 below the agreed rate; Company X must pay to BP $7 × 5,000 MT = $35,000.

2. In February the average monthly index price is equal to $230/MT, this is $10 above the agreed rate. BP pays $10 × 5,000MT = $50,000.

3. The net price after settlements will equal $220/MT.

Source: BP Oil International Ltd.

OVERVIEW OF ELECTRICITY MARKET

I wanted to make reference to the electricity markets as recent deregulation in the electricity markets has opened up power and emissions trading to international banks and organizations. Although electricity can be considered as just another energy market there are some unique elements about it which need to be understood.

(a) It cannot be stored, which means that you must have real-time balancing of supply and demand. (Imagine real-time marking-to-market but with the supply and demand flows!) The system needs to be in complete continuous equilibrium or else there will be power blackouts. NB: Hydro electricity can be stored but this is a very small amount in a global context.

(b) Electricity needs to be transported along high voltage transmission lines, often known as a 'grid'. This process can reduce the amount actually supplied by about 10 per cent as it is 'lost' in the transmission process.

(c) Flows of electricity from A to B cannot be identified.

(d) The electricity industry is often organized as a state-owned monopoly.

(e) You can have very high volatility from supply and demand spikes which can move prices from US$35 per megawatt hour to US$1,000 per megawatt hour and back again – as there is no capacity for storage.

(f) Weather and popular TV programmes can increase demand.

The spot power market

The spot markets may be organized in one of two ways, as a pool such as the Nord Pool in Scandinavia or the NYPOOL in New York, or a Power Exchange (PX), as in Poland (PPX).

1. Pool structure

There is a system operator (SO) who acts as a single buyer of electricity. The bids come from the various electricity generators in terms of prices and quantities per half-hour throughout the day, for the following day. There are two sub-structures;

(a) Either, it is only the suppliers who make bids and the SO is responsible for calculating the expected demand for each half-hour period. This provides the SMP or system marginal price, or

(b) Both buyers and sellers make bids and the SO builds up a demand function. This is fairly inelastic as demand tends to be constant whatever the price.

2. Power Exchange structure (PX)

This is a competitive wholesale market for the trading of electricity, often owned by the market participants who include generators, traders, large consumers and distribution companies. Prices are computed hourly or averaged over a day leading to an exchange index which can be become a benchmark for electricity derivatives trading.

However the system is organized, the SO does not own the generation but must manage the supply and distribution. Occasionally there is a shortfall and as it is impossible to store then additional supplies must be generated.

Table 13.5	Electricity market structure		
Country	**Date**	**Name**	
England & Wales	2001	UK Power Exchange (UKPX)	
Norway	1996	Nordpool	
Germany	2001	European Power Exchange (EEX)	
Netherlands	1999	Amsterdam Power Exchange (APX)	

Trading electricity

There are a number of alternatives;

- **Spot market**: This is really a one-day forward market which continuously rolls forward.

- **Forward market**: Anything from one year to five years – with maturities continually lengthening. This is an agreement to buy/sell a specific amount of electricity at a specific price for delivery at a specific place (and time) in the future. These are non-transferable.

- **Futures market**: Linked inevitably with Enron and other similar corporate catastrophes; this led many exchanges to de-list their electricity contracts in 2002, although they are now being re-introduced.

  - **ICE** (InterContinental Exchange) based in the UK now offers a range of electricity futures contracts linked to 'base load (off-peak)' and 'peak load' contracts.

  - **NYMEX** offers a contract on the PJM Electricity Market which settles monthly and is linked to the Pennsylvania Electric Company and Potomac Electric Company.

  - Other popular futures contracts are the 'Twin Cities on and off-peak electricity futures', this is specifically for delivery in the Twin Cities of Minneapolis and St Paul, and the Nord Pool futures contracts.

There is also a link between electricity and gas prices and this is known as the 'Spark-spread' which can also be traded independently.

■ **OTC markets:** At the time of writing it is incredibly difficult to get details and examples of OTC electricity transactions due to their proprietary nature. However they comprise:

- ■ Electricity call options – often sold by electricity generating companies to users who wish to protect their price risk.

- ■ Electricity put options – often sold by large users who wish to safeguard supply and used to generating companies to guard against price falls.

- ■ Electricity price swaps – these are typically established for a specified quantity of power that is referenced to the variable spot price at either the generator's or consumer's location.

This whole area of electricity and power derivatives is complex, niche and justifies its own publication, understandably it is therefore outside the range of this book.

'So much for derivatives being uncontrollable weapons of financial mass destruction!'

Using Derivatives in Hedge Funds

Stuart C. Fiertz
President,
Cheyne Capital
Management Limited

Introduction

Mitigating risk

Increasing exposures

Capturing tax efficiencies

Manoeuvring anonymously

Accessing restricted markets

Trading non-deliverable assets

Shifting operational burdens

Executing with greater precision

Conclusion

INTRODUCTION

While the legendary investor Warren Buffet has chosen to describe derivatives as instruments of financial mass destruction, the hedge fund community has found derivatives to be effective tools for both controlling risk and for gaining targeted investment exposures. Indeed, the ability and willingness of hedge fund managers to use derivatives is one of the key features that differentiates hedge funds from traditional investment funds. This chapter is designed to introduce readers to the broad applicability of derivatives for hedge funds and to give a demonstration of their effectiveness. The continuous development of new derivative structures means that a list that purports to be definitive will quickly become incomplete. Instead, this chapter focuses on the underlying objectives of the buyside derivatives user. Previous authors have concentrated on the cynical use of derivatives to obfuscate and thereby to take advantage of vulnerable and unsophisticated end users. No less an observer than Alan Greenspan, however, has credited derivatives in the form of credit default swaps with ensuring that the sharp 2002–2003 credit downturn did not negatively impact the overall banking system. So much for derivatives being uncontrollable weapons of financial mass destruction! Indeed, derivatives will continue to be important and effective tools for hedge funds and other investors to both mitigate risk and to gain their targeted investment exposures.

MITIGATING RISK

Risk mitigation with derivatives can take two forms. They can be used to isolate those risks consistent with a particular hedge fund strategy by hedging out unwanted risk. They can also be used to modulate the overall risk profile of a hedge fund. This type of adjustment made with derivatives can be either a temporary tactical response to changing market conditions or a more permanent structural hedge to reach a target risk profile.

The behaviour of convertible bond arbitrageurs is a useful way to illustrate the use of derivatives to isolate specific risks within a single hedge fund strategy. In its classic form, these arbitrageur will eschew taking a view on the direction of the underlying credit quality of a particular convertible bond and will use a credit default swap to neutralize the credit exposure. The convertible bond arbitrageurs may also enter into an interest rate swap to hedge out the interest rates exposure emanating from the fixed coupon and fixed redemption at maturity profile of the typical convertible bond. By contrast with their approach to credit and interest rate risk, convertible bond arbitrageurs will usually hedge out the risk of adverse equity price movements by selling short the actual shares of the companies underlying each convertible bond in the portfolio. The convertible bond arbitrageur may use derivatives on equity market indices tactically to increase or decrease equity exposure when the liquidity of the underlying shares is restricted, such as for Asian equities during US trading hours, and during periods of market dislocation where the need for a speedy execution outweighs the added basis risk of an imperfect hedge.

Long–short equity hedge fund managers will purchase shares of companies they believe will appreciate and sell short shares that they believe will decline in market value. Short selling entails first borrowing shares that are not already held in the portfolio and then selling these borrowed shares in the market. The manager then hopes to later buy back these shares at a profit at a lower price. These long–short equity managers will typically use derivatives on equity market indices, such as futures, to increase or decrease their net market exposure. Finding suitable shares to sell short is harder than finding shares to buy, both because of technical factors such as potential difficulties in locating shares to borrow and because of the innate structural disadvantage of selling short an individual share that can appreciate by an unlimited amount yet can only fall a limited amount. Hedge fund managers are therefore more likely to establish some or all of their short exposure through broad equity market indices. This pattern holds for both short-term tactical and more permanent structural trades.

Credit hedge fund managers may decide to buy protection on credit market indices so as to mitigate the risk that credit spreads in general will widen. While forgoing the opportunity to profit should spreads tighten, the hedge fund manager has isolated the targeted risk, namely the opportunity that the specific credits held in the portfolio will outperform the rest of the credit market.

Hedge fund managers that invest in debt instruments will often use interest rate swaps to reduce the duration mismatch between their assets and the funding provided either by their prime broker or through their repo lines. Such swaps are typically from fixed rate to floating rate.

Hedge fund managers are more likely than long-only managers to hedge out their currency exposure. The managers will typically use three month forward contracts, although active trading of the underlying positions and shifts in profit and loss due to market movements require frequent rebalancing trades. Exceptions to this approach include macro funds, which are designed to take directional bets on broad factors such as foreign exchange rates, commodity prices, equity markets, interest rates and foreign exchange funds, which are set up specifically to be exposed to foreign exchange rate volatility. In the emerging markets, non-deliverable forward contracts are used to hedge currencies that are not freely tradable.

INCREASING EXPOSURES

Derivatives on market indices can be an effective tool for minimizing the dilution of return potential associated with any strong inflows into a particular hedge fund. The manager can quickly get the fund up to the targeted net market exposure and then take any necessary time to build positions in the desired individual assets. As attractive assets become available and are purchased, the manager can then reduce a proportionate share of the derivative index position.

There are several forms of leverage embedded in derivatives which hedge fund managers readily use both to gain increased exposure to indices and individual securities.

Derivatives can be structured to have a highly geared pay off linked to a specific event, such as is the case with a deeply out-of-the money call option. The hedge fund manager analyses the probability of the underlying security or index reaching the strike price and then compares this likelihood with the price of the derivative contract. Another way that derivatives enable investors to take highly leveraged positions stems from the fact that futures exchanges and prime brokers generally require hedge funds to post only a relatively small amount of collateral compared with the gross exposure of the derivatives contract.

An additional advantage of derivatives is that highly leveraged positions that are in the money do not always have to leave the hedge fund investor with the potential for large, or even unlimited, losses. By investing in either index or bespoke tranches in the credit derivatives market, for example, it is possible to obtain a highly leveraged position in investment grade credit while only risking a pre-defined amount of capital. The risk profile on the downside of this derivative position compares particularly favourably with the risk profile of a similarly leveraged position in, say, cash bonds where the leverage is typically obtained through either repo financing or margin loans. Such financing arrangements are generally recourse to the investor's entire pool of assets. The derivative investor is only exposed to the original investment on the downside while the cash investor is therefore exposed to the downside on the gross size of the leveraged position.

CAPTURING TAX EFFICIENCIES

Derivatives can be used to gain useful tax efficiencies. For example, by entering into contracts for difference as an alternative to an outright purchase of shares, hedge funds can avoid paying the stamp duty attached to the physical asset in markets such as the UK while capturing the same economic exposure. This works because, at least at the moment, stamp duty is not applicable to contracts for differences. The heavy stamp duty applicable to real estate purchases can similarly be avoided through the use of property derivatives. Hedge funds managers are amongst the investors beginning to discover these particular savings.

Similarly, gaining exposure to an asset via the use of a derivatives contract such as a total return swap is a useful tool for minimizing, and in some cases totally avoiding, the application of withholding tax on periodic payments such as interest and dividends. The desired asset could be transferred to a bank, for example, that can reclaim the withholding tax while using a derivative contract to shift the economic risk of the asset back to the hedge fund. Many hedge funds are set up in tax havens, such as the Cayman Islands, and do not therefore benefit from dual tax treaties.

There are times when a hedge fund has a low tax basis and is therefore exposed to a potentially high capital gains tax liability if the manager sold this given asset at that time. Certain jurisdictions will seek to impose a withholding tax on capital gains that can not be reclaimed for untaxed vehicles like the traditional hedge fund vehicle. It may be more efficient to hedge all of the market risk of that position by entering into an offsetting derivatives contract and then retaining the underlying asset. It may therefore be possible to either defer the tax liability indefinitely or to unwind the position at a time when the tax liability is lower, such as a time when the market value of that asset has fallen to the original purchase cost. There would be no taxable gain on the onshore asset and the derivatives contracts would be unwound offshore at a profit that would generally be capital gains tax-free.

MANOEUVRING ANONYMOUSLY

Derivatives enable investors to manoeuvre anonymously in the financial markets. The credit default swap market developed in Europe from a desire of large banks to visibly support their key corporate customers by advancing large credit facilities while at the same time reducing their net economic exposure by using credit default swaps without having to disclose this activity to the borrower. In a similar fashion, hedge funds may want to remain as large holders of a particular convertible bond or loan but at the same time reduce their net exposure to the credit through credit default swaps. In order to gain favour with a particular issuer or investment bank, hedge funds may purchase a larger allocation of a new issue than they actually wish to retain. The hedge fund manager can then choose to retain the position but hedge out the economic risk anonymously via a derivatives transaction.

Until recently it was possible in the United Kingdom to gain economic exposure to the shares of a company involved in a takeover while avoiding the requirement to publicly disclose such interest. While the disclosure rules have now changed to some extent in the United Kingdom, it may still be possible to build up large undisclosed stakes in companies in markets that have a less fully developed disclosure regime.

ACCESSING RESTRICTED MARKETS

Derivatives are an effective tool for hedge funds to gain exposure to restricted markets. If a country has currency controls that will restrict the hedge fund's ability to repatriate either profits or capital, then it may be advantageous for the hedge fund to gain exposure to a targeted asset via a derivatives contract. Similarly, if there are restrictions on foreign ownership and if, as a consequence, those shares eligible for foreign share ownership trade at a significant premium to domestic shares, then the hedge fund manager may choose to secure exposure to the domestic shares through a derivatives contract with a local counterparty and then sell short the more expensive foreign share in the hope that the price of the two will converge. Given the general trend towards the progressive lifting of restrictions on foreign share ownership, this type of trade has been profitable over recent years.

TRADING NON-DELIVERABLE ASSETS

In their constant search for both uncorrelated sources of return and tools to isolate more effectively targeted sources of return potential, hedge fund managers are drawn into trading an ever widening range of risks and exposures. Some of these are only available in derivative form given their very nature. Examples of such risks include equity implied volatility, unemployment data, weather and catastrophe risk. These risks do not have a cash underlying except when securitized into tradeable units such as catastrophe bonds.

SHIFTING OPERATIONAL BURDENS

Hedge fund managers will use derivatives in order to shift the operational burden to third parties to save time, effort and costs. A primary example is the use of equity index hedges. It is easier to enter into a single derivative transaction rather than borrowing shares of potentially hundreds of companies, selling the shares of each company, managing the stock borrow over time, then buying back the shares of each company in order to unwind the position and then returning the shares to close out the stock borrow. For certain regional indices such as MSCI Europe, it may be necessary to execute numerous foreign exchange transactions as well. These operational burdens are either shifted to the counterparty of the trade if the counterparty wishes to hedge its new position, or avoided entirely if such a trade either flattens out the counterparty's own exposure or if the counterparty is looking to retain a naked un-hedged exposure. Similarly to gain exposure to an equity index, it is easier to enter into a simple derivative transaction rather than buying the shares of potentially hundreds of companies, settling these transactions and then having to sell each of the very same shares once the hedge fund manager decides to reduce the exposure to this equity index.

Credit default swap tranches allow the hedge fund manager easily to obtain a targeted degree of leverage with a customized pool of underlying investment grade corporate credits. The alternative in the cash market is to have to find dealers willing to sell either bonds or loans from each of these 100 or so corporates and then having to finance each of these positions in the repo market. The repos then need to be rolled on a periodic basis and the margin collateral continuously adjusted. The operational burden of taking a short position in the cash market is compounded by the need first to borrow the 100 corporate bonds and then maintain that borrow for an extended period of time.

Derivatives also readily allow for the alignment of payment dates so that cash can be received on the same day that either premia or interest is payable on the other side.

In the commodities market, it is generally preferable to trade in a derivative form as most hedge fund managers would not know, for example, where or how to store a ton of cocoa. Nonetheless, the attractive use of derivatives from an operational prospective does require a higher degree of up-front investment required in risk management and booking systems. There is also likely to be more work involved in moving collateral from one derivatives counterparty to another. Hedge funds also need to manage actively the amount of counterparty risk they are taking, which is likely to be for a longer term exposure than is the case with cash securities that are generally settled with delivery versus payment on a short-term cycle measured in days rather than months and even years as is the case with derivatives.

EXECUTING WITH GREATER PRECISION

One of the attractions of derivatives for hedge fund managers is the degree of precision that can be achieved. The convertible arbitrageur can enter into a credit default swap that precisely matches the maturity of the convertible bond. It is rare that a convertible bond issuer has cash straight bonds outstanding that have the same maturity date as their convertible bonds. It is even rarer to be able to borrow such bonds, if they existed, as they would be in great demand.

Derivatives also allow a hedge fund manager readily to switch particular exposures within a pool of assets without having to disturb the overall pool and its financing arrangements. Derivatives thereby allow a static pool to be actively managed. Profits can be taken and potentially loss-making positions can be neutralized. A simple example of this is when a hedge fund gains exposure to the investment grade corporate credit market through an index trade and subsequently wishes to switch out of one component credit and into another. This approach is also being applied on a more systematic basis where entire portfolios of risk are sourced as customized static pools and then actively managed through the use of either single name credit default swaps or by switching names into and out of the static pools themselves.

CONCLUSION

As has hopefully been demonstrated above, derivatives are important and effective tools that are useful to both mitigate risk and to capture upside return potential. As long as hedge funds and their managers are not using derivatives to obfuscate their risk exposures and valuations, and to thereby deceive their investors, regulators and lenders, then hedge funds should be able to continue with their largely unregulated use of these instruments. It would be unfortunate if regulators and commentators missed this point out of historic prejudice and ignorance. Perhaps a derivative will be developed that will hedge even this risk.

'... the volume and complexity of trades has continued to grow dramatically, fuelling the demand for systems which are faster, encompass more asset classes, cover the entire trade life cycle, and are easier to install and maintain and require fewer staff to support them.'

■ ■ ■

Derivatives and Technology

Chris Horsburgh
City Practitioners Ltd

Introduction and background

Hardware and software developments

Business drivers for change

Responses

Conclusion

INTRODUCTION AND BACKGROUND

Since the last edition of this book there have been many developments in the technology landscape covering the realms of both hardware and software. Devices have become faster, bigger and cheaper, communication via developments such as broadband and wireless has become quicker and more reliable and software development has widened to encompass web services and service orientated architecture (SOA). At the same time the volume and complexity of trades has continued to grow dramatically. This has fuelled continued demand for systems which are faster, encompass more asset classes, cover the entire trade life cycle and are easier to install and maintain and require fewer staff to support them. The aim of this chapter is to look at the solutions being produced to deal with these issues.

The early derivative trading systems concentrated on the mathematical side of the trade process. They enabled derivatives to be priced, the trades to be booked and standard market risk measurements to be calculated so that the risk of the portfolio could be managed. To do this the system needed to be able to build the correct yield curves, calculate the correct day counts for rollover periods. This would allow discount factors and estimated cash flows to be calculated so that instruments such as an interest rate swap could be priced. The systems were also able to price interest rate options such as caps, floors and swaptions using the Black–Scholes model. These systems would typically cover the front and middle office functions of the trading cycle.

The trades would then have to be re-keyed into a separate back office system using written information on a ticket produced by the front office. This often caused problems because these systems had been developed to handle FX and money market type trades so had no concept of handling multi-period instruments such as interest rate swaps. These problems were overcome by entering the trade as a series of cash flows.

Confirmations tended to be produced manually using a word processing package and payments were made by manually keying in the instructions into the bank's payment system. The process consisted of islands of information interconnected by manual intervention.

Banks trading derivatives had usually been trading money market, FX and fixed income previously so it was normal to find a system for each of these activities. This led to the creation of trading silos for the different product sets requiring different hardware and specialist staff to support them.

Due to the separateness of the systems, dealers had much more say in choosing which systems were used. The function of IT was to implement the system the dealer wanted. It was not uncommon for a new head of desk to arrive and request a new system because he had used it successfully previously.

There was little concept of an overall business and system architecture. Cost of ownership was only looked at in terms of the desk and cost per trade was not yet a developed concept.

The early systems such as Devon, Oberon and Quotient ran on a variety of hardware platforms such as Dos, Unix and Vax. In the main they were written in C although Devon was written in APL. The presentation layer to the user tended to be character based, often using a screen enhancing package. The first graphical user interfaces came with the next generation of systems such as Opus, Infinity and Summit and were based on XWindows. These applications also marked the transition from workstation and terminal-based applications to client server applications with a thick client running on the workstation containing most of the application logic and the database containing trade and market data running on the server.

NB: The terms thick and thin clients are widely used to describe the amount of functionality being carried out on the workstation compared with that being carried out on the server.

The predominant database package used by all these applications was Sybase. Disk space was still expensive and so the amount of information that could be stored on the server was limited.

Up until this point the vendors producing these systems had tended to be small companies founded by ex-traders or bespoke bank projects that had been spun off into commercial systems. With the growth in the market, the big vendors decided to move in and Opus and Infinity were bought by Sungard and Summit was bought by Misys.

The capacity and functionality of current derivatives trading systems has been able to increase to meet the growing volume and complexity of deals traded because of the major developments in hardware and software that have taken place in recent years.

HARDWARE AND SOFTWARE DEVELOPMENTS

Hardware developments

Faster processors, bigger disks, larger RAM cards and faster and higher resolution graphics cards have all contributed to the substantial increases in computing power that is available from current desktop and laptop personal computers. As the capacity of all these components has increased so have the prices decreased. Similar developments have occurred on the server side, with similar increases in performance and capacity, coupled with system reliability and high capacity multi-disk storage devices. In the area of communications the advent of broadband wireless and high speed dedicated internet connections has meant that fast global communications are now much more readily available and have replaced slow dial up connections and point to point leased lines.

Software developments

In the area of software, Windows XP has become a true 32 bit multi-tasking operating system. This has led to almost total extinction of client Unix workstations. The most common configuration found these days is Windows XP workstations with either Windows XP or Unix servers. The advent of Linux has led some people to speculate that this might change but evidence for this has yet to be observed. In terms of the models used by systems the client server model has been replaced by the three-tier model with a thin client on the workstation communicating with an application server which in turn is communicating with a database server. This is the model used by the majority of current derivative trading systems.

The languages in which these systems are written in have also changed. C has been replaced by C++, especially on the server side with use being made of its object orientated capability in such areas as inheritance and reusability. On the client side in addition to C++, Visual Basic and .Net technology from Microsoft are becoming more common. The widespread availability of the internet and familiarity of users with using a browser has led to the development of trading systems with browser-based clients and the take up of Java as a programming language to develop these systems. Java is a language that will run on all hardware platforms so is very suited to the internet environment which is hardware agnostic.

BUSINESS DRIVERS FOR CHANGE

The developments in hardware and software described above have enabled system vendors to build more advanced systems. It is helpful to understand the business drivers that are creating the demand for these systems.

Increased volumes and reduced spreads

This has required systems to process much greater volumes of data without any decrease in performance calling for systems with greater processing and storage power.

Increase in the variety of asset classes traded

This has been very marked especially around the areas of credit and structured trades and has required systems that can price and process these trades. It has also demanded much greater flexibility in the way in which trades can be built from constituent parts.

Exchange of information between systems

Traditionally this was done with point to point feeds between systems. These had to be changed every time a data item in the feed changed. With the advent of XML and the take up of FpML there is increasing pressure on vendors to move away from proprietary interfaces and adopt ones that will allow interchange of data using pre agreed standards such as FpML. This reduces the amount of bespoke development that has to be done to integrate a system into the overall system landscape of an institution.

The cost of ownership

Institutions are much more conscious these days of the total cost of ownership of a system. Where as previously It was the capital cost that was scrutinized now the maintenance costs, cost of hardware, cost of implementing new versions, upgrades and number of staff required to support the system are also included. This enables a more accurate total cost of ownership to be calculated.

Internal STP

With the continued desire to reduce costs and avoid re-keying of data, there is increasing pressure on vendors to expand the coverage of the asset classes they support and to provide complete front to back coverage for trade processing of those asset classes.

This has required systems to become aware of the time line of the post trade process and provide workflow capabilities so that a trade can pass through distinct stages either automatically or after having received the appropriate authorization. The ideal is that a trade can be booked, the price calculated, the trade confirmed, the risk managed, payments made and ledger entries generated. All from within the same system irrespective of where it is in the world and in what time zone it is operating but still supporting multi-legal entities and market-related end of days and batches.

There is also a continued desire to get rid of paper whether it is from confirmations generated or reports produced. The requirement is that technology provides the transfer and presentation media for this data and automates the production process.

RESPONSES

External STP

As trading volumes have increased in recent years there have been a number of initiatives that have arisen from the desire to use technology to eliminate the disagreements that can exist between counterparties regarding what they have actually traded with each other. Traditionally each side would send the other a confirmation detailing their understanding of what they thought had been traded. If this was different then there would need to be cycles of communication between the two sides until agreement was reached. Swapswire is an initiative from a number of banks who took the view that it would be much simpler for the deal to be agreed bilaterally by the two people doing the deal at the time it was done. So they developed a system that presents the details of the trade done to both sides who agree it there and then. It can be thought of in terms of using conversational software like MSN messenger. This then allows both parties to post the agreed version of the trade into their respective trade capture systems at the start of the trade processing cycle.

There have been other related services set up such as DerivServ from DTCC, TZero, ICE and Omgeo.

The trading population is continuing to expand with the types of organizations trading derivatives moving away from being dominated by the banks (the sell side) and expanding to include (the buy side), traditional asset managers, hedge funds, private trusts and high net worth individuals. The sell side is investing heavily in systems such as internet portals and messaging systems (c.f. Communicator) to enable these clients to communicate and trade with them in an automated way.

Increasing trade volumes with an ever expanding list of counterparties has led to a substantial increase in the number of payments having to be made. To reduce this both sides of the deal agree to novate the deal to a central counterparty so that each side then makes its payments to the central counterparty. If this is repeated over many deals then substantial reductions in payment volumes are achieved. In London Swapclear was set up to offer this facility with the London Clearing House acting as the central counterparty. Institutions using both Swapswire and Swapclear have reported substantial reductions in both the number of failed trades and payments and the number of staff needed to deal with their processing.

Portfolio reduction

One of the latest initiatives to appear in the market is a facility whereby two counterparties can send copies of their respective portfolios to the service provider who will then examine them and identify trades that can be netted out and cancelled without the overall risk position changing. This service was developed because it had been observed that outstanding gross volumes had experienced tremendous growth while net outstanding risk positions at banks had hardly grown at all. This indicated that there were a large number of deals which were making no contribution to the overall risk position. If these could be identified they could be terminated without changing the risk profile, thus avoiding any further processing operations. This service is provided by triOptima using their product triReduce.

All the facilities described above have only been possible because of the technology advances described earlier notably the improvements in communications, speed of processing, size of storage devices and the widespread availability of the internet and the uptake by the vendors of protocols associated with it.

CONCLUSION

We can see from the above that as trading volumes and complexities have increased, developments in technology have enabled systems to be expanded in both processing power and functionality to deal with these changes. It is a continual race between expanding business requirements and increasing system functionality. What developments then are we likely to see going forward?

Many organizations are now beginning to look at their overall system and data architecture to see if there are rationalizations that can be made. These have grown up over the years to meet changing functional requirements without any reference to an overall strategy or design principles. There is now a desire to determine an overall architecture to which logical application architectures can be mapped. This allows organizations to reduce their business processes to their fundamental components and encode logic for their reuse both internally and with outside parties. This is known as service-orientated architecture (SOA). Much is being written about this approach and the benefits that adopting it can bring especially when combined with web services. A number of the major banks are beginning to invest in this technology but recent reports suggest that it will be 5 to 10 years before the full benefits of this approach are seen in derivatives trading systems.

'There is always the possibility that the remaining unsigned, outstanding confirmations may create potential instability in the market.'

■ ■ ■

Derivatives and Documentation

Introduction

Background to the International Swaps and Derivatives Association, Inc. (ISDA)

Products covered by the ISDA Agreement

ISDA Heaven vs ISDA Hell

INTRODUCTION

I need to preface this chapter with the following statement; 'I am not a lawyer – and nothing will replace specific professional advice from an expert'. However, I do believe it is important to discuss in overview why documentation is so very important in the derivatives market. For many of us ISDA is a term that we have heard without perhaps fully understanding exactly what it means other than it is something to do with documentation. ISDA, which is an acronym for the International Swaps and Derivatives Association, Inc., is the market standard documentation for OTC derivatives transactions. When a deal is transacted over a telephone the verbal agreement is legally binding until such time as the ISDA confirmation is signed. In a perfect world the confirmation is sent very soon after the transaction is executed, hopefully within a few business days. This may present obstacles unless these confirmations are sent via electronic templates; the chapter from DTCC Deriv/Serv explains this in more detail. Increasingly as deals are executed across electronic networks confirmations are indeed generated automatically. If the evidence of a transaction is taken from the confirmation, what happens if the confirmation is unsigned and indeed remains un-signed, or what if both parties cannot agree the precise deal specifics so will not agree the confirmation? What if there is a default or a credit event? Does the deal still stand? These and other issues are why the regulators are becoming increasingly watchful. There is always the possibility that the remaining unsigned, outstanding confirmations may create potential instability in the market. At the time of writing the backlog has been reduced substantially, but it has not disappeared.

In the derivatives market all transactions are executed 'subject to docs'. This means that there is an element of trust between the market participants that the primary documentation is already agreed and in place. In the exchange-traded market, documentation is exchange specific and everyone must comply. In the OTC market, transactions may be vanilla or exotic; the counterparty may be a small bank, a corporate, a hedge fund, an insurance company, a large bank, etc., therefore documentation needs to exist to address the concerns of all the participants. In a financial organization or a bank it is the Front Office which executes the transactions; in a corporate client it will be a member of the Treasury staff who executes the deal. Naturally, these individuals are not lawyers and do not purport to be. Inevitably deals will be transacted with details which may be complete from the trader's perspective but are incomplete from the point of view of preparing documentation, e.g. what is the legal name of the entity, is it ABC Limited, ABC Incorporated, ABC Group, and what is the full address including post code, etc?

Market standard

ISDA is the market standard documentation for privately negotiated OTC transactions. Their website is very comprehensive and is worth a look, www.isda.org.

BACKGROUND TO THE INTERNATIONAL SWAPS AND DERIVATIVES ASSOCIATION, INC. (ISDA)

ISDA was originally formed in 1985 with 10 members to standardize market practice and address the documentation issues arising from a sudden upswing in the volume of OTC derivatives transactions. At that time each bank and client had their own organization specific documentation. Picture this; Bank A in the USA transacts five swaps in the morning with Bank B in the UK, each send five full sets of their own individual documentation to each other (via mail). The same issues will likely arise every time as the documentation is different. The legal team must agree changes in order for the deal to proceed, this may involve transatlantic phone calls and in extreme cases documentation sent via air courier. In the afternoon, Bank A transacts 10 swaps with Bank C in Germany. The same thing happens again; 10 full sets of documentation are dispatched but the queries and amendments will now be different. If a bank transacted with 20 different counterparties in 24 hours, it could receive 20 different versions of the documentation. In order to minimize the time spent doing the same thing over to over again, the bank lawyers in the major banks all decided to get together to try to design a set of documents which suited them, most of the time. They originally named themselves the International Swap Dealers Association; this was renamed some years ago to the International Swaps and Derivatives Association, Inc.

Between 1985 and 1987 ISDA's efforts were concentrated on just interest rate and currency swaps, culminating in the 1987 Interest Rate and Currency Exchange Agreement which was a multi-currency cross-border agreement. In 1989 and 1990 amendments were made to enable the Agreement to cover not just swaps but also caps, collars and floors and options – this document updated the 1987 agreement and eventually became the ISDA Master Agreement 1992.

In December 2001 a fresh review commenced with over 100 member firms to refresh the agreement in the light of the new market instruments and developments. This became the 2002 ISDA Master Agreement, published in 2003.

PRODUCTS COVERED BY THE ISDA AGREEMENT

At the time of writing the products covered are:

- Interest rate swaps
- Currency swaps
- Forward rate agreements
- Commodity swaps
- Equity and equity index swaps
- Options
- Foreign exchange
- Caps, collars, floors
- Credit derivatives
- Bullion
- Weather derivatives
- Inflation derivatives

Structure of the documentation

Although we refer to the ISDA Master Agreement, this suggests it is a single document, but in fact it consists of three separate sections and all three are required for a complete set of documentation:

1. The ISDA Master Agreement

This is a 'boilerplate' agreement which means that in practice it is pre-printed and is not altered or amended. It has 14 sections covering:

- Interpretation
- Obligations
- Representations
- Agreements
- Events of default and termination events
- Early termination
- Transfer
- Contractual currency
- Miscellaneous
- Offices: Multibranch parties

- Expenses
- Notices
- Governing law and jurisdiction
- Definitions

2. The Schedule

This is how the Master Agreement is amended; this is where the lawyers come in, it is what the ISDA negotiators negotiate. This is usually divided into six parts covering:

Part 1 – Termination provisions

Part 2 – Tax representations

Part 3 – Agreement to deliver documents

Part 4 – Miscellaneous

Part 5 – Other provisions

Part 6 – Foreign Exchange Transactions and Currency Options

NB: the ISDA Master and the Agreement Schedule need only be negotiated once, but a separate confirmation is required for each individual transaction.

3 The Confirmation

A confirmation is required for each individual transaction and will reference the particular Master Agreement and Schedule. Since 1991 ISDA has issued a set of Definitions booklets and these are used to clarify the language used in the Confirmations. A typical confirmation will include:

- Relevant ISDA definitions and references to an executed ISDA Master Agreement. If this has not yet been negotiated a 'vanilla' ISDA is considered by lawyers to exist. In essence, an ISDA master with no agreed schedule.
- Economic details of the trade such as, trade date, effective date, maturity date, who is the payer/receiver, or buyer/seller, payment calculation terms, timing and mechanics and offices through which payments will be made.
- Any amendments to the specific deal.

The ISDA Master forms a single agreement between the parties. Where there is inconsistency between the confirmation and the ISDA Master Agreement, the confirmation will prevail (unless the Agreement Schedule says otherwise).

Practical issues

In my personal opinion, I cannot stress enough how important it is for both parties to an OTC derivative transaction to agree to the basic documentation before dealing. This will entail showing it to your own in-house lawyers – before signature. If you do not have an in-house lawyer it is worth sending the papers out to a specialist firm. Beware of the phrase, 'don't worry, just sign here it is a standard document'. The ISDA Master Agreement might be, but the Agreement Schedule you may have been sent may be different from bank to bank.

Also, do not underestimate how long it may take to negotiate the Schedule – weeks and occasionally months is normal.

The ISDA Master Agreement can be set up to be:

- a single-branch agreement – e.g. HSBC, London, or a
- multi-branch agreement – e.g. HSBC, London, New York, Tokyo.

ISDA HEAVEN VS ISDA HELL

This is rumoured to be an old ISDA story. Virgil and Dante visit ISDA Heaven, they see lots of people in large airy offices, negotiating ISDA Master Agreements with telephone, e-mail, internet and fax links. They then visit ISDA Hell, and they see lots of people in large airy offices, negotiating ISDA Master Agreements with telephone, e-mail, internet and fax links.

Dante is looking perplexed and says to Virgil, 'I cannot see what the difference is, they both look the same', 'Yes', Virgil replied, 'but with one major difference – in ISDA heaven the documents get signed!'

For those who may be interested in further reading an excellent book is *Mastering the ISDA Master Agreements*, (1992 and 2002), 2nd edition, by Paul Harding, published by Financial Times Prentice Hall, 2004.

'…we will almost certainly look back on this time as a sea change in the operating model for OTC derivatives, leading to a new era in the processing environment.'

■ ■ ■

A Brief History of Straight Through Processing (STP) for OTC Derivatives

Bill Hodgson
Depository Trust & Clearing Corporation

What is STP?

Automation drivers and priorities

Message formats

Central clearing for OTC products

Innovation in trade capture and confirmation

Fundamental issues in processing OTC products

The future of STP for OTC contracts

The 'backlog'

A central infrastructure for the OTC markets:
Trade Information Warehouse

Conclusion

WHAT IS STP?

Before we get to the history part, just what is straight through processing (STP) anyway? There are many definitions and ways to describe STP, one is this:

Definition   **Straight through Processing** (STP) enables the entire trade process for capital markets and payments transactions to be conducted electronically without the need for re-keying or manual intervention, subject to legal and regulatory restrictions.

This definition is a good start, but it fails to note that piecemeal electronic processing, which is not integrated within and across firms, does not deliver true STP. For instance, a firm captures over-the-counter (OTC) derivatives contracts in its main books and records system where the data model and business process fully represents the true nature of the actual contracts being executed. The firm then feeds the individual cash payments to its settlement team, which also receives payments from other business units outside the OTC market. The settlements team obliges in making the cash movements occur, but can not easily respond to the need for OTC trades with multiple flows on the same day (e.g. a rate swap or currency swap with an exchange) to be settled as a group (either net or at least all or nothing), nor can the settlements group respond when a credit issue occurs in a margin call and the OTC team need payments suspended.

For OTC derivatives, STP exhibits a number of specific characteristics:

- All the systems in the processing chain have an appropriate level of functionality built in to represent the unique nature of the OTC contracts being processed.

- The process flow cleanly discriminates the need for humans to be involved such that intervention is only necessary for well-defined exceptions, or at key control points in the process.

- Information about the contracts is integrated across the systems such that a unique contract reference will enable humans to use information in different systems environments quickly and easily.

- No step in the process from trade execution to settlement involves data being moved between systems by humans (apart from the initial trade capture if necessary).

- All the systems in the chain have a true representation of the contract, or at least relevant components of the contract, and do not fudge the trade into an alien trade structure (e.g. two bond legs to represent an interest rate swap with no linkage between them other than a comment field).

- The processing systems integrate to support the life cycle events on an OTC contract.

AUTOMATION DRIVERS AND PRIORITIES

The first STP priority for firms trading and settling OTC products is to automate their internal processes before thinking about how to integrate between firms. The primary concern of firms using the OTC market is the accurate capture and processing of the contracts they have entered into. The top 20 firms in the market by now have spent hundreds of millions of dollars over the past 20 years in a cycle of expansion and consolidation as each new wave of OTC products matured.

The evidence from the major firms is that:

- A single system within each firm will not do it all (although some of the more recent systems do a great deal).

- The different centres of expertise within each firm have different processing needs, e.g. traders, credit risk, market risk, accounting, prime brokerage, settlement and confirmations to name a few.

- There are new products or variations on existing products each year; the OTC market is never static and its complexity continually increases, as do the operational risks with these activities.

- Trade volumes nearly always go up.

- Innovation keeps occurring in the services market, e.g. trade tear-up services.

All these factors drive continuous change in the processing platforms for OTC products.

For small firms trading derivatives, such as hedge funds, the need for an 'all in one' package is ever more pressing as they rarely have the resources to build, maintain and refresh such a complex processing environment.

MESSAGE FORMATS

At the inception of the OTC market, the contracts were really only message formats, not standardized in any way. As a result, FAX was the only method quickly to express the terms of a contract and deliver them to the counterparty for review and confirmation. As with any product, standardization provided the driver for the first major innovation in STP *between firms* with the introduction of SWIFT messages for OTC derivatives.

The MT360 message enabled SWIFT customers to prepare a fully electronic message expressing the terms of a single currency interest rate swap, and have it delivered securely and reliably to their counterparty. Assuming every firm could produce and consume MT360 messages, the FAX machine should lie idle for products supported by the MT360 and any other MTxxx message defined by SWIFT.

An overview of an MT360 message

Table 17.1 describes a portion of an MT360 message, and in this example the fixed leg of an interest rate swap.

Table 17.1	Group	Block	MT360 Tag	Field name	Example
	Fixed leg				
			37U	Fixed Rate	4.1234
			37N	Details of Interest Rate	Free text
			17F	Period End Date Adjustment Indicator	Y
			14D	Day Count Fraction	ACT/360
			14A	Business Day Convention	MODF
		Financial centres			
			18A	Number of Repetitions (Centres)	1
			22B	Financial Centre	USNY
		Payments			
			18A	Number of Repetitions (Payments)	10
			30F	Payment Date	05 Jun 06
			32M	Currency, Payment Amount	USD 4,123,400

(When encapsulated in a file for transmission, each field is on a line in this format: ':37U:4.1234'.)

Each field has a tag identifying the contents and is defined in the MT360 rule book. The format of each field value is defined by SWIFT and is validated upon entry to their network. No invalid data is allowed into the network. Please refer to http://www.swift.com/ for more information.

The second innovation, also delivered by SWIFT, was a service automatically to compare a pair of MTxxx messages and enable two firms to understand and resolve differences between the contract terms. Hence the introduction of the SWIFT Accord service which became the first piece of infrastructure for the OTC derivatives market provided centrally, rather than focused on the internal processing demands of firms.

The MTxxx message format was designed before the Internet became ubiquitous along with the innovations in complex data representation including the needs for printing (SGML and PostScript), web pages (HTML) and then the generic format (XML), which fundamentally underpin many 'dialects' such as Financial products Markup Language (FpML).

As the OTC market developed, the needs for communication within firms between their own systems soon outgrew the ability of simple 'flat files', MTxxx messages or even relational databases to represent the complex interrelationships within an OTC contract, and a better solution was needed. In 1997 JPMorgan began a 2-year project developing a prototype XML representation of an interest rate swap, this evolved into FpML, now the de facto standard for the entire OTC market to record and transmit the terms of OTC contracts. See http://www.fpml.org/history.html for more details.

FpML began as an independent organisation with a wide membership of OTC derivatives users to develop the standard. In 2001 the FpML product was merged into ISDA to combine the strengths of the trade association with the technical assets of FpML.

An extract from an FpML document

```
<calculationPeriodAmount>

    <calculation>

        <notionalStepSchedule>

            <initialValue>10000000.00</initialValue>

            <currency>USD</currency>

        </notionalStepSchedule>

    </notionalSchedule>

    <fixedRateSchedule>

        <initialValue>0.04123</initialValue>

    </fixedRateSchedule>

    <dayCountFraction>ACT/360</dayCountFraction>

    </calculation>

</calculationPeriodAmount>
```

The fragment above is a small part of a complete FpML 'document', as they are called. In the example above the notional is 10,000,000 USD, but expressed as the first (and only) step in a notional sequence in this trade. (A sequence would be used to represent an amortizing or accreting notional to match the change in notional on a loan.) Additionally the fixed rate on the swap is shown as 0.04123, a percentage according to the rules of FpML. Compared with an MT360 message, the fields have a readable English name, and are structured in blocks of data, such as 'calculationPeriodAmount'. The definition of the structure of FpML is itself defined using XML, the definition is called a schema. More information on the fundamentals of XML can be found at http://www.w3.org/XML/.

An FpML message is verbose in using words to label the data fields, more flexible in representing complex data structures, has wide OTC product coverage and is an industry 'open' standard usable for free by anyone. Almost anyone involved in OTC derivatives can become involved in the development of the FpML standard via the committee structure.

CENTRAL CLEARING FOR OTC PRODUCTS

Comparing the processing environment for OTC products with those traded 'on exchange' it is clear that the costs and risks incurred are quite different. During the late 1990s the London Clearing House used its expertise in providing central counterparty (CCP) services for exchange-traded products to deliver the first (and so far only) CCP service for OTC interest rate swap products, SwapClear. SwapClear mutualizes the risks of processing OTC contracts using margining and a multiple protection mechanisms to provide greater certainty of settlement compared with the non-cleared environment. SwapClear was launched with a fully integrated link from SWIFT Accord, sending fully matched interest rate swaps for registration and clearing via the SWIFT network.

INNOVATION IN TRADE CAPTURE AND CONFIRMATION

Following the innovation in messaging brought by FpML, and through a desire by the industry to simplify the capture of OTC trades, the SwapsWire business was launched providing a fundamentally new process for traders to capture, agree and confirm the terms of trades. SwapsWire was the first OTC infrastructure project to place software directly on the traders' desktops – electronic trading of OTC products remains an elusive goal still being pursued by a number of firms. SwapsWire's initial service was for interest rate derivative contracts and has since expanded to cover more products, and to have an integrated link to the LCH.Clearnet SwapClear service.

There are now many firms investing to provide solutions in the OTC trade capture space, some through electronic trading, some through trade capture, and some through the OTC trade brokers. Examples are MarketAxess and TradeWeb, which offer electronic screen-based trading of credit contracts; TZero, which offers electronic capture of trades executed by telephone; MarkIt / Communicator, which provides a way to migrate FAX-based information flow into a web-based environment alongside full electronic confirmation via Depository Trust and Clearing Corporation's (DTCC) Deriv/SERV.

In the packaged software market, firms such as Summit and Calypso have built fully integrated interfaces into DTCC Deriv/SERV enabling a firm to capture, confirm and process trades on a single platform.

In the process automation market, Scrittura and Thunderhead offer solutions aimed at the confirmations process in particular that connect a firm's systems and process flow to DTCC Deriv/SERV.

Firms such as Globe Ops and Coretexa are investing to build services to enable hedge funds to outsource their processing (Globe Ops) or integrate their connectivity into a single platform (Coretexa) for the buy-side market.

Last but not least is a service from MarkIt – the Reference Entity Database (RED). The reference entities and securities traded as the underlying instruments on credit contracts must be precisely defined for protection to be effective. MarkIt provides a database of 'scrubbed' data within which unique pairs of reference entities and bonds are allocated a 9-digit 'CLIP' code – which traders can then use to accurately capture the trade. The DTCC Deriv/SERV service contains a copy of the RED database and fully supports confirmation using the RED codes. For more information see http://www.markit.com/.

FUNDAMENTAL ISSUES IN PROCESSING OTC PRODUCTS

Despite the investment by firms to automate OTC contracts, the rapid growth of the OTC market has meant that:

- Settlement error rates are hard to reduce.

- Timeliness and accuracy of confirmation are hard to achieve simultaneously.

- Product and process complexity has raced ahead of automation, keeping firms in continuous 'catch-up' mode.

- Market innovation has put heavy demand on human expertise and skill.

In this environment, the major dealers have seen that hiring ever more people does not address these fundamentals, and that a new approach utilizing centralized infrastructure is a way finally to put the OTC market on a stronger footing for processing the commoditized products, leaving firms to devote their expensive human expertise to the customized and tailored OTC contracts.

THE FUTURE OF STP FOR OTC CONTRACTS

In 2003 the Depository Trust and Clearing Corporation (DTCC) entered the OTC market with a confirmation service for credit derivatives branded as Deriv/SERV. Today, Deriv/SERV is the recognized global standard in the post-trade processing of credit derivatives.

This service uses FpML and a web-based user interface to achieve trade confirmation. The basic principle is that the two parties to a trade enter the 20 or so key data items representing a credit contract into DTCC Deriv/SERV, which then compares the two parties' entries, and enables them to resolve differences. DTCC Deriv/SERV offers two modes, affirmation whereby one party alleges a trade and the other responds, and two-sided matching, which is preferred by many firms that want to see evidence of the existence and terms of a contract expressed in a public place, in the event of a dispute.

By mid-2006, more than 600 firms had signed on to DTCC Deriv/SERV, including customers in 25 countries across UK/ Europe, the Americas, Asia and Australia. This, includes all the major dealers in OTC products, as well as a rapidly growing number of investment managers and hedge funds. In addition, the platform has evolved to offer support for both credit, rates and equities contracts.

From 2004 onwards the volume of trading in credit contracts created a new challenge for back offices, settling the many payments due on each quarterly roll date. Single name Credit Default Swaps and Credit Default Index trades almost all pay their premium on the 20th of each quarter. Most other OTC contracts make payments relative to the Effective Date of the contract, and settle on any day during the year. This means that as the number of contracts grows, there is a one to one increase in the number of payments and number of nostro reconciliation breaks for the quarterly payment dates.

Firms worked with DTCC to build a payments pre-matching service, which they use to compare and match their payments in advance of settlement. At the end of 2003 the service matched 80,000 payments with a final match rate of 79 per cent, in Q2 2006 (2 years later) the figures had risen to 1.6 million payments with a 97 per cent fully matched rate. An additional benefit of pre-matching is the ability to calculate net settlement amounts. Using matched payments the service calculates the bilateral net settlement amounts for firms. These bilateral amounts are then used by the firms to carry out net settlement, reducing the number of payments by up to 90 per cent and reducing the operational risks and costs accordingly.

Whilst automation of the confirmation and payments process reduces operational risks further, the next step the industry has chosen to take is to look to DTCC to develop a central Trade Information Warehouse to become the global infrastructure for the OTC market. The goal is to bring increased accuracy, cost savings and reduced risk to the post-trade processing of OTC derivatives.

THE 'BACKLOG'

During 2005 significant attention was brought to the 'backlog' of confirmations in the credit derivatives market. The backlog comes from three issues: the first a lack of full use of any electronic confirmation service by most dealers and the second the absence of signed master confirmation agreements. The third issue needs some explanation.

An underlying operational problem relates to secondary trading of credit contracts by buy-side firms by which they trade in and out of contracts during a single day, taking profits from intraday price movements. One way to benefit from the price change in a contract is to 'sell it' to a third party in return for a fee payment. The legal terminology involves an assignment (or novation) with a transferor (stepping out of a trade), a transferee (stepping into a trade) and the remaining party (who sees their counterparty change from one to the other).

Typical Assignment (Novation) example

Figure 17.1

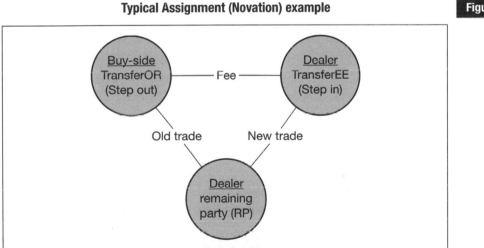

Using common practice the firm stepping out would terminate the trade within its own systems, and the stepping in party would create the new trade. Unfortunately the legal basis of an assignment means the transaction is *not* legally binding until all three parties sign the documentation (whether on paper or electronically), leading to a situation where the remaining party would expect to receive payment from the original party (the transferor/step out) but, in fact, sees a payment in its bank account from the transferee (step in), leading to an investigation to resolve the nostro re-conciliation problem.

In early 2005 the United Kingdom Financial Services Authority and, in mid 2005, 14 national regulators chaired by the Federal Reserve Bank of New York (the 'Fed') became aware that the paper process for completing assignments was significantly lagging behind the actual books and records of the firms involved, leading to a risk that should a credit event occur on a credit default contract, all three parties would not have legal certainty on who the two parties were to the trade, and therefore how to settle the defaulted trades.

Fourteen dealers became engaged in a dialogue with the national regulators group to address this situation. The dealers put forward a voluntary action plan which involved:

- Reducing the backlog with quantifiable targets against time;
- Utilizing all the functionality of electronic confirmation services primarily DTCC Deriv/SERV;
- Obliging any buy-side firm executing four or more credit contracts per month to join the DTCC Deriv/SERV service.

Additionally DTCC embedded a standard master confirmation into its legal operating procedures for use on a trade by trade basis, and ISDA developed an industry standard settlement Matrix as a legal framework for confirmations which was also supported by DTCC during 2006. To learn more, visit the Fed website at http://www.ny.frb.org/.

Whilst the DTCC Deriv/SERV service provided a solution to assignments, trade confirmation, and extended into payment matching, rates and equity contracts, the initiative announced in 2006 is to build an integrated Trade Information Warehouse to process OTC contracts from trade capture through to settlement. For more information see http://derivserv.dtcc.com/.

A CENTRAL INFRASTRUCTURE FOR THE OTC MARKETS: TRADE INFORMATION WAREHOUSE

Today, counterparties to credit derivatives contracts (and most other OTC derivatives contracts) handle all administration between themselves on a bilateral basis. In other words, each party must continually 'sync up' with each of its counterparties over the life of every contract, keeping track of post-trade events, such as assignments, amendments, terminations and notional adjustments. This requires considerable manual processing relying on faxes, emails and phone calls.

The warehouse addresses two critical problems that continue to plague the industry: 1. maintaining reliable, up-to-date contract records, and 2. efficiently processing the flow of information, payments, netting and other post-trade events associated with contracts, that are aligned with operational risks.

The concept of the Trade Information Warehouse is to provide a processing environment with similar characteristics to that of the exchange-traded market but for OTC contracts. Key features will be:

- Global: Provides a solution without regional silos.

- Maximum trade population capture: gathers the entire market into one place to standardize and simplify processing.

- Extensible design: Designed initially for credit derivatives with the ability to extend into other asset classes such as rates and equities, in time.

- Standard downstream processing: Implements the effects of lifecycle events in a single agreed way.

- Life-cycle support: Supports the entire life-cycle and processing features of OTC contracts.

- Inclusive: Involves the entire community, including the needs of sell-side dealers, hedge funds, investment managers, custodians, asset managers, depositories, and settlement services.

- Multiple input sources: Enables capture of the trade from any platform, such as e-Trading, trade Affirmation and trade Confirmation platforms.

- Prescriptive user participation: Drives the market to a single operating model and eliminates costly and unnecessary differences between firms.

- Open architecture: Ensures innovative third-party solutions can connect and leverage from the warehouse infrastructure.

Figure 17.2 maps out the Trade Information Warehouse. When complete it will provide:

- Automated legal trade confirmation for a wide range of OTC contract types.

- Tie-out of all other OTC contract types where a legal template has not yet been implemented.

- Maintenance of the 'current state' of the contract, as a result of all business events (such as partial terminations, assignments, etc.).

- Calculation, maintenance and adjustments to the cashflow schedule for fully supported contracts, cashflow matching for tie-out records.

- Automation of credit event triggering, corporate actions and other centralized effects on trades.

- Automated central settlement of the amounts calculated by the warehouse via the settlement agent.

Figure 17.2   **Trade Information Warehouse schematic**

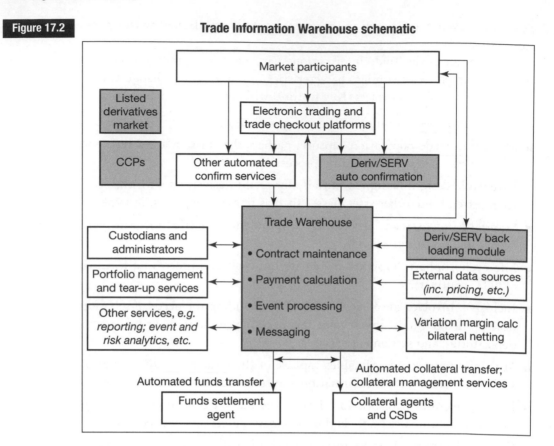

The construction of the Trade Information Warehouse began in 2006 and will be implemented in multiple phases in partnership with the 20 largest dealers, representation from asset managers and hedge funds, investment managers, asset managers and global custodians.

In addition to significant cost and risk reductions due to the automated administration of contracts, the benefits of the Trade Information Warehouse can be summarized as:

1. The first time a fully transparent data set of the contract terms is available to the industry leading to an absence of disputes, and a fundamentally better way to respond to credit events in the market.

2. Payments for trades in the Warehouse are always complete and correct via the settlement agent service compared with the current process in the current bilateral environment.

3. Removes bilateral reconciliations such as payments, margin calls, portfolio reconciliations.

4. Standardizes the processing and calculations rules for products.

5. Applies a common operating model for all market participants.

6. Reduces nostro fees through bi-lateral net settlement.

7. Eliminates nostro breaks for all trades in the Warehouse.

8. Expands the accessibility of the OTC market by eliminating operational risks.

CONCLUSION

The OTC market, which is approximately 25 years old, is still new compared with the listed exchanges or cash markets around the world, yet has outstripped every other market in terms of innovation and growth rates due to the fundamental building blocks being offered, and the flexibility of the available financial solutions.

The evolution of projects such as the Trade Information Warehouse reflects the interest firms see in continuing to reduce costs and risks in the post-trade environment, therefore enabling further expansion of the OTC market to more participants.

In another 25 years' time, we will almost certainly look back on this time as a sea change in the operating model for OTC derivatives, leading to a new era in the processing environment.

'The compliance function (and the risk function) must be alert to the danger of ethical creep, or a shifting in the acceptable level of ethics due to a familiarity with the regulations and the innovative atmosphere in a derivatives practitioner, leading to a diminishing of the ethical hurdle over time.'

■ ■ ■

Risk and Compliance
for Derivatives

Tony Blunden
Chase Cooper Limited

Introduction

Governance

Risk management practice

Compliance practice

Conclusion

INTRODUCTION

The risk and compliance functions in a derivatives organization have a very broad brief. The content of that brief is primarily determined by whether the organization enters into OTC derivatives, exchange-traded derivatives, structured projects involving derivatives or any combination of the three. The practical scope of the risk and compliance functions can vary greatly between two similar organizations depending on how responsibility is shared between the compliance, legal, internal audit, risk management and operations functions.

All financial services organizations in the UK are regulated by the Financial Services Authority (FSA) under the financial services and markets legislation. The FSA replaced a number of regulatory organizations that existed under previous UK regulatory regimes. It has promulgated regulatory principles which must be complied with and which stem, in the main, from normal corporate ethics. It continues to produce/update a comprehensive rulebook covering such areas as financial rules, client money and assets, conduct of business rules, complaints and arbitration and enforcement. Inevitably regulators' rule books influence and are influenced by other interested parties outside of their countries[1] and, in the European Union, by its directives.[2] It is ultimately the responsibility of the chief executive of any UK derivatives organization to ensure adherence to these rules. However, the chief executive will generally assign some or all of the responsibility to business management, to risk management and to compliance, although it is recognized that the prime influence on a firm's risk and compliance culture is the leadership of that firm.

GOVERNANCE

It is essential to have good governance in any organization and particularly in a derivatives practitioner. For risk and compliance to operate effectively in a derivatives environment requires clear guidelines and procedures to enable all staff to understand the organization's appetite for risk and the ways in which the organization complies with the regulations required of it. This need not be onerous although it is important that it is documented

---

[1] Such as the Basel Committee on Banking Supervision ('Basel'), the Committee of European Securities Regulators ('CESR') and the Committee of European Banking Supervisors ('CEBS').

[2] Such as the Investment Services Directive ('ISD'), the Banking Supervision Directive ('BSD'), the Capital Requirements Directive ('CRD') and the Markets in Financial Instruments Directive ('MiFID').

and disseminated. Typically, governance around risk and compliance will comprise documented policies and procedures, a framework that conceptually explains the high level policies, terms of reference for various committees, working groups and departments, and responsibilities of various bodies and people in the firm. Generally, a derivatives organisation will have separate risk management and compliance functions in order to ensure that both are independent, properly established and able to assess effectively the firm's compliance with its internal policies and procedures and with external regulation. Additionally, this helps to ensure that no one member of staff or department is able to trade, settle and report a derivatives transaction and it helps to eliminate conflicts of interest. A clear division of duties can also help to ensure that an organization receives objective and accurate information on the risks faced by the organization and the adequacy of its compliance systems.

Effective governance procedures will make clear the reporting information flows in an organization and will also, typically on an annual basis, require an evaluation of the adequacy and effectiveness of the risk and compliance systems and procedures. Risk reports are often made on a monthly basis to senior management whereas compliance reports are more usually quarterly. Board level policies for risk and compliance will also include a clear statement of the Board's approach to risk management and compliance including its appetite, a clear organizational structure including roles and responsibilities, a brief description of the processes used by the organization to manage risk and compliance and, often, a glossary of risk and compliance terms so that all staff are aware of the meaning of commonly used terms.

Role of risk management

The task of ensuring that senior management are effectively and appropriately advised falls to risk management; this includes identifying and managing the risks to which the organization is subject. Particularly in a derivatives organization, the complexity of the risks is significant and the senior management may require considerable technical help in fully understanding the risks to which the organization is exposed. Although not all senior management will be conversant with the sometimes difficult mathematics involved with many derivatives, it is critical that at least two members of the Board understand fully the principles, assumptions and choices involved. This may require substantial training for board members who may be unfamiliar with the mathematical concepts involved. However, if the risk management reports are to be properly reviewed and understood the training is unavoidable.

In some organizations there may be a specialist technical unit typically staffed with PhD mathematicians who have considerable experience in modelling with complex sets of derivative equations. The unit will have specific responsibility for market risk and will either be attached to risk management itself or maybe part of a product control function. It will not be part of the trading function, will not report into trading and will provide independent challenge to and validation of the trading P&L. Where such a technical unit exists, it has more recently become involved in credit risk modelling and very recently involved in operational risk modelling.

In many organizations, the difference between the credit processing function and credit risk management is often confused or misunderstood. Credit risk management's role is to ensure that credit granting is based on sound and well-defined criteria and that appropriate reporting against these criteria is available to senior management. The process for approving, amending, renewing and refinancing credits may be carried out by credit risk management but is often carried out by a separate credit processing function.

Responsibilites of risk management

The fundamental responsibility of risk management is to have proper arrangements for identifying, assessing, monitoring and managing the risks to a firm's business. These arrangements will cover market risk, credit risk and operational risk at a minimum. Other possible risks which may be covered are liquidity risk (sometimes jointly with Finance), group risk (also covered by the Strategy function) and insurance risk (where insurance has been used in a derivative transacted by the organization and jointly with the actuary where one exists). As the arrangements differ in detail for each type of risk, they are covered in considerable detail in 'Risk management practice' on page 367.

Role of compliance

The task of ensuring that an organization complies with the rules of any relevant regulatory authority is paramount for the compliance function. A practitioner should promote within itself a culture of compliance, a responsibility which should be taken by the chief executive and the highest levels of management, because the culture of an organization flows from the attitudes of those at the top. The compliance culture can then be expected to filter downwards throughout the practitioner. Clearly, the compliance function assists senior management in instilling a positive view of compliance.

However, compliance may also be responsible for ensuring that the organization adheres to the rules of any exchanges of which the practitioner is a member and the applicable rules of any exchange on which it transacts.

Additionally, it may fall to the compliance function to assist the legal and/or HR functions in ensuring that the organization adheres to any relevant legislation in any country in which it operates or has counterparties. It is not unusual for the compliance function to carry out work to test controls similar to that which the internal audit function carries out. Even if an organization has a separate internal audit department, both the compliance function and the internal audit department should work closely together and, at the very least, the compliance function should be copied on all internal audit reports.

Additionally, the compliance function of a derivatives institution often undertakes operational risk management work. As with internal audit, if a separate operational risk management function exists, both the compliance function and the operational risk function should work closely together. The identification and mitigation of compliance operational risk is a normal part of the work of a compliance function.

The compliance function (and the risk function) must be alert to the danger of ethical creep, or a shifting in the acceptable level of ethics due to a familiarity with the regulations and the innovative atmosphere in a derivatives practitioner, leading to a diminishing of the ethical hurdle over time. This situation is very difficult to detect and may only become clear in situations of extreme stress. Regular training on compliance issues may act as a counterbalance together with strong senior management awareness of ethics as well as compliance matters. Further control over ethical creep can be achieved by the regular maintenance of legal opinions and open communications with the regulator.

Transacting in derivatives also raises a large number of technical issues, and compliance with specific regulations often requires the production of reports and the performance of regulatory duties on a daily basis. It is often considered preferable for the compliance function to overview these reports rather than to prepare them, as this then frees it up for alternative work and allows an element of independent review.

Responsibilities of compliance

There are three principal responsibilities of a compliance function:

- to create and maintain internal rules and procedures to facilitate observance of any relevant regulations;
- to monitor activities within all parts of the organization on a regular basis, and to ensure that business is conducted in accordance with those regulations;
- to liaise with sales, marketing and trading staff to influence the design of new products before those products are launched.

The greatest value added in the compliance function of a derivatives practitioner is in the third responsibility. Timely intervention by the compliance function is more likely to result in an innovative product that is suitable for the firm to market and appropriate for the target client base.

Other general responsibilities include promoting the awareness and the understanding of compliance rules within the organization, resolving questions of compliance difficulty as they arise and following up any actual or potential, regulatory or related problems uncovered by the monitoring programme or otherwise to ensure that corrective action is taken where necessary.

A regulator's conduct of business rules often provide a good overview of how derivatives business should be conducted. They generally cover a variety of topics ranging from advertising and marketing to customer agreements, customer relations and customer dealing. They often also cover the wider issues including market integrity (for example, insider dealing) and more general aspects of compliance (for example, personal account transactions). All derivatives practitioners should adhere to these rules, and the spirit of these rules, at all times.

One area of responsibility on which there is no industry consensus is whether or not the compliance function has primary responsibility for liaison with the regulator. While this may seem a natural and logical responsibility for the compliance function, some firms view their overall relationship with their regulator as a strategic business responsibility and place this within the chief executive's office. Alternatively, if the operational risk management department has responsibility for strategic business risk then responsibility for the overall regulatory relationship may be placed within this department. It is, however, undeniable that the greatest day-to-day knowledge of how a regulator will react to a given problem will reside in the compliance function. This knowledge is inevitable, especially in a derivatives practitioner, as much day-to-day liaison with the regulator takes place at a working level in the compliance function.

The risks faced by a derivatives practitioner are of a complex nature, and a comprehensive and effective system of internal controls is essential. Such controls are invaluable in assisting the compliance function to perform its duties, and it must take responsibility in this area together with other risk and control-orientated departments such as operational risk management, finance and internal audit. A great deal has been written about internal controls in banks and there is a general agreement that a thorough system of internal controls is a fundamental requirement for sound management.

In addition to these, there are very many specific responsibilities which may fall to the compliance function and some of these may require work to be performed on a daily basis. Examples of such responsibilities are trade reporting (many transactions need to be reported to the regulatory authority within 24 hours of execution), equity position monitoring (holdings in equities above certain percentages may need to be reported to a variety of entities, for example, the company whose equity is held or the exchange on which it is traded, if applicable, according to the legislation of the relevant country) and exchange-traded derivative position monitoring (such positions should be monitored both in the light of any position limits set by the exchange, and with relevance to internal control).

RISK MANAGEMENT PRACTICE

As noted in the responsibilities of risk management section above, the detailed practices for market risk, credit risk and operational risk vary considerably. Although each practice is aimed at identifying, assessing, monitoring and managing the risks to an organization's business the methodology used is dependent on the particular type of risk. This is due to the different degrees of development in the management of each risk which is largely due to the amount of time and effort that the industry has applied to managing that particular risk. This means that market risk has well recognized and accepted standards covering clearly defined products and using, in many cases, complex mathematical formulae. Although credit risk has been around since banks started lending money, the development of a recognized credit risk methodology is arguably more recent than that of market risk. This leads to a methodology that is continuing to evolve but which is now generally recognized. In contrast, operational risk has only been explicitly recognized for around a decade and is therefore relatively nascent in its development. Notwithstanding this, operational risk has clearly defined high-level processes which are being implemented in a variety of ways by the industry.

Market risk practice

Market risk is the possible loss to the organization resulting from market movements relating to on- or off-balance sheet positions. The detailed governance relating to derivatives market risk tends to reside within an organization's approach to its modelling and to the data that is used in the models. It, of course, also covers detailed limits by desk, trader and derivatives product. Internal reporting of derivatives market risk is also inextricably linked to the models used by most derivatives organizations.

There are two methods of measuring market risk for derivative practitioners. By far the most common is the use of an internal measurement model. The other method, the so-called standardized approach, is mentioned for the sake of completeness as it is rarely used in the derivatives world except where there are very few transactions in an organization.

In the standardized approach, the derivatives are decomposed into positions in the relevant underlying products and a risk figure for general and specific market risk is calculated using standard formulae. The starting figures used in this calculation are typically the principal underlying amounts or the notional underlying amounts and the sensitivity of the derivative to market risk is therefore inherently limited, given that no direct reference is made in the standardized approach to current or future market prices. The standardized approach therefore reduces all products to standard product measurements, and is consequently inappropriate for the majority of derivative products which are inevitably complex in nature, inherently difficult to standardize and inescapably require reference to current market prices for accurate valuation purposes. Precise assessment is required in most derivative organizations as the profit or loss on the derivatives position is included immediately within the organization's profit and loss account.

Today there are many off-the-shelf mathematical models available for internal derivative market risk calculation and they are suitable for a wide variety of derivative organizations. However, the ability to calculate mathematically the market risk of a derivatives portfolio should only be regarded as the starting point of a complete market risk measurement system. The management of the traders and of the trades is of more importance than a statistical calculation of a market risk figure. The assessment of the quality of the market risk management of an organization that has implemented a mathematical measurement model is generally carried out in reference to several areas:

- Model implementation, which involves points such as the integrity of the implementation and the numbers of staff skilled in the use of complex models in all parts of the organization.

- Qualitative standards, which involve an organization having an independent risk control function, the production and analysis of daily reports, the regular back testing program, the integration of the models output into the day-to-day planning and control in the organization, documented policies and procedures, independent review of the standards by the organization's internal audit function.

- Quantitative standards, which involves a daily value at risk calculation based on a 99 centile 10-day holding period, a sample period of at least one year, frequently updated data sets, sound reasons the correlations were used, and back testing on the hypothetical or actual trading outcomes.

- Market risk factors, which capture the inherent market risks in the organization's portfolio including relevant yield curves, spread risks, foreign currency factors and equity market factors such as sector betas and individual equity gammas.

- Stress testing, which identifies events or influences that could greatly impact an organization and includes low probability events in all major types of risk, linear and non-linear characteristics, quantitative and qualitative aspects of market disturbances, correlations approaching one or minus one and other unlikely but plausible occurrences.

- Model validation, which involves validation of the processes, formulae and data flows used in the model by a function independent from the trading function.

Credit risk practice

Credit risk is the potential loss that an organization may incur when a borrower or counterparty fails to meet its obligations in accordance with the agreed terms. The credit portfolio of a derivatives institution is generally divided into two portions: the trading book and the non-trading book. The trading book portion of the credit portfolio is assessed as a market risk position unless the model in use fails to assess specific market risk. In this case an adjustment for credit risk is made within the credit risk calculation. The non-trading book part of the credit portfolio comprises the organization's exposure to borrowers and counterparties.

Although credit risk modelling is less well-developed than market risk, many derivatives organizations use credit risk models to assess their credit risk. There will be very few derivatives organizations using the Basle standardized approach to credit risk and this is again mentioned for the sake of completeness. Given the likely extensive use of modelling, detailed credit risk governance is again referenced to a derivatives organization's use of the model and data sets and of the reports from the model. However, the credit risk management framework will refer to both the internal and external data, to analyses of the portfolio and validation of the credit risk including mitigation of the gross credit risk.

Before referring to modelling, it is important to consider the data sets that are used. These are generally broken down into internal data and external data. Internal credit data relates to both transactional data including client positions, collateral and netting agreements and to static data including client credit scores and product evaluations. External data is provided to a derivatives organization by specialist data providers and rating agencies and includes credit spreads, credit ratings, default rates, recovery rates, volatilities and correlations.

In the standardized approach, the derivatives are assessed for their exposure value with reference to whether they are in the balance sheet or off-balance sheet, whether they are in the trading book or in the non-trading book, the type of instrument and the type of counterparty. A credit risk figure is calculated using standard exposure classes, multiples and risk weights. As with market risk this approach has little sensitivity to actual credit risk, given that no direct reference is made in the standardized credit risk approach to current or future market prices. The standardized credit risk approach is consequently inappropriate for the majority of derivative products which are inevitably complex in nature, inherently difficult to standardize and inescapably require reference to current market prices for accurate credit risk valuation purposes.

In addition to market risk calculation models, there are also many credit risk models available off-the-shelf. However, compatibility and completeness of data is a frequent problem for many organizations. As noted above there are a considerable number of data required in order to assess credit risk, particularly in a derivatives organization. In common with market risk, it is not sufficient for an organization simply to use a credit risk mathematical model. The organizational structure around model and the organization's understanding and use of the models results are far more important than simply deriving a mathematical exposure figure. The assessment of this is again carried out by reference to several areas:

- Operational control, which includes an independent, adequately staffed function with a separate reporting line from the functions responsible for originating or renewing credit exposure, sound credit risk policies, processes and systems, prior assessment of a borrower or counterparty's creditworthiness before credit commitment, active involvement of the Board and senior management, and Board awareness of the limitations and assumptions of the credit model.

- Credit limits, which include consistent and well disseminated limits often involving daily and intraday usage calculations at a gross and net (of collateral) level, portfolio and counterparty level exposure calculations and limits set by groups of related counterparties, industries and markets.

- Stress testing, which involves unlikely but plausible events such as changes to economic conditions, concentrations and the risk that liquidating the organization's own positions (either proprietary or through counterparty default) moves the market against it.

- Independent review, which involves the adequacy of the credit risk management system and process, the organisation of the credit risk function, the approval process for risk pricing, the accuracy and completeness of the data, volatility and correlation assumptions including the risk transformation calculations.

- Credit reporting, which involves the dissemination of the usage of credit limits including current gross and net exposure and calculations using typical industry measures such as probability of default, loss given default and exposure at default.

- Other areas such as the integrity of the modelling process and further model validation through the use of shocks and backtesting.

Operational risk practice

Operational risk is the possible loss to the organization resulting from inadequate or failed internal processes, people and systems or from external events. Although there is no clear industry recognized methodology covering operational risk (as there is in market risk and is becoming in credit risk), it is generally acknowledged that there are six main processes to operational risk: governance, risk and control assessment, key risk indicators, loss causal analysis, modelling and reporting.

■ Governance involves the direction and review by senior management of operational risk within the organization. A Board approved operational risk policy together with terms of reference for the relevant bodies and a framework is also often developed. Many different frameworks exist and they all have in common a description (whether pictorial or in words) of how the identification, measurement, monitoring and management of operational risk will occur within the organization. A timeline that indicates the intermediate milestones for the progression of each of the processes is also often drawn up during the governance phase of operational risk management. This, of course, allows senior management to manage and review the development of operational risk processes within the organization and to set and influence the speed of the development.

■ Risk and control assessment involves the identification and subjective measurement of operational risks and their mitigators. This is often the first process of operational risk management that is carried out by an organization. Although a first risk and control assessment is almost always subjective, it can be of significant business value if it is linked to the strategic objectives of the business. As risk assessments progress and the links between losses and indicators are established, the assessments become more influenced by objective data. However, a continued focus on the business objectives will help to ensure buy-in and use at the most senior levels of management.

■ Key risk indicators involve the process of identification, capture and analysis of metrics of key risks (and controls). This is achieved by linking the metric identification process to the risks and controls already identified by the firm in previous risk assessments. This naturally enables a focus on the key risks (as identified by the risk and control assessment) and provides clear assistance in easily recognising predictive indicators. Given a link of risks to the business objectives, the key risk indicators allow senior management to assess the likelihood (or otherwise) of meeting its own strategic plan. Such devices are excellent for embedding operational risk management within a firm.

- Loss causal analysis includes the identification, capture and analysis of both internal and external events arising from the occurrence of operational risks. There are significant benefits from understanding the causes of the losses and from linking the causes to the risks already identified by the organization in its risk and control assessments. Both internal and external losses can be used by organizations in causal analysis, although inevitably the external loss analysis will be more difficult as the control environment that failed will be less understood. The use of this analysis of objective data to challenge the subjective nature of the risk and control assessment is vital to coherent and comprehensive operational risk management.

- Modelling concerns the mathematical analysis of the effects of operational risks on an organization. It is very helpful that the Basel Committee on Banking Supervision (in its International Convergence of Capital Measurement and Capital Standards, June 2004) and the FSA (in its CP05/3, January 2005) finally acknowledged that the internal control environment of a firm and scenario analysis are both valuable components of an operational risk model. (For the sake of completeness, the other two components of an operational risk model are internal loses and external losses.)

  Both risk and control assessments and key risk indicators can be used in modelling operational risk and can add significantly to the business benefits that can be derived from such modelling. As well as a capital figure that can be used for capital allocation to business lines, a model that uses risk and control assessments can assist in a cost benefit analysis of the controls used by a firm. Challenges can be made to the effectiveness of the controls, given the size of a particular risk, and to the allocation of resources for each control.

- Reporting allows the immediate above four processes (i.e. risk and control assessment, losses, key risk indicators and modelling) to be brought together in a coherent manner for use by all levels of management to supervise and control operational risk. In practice, reporting must be tailored to the needs of the receiver. The Board of Directors generally are interested in operational risk reports that address their interests, i.e. strategic risks (and controls) and significant exceptions to lower levels of risk across the entire organization. Department heads, on the other hand, are relatively tightly focused on their own risks but often require considerable detail on those risks. Much reporting often also focuses on the risks, without thought for the linked controls and action plans that can demonstrate a firm's commitment to using operational risk management to enhance the firm's business decisions.

The six main operational risk management processes of governance, risk and control assessment, losses, key indicators, modelling and reporting are fundamentally entwined with each other.

COMPLIANCE PRACTICE

OTC derivatives industry

There are some areas where OTC derivatives practitioners face substantially different risks from those involved with exchange-traded products. This is primarily because almost all of the parameters of an OTC derivative may be individually tailored and negotiated and agreed between the counterparties to the transaction (as an example, in the case of options, the maturity, strike and size may be negotiated). In addition, because many OTC derivatives may be tailored to meet the specific needs of the counterparties to the transaction, certain OTC derivatives may be more complicated and less standardized than those traded on regulated exchanges.

The general marketing and trading activities of OTC derivatives practitioners have featured regularly in the financial (and non-financial) press. In addition a number of reports have been written attempting to offer guidelines for best business practice. Although issued in the 1990s, these reports have stood the test of time and are still largely followed today. One report was issued by the G30 in July 1993 entitled 'Derivatives: Practices and Principles'. This report focuses on major risks and gives brief guidance on, for example, the role of senior management, marking-to-market, market valuation methods, measuring market risk and stress simulations.

Another report was issued in March 1995 entitled 'A Framework for Voluntary Oversight of the OTC Derivatives Activities of Securities Firm Affiliates to Promote Confidence and Stability in Financial Markets'. This was prepared by the Derivatives Policy Group, which includes representatives from CS First Boston, Goldman Sachs, Lehman Brothers, Merrill Lynch, Morgan Stanley and Salomon Brothers with Cleary, Gottlieb, Steen & Hamilton as counsel. This report focuses on management controls, enhanced reporting (for example, on credit risk), evaluation of risk in relation to capital, and counterparty relationships.

Yet another report was issued in 1995, in August, entitled 'Principles and Practices for Wholesale Financial Market Transactions'. This report includes input from six trade associations and was coordinated by the Federal Reserve Bank of New York. It is intended to provide a voluntary code of conduct for participants in the wholesale OTC markets in the USA and includes major sections covering financial resources, participants, policies and procedures, mechanics of transactions and standards of transactions. Even though this report is directed at participants in the USA, as a general set of principles and practices it has been suggested that it might also prove of use to UK derivatives practitioners.

As noted already, the compliance function of a derivatives practitioner will be more heavily involved in the design of new products than its equivalent in a non-derivatives firm. This is particularly so in an OTC derivatives or structured products practitioner, where each new transaction is effectively a new product because of its bespoke nature. Additionally, the compliance procedures of such an institution are likely to cover more material than the regulators' rules and may include substantial guidance on the appropriateness and suitability of OTC derivatives and structured products that include derivatives. In addition, compliance procedures relating to such complex products are also likely to include guidance on ethical conduct.

It should be noted that many regulators have a principle of self-responsibility within their rules or guidance, particularly in relation to institutional investors (i.e. clients that are large or are not individuals). Generally, guidance relating to such a principle is linked either to 'know your counterparty' rules or to a requirement to observe high standards of integrity and dealing and to act with due skill, care and diligence. Occasionally, a regulator may be more explicit, as with the Japanese Financial Supervisory Agency's June 1998 guideline, and require a practitioner to provide a straightforward written explanation of the contents and associated risks of the product or transaction, taking into account the knowledge and experience of the counterparty.

With regard to the principle of self-responsibility, it should also be noted that the obligation for the adequate disclosure of the financial position of the counterparty rests with the counterparty and its external auditors. In particular, the external auditors are required each year to certify that audited accounts present a true and fair view of the financial condition of the counterparty.

Notwithstanding all this it remains good practice to refer unusual OTC derivative transactions to a local law firm for review before contacting the prospective counterparty. Once the counterparty shows interest in the transaction it is also good practice to encourage the counterparty to discuss the transaction with its external auditor and other professional advisers and with its regulator, if appropriate. Steps should also be taken to ensure that a sufficiently high level of senior management of the counterparty is aware of an OTC derivatives transaction (the more complex the transaction, the higher the level of senior management, including possibly the Board of Directors). Approval at the relevant level and from the relevant departments of the practitioner should also be required.

Although institutional investors should be able to assess properly any OTC derivative, it remains in the practitioner's interest to sell derivatives that are appropriate. There is a need to protect the practitioner from the adverse publicity which accompanies the sale of perceived inappropriate products, even if the commentary is unwarranted or incorrect. However, the derivatives practitioner plays a guessing game in attempting to determine which products will be found to be inappropriate at some time in the future by regulators or politicians who may not even be in office at the time of the sale.

Sensitivity analyses can play a useful role in explaining the effects of a complex OTC derivative to a counterparty. The analysis can take the form of either a spreadsheet or a graph. In either form care should be taken that possible profits and losses (or balance sheet effects, where applicable) are properly and clearly identified and that there is a fair representation of possible outcomes showing both upside and downside exposures. However, it should be made clear to the counterparty that the provision of a sensitivity analysis does not mitigate the counterparty's responsibility to evaluate the OTC derivative independently or to consult with appropriate professional advisers, both internally and externally.

Assumptions will need to be made in order to produce an analysis that is not excessively complicated. Care should be taken to make reasonable assumptions that are clearly stated and that do not present a misleading picture of the potential risks and benefits of the scenarios analysed. While assumptions should take into account historical movements these should not be followed slavishly. Allowances must be made for movements which might seem extreme today but, for a transaction with a ten-year life, may be viewed as normal in, say, seven years.

Although the organization is, by definition, skilled in derivative products, attention should be paid to the overall exposure of the firm to the operational risks of complex and OTC derivatives as well as the market and credit risks. The compliance operational risks will include the relevance of the transaction to the counterparty and the transaction's size in relation to the counterparty's accounts.

It is also important that communications with the counterparty, whether oral or written, should not withhold information. This can happen either through failing to mention relevant information or through failing to correct previous information when subsequent events render that information itself false or misleading. Additionally, care must be taken not to present half-truths or rumours as qualified statements of fact.

While evolutionary rather than revolutionary in nature, the derivatives industry has created two completely new product categories in credit derivatives and insurance derivatives. These categories are in response to counterparties' needs and have developed, and will continue to develop, as the counterparties themselves, as well as the derivative practitioners, identify new uses. The practices outlined here are equally appropriate for credit and insurance derivatives, although careful monitoring will need to take place in order to identify possible additional procedures.

Crime and derivatives

Aside from ensuring compliance with applicable legislation and regulation, the compliance function should take an active role in the prevention and, if this fails, the detection of crime committed against the organization. Such crime may be committed either by employees or by counterparties. Even if an organization believes that all its employees are honest, all internal controls should be designed with the possibility of crime in mind. It should be recognized that a practitioner will have a cross-section of the community in it and as such will have some potentially dishonest employees. The practitioner will seek to have robust controls to make it harder for such employees to join the firm and to reduce in a cost-effective manner the chance of their being successful. This is again an area of responsibility shared with other functions such as a fraud unit and with operational risk management.

The most likely source of crime that most banks will suffer is crime committed by an employee for his or her own financial benefit. This financial benefit may be sought in a number of ways: there may be attempts at the direct theft of cash – through the misappropriation of funds; there may be attempts at increasing salaries or bonuses – through the mismarking of books or through irregular sales techniques; or there may be insider dealing – through the use of privileged or confidential information for profit.

Apart from the desire for financial benefit, an employee may be driven to crime to cover up an error (perhaps in the misguided belief that this will save his or her job), to gain promotion, or as a result of blackmail. Crimes committed for these reasons are often harder to guard against and detect, simply because they are often less logical.

Crime, of course, is not the sole preserve of the employee. Counterparties may also commit crime against an organization and, once again, it may fall to the compliance function (with assistance from the legal and marketing functions where applicable) to oversee the implementation of safeguards. Many instances of counterparty crime may not cause a problem of detection. The counterparty may deny that a trade was undertaken, claim that the individual acting on its behalf did not possess the relevant authority to transact on its behalf, or claim that the derivatives practitioner failed to adhere to the appropriate marketing or dealing techniques. Procedures such as routine telephone taping of external calls and prompt execution of legal documents together with effective execution procedures can reduce the likelihood of counterparty crime.

Crime is, undeniably, more difficult to detect where there is fraudulent collusion. Such collusion may be between two employees or between an employee and a counterparty. All internal controls must be developed with the possibility of fraudulent collusion in mind. But, it must always be remembered, with sufficient collusion internal controls will always fail! It is therefore essential that management, the compliance function and all the employees do not rely solely on these controls but maintain a vigilant and inquiring mind at all times. Most importantly, an unusual occurrence must not be explained away in the most convenient way by those involved, for example, as a clerical error. *All* unusual occurrences should be investigated. The answer which management wants to hear is not necessarily the right one.

Money laundering

In April 1994 the UK introduced legislation aimed at preventing money from being laundered in or through the UK and the FSA has since taken responsibility for this. Many financial institutions already had comprehensive 'know your customer' procedures in place and, in most cases, the legislation and subsequent guidelines and rules served to formalize what was already standard practice for many organizations. The prevention of money laundering in derivatives organizations often falls to the compliance department.

There is a possibility that money launderers may focus their attention on the derivatives markets and, in particular, the OTC derivatives markets. There are numerous reasons why this is the case. For example, OTC derivatives transactions may be of high value and of short duration (either because the hedge is only required for a short period or because the original transaction is cancelled as the underlying markets move). Additionally, the OTC derivatives markets are global and transactions involving a number of different financial centres are not as unusual as in other financial markets.

There are various commonly discussed events which, it has been suggested, should be cause for a closer review with regard to money laundering. Some of these are:

- requests for payments to third parties which have no relationship to the original counterparty;
- settlement instructions that are changed at the last minute;
- collateral being delivered from one account and returned to another account;
- constant assignment or cancellation of transactions;
- dissolution, voluntary liquidation or similar of a counterparty soon after a transaction has occurred;
- dealing through a large number of 'offshore' jurisdictions.

To assist in compliance with its relevant obligations regarding money laundering, the OTC derivatives practitioner in the UK can look to a number of documents and, in particular, the relevant guidance notes issued by the Joint Money Laundering Steering Group. These guidance notes cover details such as the requirements of UK law, internal controls, policies and procedures, identification procedures, record keeping, recognition and reporting of suspicious transactions, and education and training. Such guidance notes need to be adapted for individual circumstances.

MiFID

The Markets in Financial Instruments Directive comes into force throughout the European Union in November 2007. For derivatives organizations in many countries, there will be a fundamental change in the way that they operate. The Directive covers many areas of risk management and compliance (governance, sales, marketing and trading) that are already part of many derivative organizations in the UK and the USA. However, even derivatives organizations in these countries will have to be clear in their documentation of their compliance with MiFID. In brief, areas covered by the Directive include:

- Governance
  - Functional independence for risk and compliance
  - Documented compliance policy
  - Arrangements for monitoring adherence to the policy
  - Management of conflicts of interest and personal transactions
  - Proportionate resources allocated to business continuity
  - Sufficient control over outsourced processes
  - Appropriate record keeping and reporting.

- Sales and marketing
  - Know your customers' procedures
  - Suitability and appropriateness of products for customers
  - Three different types of client classification
  - Client disclosure requirements
  - Information about the firm to be given to customers
  - Details to be in client agreements
  - Reporting of transactions to customers.

- Trading
  - Best execution for customers
  - Safeguarding of client assets
  - Requirements to be a systematic internaliser and a multilateral
  - Trading facility
  - Pre-trade and post-trade transparency for customers.

CONCLUSION

The risk and compliance functions of a derivatives organization have responsibilities both externally (for example to regulators, exchanges and shareholders) and internally (for example by way of the implementation or review of internal controls and the prevention or uncovering of crime). However, the precise responsibilities of the risk and compliance functions should be seen as dynamic, being constantly amended and updated to take account of the derivative industry's innovation and to comply with the regulators' reactions to the industry's innovation. The regulators and the industry are forever evolving!

'The main approaches to accounting for derivatives are:

■ mark-to-market or fair value accounting

■ accruals accounting

■ hedge accounting.'

■ ■ ■

First Principles of Accounting for Derivatives

Deborah Morton-Dare
ACA, BSc

Introduction

Fundamental accounting concepts

Reporting requirements

Fair value and mark-to-market accounting

Accruals accounting and amortized cost

Fair value vs hedge accounting

Accounting treatment

International standards

Conclusion

INTRODUCTION

This chapter provides an introduction to the accounting for derivatives. The principles of accounting and bookkeeping are a large topic in themselves so this chapter assumes that the reader has a basic knowledge of double-entry bookkeeping.

Typically, there are two circumstances where the reader may need to have a knowledge of accounting for derivatives:

- In order to review, understand or prepare accounts. In these circumstances it is important to have an understanding of the disclosure requirements for derivatives.

- In order to make the bookkeeping entries required to account for a derivative transaction that has been undertaken.

This chapter covers the basic accounting principles, the detailed bookkeeping entries required for different types of instruments, and discusses the application of international accounting standards and disclosure requirements. At the end an overall approach to accounting for a new derivative transaction is set out.

FUNDAMENTAL ACCOUNTING CONCEPTS

Financial Reporting Standard (FRS) 18 gives the basic accounting principles to be used as a guide for accounting treatment.

Two concepts have been given particular prominence in FRS18 as being part of the bedrock of accounting and therefore critical to the selection of accounting policies.

- *Going Concern* – Accounts are prepared on the basis that the enterprise will continue in operational existence for the foreseeable future. This means in particular that the profit and loss account and balance sheet assume no intention or necessity to liquidate or curtail significantly the scale of the operation.

- *Accruals* – The accruals basis of accounting requires the non-cash effects of transactions and other events to be reflected, as far as is possible, in the financial statements for the accounting period in which they occur, and not, for example, in the period in which any cash involved is received or paid.

The objectives against which an entity should judge the appropriateness of accounting policies to its particular circumstances are:

- relevance;
- reliability;
- comparability; and
- understandability.

Another two accounting concepts are desirable qualities of financial information rather than part of the bedrock of accounting. The FRS therefore discusses them in the context of the objectives against which an entity should judge the appropriateness of accounting policies to its particular circumstances.

- *Consistency* – There is consistency of accounting treatment of like items within each accounting period and from one period to the next.
- *Prudence* – Revenues or profits will not be anticipated, but only accounted for when ultimate realization can be assessed with reasonable certainty. Conversely, provision is made for expenses or losses as soon as they are identified, even if precise quantification is difficult.

REPORTING REQUIREMENTS

The derivatives industry is probably the most global industry that exists today. A derivative user in one country might order a futures trade via a broker in another country which gets executed in yet another country. Until recently the disclosure requirements were different in most countries. Often, an international company or financial institution would have had to report in several different accounting jurisdictions.

Accounting standards governing financial instruments

All listed companies in Europe will be producing group accounts in compliance with International Financial Reporting Standards (IFRS) and International Accounting Standards (IAS) for accounting periods starting on or after 1st January 2005. As a result accounting for financial instruments will be in compliance with IAS 32 and IAS 39. UK GAAP has not had an accounting standard dealing with measurement and accounting treatment of financial instruments, only a standard dealing with disclosure. This will mean that there will be significant changes in the treatment of financial instruments in some UK listed company's accounts. Clearer and more stringent rules will apply relating to the distinctions between the effect and treatment of different financial instruments. It should be noted that some instruments which have previously been accounted for as a hedge may now not qualify. The key requirements of these standards are discussed below.

The main approaches to accounting for derivatives are:

- mark-to-market or fair value accounting;
- accruals accounting;
- hedge accounting.

FAIR VALUE AND MARK-TO-MARKET ACCOUNTING

Mark-to-market (MTM) is the term used to describe the market value of open positions held. Any movement in value will result in an unrealized profit or loss on that position.

Mark-to-market accounting values derivatives transactions at the economic or market value of the transaction. This market value is often very different from the impression that you might get from considering the immediate cash flows from a derivatives transaction. For example, cash could be paid out on the next payment of a swap even though it has a positive mark-to-market.

Financial Reporting Standard (FRS) 13, 'Derivatives and other Financial Instruments: Disclosures', is discussed at the end of the chapter. This defines fair value as:

> 'The amount at which an asset or liability could be exchanged in an arm's length transaction between informed and willing parties, other than in a forced or liquidation sale.'

ACCRUALS ACCOUNTING AND AMORTIZED COST

Many financial instruments are accounted for on an accruals basis, in line with the fundamental accounting concept just defined. For example, a simple loan is typically accounted for as the payment of some principal at the beginning and the end of the loan. During the life of the loan there may be interest payments made, which are normally accrued for over the period between each interest payment. The balance sheet value of the loan will therefore be the principal amounts plus any accrued interest. This value is likely to be different from the market value of a similar instrument such as a bond that has an identifiable market value.

Many derivatives when broken down into their constituent parts can be viewed as if they are made up of simpler financial instruments. For example, a cross-currency swap is essentially a loan in one currency, combined with a deposit in another. It is therefore possible to account for a cross-currency swap as a loan or a deposit on the balance sheet.

FAIR VALUE VS HEDGE ACCOUNTING

One major reason for using derivatives is to provide a hedge against other transactions. For example, a bank may make a five-year fixed rate loan but fund the loan with a floating rate deposit. The bank is therefore exposed to interest rate risk if the rate on deposit increases. The bank could use an interest rate swap to hedge this risk.

It is important that the loan, deposit and interest swap are accounted for on a consistent basis, in line with the fundamental accounting concept defined earlier. For example, if the loan and deposit are accounted for on an accruals accounting basis, while the swap is marked-to-market then the loans and deposit will show a relatively constant value in the balance sheet over time while the swap would fluctuate from day to day. This will give a misleading impression of the economics of the transaction.

In order to avoid this kind of problem all the components of this transaction must be accounted for on the same basis. In this example, one approach would be to account for the loan, deposit and swap on an accruals basis. An alternative approach is to account for all of the transactions on a marked-to-market basis.

ACCOUNTING TREATMENT

When considering the appropriate accounting treatment of derivatives, it is necessary to focus first on the way in which they are used by the reporting entity, considering the management's intention when entering into the transaction. The following distinctions are made:

■ Transactions entered into for trading purposes – fair value accounting. If an instrument has been entered into for trading or for speculative positions, then fair value or mark-to-market accounting will be appropriate. This results in the asset or liability being shown and any gains or losses arising from changes in the fair value being recognized immediately in the profit and loss account.

■ Transactions entered into for hedging purposes – hedge accounting. A hedge is an instrument that individually, or with other instruments, has a value or cash flow that is expected to move inversely with changes in the value or cash flows of the position being hedged. The intention of entering into a hedge is to reduce or offset a risk to which the entity is exposed. Any gains or losses on the hedge should, therefore, be matched to the same period and accounted for on the same basis as the transaction that is being hedged. This is the application of the accounting concept of matching and accruals.

The significance for accounting of the distinction made is to show a true and fair view in the accounts of the commercial effect of the transaction and whether it gives rise to changes in assets, liabilities, gains or losses for the entity undertaking it. The preference of the Accounting Standards Board (ASB) in the UK is to use fair value accounting unless it does not give a true and fair view. The application of this method of accounting will be illustrated throughout the chapter. Alternative methods are discussed at the end of the chapter.

Determining accounting events

All financial instruments have several accounting events over their lifetime. Accounting events involve:

- cash flows – either money is received or paid
- the creation of future cash flows which are:
  - an asset or liability, or
  - a gain or loss.

The first step in the accounting treatment for a financial instrument is to determine the accounting events involved, and whether these give rise to cash flows or whether they involve an accrual for a future cash flow, either an asset or liability, gain or loss.

Accounting for cash flows is normally an operational accounting event and is usually simple to account for, as the value is known. If the accounting event does not involve cash, valuations will have to be made and this can involve far more complex issues. Valuations of assets and liabilities, gains and losses are normally made by financial accounting departments, often as part of financial reporting requirements. Valuations will usually involve the instrument being marked-to-market. More complex issues over valuations are not covered in this chapter.

The accounting events involved during the lifetime of an instrument will be illustrated by looking at examples of accounting for swaps, financial futures and options. The basic principles illustrated can be applied to accounting for all financial instruments.

It is assumed in all the following examples that the instrument is marked-to-market.

Accounting for swaps

The different types of swaps that exist are discussed in detail in other chapters. To illustrate the key principles of the accounting treatment we will look at an interest rate swap and a cross-currency swap.

Interest rate swaps – accounting events involved

For interest rate swaps the first accounting point to note is that on deal date there is no exchange of principal and so the accounting is not for a cash flow, but for a trading asset or liability which will need to be marked-to-market periodically. There will then be periodic payments for interest rate differentials and these will be cash flow accounting events.

The accounting that follows is for an interest rate swap sold by a bank for trading purposes. The accounting for interest rate swaps entered into for dealing or speculative purposes is on an accruals basis with the asset or liability marked to market, the resulting profit or loss being taken to the profit and loss account in the period in which it arises.

Deal date and each reporting date:

DR/CR market value swaps

DR/CR P&L

Each swap payment/receipt date:

DR/CR net settlement

DR/CR cash

On 1 April, 2004, you enter into a one-year interest-rate swap to receive fixed at 7.8 per cent pay floating interest rate swap. The floating leg pays 6-month LIBOR + ten basis points (0.1 per cent). The notional principal amount is £15 million. Coupons are paid semi-annually. **Example**

LIBOR is 7.5 per cent on 1 April, 2004 (this will be paid in October 2004 in arrears) and 8.0 per cent on 1 October, 2000 (paid in April 2005 in arrears).

It is marked-to-market with a value of:

GBP 15,000 on 30 April, 2004

At 30 April, 2004:

DR MTM swaps   15,000

CR P&L   15,000

Swap receipt on 1 October, 2004 on April, 2004 rate.

Receipt amount (7.8% − 7.5% − 0.1%) × 15,000,000 × 181/365 = £14,959

DR cash   14,959

CR P&L   14,959

Note that the mark-to-market on 1 October, 2004, will automatically drop by exactly £14,959 to reflect the receipt of the payment.

DR P&L	14,959
CR MTM swaps	14,959

On 1 April, 2005, the value of the swap has reversed and there will be a swap payment on the October 2004 rate.

Payment amount $(7.8\% - 8.0\% - 0.1\%) \times 15,000,000 \times 182/365 = 22,438$

DR P&L	22,438
CR cash	22,438

Mark-to-market valuation

The mark-to-market valuation of interest rate swaps estimates the net present value of future cash flows expected to arise under each swap at current market interest rates. Future cash flows and the notional principals should be discounted to a present value using zero-coupon yield curve rates.

The future cash flows for the fixed rate leg are obviously known. The future cash flows of the floating rate leg are determined by future interest rates, which are not known. The market value therefore has to be calculated from the next known cash flow. This is based on the rate set at the beginning of the interest period, as illustrated in the previous example.

Other factors which need to be taken into account in the marked-to-market valuation are future credit risks, any significant future administration costs and close out costs. Any provisions needed will reduce the marked-to-market valuation and be taken to the profit and loss account.

Cross-currency swaps – accounting events involved

The first accounting point to note for cross-currency swaps is that, unlike interest rate swaps, on deal date there is an exchange of principal and so the accounting is for a cash flow. On deal date the counterparties will exchange principals in one currency for another, exchanging a debt raised in one currency into a liability in another. The rate of exchange is normally the spot rate at the date of the transaction. The resulting asset or liability will be periodically marked-to-market.

As with interest rate swaps, periodic payments are then exchanged over the term of the swap based on the agreed interest rates on the principal amounts in the different currencies. The interest can be fixed to floating; fixed to fixed; or floating to floating. These cash flows are accounted for as with interest rate swaps.

At maturity, the counterparties re-exchange the principal amounts at the same exchange rate agreed at the outset of the transaction and so there is another cash flow to account for.

Mark-to-market valuation

The mark-to-market valuation of cross-currency swaps estimates the net present value of future cash flows expected to arise under each swap at current exchange rates and current interest rates in each currency with the resulting profit or loss being taken to the profit and loss account.

The future cash flows for a fixed rate leg are obviously known. The future cash flows of a floating rate leg are determined by future interest rates, which are not known. The market value therefore has to be calculated from the next known cash flow. This is based on the rate set at the beginning of the interest period, as illustrated in the interest rate swap example.

Other factors which need to be taken into account in the marked-to-market valuation are future credit risks, any significant future administration costs and close-out costs. Any provisions needed will reduce the marked-to-market valuation and be taken to the profit and loss account.

Cross-currency swap accounting

The accounting that follows is for a cross-currency swap sold by a bank for trading purposes.

The basic principle behind the accounting is that there is a loan with one set of terms and a deposit with another, the difference being with a swap the resulting balance sheet and profit and loss figures should be netted off.

Deal date – mark-to-market:

DR/CR   Market value currency 1 leg

DR/CR   P&L currency 1 leg

DR/CR   Market value currency 2 leg

DR/CR   P&L currency 2 leg

Value date first principal exchange:

DR   Currency 1 cash

CR   Currency 1 cross-currency swaps

DR   Currency 2 cross-currency swaps

CR   Currency 2 cash

Each swap payment date:

DR/CR   Currency 1 P&L

DR/CR   Cash currency 1

DR/CR   Currency 2 P&L

DR/CR   Cash currency 2

Maturity – principal exchange:

DR   Currency 1 cross-currency swaps

CR   Currency 1 cash

DR   Currency 2 cash

CR   Currency 2 cross-currency swaps

Example

On 1 April, 2004, you enter into a one-year cross-currency swap to receive USD fixed at 5.1% and pay GBP 6-month LIBOR floating interest rate swap. The notional principal amount is USD 20 million and GBP 12,121,212. Coupons are paid semi-annually.

GBP LIBOR is 7.5% on 1 April, 2004, and 8.0% on 1 October, 2004. The USD/GBP exchange rate is 1.65 on 1 April, 2004.

The mark-to-market on 30 April, 2004, is as follows:

USD leg:	19,950,322	
GBP leg:	11,878,787	

Initial principal exchange

DR USD cross-currency swaps	USD 20,000,000	
CR USD cash		USD 20,000,000
DR GBP cash	GBP 12,121,212	
CR GBP cross-currency swaps		GBP 12,121,212

MTM at 30 April, 2004

DR P&L USD	USD 49,678	
CR MTM swaps USD		USD 49,678
DR MTM swaps GBP	GBP 242,425	
CR P&L GBP		GBP 242,425

Swap payment on 1 October, 2004

Swap receipt: 5.1% $\times$ 20,000,000 $\times$ 181/365 = USD 505,808

Swap payment: 7.5% $\times$ 12,121,212 $\times$ 181/365 = GBP 450,809

DR cash	USD 505,808	
CR P&L		USD 505,808
DR P&L	GBP 450,809	
CR cash		GBP 450,809

Swap payment on 1 April, 2001

Swap receipt: 5.1% $\times$ 20,000,000 $\times$ 181/365 = USD 505,808

Swap payment: 8.0% $\times$ 12,121,212 $\times$ 181/365 = GBP 480,863

DR cash	USD 505,808	
CR P&L		USD 505,808
DR P&L	GBP 480,863	
CR cash		GBP 480,863
Final principal exchange		
DR USD cash	USD 20,000,000	
CR USD cross-currency swaps		USD 20,000,000
DR GBP cross-currency swaps	GBP 12,121,212	
CR GBP cash		GBP 12,121,212

Accounting for futures

A futures contract is an obligation to buy or sell a specific amount of a financial instrument or commodity or a security at a specific time, with the contract traded on an exchange.

Futures contracts – accounting events involved

At inception of the contract no monetary entry is made for the underlying value of the commodity itself. Both parties to the contract have to deposit an initial margin with the clearing house. This cash flow is accounted for and a trading asset recorded.

During the period when the contract is open, a daily mark-to-market valuation is accounted for and an adjustment made to the trading asset or liability account. The net price difference with the previous day's valuation is settled in cash with the clearing house as a variation margin. The party showing a loss will have to pay a variation margin to the clearing house; the party showing a profit will receive a variation margin from the clearing house.

When the contract is closed the resulting cash flows are accounted for. Most contracts are matched off with a reverse contract before the settlement date.

Deal date – Initial margin paid:

DR   Trading assets – futures margin account

CR   Cash

Daily mark-to-market:

DR/CR   Trading assets – futures margin account

DR/CR   Profit and loss

Accrual for variation margins due or owed:

DR/CR   Trading assets – futures margin account

DR/CR   Sundry assets/liabilities

Settlement of variation margins received or paid:

DR/CR   Sundry assets/liabilities

DR/CR   Cash

Example   A broker buys long 1 platinum (50 troy oz) 6 months @ £690.

Value date: deposit initial margin

Initial margin @ (£34,500 × 5%)

DR trading assets – futures margin account – initial margin	1725	
CR cash	1725	

Daily mark-to-market

End of trading Day 1: platinum falls to £689 giving rise to loss of £1 × 50. This becomes a liability to pay the variation margin to the clearing house.

DR P&L	50	
CR trading assets – futures margin account		50

Accrual for variation margins owed

DR trading assets – futures margin account – variation margin		50
CR sundry liabilities – variation margin		50

Settlement of variation margin

DR sundry liabilities – variation margin	50	
CR cash		50

Closure of contract

If contract is closed @ £690

DR cash	1725	
CR trading assets – futures margin account		1725

Accounting for options

The right, but not the obligation, for the buyer of an option to buy or sell a specific asset or index at a pre-determined price at a specified future date or period. The buyer pays a premium for the option.

Options are accounted for on a mark-to-market basis as with other instruments. It is important to remember the possible values of an option position. If the company has sold an option, the value of the deal can never be greater than the premium received; however, the downside is unlimited. Likewise, if the company has bought an option the value can never be less than the premium paid.

Accounting

The accounting that follows is for an option sold.

Deal date:

DR cash premium received

CR options dealing account

Each reporting date:

DR/CR options dealing account mark-to-market movement

DR/CR P&L

On exercise if out of the money for the company

DR options dealing account

CR cash

On 1 January the company sells a £50,000 3-month FT-SE 100 put option with a strike price of 3,000. It is exactly at the money and the premium is £4,000.

Example

On 31 January the FT-SE has gone to 4,000 and the time value is £2,000.

On 28 February the FT-SE is at 2,000 and the time value is £1,000.

On 31 March, the exercise date, the market price is 3,000 exactly.

At 1 January

DR cash	4,000	
CR option dealing account		4,000

At 31 January

DR option dealing account	2,000	
CR P&L		2,000

At 28 February

MTM of contract = 50,000/3000 × 2,000 = 33,333

Decrease in intrinsic value 50,000 − 33,333 = 16,667

Total value = 16,667 + 1,000 = 17,667

Adjustment to balance sheet value = 17,667 − 2,000 = 15,667

DR P&L	15,667	
CR options dealing account		15,667

At 31 March

Exercise value = 0

Time value = 0

Option is not exercised

DR option dealing account	15,667	
CR P&L		15,667

INTERNATIONAL STANDARDS

Overview of accounting guidelines

International Accounting Standards

IAS 32 – Financial Instruments: Disclosure and Presentation
IAS 39 – Financial Instruments: Recognition and Measurement

The standards are amongst the most complex of accounting standards but must be applied by most public companies in Europe from 2005. The standards apply not only to complex financial instruments, such as derivatives, but also to more straightforward instruments, such as trade debtors, trade creditors and long-term debt. Both standards continue to be under development and the intention for further revisions to be made.

The adoption of the standards by UK companies is likely to result in significant changes to existing practice, but the main intention is to significantly enhance the transparency of the use of financial instruments by companies. A major result will be greater volatility in profit or loss and equity and this will require preparers of accounts to communicate the meaning of this to users of the accounts.

Background

The IASC recognized that although there was a need to develop a comprehensive standard, this would take a considerable amount of time to achieve, and therefore issued IAS 39 as an interim statement in 1997. This has subsequently been updated and revised.

The main proposals of IAS 39 were:

- All financial assets and liabilities held for trading, all derivatives and certain other financial assets to be measured at fair value.
- All other financial instruments are to be measured at amortized cost.
- It also requires transaction that are to attract hedge accounting treatment:
  - to be pre-designated as hedges;
  - to meet certain minimum hedge effectiveness criteria,
  - to meet certain other requirements;
  - and to be accounted for in the way specified in the standard.

The key principles behind IAS 32 and 39

A summary of the principles that underlie the approaches of the two standards is a useful overview to help understand the rules that are detailed and complex.

1. Financial instruments and non-financial derivatives create rights and obligations that meet the definitions of assets or liabilities and, as a result, should be recognized in financial statements, not retained 'off balance-sheet'.

2. Fair value is the most relevant measure for financial instruments and the only relevant measure for derivatives.

   Therefore, derivatives falling within the scope of IAS 32 and 39 are always measured at fair value, even when other exceptions are made, e.g. hedge accounting. For other financial instruments fair value is used when reliable and most relevant.

3. Only items that meet the definitions of assets and liabilities should be recognized as such in the balance sheet.

   Gains or losses resulting from changes in fair values do not have the essential characteristics of assets or liabilities so should be reported in the profit or loss or in equity.

4. Special accounting for items designated as being part of a hedging relationship should be provided only for qualifying items.

   A hedging relationship only qualifies when it is:

   (a) Clearly defined by designation and documentation;

   (b) Reliably measurable; and

   (c) Actually effective.

Two further principles underlie hedge accounting:

(a) Since the objective of hedge accounting is to reflect gains and losses on exposures managed together in the profit or loss at the same time, to the extent that a hedging relationship is effective, the offsetting gains and losses on the hedging instrument and the hedged item should be recognized in profit or loss at the same time.

(b) To the extent that a hedging relationship is not effective, the profit or loss effects of that ineffectiveness should be recognized in profit or loss immediately.

Applying the standards

STEP 1: Identify all financial instruments

Financial instruments include cash, trade debtors and creditors, loans receivable and payable, investment in stocks and bonds as well as derivatives. Derivatives might also be embedded in another type of instrument, embedded derivatives appear as a feature in a conventional contract that changes key elements of the contract in response to changes in a specified rate, price, index, etc. For example, investments in convertible debt and loans where the interest payments or possible the final principal amount are linked to changes in the price of a commodity, equity or currency other than that in which the debt or loan is denominated.

STEP 2: Classify all financial instruments in one of the following categories:

Financial assets and financial liabilities at fair value through profit or loss

All derivatives and any asset in which the company is actively trading are in this category.

Held to maturity investments

Fixed maturity financial assets with fixed or determinable payments that the company has the positive intention and ability to hold to maturity. If there are significant sales of assets in this category before maturity it is necessary to reclassify all financial assets into the available-for-sale category, unless the reason for the sales is outside the company's control.

Loans and receivables

Non-derivative financial assets with fixed or determinable payments that are not quoted in an active market, there is no need for a fixed maturity, e.g. trade debtors.

Available-for-sale

All assets that are not classified in the categories above. For example, investments in equity instruments since these may only be classified as at fair value through profit or loss or available for sale, also debt instruments that an entity does not wish to classify as held to maturity.

STEP 3: Record the financial instrument on the balance sheet

Initial measurement is at their fair value when the company becomes a party to the contract creating the item, most of the time this is the cash paid or received. However, if it is constructed in a way which confers an apparent benefit on one of the parties fair value must be determined with reference to fair value prices for the risks involved. In many cases this involves discounting future cash flows at a fair market rate.

STEP 4: Measure the instrument subsequently, recognize gains and losses

This will depend on the classification chosen in step 2. The subsequent accounting is as follows:

- All financial assets and financial liabilities classified as at fair value through profit or loss, including all derivative and all available-for-sale financial assets, are measured at fair value. Resulting gains and losses are included in profit or loss in the period in which they arise.

- Held to maturity investments, loans and receivables and financial liabilities other than those classified as at fair value through profit or loss are measured at amortized cost. This will probably be the same as past accounting practice. Amortization of premiums or discounts using the effective interest method, and losses due to impairment are included in current period profit or loss, as are most foreign exchange gains and losses. Other gains and losses are recognized only on removal of the instrument from the balance sheet.

- Available-for-sale financial assets – gains and losses other than impairment losses and foreign exchanged gains and losses are included in equity until the asset is removed from the balance sheet. The premium or discount recognized on acquisition of a fixed income security is amortized to profit or loss as interest income or expense using the effective interest method. Losses due to impairment and foreign exchange gains and losses are included directly in profit or loss.

- Investments in equity instrument for which fair value cannot be reliably measured are measured at cost. Gains and losses on financial liabilities are recognized in profit or loss, whereas those classified as equity are recognized in equity.

STEP 5: Provide the disclosures

Disclosure requirements include not only information about the financial instruments themselves, but also the manner in which a company uses financial instrument in financial risk management.

Hedge accounting

Hedge accounting is always optional, there is no requirement to adopt hedge accounting.

Steps in hedge accounting process:

Step 1: Understand risk exposures and their effect on financial statements.

Step 2: Designate and document the hedge relationship.

Step 3: Account for the hedging relationship.

- Two primary types of hedging relationship:
  - Fair value hedge – all gains and losses are recognized in current period profit or loss, along with adjustment to the carrying amount of the hedged item for the gain or loss attributable to the hedged risk.
  - Cash flow hedge – the portion of the gain or loss on the hedging item determined to be effective is recognized in equity.

Step 4: Discontinue hedge accounting.

- If the hedging relationship becomes ineffective or is otherwise terminated. Usually it is ceased on a prospective basis.

Step 5: Provide disclosures.

CONCLUSION – AN APPROACH TO ACCOUNTING FOR A NEW DERIVATIVES TRANSACTION

In conclusion, this chapter sets out a step-by-step approach to accounting for a new derivatives transaction.

1. Determine the reason why the organization has entered into the transaction. This will help determine the correct accounting treatment for the transaction. A transaction that is clearly for trading purposes or is hedging transactions that are marked-to-market will normally be marked-to-market. If a transaction is a hedge and the items being hedged are accounted for on an accruals basis then it may be appropriate to use hedge accounting.

2. Check your local jurisdictions reporting requirements and determine how to apply them, based on your knowledge of the transaction.

3. Identify and account for any initial entries required at the date the deal was executed.

4. Identify an account for any initial cash flows, such as the principal exchange on a cross-currency swap, or initial margin on a future.

5. Identify and account for an interim cash flows that may occur. These might include swap coupon payments or variation margin.

6. At each reporting date value the derivative either on a mark-to-market basis or on an accruals basis.

7. At the end of the life of the transaction account for the closing entries.

At each reporting date you should make sure that the valuation is reasonable, given what you know of the commercial intention of the transactions. If you are using hedge accounting you should ensure that, if you look at the total profit of all the related transactions, they have produced the correct overall profit.

Glossary

Abandon Where an option holder chooses not to exercise his option.

ABS A security collateralized by loans, leases, unsecured receivables or installment contracts on personal property, automobiles or credit cards. The cash flows generated by the underlying obligations are used to pay principal and interest to the ABS holders.

Absolute Risk The volatility of total returns.

Acceptance Short-term debt instrument, drawn on a bank for future payment.

Accreting Loan A loan where the principal increase in stages as capital is required.

Accrued Interest Interest that has been earned but not yet paid.

Actuary A statistician who calculates risk. Usually employed by an insurance company.

ADR American Depositary Receipts, see **Depositary Receipts**.

AIM Alternative Investment Market. For small young and growing companies opened by the Stock Exchange in June 1995.

American Style An option that may be exercised into its underlying instrument on any business day until expiry.

Amortizing Loan A loan where the principal reduces in stages as capital is repaid.

Arbitrage The purchase or sale of an instrument and the simultaneous taking of an equal and opposite position in a related market, for profit.

Arbitrageur A trader who takes advantage of profitable opportunities arising out of pricing anomalies.

At-Market An order to buy/sell at the current trading level.

At-The-Money Option (ATM) An option with an exercise price at the current market level of the underlying. For example, this could be ATMF – At the Money Forward.

Audit Inspection of a company's books by independent accountants.

Average Rate Option An option where the settlement is based on the difference between the strike and the average price of the 'underlying' over a predetermined period. Also known as Asian options.

Backwardation When the spot or near-term price of a commodity is higher than the forward price.

Bankers Acceptance Bill of exchange accepted by large banks. B/As bear interest for periods of three to six months. B/As constitute an irrevocable primary obligation of the drawer and of any endorsers whose names appear upon them. B/As primarily serve to finance imports and exports.

Basis Point One hundredth of one percent (0.01%).

Basis Risk When relationships between products used to hedge each other change or break down.

Bear Market A falling market.

Best The broker can buy or sell at the 'best' price available at his/her discretion.

Bid The wish to buy.

Big-Bang October 27th, 1986, the stock exchange's new regulations were introduced and the automated price quotation system.

Black and Scholes The original option pricing model used by many market practitioners, written by Black and Scholes in 1972, (see Scholes–Merton).

Blue Chip Large established company – in China known as 'Red Chips'.

Bond A borrower of funds issues a bond stipulating the amount of payments to a lender. Bonds normally carry a fixed interest rate but may be linked to a floating rate (FRN).

Bond Rating A rating given to a bond as the likelihood that the borrower will default on the interest and principal payments.

Brady Bonds Eurobonds issued by the government of a developing country refinancing its debt to foreign commercial banks, under a Brady-type agreement. The agreement is characterized by introduction of an IMF plan and the opportunity for the creditor to exchange its debt against a set of instruments that comprise various original financial solutions aimed at satisfying both counterparts of the deal. Brady bonds' main features are collateralization, debt reduction, debt-equity conversion, underwriting against new money and options on oil revenues.

Broken Date A value date that is not a regular forward date.

Broker An individual or a firm that acts as an intermediary, putting together willing sellers and willing buyers for a fee (brokerage).

Bull and Bear Bond Fixed interest bond, whose value at maturity is dependent on the performance of a stock market index. The issue is divided into two parts: a bull bond and a bear bond. The bull bond's redemption value rises if the market index increases and declines if the index decreases. Conversely, the bear bond has a higher redemption value if the stock market weakens and a lower value if stock prices rise.

Bull Market A rising market.

Call Option An option that gives the holder (buyer), the right but not the obligation to buy the underlying instrument at a pre-agreed rate (strike rate) on or before a specific future date.

Callable Bond The issuer has the right to redeem the bond at a specified earlier date than the one originally fixed as the final maturity.

Capital Growth Bond Issue price at par (100%) with redemption at a multiple of that amount.

Capitalization Issue An issue where funds from a company's reserves are converted into shares and offered free of charge to the shareholders.

Capped FRN FRN with a maximum interest rate.

CaR Capital at risk.

Cash Settlement Where a product is settled at expiry, based on the differential between the fixed/guaranteed price and the underlying instrument.

CCP Central Counterparty set up by the Stock Exchange, to remove credit risk when buying/selling shares.

CD Certificate of Deposit: A tradable deposit issued by banks and building societies.

CDO Collateralized Debt Obligation: a security based on a mix of debt and credit risk. Different layers are often referred to as 'tranches' or 'slices', each having different maturity and risk.

CFD (equity) Contract for Difference. A derivative product to trade the price differential over an indefinite time period of a specified number of shares.

CFD (oil) Contract for Difference. A derivative product used to manage the price risk between 'dated Brent' and the first front month.

CLS Continuous Linked Settlement: a new way to settle FX and Currency trades through CLS Bank and minimize Herstatt risk.

CMO Collateralized Mortgage Obligation: a debt security based on a pool of mortgages.

Compound Option An option on an option. The holder (buyer) has an option to purchase another option on a pre-set date at a pre-agreed premium.

Convertible Bond Bond/note, which can be converted for newly, issued shares or bonds at pre determined prices during specified periods of time.

Convertible Rate FRN An issue, which carries the option to convert either from an initial floating rate note into a fixed rate bond, or from a fixed rate bond into a floating rate note. This provides ways in which investors and borrowers can speculate and/or hedge against the future course of interest rates.

Counterparty Risk When counterparties are unwilling/unable to fulfil their contractual obligations.

Covered Warrant A warrant issued by a party other than the originator or issuer of the underlying asset.

Covered Writing Where an option is sold against an existing position.

CP Commercial Paper: an unsecured IOU issued by large companies and banks.

Coupon Rate The fixed rate of interest on a bond.

Credit Risk The uncertainty associated with the financial condition of a company.

CREST The paperless share settlement system. CREST is operated by CRESTCo and was introduced in 1996.

Cross Rate The exchange rate for one non US dollar currency against another non US dollar currency, e.g. CHF/JPY.

Dated Brent A physical oil cargo becomes dated when it has been allocated a loading date.

Day Trade A position opened and closed within the same trading day.

Deep Discount Bond This is a bond with issue price significantly below maturity price, due to lack of coupon or a coupon below market rate.

Default Failure to perform on a foreign exchange transaction or, failure to pay an interest obligation on a debt.

Default Risk The uncertainty that some or all of an investment may not be returned.

Depositary Receipts Certificates which represent ownership of a given number of a company's shares, which can be listed and traded separately from the underlying shares, e.g. ADR's and GDR's.

Derivatives Risk management instruments that are 'derived' from the underlying markets (e.g. equity, bonds, FX, commodity). The main derivative instruments are futures, options and swaps.

Dividend The part of a company's profits which is distributed to shareholders, usually expressed in pence per share.

Discount The margin by which the purchase price is cheaper than the redemption price.

DMO Debt Management Office. An executive agency of the treasury, responsible for issuing Gilts to fund the Government's borrowing.

DOL Daily Official List. The daily record setting out the prices of all trades in securities conducted on the Exchange.

Drop-Lock Bond The drop-lock bond (DL bond) combines the features of both a floating and a fixed rate security. The DL bond is issued with a floating rate interest which is reset semi-annually at a specified margin above a base rate, such as 6-months LIBOR. This continues until such time as the base rate is at or below a specified trigger rate on an interest fixing date or, in some cases, on two consecutive interest fixing dates. At that time the interest rate becomes fixed at a specified rate for the remaining lifetime of the bond.

Dual Currency Bond A dual currency bond is a hybrid debt instrument with payment obligations over the life of the issue in two different currencies. The borrower makes coupon payments in one currency, but redeems the principal at maturity in another currency in an amount fixed at the time of the issue of the bonds. The price of the bonds in the secondary market is indicated as a percentage of the redemption amount.

ECP Euro commercial paper is an unsecured general obligation in the form of a promissory bearer note, issued on a discount or interest-bearing basis by large commercial and industrial organizations. Maturities of ECP range from a few days up to one year, with most 182 days. ECP provides a flexible alternative to short-term finance credit lines with commercial banks and the rate for prime issuers is usually set at a small margin above that offered by prime bank money market securities of comparable maturities.

EDR Euro Depositary Receipts. A certificate representing ownership of the issuer's underlying shares. The EDR is denominated and quoted in euros.

End/end A transaction for settlement on the last business day of a month against the last business day of a future month.

Equity The risk-sharing part of a company's capital, usually made up of 'ordinary shares'.

ETF Exchange-Traded Funds. Known in the USA as Index Shares. Stock Exchange quoted fund portfolios designed either as index trackers (Index Funds) or as managed stock baskets (Actively Managed Funds).

Eurobond Bond issued by a borrower in a foreign country, denominated in a eurocurrency (e.g. US dollar, Canadian dollar, yen, euro, French franc, etc.), underwritten and sold by an international syndicate of financial institutions.

Euronote A short-term, negotiable bearer promissory note usually issued at a discount with maturities of less than one year. (Issued in bearer form; may be held as a global certificate.)

European Style An option which may only be exercised on the expiry date (see **American Style**).

Exchange Regulated exchanges include, LIFFE, CME, ICE, etc.

Exchangeable Bond Bond/note, which can be exchanged for existing shares or bonds of a third party at, pre-determined prices during specified periods of time.

Exchange Traded A transaction where a specific instrument is bought or sold on a regulated exchange, e.g. futures.

Exercise The conversion of the option into the 'underlying'.

Exercise Price Strike Price The price at which the option holder has the right to Buy/Sell the underlying instrument.

Extendible Bond The investor has the option at one or several fixed dates to extend the maturity.

Exotic Options New generation of option derivatives, including, Look-Backs, Barriers, Baskets, Ladders, etc.

Expiry The date after which an option can no longer be exercised.

Expiration Date The last date on which an option can be exercised.

Fair Value For options, this is calculated by an option pricing model such as that written by Black and Scholes. For futures, it is the level where the contract should trade, taking into account cost of carry.

Fixed Interest Securities Securities which attract a fixed rate of interest each year.

Flip-flop FRN FRN which combines an FRN with a very long final maturity, or even a perpetual issue, and an investor option to convert after a specified period into a short-dated FRN, which typically pays a lower margin over LIBOR than the original issue. The investor further has the option at a later date to convert back into the initial issue before redemption of the short-dated note.

Floatation When a company's shares are issued on the Exchange for the first time.

Foreign Bond Securities, for example Yankee, Samurai, Shogun, Shibosai, Bulldog, Matador and Daimyo bonds, issued by a borrower in a domestic capital market other than its own, usually denominated in the currency of that market, underwritten and sold by a national underwriting and selling group of the lenders' country. (Usually issued in bearer or registered form.)

Forward Foreign Exchange All foreign exchange transactions with a maturity of over two business days from transaction date (see **Short Dates**).

Freddie Mac Federal National Mortgage Association (FNMA).

FRN Floating Rate Note – FRNs are medium to long-term debt obligations with variable interest rates, which are adjusted periodically (typically every one, three or six months). The interest rate is usually fixed at a specified spread over one of the following specified deposit rates:

- LIBOR: London Interbank Offered Rate.
- LIBID: London Interbank Bid Rate.
- LIMEAN: London Interbank Mean Rate (average of LIBOR and LIBID).

FSA Financial Services Authority. Regulates the financial services industry under the Financial Services and Markets Act 2000.

Futures A futures contract is a contract to buy or sell a standardized amount of an underlying instrument at a future date at a pre-determined price. Trading at a recognized exchange (e.g. Euronext.liffe).

GDR Global Depositary Receipt (see **Depositary Receipts**).

GEMMs Gilt-edged market makers.

Gilt Gilt-edged securities are debt instruments issued by the UK Government.

Ginnie May Government National Mortgage Association (GNMA).

Global Bond International issue placed at the same time in the euro and one or more domestic markets with securities fungible between the markets.

Gross Redemption Yield (GRY) See **Yield to Maturity**.

Guaranteed Bond Guaranteed bonds have their interest, principal or both guaranteed by another corporation. It is very common that a parent company guarantees bonds issued by subsidiaries.

GUN A floating rate note facility akin to a RUF whereby a group of banks (grantors) undertake to purchase any notes put back to them by investors on any ERN interest rate fixing date. Put notes are then auctioned out to the market by the grantors.

Hedge A transaction that reduces or mitigates risk.

Historical Volatility An indication of past volatility in the market place.

Holder The buyer/owner of an option.

Herstatt Risk The failure to settle one side of an FX trade by value date. Named after bank where this failure occurred in 1974 (see also CLS).

Implied Volatility The volatility implied by the market price of the option.

Indication Only Quotations which are not firm.

Index A relative expression of the weighted value of a group of securities used as a performance indicator.

Insider Dealing The purchase or sale of securities (or other financial instruments) by someone who possesses 'inside' information, likely to affect the price of the instrument in the market. In the UK such deals are a criminal offence.

International Bond Bond issued by a borrower in a foreign country. International bonds include foreign bonds, parallel bonds and eurobonds.

In-the-Money Option (ITM) An option with an exercise price more advantageous than the current market level of the underlying.

Intrinsic Value One of the components of an option premium. The amount by which an option is in-the-money.

Investment Trust A collective investment fund in the form of a listed company which holds a portfolio of securities on behalf of its shareholders.

ISDA International Swaps and Derivatives Association Inc. Many market participants use ISDA swap documentation.

Junk Bond High risk, low rated speculative bonds.

LCH Clearnet The London Clearing House: A central counterparty set up to remove credit risk on exchange traded transactions.

LIBOR The London Inter-Bank Offered Rate. The inter-bank rate used when one bank borrows from another. It is also the benchmark used to price many Capital Market and Derivative transactions.

LIBID The London Inter-Bank Bid Rate. The rate where one bank will lend to another.

LIFFE London International Financial Futures Exchange, now owned by Euronext.

Limit Order An order given at a certain price.

Liquid Market An active market place where much selling and buying occurs with minimal price concessions.

Liquidation The closing of an existing position.

Liquidity The ease with which an item can be traded on a market.

LYON Liquid Yield Option Note – A LYON combines the features of a zero-coupon bond with those of a convertible bond. The zero coupon bond pays no interest until it is redeemed at or before maturity; the difference between the issue price and the redemption price represents the accrued interest. In addition, the LYON bond may be converted by the holder, into the stock of the issuing corporation within a specified period and at a specified conversion price.

Listed Company A company whose securities have been admitted to the Daily Official List (DOL).

Listing Particulars A prospectus which details what the Stock Exchange requires a company to publish about itself and its securities before they can be admitted to the main market.

Long More purchases than sales.

LSE London Stock Exchange.

Mandatory Quote Period The time when market-makers on the LSE's SEAQ and SEAQ International computers are obliged to make firm two-way quotes for the securities in which they are registered.

Mark-to-Market A process whereby existing positions are revalued on a daily basis.

Market Maker An authorized trader, obliged to make firm two-way quotes in financial instruments during trading periods.

Mezzanine Finance See Subordinated Debt.

Mine Where a dealer takes the offer which has been quoted by a counter-party. It must be qualified by the amount.

Mini-max FRN (or collared) FRN with a minimum and a maximum interest rate.

Mismatch FRN FRN having a coupon structure re-fixed more often and for different maturities than the interest periods, e.g. the interest rate is based on 6-months LIBOR but adjusted every month.

Mortgage Backed Security Debt security backed by a pool of mortgages.

MTN Medium-term note. An unsecured note issued in a Euro-currency with a maturity of three to six years.

Naked Option An option position taken without having the underlying.

New Issue An issuer coming to the market for the first time.

Nominated Advisor Compulsory Exchange approved advisor for AIM companies.

NMS Normal Market Size. Calculated for each security, based on a percentage of daily turnover. The percentage is set at 2.5 per cent and intended to represent the normal institutional bargain.

Notice of Exercise Notification by telex, fax or phone which must be given irrevocably by the buyer to the seller of the option prior or at the time of expiry.

OEIC An Open-Ended Investment Company governed by a trust deed or memorandum with specific investment objectives. The funds are pooled under management and the price of units is based on net asset value.

Offer The wish to sell.

Offer for Sale A method of bringing a company to the market. The public can apply for shares directly at a fixed price. A prospectus giving details of the sale must be published in a national newspaper.

Option An agreement between two parties that gives the holder (buyer), the right but not the obligation to buy or sell a specific instrument at a specified price on or before a specific future date. On exercise the seller (writer) of the option must deliver, or take delivery of the underlying instrument at the specified price.

Orders Firm order given by a dealer to a counterparty to execute a transaction under certain specified conditions, e.g., limit order, stop loss order, etc.

Order Book Otherwise known as SETS (Stock Exchange Trading System). Introduced on October 20th, 1997, the electronic order book automatically executes orders when bid and offer prices match.

Ordinary Share The most common form of share. Holders may receive dividends on the recommendation of directors. Known in the USA as 'common stock'.

Over the Counter (OTC) A bilateral transaction between a client and a bank, negotiated privately between the parties.

Out-of-the-Money option (OTM) An option with an exercise price more disadvantageous than the current market level of the underlying. An Out-of-the-Money option has time value but no intrinsic value.

Outright The purchase or sale of a currency for delivery on any date other than spot.

Overnight Transaction for settlement tomorrow, taken out today.

Par Where the price is the same at purchase and redemption.

Perpetual bond These are bonds, which are due for redemption only in the case of the borrower's liquidation. Usually the terms and conditions provide a call option at a premium. The interest rate can be fixed for the whole maturity or only for an initial period (e.g. ten years). For each subsequent period the interest is reset as provided in the terms and conditions.

Point/pip The last decimal place of the quotation.

Portfolio A collection of securities owned by an investor.

POTAM Panel on Takeovers and Mergers. UK regulatory body.

Preference Shares Normally fixed income shares, where holders have the right to receive dividends before ordinary shareholders. In the event of liquidation preference shareholders rank above ordinary shareholders.

Participating preference shares – These preference shares have further rights, which are normally linked to the relevant company's profits or dividend payment on ordinary shares.

Other preference shares – These will have the rights of standard preference shares, but may also be:

- Cumulative – i.e. income arrears are carried forward to the next payment date.

- Convertible – into ordinary shares.

- Redeemable – at a fixed date or contingent on a special event, or

- Permanent – not redeemable except at issuers option.

- Callable – can be repurchased by its issuer at a specified price.

- Protected – has its dividend guaranteed in the event that the corporation does not earn a profit.

- Participating – allows its holders to receive dividends in addition to the fixed amount in years when the ordinary dividend exceeds a certain level.

- Prior preferred – has senior rights over other classes of preferred stock.

Premium-options The cost of the option contract. It is made up of two components, intrinsic value and time value.

Premium The margin by which the purchase price is more expensive than the redemption rate.

P/E Ratio Price/Earnings Ratio. A measure of investor confidence, normally the higher the figure the higher the confidence. Current share price divided by earnings per share.

Price Transparency Where a transaction is executed on the floor of an exchange, and every participant has equal price.

Primary Market The function of a stock exchange in bringing securities to the market for the first time.

Privatization Conversion of a state-run company to public limited liability status.

Private Company A company which is not a public company and cannot offer its share to the public.

Put Option An option that gives the holder (buyer), the right but not the obligation to sell the underlying instrument at a pre-agreed strike rate (exercise rate) on or before a specific future date.

Puttable Bond The investor has the right to require redemption of the principal at a specified earlier date than the one originally fixed as the final maturity.

Registrar An organization responsible for maintaining a company's share register.

Repo Sale and repurchase agreement. Used by many Central Banks as a method of managing liquidity in the money markets. Banks trade repos and reverse repos in many products but mainly bonds.

Retractable Bond Issue carrying the option (for both the issuer and the investor) for early redemption at one or several fixed dates.

Reverse Convertible Bonds Convertible bond that may be redeemed at the issuer's decision against existing shares of an underlying company which has no economical relation with the issuer or the guarantee of the bonds.

RIE Recognized Investment Exchange, meeting FSA requirement.

Rights Issue An invitation to existing shareholders to purchase additional shares in the company, normally at a discount.

Risk The volatility of expected outcomes.

RNS Regulatory News Service. To ensure that price sensitive information from listed, AIM and certain other bodies, is disseminated to all RNS subscribers at the same time.

Rollercoaster Loan A loan with both accreting and amortizing elements (see **Accreting** and **Amortizing Loan**).

RUF Revolving underwriting facility, sometimes called a Note-Issuance Facility (NIF). This is a medium to long-term finance instrument, which allows the borrower, by issuing short-term paper, to benefit from cheaper short-term funds.

Scholes–Merton The Nobel prize winning revision of the Black–Scholes option pricing model.

SEAQ The Stock Exchange Automated Quotation system for UK securities. A continuously updated computer database containing price quotations and trade reports for UK securities.

SEAQ International Stock Exchange Automated Quotation System for International securities.

SEATS plus Supports the trading of all AIM and listed UK equities whose turnover is insufficient for market makers or SETS.

SETS Stock Exchange Trading Service. Otherwise known as the Order Book.

SETSmm SETSmm is a SETS-style order book supported by market makers for FTSE 250 securities not trading on SETS, all UK FTSE Eurotop 300 securities and Exchange Traded Funds (ETFs).

SFA Securities and Futures Authority. The self regulating organization (SRO) responsible for regulating the conduct of brokers and dealers in securities, options and futures. Now included within the FSA.

Short More sales than purchases.

Short Dates Foreign exchange deals for a broken number of days up to the one month date.

SICAF (Société d'investissement à capitale fixe) A share representing one part of ownership in a fixed capital investment company.

SICAV (Société d'investissement à capital variable) A SICAV share represents part of ownership in an open-ended investment company with a variable capital.

Sinking Fund Payments made by the borrower on a regular basis to a special account to set aside the necessary funds for the redemption of its long-term debt. In the euromarket, borrowers can meet their requirements through purchases in the open market or through drawings by lot.

SMF The Securities Masterfile provides up-to-date information on securities traded on UK and international markets.

SSN Stock Situation Notices which contain extensive details of a corporate action.

Sold Short Someone who has sold a commodity without previously owning it (short sell).

Spot Foreign Exchange A transaction to exchange one currency for another at a rate agreed today (the spot rate), for settlement in two business days time.

Spot/next Swap transaction for settlement on the second business day against the third business day after the transaction date.

Spread The difference between buying and selling rates.

Square Purchases and sales of an asset are equal.

Step Up/Step Down Bond Rate will go up and/or down as indicated in the terms and conditions of the notes.

Stockbroker An Exchange member firm which provides advice and dealing services to the public and which can deal on its own account.

Stop Loss Order Becomes an order at best after a certain rate has been reached or passed or dealt, depending upon the specified conditions previously agreed between the parties.

Strike Price/Exercise Price The price at which the option holder has the right to Buy-or-Sell the underlying instrument.

Subordinated Debt Subordinated debt (sometimes called mezzanine finance) has many of the characteristics of both debt and equity. A subordinated creditor agrees to rank after senior creditors but before ordinary shareholders in a winding-up. For regulatory purposes certain forms of subordinated debt issued by financial institutions may be treated, like equity, as 'primary capital'.

Swap A derivative risk management tool.

Swaption An option into a pre-determined swap transaction. Options can be 'payers' or 'receivers' on the swap which itself can be American or European.

TechMARK Launched November 1999. This market groups together technology companies from across the main market. It has its own indices, the FTSE techMARK 100 and FTSE techMARK Allshare.

Technical Analysis A graphical analysis of historical price trends used to predict likely future trends in the market. Also known as 'charts'.

Theoretical Value The fair value of a futures or option contract (see **Fair Value**).

Time Value The amount (if any), by which the premium of an option exceeds the intrinsic value.

Tom/next A transaction for settlement on the next business day after tomorrow.

Touch The best buying and selling prices available from a market makers on SEAQ and SEAQ International in a given security at any one time.

Traded Option Treasury Bond An option contract bought or sold on a regulated exchange. Bond issued by the US Treasury – longer than 10 years.

Treasury Bill Short-term security issued by the US Treasury.

Trillion One thousand billion (12 zeroes).

TRUF Transferable revolving underwriting facility (TRUF). Similar to a RUF, but the underwriting bank's contingent liability (back-up line) to purchase notes in the event of non-placement by the borrower is fully transferable.

UKLA United Kingdom Listing Authority. A capacity assumed by the FSA from the LSE, as the competent authority for a UK listing.

UK Treasury Bill Short-term security issued by the UK Treasury.

Underlying An asset, future, interest rate, FX rate or index upon which a derivative transaction is based.

Underwriting An arrangement by which a company is guaranteed that an issue will raise a given amount of cash. Underwriters undertake to subscribe for any of the issue not taken up. They charge commission for this service.

Unit Trust A collective investment in the form of a trust which holds a portfolio of securities on behalf of the investors who hold units in the trust. Known in the USA as Mutual Funds.

USF Universal Stock Futures. Quoted on LIFFE, single share futures contracts covering a range of different shares from a number of countries and sectors.

VaR Value at risk: a statistical measure used for risk management.

Volatility One of the major components of the option pricing model, based on the degree of 'scatter' of the underlying price when compared to the 'mean average exchange rate'.

Value Today Same day value.

Value Tomorrow Value the next working day or business day.

Variable Rate Note FRN; where the margin over the reference rate is fixed by the issuer and the re-marketing agent several days prior to the following interest period. The holders, during a pre-determined period of time, have the right to either bid for the new applicable margin over the reference rate or (under certain conditions) put the notes to the arranger (but not the issuer) on the following interest payment date.

VWAP Volume Weighted Average Price, which is calculated by dividing the value of trades by the volume over a given period. A closing 10 minute VWAP is used to calculate set closing prices on the order book.

Warrant An option which can be listed on an exchange, generally longer than one year. Many capital market issues have warrants embedded in them.

Writer The seller of an option.

Yard One thousand million (billion).

Yellow Strip The yellow band on a SEAQ screen which displays the highest bid and the lowest offered price that competing market makers are offering in a security. It is known colloquially as the 'touch' or 'yellow strip' price.

Yield The return earned on an investment taking into account the annual income and its present capital value. There are a number of different types of yield, and in some cases different methods of calculating each type.

Yield Curve A curve showing interest rates at a particular point in time for securities with the same risk but different maturity dates.

Yield to Maturity The annualized rate of return if a bond is held to maturity, often known as Gross Redemption Yield (GRY).

Your Risk Quoted rates are subject to change at the risk of the receiver.

Yours Opposite to mine. The dealer gives at the bid which has been quoted by the counterparty. It must be qualified by the amount.

Zero Coupon Bond This is a Bond without a coupon providing interest payments. Zero coupon bonds have an issue price well below 100% with repayment on maturity at face value or par. The investors' return is the difference between the issue price and redemption value.

Taylor Associates run programmes and tutorials in the following areas:

Technical Skills

- Capital Markets
- Dervatives
- Treasury and Banking
- Foreign Exchange
- Fixed Income
- Securitization
- Equities
- Technical Analysis

- Wealth Management
- Fund Management
- Mergers and Acquisitions
- Portfolio Management
- Credit Evaluation
- Risk and Risk Management
- General Finance and Accounting
- Law

Management Skills

- Diversity – combating sexual, racial, age, disability, sexual orientation and religious discrimination
- Diversity – harassment and bullying
- Team Building
- Sales and Communication skills
- Presentation and Writing skills
- Coaching
- Assertion and Managing Difficult Staff

For further details contact:

Francesca Taylor

Tel: 01372 841096

e-mail: info@taylorassociates.co.uk

Web: www.taylorassociates.co.uk

Index

accounting for derivatives, first principles for, 381–99
  accounting standards governing financial
      instruments, 383–4
  accruals, 382–3, 384
  amortized cost, 384
  consistency and prudence, 383
  cross-currency swaps, 388–91
  events, determining accounting, 386, 387–9
  fair value, 384, 385
  futures, 391–2
  going concerns, 382
  hedge accounting, 384, 398
  interest rate swaps, 387–8
  International Accounting Standards (IAS), 394–8
  mark-to-market accounting, 384, 388, 389
  options, 392–3
  reporting requirements, 383–4
  swaps, 386–91
American options, 44–5, 185
arbitrageurs, 7–8 , 322–3
assets, meaning and types of, 2. *see also* underlying
     assets
Asian options, 45, 210

back-to-back loans, (figs 10.18, 10.19), 212–13
bankruptcy, 155
barrier options, 211
benchmarking, 6, 34, 135–41
  additional benchmarking at month-end, 138
  BBA LIBOR fixing, 136
  credit default swaps, 136–7, 139
  daily benchmarking, 136–7
  dealer contributed data points against composite,
     snapshot of, (Fig 7.1), 137
  exchange-traded markets, 137
  financial benchmarking, 136–0
  Financial Services Authority, 139
  interest rate caps and floors, 103, 104
  International Accounting Standards, 138
  iTraxx Europe, 163
  Markit Annual Scorecard, 140–1
  Markit's Totem service, 138
  monthly Fed metrics, 139–40
  oil prices, 290
  operational risk measurements, 138–40
  over the counter (OTC) derivatives markets, 135–41
  regulators, 139
  strike price, 45
Bermudan options, 45, 210
binary options (digital options), 285–6

call and puts, 42–3

capped call (Fig 12.4), 282–3, 285
capital adequacy, 76
CHF call option – long call, (Fig 10.4), 191
CHF call option – short call, (Fig 10.5), 191
CHF put option – long put, (Fig 10.6), 192
CHF put option – short put, (Fig 10.7), 192
currency options, reduced premium
     strategies and, 203–6
exchange-traded energy option contracts, 305
OTC (over the counter) currency options, 183, 186,
     192–3, 196, 202
premium-determinants, 89
profit/loss profile of long put strategy, (Fig 4.11),
     56
profit/loss profile of short call option
     strategy, (Fig 4.10), 55
profit/loss profile of short put strategy (Fig 4.12),
     56
put/call parity, (Fig 10.8), 193, 206
stock index options, 253
callable swaps (cancellable swaps), 131
capital protected growth products, constructing,
     277–9
caps, *see* interest rate caps and floors
cash collateralized debt obligations (CDOs) (Fig 9.6),
     168
Central Counterparty Model (CCP), 5, 101
Chicago Board of Trade, 63
Chicago Mercantile Exchange (CME), 4, 63
clearing, 4–5, 69, 352
cliquets and reverse cliquets (ratchet options), 284–5
CME E-quivalents, (Fig 10.27), 225
CME S&P 500 (Tab 11.5), 247
collars *see* currency collar options (cylinder options),
     interest rate collars
collateralized debt obligations (CDOs), 167–73
  cash CDOs (Fig 9.6), 168
  classification, 172–3
  credit risk, 167–8
  ratings, 171–2
  special purpose vehicles (SPVs), use of, 168–9
  synthetic CDOs, (Fig 9.7), 169–70
  tranche,
    characteristics, 170
    loss allocation example, (Fig 9.9), 171
    loss prioritization in CDO capital
      structure, (Fig 9.8), 170
    rating, 171–2
commodity derivatives, 289–319, *see* exchange-related
     energy derivatives, exchange-traded energy
     option contracts, OTC oil swaps, OTC or
     'off-exchange' energy derivatives

commodity derivatives (*continued*)
  crude oil prices, (Fig 13.2), 294
  electricity market, 217–19
  oil market, background to the, 291–4
  West Texas Intermediate (WTI), (Fig 13.1), 293
complex credit sector, 173
compliance, 373–8
  crime and derivatives, 376–8
  Markets in Financial Instruments Directive, 378
  money laundering, 377–8
  OTC derivatives practice, 373–5
  risk, 364–6
coupon swaps, 121
credit, *see* credit default swaps, credit derivatives,
      credit options, credit risk
credit default swaps, 149–58, 162, 327
  benchmarking, 136–7, 139
  cash flows, (Fig 8.3), 152
  contract details, 154–6
    credit events, 155–6
    deliverable obligations, 156
    ranking pari passu, 156
    reference entity, 155
    reference obligations, 155
    settlement, 156
    underlying assets, 149
  credit events, 150–4
  credit rating of probable swap counterparties, 157
  delivery, 153, 156
  growth, (Fig 8.1), 144–5
  hedging example, 150–2, 153
  insurance and, distinction between, 149–51
  LIBOR, 151
  maturity, 157
  pricing via assets swaps, (Tables 8.2), 152
  probability of default, 157
  protection buyers and sellers, motivations of, 157
  settlement timeline, (Fig 8.4), 153
  single name, 144
  spread, 151
  trading example, 153
  underlying assets, (Tables 8.2, 8.3), 150–1, 154
credit derivatives, 143–59, *see also* credit default swaps,
      credit options, total rate of return swaps
  credit risk, 145–6, 148
  default data, 148
  first deals, 148
  hedge funds, 144–5
  London market, reasons for primacy of, 148
  range of, 148–59
  ratings, (Table 8.1), 147, 148
  risk management, 144
  style of trading, 146–7
  subdivisions of markets, 146
  turnover, 144
  underlying assets, 146
credit events, 150–6
  bankruptcy, 155
  failure to pay, 155
  obligation acceleration and default, 155
  repudiation/moratorium, 155
  restructuring, 156
credit indices, 162–7, *see also* iTraxx Europe

benefits of, 162
  CDX, 162–3, 166
  credit default swaps, 157
  credit fixings, 166
  Creditex, 166–7
  index protocol, 166–7
  Markit, 166–7
credit ratings, (Table 8.1), 147, 148, 171–2
credit risk, 145–6, 369–70
  bank and customer, 34–6
  client specific risk, 145
  collateralization, 145, 166–7
  credit derivatives, 148
  currency swaps, 223
  equity index swaps, 266
  exchange-traded futures contracts, 299
  forward rate agreements (FRAs), 78–9
  hedge funds, 145
  insurance, 145
  interest rate swaps, 117, 120
  investment banks, 145
  liquidity, 33
  market risk, 145
  modelling, 369–70
  OTC (over the counter) instruments, 5
  OTC (over the counter) oil swaps, 314
  protection buyers and sellers, 145–6
  short-term interest rate futures (STIR), 65–6
  total return swaps, 159
crime and derivatives, 376–8
currency collar options (cylinder options), (Table 10.4),
      203–6
  cost, 204
  insurance, 204
  multiple products, 204
  outcome, 205–6
  profit potential, 204
  reduced premium strategy, 203–6
  zero-cost collar option, (Fig 10.16), 206
currency derivatives, 175–227, *see also*
      currency options, reduced premium strategies
      and, currency swaps, over-the-counter cur-
      rency options
  Asian options, 210
  Bermudan options, 210
  exchange rates, 176–7
  hedging, 176–8
  knock-ins (barrier options), 211
  range of, (Table 9.1), 178
  risk, 176–7
  short and long-term exposures, 176
  simple exotic structures, 210–12
currency options, reduced premium strategies and,
      202–10
  bank, setting up a facility with a, 209–10
  currency collar options (cylinder options), 203–6
  out of the money options, 203
  participating forwards, 207–8
  put/call parity, 206
currency swaps, (Fig 10.20) 212–26
  accounting, 388–91
  back-to-back loans (Figs 10.18, 10.19), 212–13
  bypass mechanism, 216–17

cash flows (Figs 10.22, 10.24, 10.26), 215–16
confidentiality, 216
credit risk, 223
cross-currency swaps, 388–91
exchanged traded instruments, 223–8
fixed versus floating interest rate swaps, (Fig 10.23), 218
forward foreign exchange, comparison with, (Fig 10.25), 220–1
hedging with fixed/floating currency swap (Fig 10.24), 219–20
initial exchange, cash flows in the swap with, 215–16
initial/final exchange of principal, 217
interest rate swaps, 214–15, 218
LIBOR, 219
liquidity, 218
maturity, 216
new or existing obligations, 217
outright forwards, 221–2
parallel and back-to-back loans (Fig 10.18), 212–13
principal and interest obligations (Fig 10.21), 215
quotations, 219
range of swap types, 218
risk, 222
size, 216
tripartite swaps, 218
true derivatives, 217
when to use, 222
cylinder options, see currency collar options (cylinder options)

day counts, 17–18
dealing with derivatives, 34–7
    bank and customer credit risk, 34–6
    client relationships, 36
    counterparty, choosing the, 35–6
    exchange-traded transactions, 36
    gearing, 36–7
    OTC transactions, 34–5
definition of derivatives, 2–3
Delta options, (Figs 10.12, 10.13), 198–200
digital options (bunary options), 285–6
documentation and derivatives, 339–44
Dow Jones Index, 233
DTCC Deriv/SERV, 353–6

efficient portfolio management, 266
EFP (Exchange of Futures for Physicals), 297
electricity market, 317–19
    electricity market structure (Table 12.5), 318
    forward market and futures market, 318–19
    OTC markets, 319
    pool structure, 317
    power exchange strcuture (PX), 318
    spot power market, 317–18
    trading, 318–19
electronic processing, see straight through processing (STP) for OTC derivatives
electronic trading, 4, 63–4, 69, 353
energy, see oil
equity based retail products, development of UK and European markets for, 275–7
equity derivatives, 229–71, see also equity index swaps,

single stock options, stock index futures, stock index options
    auto-callable or early release, 284
    calculation of income level, 280–1
    capital protected growth products, constructing, 277–9
    capped call (Fig 12.4), 282–3, 285
    cliquets and reverse cliquets (ratchet options), 284–5
    development of market, 275–7
    digital option (binary option), 285–6
    equity indices, 233–5
    fees, 278
    FT-SE 100 between 1990 and 2006, (Fig 12.1), 274
    futures, 232
    hybrids, 235
    income paying capital at risk products, 280
    interest rates (Fig 12.3), 277–8
    investment products, creating attractive, 273–87
    minimum return, 281–2
    option costs, 279
    options, 232–3
    OR structure, definition of, 282
    payoff of an OR structure, (Fig 12.4), 282
    pricing factors, summary of, 279
    risk to capital, 281
    single stocks, 231–2
    structural variations, common, 281–6
    swaps, 233
    systemic and unsystematic portfolio risk, (Fig 11.1), 232
    underlying assets, (Table 12.1), 281
equity index swaps, 263–71
    cash flows, (Fig 11.4, 11.5), 265, 268
    collateral, 266
    cost effectiveness, 265
    credit risk, 266
    efficient portfolio management, 266
    foreign index, exposure to a, 266
    index tracking, 265
    interest rates, 263–4
    LIBOR, 265
    LIBOR rates and day count, (Table 11.11), 269–70
    net cash settlement, 265
    principal amounts, 266–7
    resets, 267
    synthetic stock market investment example (Fig 11.5, Table 11.11), 267–70
equity indices, 233–5
    list of major indices, 234–5
equity investment, 274–5
equity options – abbreviated contract specification (Table 11.9), 259
E-quivalent, 224
Euribor, (Table 5.6), 73–4
Euro markets, 14
Eurodollar FRA hedge, (Fig 5.9), 84–5
Eurodollar interest rate options to hedge investments, (Fig 5.12), 93–4
Euronext-LIFFE, 4, 63–4, 69–70
European options, 45, 185
exchange of futures for physicals (EFPs), 297
exchange-traded energy derivatives, 250–1, 295–301
    Central Counterparty, 4

exchange-traded energy derivatives (*continued*)
  Clearing House, 4–5
  contract specifications, 4
  electronic screen-based trading, 4
  exchanges, list of, 295
  futures contracts, 295–301
  LCH.Clearnet Ltd, 4–5
  open outcry, 4
  over the counter instruments, 4–5
  prices, 295–301
exchange-traded energy option contracts, 302–7
  cost of carry, 305
  exercise, 304
  expected market volatility, 305
  hedging with an option on light sweet crude oil,
      306–7
  insurance protection, 303
  maturity, 304
  NYMEX light sweet crude oil option – abbreviated
      contract specification (Table 13.3), 303
  premium determinants, 304–7
  profit potential, 303
  put or call, 305
  sell-back, 303
exchange-traded futures contracts, 295–301
  Brent futures hedging transaction, 299
  credit risk, 299
  crude oil prices, inflation adjusted monthly, (Fig
      13.3), 296
  energy derivatives, 295–301
  exchange of futures for physicals (EFPs), 297
  gas oil futures closing prices, (Fig 13.4), 300
  hedging techniques (Table 13.1), 297, 299
  IPE Brent Crude oil future – abbreviated contract
      specification (Table 12.2), 301
  market operations, 298
  pricing, 298
  profit from the futures hedge, 301
exchange-traded instruments
  benchmarking, 137
  Central Counterparty Model (CCP), 5
  CME E-quivalents, (Fig 10.27), 225
  currency swaps, 223–8
  dealing with derivatives, 36
  energy derivatives, 295–301
  financial futures contracts (exchange–traded),
      63–75
  foreign exchange futures, 223–4
  futures contracts, 295–301
  options, 41
  outcome, 226
  profit or loss, 226
  simplified contract specification for CME British
      Pound future, (Table 10.5), 224
expiry date, (Fig 4.1), 44, 45

fees, 13, 278
financial futures contracts (exchange-traded), 63–75
  brokers, 74–5
  central counterparty, LCH.Clearnet as,
      (Fig 5.4), 69
  clearing, 69
  delivery, 64, 66–7
  electronic trading, 63–4, 69
  Euronext-liffe, 63–4, 69–70

  forward rate agreements, compared with,
      (Table 5.7), 86
  fungibles, 63
  futures trading transactions, example of, 67–8
  hedging, 71–2, 74–5
  initial margins, 70, 74–5
  LCH.Clearnet Ltd, (Fig 5.4), 69–71
  LIBOR, 66–7
  market structure, 69–74
  matching, 69
  short term interest rate futures contracts (STIRS),
      65–7
  specification, 64, 66
  trade registration system (TRS), 69–70
  variation margins, 70–1, 75
financial maths, 18–21
  Discount Factor (DF), 21
  Future Value (FV), 19
  Present Value (PV), 20–1
  Time Value of Money (TVM), 18–19
Financial Services Authority, 139, 356, 362, 377
fixed/floating interest rate swaps, 121–2, 122–7
forward foreign exchange
  currency swaps, comparison with, (Fig 10.25),
      220–1
  OTC (over the counter) currency options,
      comparison with, (Table 10.3), 187
forward interest rates, calculating, 22–3
forward rate agreements (FRAs) (OTC), 31–2, 54–5,
      75–86
  buyers and sellers, 77
  capital adequacy, 76–7
  cash settlement, 78
  counterparty credit risk, 78–9
  credit lines, 85
  Eurodollar FRA hedge, (Fig 5.10), 84–5
  financial futures, comparison with,
      (Table 5.7), 86
  hedging with sterling FRAs, 80
  implied forward rates (Fig 5.5), 76
  important dates, (Fig 5.6), 79
  insurance, 78
  interest rate options, comparison between, (Table
      5.8), 96
  interest rate swaps, 117
  interest rates, 75–7, 81, 84–5
  levels, indications of, (Fig 6.14), 130
  LIBOR, 75, 78, 81, 84–5
  market structure and operations, 78–80
  multiple settlement interest rate   derivatives, (Fig
      6.2), 101
  outcome, 81–5
  profit potential, 78
  quotes, (Fig 5.7), 81
  settlement amounts, example of, (Fig 5.8), 82
  strategy, 80–1
  US dollar FAR rates, (Fig 5.9), 83–4
  zero cost, 78
forward rates, 21–4, *see also* forward rate agreements
      (FRAs) (OTC)
  calculating, 21–4
  commodity, calculating for a, 23–4
  fair value calculations, 21–2
  forward/forward rates, 23
fraudulent collusion, 376–7

FT Actuaries All Share Index (FTA), 233
FT Ordinary Share Index (FT30), 233
FT-SE 100 (Footsie), (Table 11.2, 11.7) 233
   equity derivatives, 274, 281
   equity index swaps, 263–71
   reference level, 281
   stock index futures, 236–46, 249
   stock index options, 249–52, 258
fundamentals of derivatives
   benchmarks, 34
   dealing with derivatives, 34–7
   fair value, 34
   liquidity and credit risk, 33
   range of derivatives, 30
   settlement, 31–2
   triggers, 3
   underlying assets, understanding, 33–4
   vanilla trade, definition of, 30–1
fungibles, 63
futures
   accounting, 391–2
   CME British Pound future, simplified contract
      specification for, (Table 10.5), 224
   electricity market, 318–19
   equity derivatives, 232
   exchange-traded energy derivatives, 295–301
   exchange-traded futures contracts, 295–301
   financial futures contracts (exchange–traded),
      63–75
   foreign exchange futures, 223–4
   short term interest rate futures contracts (STIRS),
      65–7
   stock index futures, 235–49

Gamma (Fig 10.13), 200
gas oil futures closing prices, (Fig 13.4), 300
gearing, 36–7, 261
governance, 362–7, 371, 378

hedge funds, 321–8, see also hedging
   credit derivatives, 144–5
   credit risk, 145
   Eurodollar FRA hedge, (Fig 5.10), 84–5
   exposures, increasing, 324
   manoeuvring anonymously, 325–6
   mitigating risk, 322–3
   operational burdens, shifting, 326–7
   precision, executing with greater, 327–8
   restricted markets, accessing, 326
   tax efficiencies, capturing, 324–5
   trading non-deliverable assets, 326
hedging, 2, see also hedge funds
   accounting, 384, 398
   Brent crude exposure with no oil swap, 315
   Brent futures hedging transaction, 299
   credit default swaps, 150–3
   currency derivatives, 176–8
   delta, 199
   Eurodollar interest rate options to hedge
      investments, (Fig 5.13), 93–4
   exchange-traded energy option contracts, 306–7
   exchange-traded futures contracts, (Table 13.1),
      297, 299
   financial futures contracts (exchange–traded), 71–2,
      74–5

fixed/floating currency swap (Fig 10.24), 219–20
fixed/floating interest rate swaps, (Fig 6.8) 122–7
hedgers, 7
interest rate caps and floors, 106–8
interest rate collars, sterling, 113–15
interest rate swaps, 117, 122–8
multiple settlement interest rate derivatives, (Fig
   6.1), 100
OTC (over the counter) currency options, 179–80,
   187–9
OTC (over the counter) or 'off-exchange' energy
   derivatives, 311
premium-determinants, (Figs 5.13, 5.14), 90–1,
   93–4
receivables, 187–9
short term interest rate futures (STIR), 71–4
sterling FRAs, with, 80
sterling interest rate options, 90–1
stock index options (Table 11.8, Fig 11.2), 255–7

IAS, see International Accounting Standards (IAS)
in/at/out of the money, concept of, (Table 10.2), 183
index tracking, 265
indices, 233–5, see also credit indices
interest rate caps and floors, 102–9
   benchmark rate, 103, 104
   buyers and sellers, 103
   call and put, 103
   credit risk, 109
   expected market volatility, 105–6
   hedging with sterling interest rate cap (Fig 6.3),
      106
   hedging with US dollar interest rate floor (Fig 6.4),
      107–8
   interest rate collars, 110, 113–16
   LIBOR, 103–9
   maturity, 105
   outcome, 108
   premium determinants, 103–9
   price, 104–6, 109, 115
   strike price versus underlying price, 104–6
   strip, 102
   underlying assets, 103
interest rate collars, 104–5, 110–16
   cash market linked, 112
   cash settlement, 112
   credit line, 116
   hedging with sterling interest rate collar, (Fig 6.7),
      113–15
   insurance, 110–12, 116
   interest rate caps and floors, 110–16
   LIBOR, 112–13
   multiple exercise, 112
   multiple settlement interest rate products, 116
   premium, reducing the, 110–11, 116
   price, 115
   profit potential, 112
   single settlement interest rate options, 116
   sterling cap prices, (Fig 6.5), 113
   sterling floor prices, (Fig 6.6), 113
   zero cost collars, 115
interest rate derivatives, 59–97, see also
      financial futures contracts (exchange-traded),
      forward rate agreements (OTC), interest rate
      options (OTC) derivatives

interest rate derivatives (*continued*)
  background and development, 60–2
  interest rate risk, meaning of, 60–2
  maturity profile (Fig 5.1, Table 5.2), 61
  multiple settlement interest rate   derivatives
      99–133
  range of (Table 3.1), 60–1
  risk management techniques, pattern of (Table 5.3),
      62
  scope of operation (Fig 5.2), 62
interest rate futures contracts (STIRS), *see* short term
      interest rate futures contracts (STIRS)
interest rate options (OTC), 87–97
  cash market linked, 88
  cash settlement, 88
  deferring payment of premium, 96
  Eurodollar interest rate options to hedge
      investments, (Fig 5.13), 93–4
  forward rate agreements, compared with, (Table
      5.9), 96
  premium determinants, 87–97
  profit potential, 88
  sell back, 88
  single settlement interest rate options, 116
  strip, 87
  underlying assets, 87
interest rate swaps, 102, 116–33
  absolute advantage, 125
  accounting, 387–8
  actual swap, (Fig 6.11), 126
  background, 117–20
  basis swap, (Fig 6.12), 128
  callable swaps (cancellable swaps), 131
  cash settlement, 120
  comparative advantage, 118–19, 121, 124
  coupon swaps, 121–2
  credit line, 117, 132
  credit risk, 117, 120
  currency swaps, 214–15, 218
  fixed/floating interest rate swaps, 119, 121–7, 218
  forward rate agreement levels,
      comparison with, 117
      indications of, (Fig 6.13), 130
  funding optimization, 120
  global OTC derivatives market, amounts
      outstanding on, (Table 15.1), 118
  hedging, 117, 124
      sterling basis swap, 127–8
      US dollar swaps, with, (Fig 6.8), 122–7
  information, summarizing the, 124–5
  insurance protection, 120
  interest rate flows, (Figs 6.9, 6.11, 6.12), 123
  interest rates, summary of, (Table 6.2), 124–5
  interest, receipts and payments of,
      (Table 6.3), 126–7
  LIBOR, 117–19, 122–8, 133
  maturity, 117, 119
  negotiating deals, 129–30
  new or existing obligations, 120
  outcome, 123, 126
  overnight swaps, 131–2
  premiums, 116–17, 120
  prices, 129, 133
  risk management, 117
  single currency basis swaps, 127

sterling swap quotations, (Table 6.4), 129
  swap pricing, 128–9
  swap variants, 130–2
  swaptions, 130–1
  swapping interest flows with intermediary bank,
      (Fig 6.10), 125
  types of, 119, 130
  vanilla swaps, 121–2
  volatility, 129–30
interest rates, *see also* interest rate swaps
  calculation of, 17–18, 22–3
  capital protected growth products, 277
  caps and floors, 102–9
  collars, 104–5, 110–15
  derivatives, 59–97, 277–8
  equity derivatives, (Fig 12.3), 277–8
  equity index swaps, 263–4
  forward interest rates, calculating, 22–3
  forward rate agreements (FRAs), 75–7, 81, 84–5
  LIBOR, 32
  options (OTC), 87–96, 184–5
  yield curves, 25–6
International Accounting Standards (IAS), 394–8
  application, 396–8
  background, 394–5
  balance sheet, recording financial instruments on,
      397
  benchmarking, 138
  classification of financial instruments, 396–7
  disclosures, 398
  fair value, 396
  gains and losses, 397–8
  hedge accounting, 398
  held to maturity investments, 396
  IAS 32 – disclosure and presentation, 394–6
  IAS 39 – recognition and measurement, 394–6
  identification all financial instruments, 396
  loans and receivables, 396–7
  measurement of instruments subsequently, 397–8
International Swaps and Derivatives Association, *see*
      also ISDA Agreement
IPE Brent Crude oil future – abbreviated contract
      specification (Table 12.2), 301
ISDA Agreement, 340–4
  confirmation, 343
  Master Agreement, 342–4
  products covered by, list of, 342
  schedule, 343
  structure of, 342
iTraxx Europe, 162, 163–6
  benchmark, 163
  construction process, (Figure 9.1), 163
  credit events, (Figs 9.3, 9.4), 164–5
  credit fixings, 166
  European Platform, (Fig 9.2), 164
  index issue date, investing after the, 165–6
  index mechanics, (Fig 9.5), 163–4
  International Index Company (IIC), 163
  Reference Entities and Reference Obligations, 163

knock-ins (barrier options), 211

LCH.Clearnet Ltd, 4–5, (Fig 5.4), 69–71, 352
LIBOR, 15–17
  banks, whether it is just for, 17

benchmarking, 136
credit default swaps, 151
currency swaps, 219
equity index swaps, 265, (Table 11.11), 269–70
financial futures contracts, 66–7
fix, 16 (Fig 2.1)
forward rate agreements (FRAs), 75, 78, 81, 84–5
forward rates, calculation of, 23–4
interest rate caps and floors, 103–9
interest rate collars, 112, 114
interest rate swaps, 117–19, 122–8, 133
interest rates, 32
premium determinants, 91–2
rates and day count, (Table 11.11), 269–70
role and use of, 15–17
total return swaps, 158
liquidity and credit risk, 33
loans and receivables, 396–7
London Interbank Offered Rate, see LIBOR

market fundamentals, 11–27
day counts, 17–18
financial maths, 18–21
forward rates, calculating, 21–4
income, how banks generate, 12–13
key assumptions, 14–15
LIBOR, 15–17
marking to market (MTM or M2M), 24–5
yield curves, 25–6
market volumes, 6
Markets in Financial Instruments Directive, 378
marking to market (MTM or M2M), 24–5, 384, 388, 390
Markit, 138, 140–1, 353
message formats in STP processing, 349–52
FpML document, 351–2, 354
MT360 message, overview of, 350–1
money laundering, 377–8
monthly Fed metrics, 139–40
multiple settlement interest rate derivatives 99–133
Central Counterparty model, 101
credit lines, 101
forward rate agreement rates for a strip, (Fig 6.2), 101
hedging, longer maturity risk and, (Fig 6.1), 100
interest rate caps and floors, 102–9
interest rate collars, 110–16
interest rate swaps, 102, 116–33
strip, 100–1
SwapClear, 101

NASDAQ 100 Index, 234
notional principal amount (NPA), 6

off-balance sheet instruments, 3
'off-exchange' energy derivatives, see OTC (over the counter) or 'off-exchange' energy derivatives
offshore markets, 14
oil
Brent futures hedging transaction, 299
exchange-traded energy derivatives, 295–301
exchange-traded energy option contracts, 302–7
gas oil futures closing prices, (Fig 13.4), 300
IPE Brent Crude oil future – abbreviated contract

specification (Table 12.2), 301
market, background to, 291–4
oil caps, 311
OTC (over the counter) oil swaps, 313–16
OTC (over the counter) option products, 308–13
OTC (over the counter) or 'off-exchange' energy derivatives, 307–13
prices, 290–4
operational risk management for derivatives, 138–40
Option Greeks, 198–201
Delta (Figs 10.12, 10.13), 198–200
Gamma (Fig 10.13), 200
Theta, 200–1
time and value decay, (Fig 10.14), 201
Vega, 201
option mechanics, 52–6
OTC (over the counter) currency options, 189–92
profit/loss profile of long put strategy, (Fig 4.11), 56
profit/loss profile of physical gold position (Fig 4.8), 54
profit/loss profile of short call option strategy, (Fig 4.10), 55
profit/loss profile of short put strategy (Fig 4.12), 56
variable inputs for option pricing calculations (Fig 4.7), 53
options
accounting, 392–3
American options, 44–5, 185
Asian options, 45, 210
barrier options, 211
basic concepts, 39–57
Bermudan, 45
buyers or holders, 40
contracts, 40
costs, 279
currency options, 178–210
digital option (binary option), 285–6
energy option contracts, exchange-traded, 302–7
equity derivatives, 232–3
European options, 45, 185
exchange-traded, 41, 302–7
interest rate options (OTC), 87–96
mechanics, 52–6, 189–92
Option Greeks, 198–201
option premium versus maturity, non-linear relationship of, (Fig 4.1), 44
OTC (over the counter) currency options, 178–202
OTC (over the counter) or 'off-exchange' energy derivatives, 308, 311–13
pricing, 52
risk, 40
sellers or writers, 40–1
single stock options, 259–63
stock index options, 249–58
OR structure, definition of, 282
OTC (over the counter) currency options, 178–202
American options, 185
amount, 181
bank, setting up a facility with a, 209–10
basic workings, 193
best and worst case, (Fig 10.2), 189
buyers and sellers, 186

OTC (over the counter) currency options (*continued*)
   calls and puts, 183, 186, 192–3, 196, 202, 206
   cash position, (Fig 10.3), 190
   currency collar options (cylinder options), 203–4
   early exercise, 194–5
   European options, 185
   exchange rates, 178–80, 183
   forward foreign exchange, comparisons with (Table
      10.3), 187
   hedging, 179–80
      receivables and, 187–9
   in/at/out of the money, concept of,
      (Table 10.2), 183
   insurance protection, 182
   interest rate differentials, 184–5
   maturity, 183
   Option Greeks, 198–201
   option mechanics, 189–92
   out of the money options, 203
   participating forwards, 207–8
   premiums,
      determinants, 182–5
      reduced premium strategies, 202–10
   profit and loss profile,
      cash position, (Fig 10.3), 190
      CHF call option – long call, (Fig 10.4), 191
      CHF call option – short call, (Fig 10.5), 191
      CHF put option – long put, (Fig 10.6), 192
      CHF put option – short put, (Fig 10.7), 192
      put – call parity, (Fig 10.8), 193
      speculate, using options to, (Fig 10.9), 195
   profit potential, 182
   risk management, 178–9
   sell-back, 182
   speculation, use for, 194, 195
   strategy, 194
   strike, 181–3, 208–9
   underlying price, strike price versus, 182–3
   vanilla options, 180–1
   volatility (Fig 10.1), 183–4
      ATM call options, 202
      historical, 184
      implied, 184
      long straddle, (Fig 10.10), 196
      short straddle, (Fig 10.11), 197–8
      strategies, 196–8
      trading, 195–6
   whether to exercise option, 181
OTC (over the counter) instruments
   advantages of, 5
   benchmarking, 135–41
   Central Counterparty Model (CCP), 5
   compliance, 373–5
   credit risk, 5
   dealing with derivatives, 34–5
   electricity market, 319
   exchange-traded instruments compared with, 4–5
   forward rate agreements (FRAs) (OTC), 75–86
   global OTC derivatives market, amounts
      outstanding on, (Table 15.1), 118
   oil swaps, 313–16
   OTC (over the counter) currency options, 178–202
   OTC (over the counter) or 'off-exchange' energy
      derivatives, 307–13

straight through processing (STP) for OTC
   derivatives
   vanilla products, 5
OTC (over the counter) oil swaps, 313–16
   cash flows, 315
   cash or physical settlement, 314
   credit risk, 314
   diesel, using a swap to fix the price of, 316
   funding optimization, 314
   hedging a Brent crude exposure with no oil swap,
      315
   insurance protection, 314
   oil swap (Fig 13.7), 316
   premiums, 314
   settlement, 316
OTC (over the counter) option products, 308–13
OTC (over the counter) or 'off-exchange' energy derivatives, 307–13
   energy cap, payments under, (Fig 13.6), 312
   expected market volatility, 310
   market conditions, 310
   maturity, 310
   oil caps, 311
   option products, 308
   OTC option products, 311–13
   outcome, 311
   strategy, 311
   strike price, 310
out of the money options, 203
outright forwards, 221–2
over the counter, *see* OTC (over the counter)
   instruments

parallel and back-to-back loans (Fig 10.18), 212–13
participating forwards, (Fig 10.17), 207–10
power exchange structure (PX), 318
premium-determinants, 88–96
   call or put, 89
   Eurodollar interest rate options to hedge
      investments, (Fig 5.13), 93–4
   exchange-traded energy option contracts, 304–7
   expected market volatility, 89
      Eurodollar interest rate options, (Figs 5.13,
      5.14), 93–4
      sterling interest rate options, 90–1
   increase in premium, 89
   interest rate caps and floors, 103–8
   interest rate options (OTC), 87–97
   LIBOR, 91–2
   maturity, 89
   OTC (over the counter) currency options, 102–5
   price versus strike price, underlying, 89
   sterling interest rate option,
      effective borrowing costs for, (Fig 5.11), 91
      examples, (Fig 5.12), 92
   stock index options, 253–5
premiums, *see also* premium-determinants
   fair value, 46
   interest rate collars, 110–11, 116
   intrinsic value, 45
   meaning, 45
   stock index options, 250–1, 258, 263
   time value, 46
   volatility, 46–51

price
    black box concept, 52
    capital protected growth products, 279
    credit default swaps (Fig 9.2), 152
    crude oil prices (Figs 13.2, 13.3), 295, 296
    data, importance of, 14
    equity derivatives, 279
    exchange-traded futures contracts, 295 301
    exercise price, 43
    gas oil futures closing prices, (Fig 13.4), 300
    interest rate caps and floors, 104–6, 109, 115
    interest rate collars, 113, 115
    interest rate swaps, 129, 133
    oil, 290–4
    options, 52
    risk, 2
    short-term interest rate futures (STIR), 65
    stock index futures, 237
    strike price, 43, 45, 89, 104–6, 182–3, 310
    swap pricing, 128–9
    underlying assets, of, 2–3
    variable inputs for option pricing calculations
        (Fig 4.7), 53
private clients, 7
puts, see call and puts

quotations, 219

range of derivatives, 4–5
ratchet options, 284–5
ratings, (Table 8.1), 147, 148, 171–2
reduced premium strategies, currency options and,
    202–10
repo transactions, 159
retail market, 7
risk, 2, 361 73, see also credit risk, risk
        management
    assessment, 372
    benchmarking, 6
    compliance, role and responsibilities of, 364–6
    currency derivatives, 176–7
    currency swaps, 222
    equity investment, 274
    governance, 362 7, 371
    hedge funds, 322–3
    interest rate risk, meaning of, 60–2
    key risk indicators, 371
    modelling, 372
    operational risk measurements, 138–40
    operational risk practice, 371 2
    options, 40
    over the counter, 5, 313–14
    price, 2
    reporting, 372
risk management
    credit derivatives, 144
    interest rate swaps, 117
    market risk practice, 367–9
    OTC (over the counter) currency options, 178–9
    practice, 367–72
    role and responsibilities of, 363–4
    techniques, patterns of, (Table 5.3), 62

S&P 500, 234
settlement

    amounts, example of, (Fig 5.8), 82
    cash versus physical settlement, 32
    iTraxx Europe, 165
    single versus multiple settlement, (Table 3.2) 31–2
shares, see equity derivatives
short selling, 14–15
short-term interest rate futures (STIR), 65–7
    action, 67
    contracts, 65
    credit risk, 65–6
    Euribor, (Table 5.6), 73–4
    hedging, 71–4
    market operations, 65
    outcome, 67
    pricing, 65
    profit or loss, 68
    sterling futures, 71–2
    three-month sterling abbreviated contract
        specification, (Table 5.4), 66
    tick values, (Table 5.5) 68
    trading units, (Table 5.5), 68
    transactions, 67–8
single currency basis swaps, 127
single settlement interest rate derivatives, see financial
        futures contracts (exchange-traded), forward
        rate agreements (OTC), interest rate options
        (OTC)
single stock options, 259–63
    covered call, example of a, 261–2
    equity options – abbreviated contract specification
        (Table 10.9), 259
    exercise, 260
    flexibility, 261
    insurance protection, 260
    leverage (gearing), 261
    physical settlement, 260
    premium determinants, 261–2
    profit and loss profile (Fig 10.3), 262
    profit potential, 260
    sell-back, 260
smiles, skew and surfaces, (Fig 4.5), 50–1
speculate, using options to, (Fig 10.9), 194, 195
speculators, 2
spot power market, 317–18
sterling interest rate options, (Figs 5.11, 5.12), 90, 91
stock index futures, 235–49
    administration, 249
    cash futures relationship, 244–5
    cash settlement, 238
    CME S&P 500 (Table 11.5), 247
    contract specification (Table 11.2), 238–9
    contracts, 237–8
    documentation, 248
    FT-SE 100 (Table 11.2), 195–7, 236 48
    hedging with FT-SE 100 (Table 11.3), 242–4
    initial and variation margins, 240–5
    margin account, 241
    market, 237
    market operations, 238, 240
    market structure, 240
    pricing, 237
    S&P 500 futures, 247
    stock betas (Table 11.4), 245–8
    using index futures, 238–9

stock index options, 249–58
  cash settlement, 253
  cost of carry of the position, 255
  definition, 250–2
  expected market volatility, 255
  FT-SE 100,
    index option European style exercise, (Table 11.6), 250
    margin flow, summary of, (Table 11.7), 252
  hedging (Table 11.8, Fig 11.2), 255–7
  insurance protection, 253
  margin flow on FT-SE 100 (Table 11.7), 252
  margined premium, 251–3
  maturity, 254
  premium determinants, 253-5
  profit and loss profile, (Fig 11.2), 257
  profit potential, 253
  put or call, 254
  sell back, 253
  volatility, 255
stocks and shares, see equity derivatives
straight through processing (STP) for OTC derivatives, 347–59
  backlog, 355–6
  central clearing, 352
  central infrastructure, 356–9
  future of STP for OTC contracts, 354–5
  history of, 347–59
  life cycle of trade (Fig 1.1), 9
  message formats, 349–52
    FpML document, extract from, 351–2, 354
    MT360 message, overview of, 350–1
  Reference Entity Datablease (RED), 353
  technology, 335–7
  trade capture and confirmation, innovation in, 352–3
  trade information warehouse (Fig), 356–9
  within or between firms, 349
strike price or exercise price, definition of, 43
structured retail product market in 21st century, (Fig), 276–7
SwapClear, 101, 352
swaps, see also credit default swaps, currency swaps, interest rate swaps
  accounting, 386–91
  equity derivatives, 233
  equity index swaps, 263–71
  OTC (over the counter) oil swaps, 313–16
  total return swaps, 158–9
  vanilla, 121–2
swaptions, 120
synthetic CDOs, (Fig 9.7), 169–70
synthetic stock market investment example (Fig 11.5, Table 11.11), 267–70
systemic and unsystematic portfolio risk, (Fig 11.1), 232

tax efficiencies, capturing, 324–5
technology and derivatives, 331–7
  asset classes traded, increase in variety of, 335
  business drivers for change, 334–6

datableases, 333
exchange of information between systems, 335
external STP, 336–7
hardware, 333–4
internal STP, 335–6
languages, 334
ownership, cost of, 335
portfolio reduction, 337
responses, 336–7
software, 334
volumes and reduced spreads, increased, 334
Theta, 200–1
total return swaps, 158–9
  credit event and no contingent payment, where there is no, 159
  credit risk, 159
  LIBOR, 158
  maturity, 159
  payers and receivers, 159
  repo transactions, 159
  total rate of return swap, (Fig 8.5), 158
  underlying assets, 158
trade capture and confirmation, innovation in, 352–3
trade information warehouse (Fig), 356–9
traders, 2, 7
trading, example of, 12–13
tripartite swaps, 218

underlying assets
  classes, (Tables 3.3, 3.4), 33–4
  credit default swaps, 149, 154
  credit derivatives, 146
  expiry date, 44
  interest rate caps and floors, 103
  list of derivatives and their underlying assets, (Table 1.1), 3
US dollar FAR rates, (Fig 5.8), 83–4
users and uses of derivatives, 3–4, 7–9

value date, meaning of, 44
vanilla trade, 5, (Table 3.1), 30–1, 121–2, 180
Vega, 201
volatility, (Fig 4.2)
  exchange-traded energy option contracts, 305
  input, 46
  interest rate swaps, 129–30
  linear relationship of option premium versus volatility, (Fig 4.4), 50
  normal curve, effect of different volatility levels on shape of, (Fig 4.3), 49
  OTC (over the counter) currency options, (Fig 10.1), 183–4, 195–8, 202
  premium-determinants, 89
  premiums, 46–51
  smiles, skew and surfaces, (Fig 4.5), 50–1
  statistical definition, 47

yield curves, (Fig 2.3), 25–6

zero-cost collar option, (Fig 10.16), 206